ALTERNATE CURRENTS

D1736081

ALTERNATE CURRENTS

Reiki's Circulation in the Twentieth-Century North Pacific

Justin B. Stein

University of Hawai'i Press
Honolulu

Library of Congress Cataloging-in-Publication Data

Names: Stein, Justin B., author.
Title: Alternate currents : Reiki's circulation in the
twentieth-century North Pacific / Justin B. Stein.
Description: Honolulu : University of Hawai'i Press, [2023] |
Includes bibliographical references and index.
Identifiers: LCCN 2023013326 (print) | LCCN 2023013327
(ebook) | ISBN 9780824895662 (trade paperback) |
ISBN 9780824894917 (hardback) | ISBN 9780824896409 (pdf) |
ISBN 9780824896416 (epub) | ISBN 9780824896423
(kindle edition)
Subjects: LCSH: Takata, Hawayo Kawamuri, 1900–1980. |
Reiki (Healing system)—Hawaii. | Reiki (Healing system)—
Japan. | Reiki (Healing system)—Northwest, Pacific.
Classification: LCC RZ403.R45 S745 2023 (print) |
LCC RZ403.R45 (ebook) | DDC 615.8/52—dc23/eng/20230607
LC record available at https://lccn.loc.gov/2023013326
LC ebook record available at https://lccn.loc.gov/2023013327

Cover photo: Hawayo Takata standing on the porch of her home
clinic, Hilo, circa December 1940. Published with permission of
Special Collections, University of California, Santa Barbara.

For my parents and
in memory of
Yoshinaga Shin'ichi-sensei (1957–2022)

Contents

Acknowledgments

Reiki's development is often ascribed to a small number of individuals—Usui Mikao, Hayashi Chūjirō, Hawayo Takata, and Phyllis Lei Furumoto—but in a sense it was coproduced by the communities in which these figures were embedded. Similarly, though my name appears alone on its cover (and I, like those figures, spent countless hours working on it), this book came into being thanks to a network of mentors, collaborators, interlocutors, and supporters, to whom I am deeply indebted. In the following pages I acknowledge the contributions of a few dozen people to whom I am particularly grateful. My sincere apologies to anyone overlooked.

Three groups of interlocutors have been so invaluable to the research and writing of this book that I am tempted to call them collaborators. First are the Reiki students, the Reiki Masters, and their families who spoke with me about their experiences with Reiki and Hawayo Takata. Many of these names appear repeatedly in the text itself, but special thanks are due to some who answered questions for hours, replied to ceaseless emails and phone calls from a researcher trying to clarify information, and granted follow-up interviews after a robbery caused me to lose data. Takahashi Ichita, Kondō Masaki, the Nagao-Kimuras, the Yudas, the Kuramoto-Ledesmas, Sally Okura Lee, the Ventos, Shannon Mackler, Vivian Kimura, the Twan-Beacham-Beauregards, Rick Bockner, Harue Kanemitsu, Chelsea Van Koughnett, Gretchen Munsey, Natalie Weeks, Walter Quan, Paul Guillory, and Olaf Böhm unceasingly stunned me with their generosity. I offer them all a heartfelt *gasshō*.

Next, a particular group of Reiki Masters deserve special recognition for their ongoing support of this project. Phyllis Lei Furumoto, Joyce Winough, and Paul and Susan Mitchell invited me and Robert Fueston into their lives to form "the archive team." I was honored to work with this group over about two years, organizing and digitizing the personal papers of Hawayo Takata, now largely housed in the American Religions Collection at the University of California, Santa Barbara. It was invaluable to have this group of longtime Reiki Masters, three of whom studied with Hawayo Takata, as conversation partners while working through these materials. I am particularly grateful to Susan Mitchell for carefully reading through the entire draft and sharing her comments.

Third, I am indebted to two intersecting networks of scholars researching Reiki. The first, in Japan, was organized by the incomparable Yoshinaga Shin'ichi, who tragically passed away shortly before the completion of this manuscript. Yoshinaga-sensei's generosity and erudition profoundly influenced the development of this research, and it is to him that I codedicate this book. Along with Yoshinaga-sensei, my closest collaborator has been Hirano Naoko, with whom I traveled to Hilo to interview Japanese Americans who learned Reiki from Takata in the 1930s and 1940s, located Japanese-language articles from Honolulu newspapers, and developed the idea that, from its beginning, Reiki has been a product of dialogue between Japanese and Americans. Additionally, Jojan Jonker, Dori Beeler, Liad Horowitz, and Robert Fueston have been excellent conversation partners over the years; special thanks to Jojan and Liad for reading an early draft manuscript and providing me with copious notes.

Thank you to my editor, Masako Ikeda, for giving this project a chance despite initial suspicion of Reiki as a subject, and for your patience as I juggled this project with the demands of a new job and the ordeal of the COVID-19 pandemic. Thank you to the two anonymous reviewers for your detailed comments; the book benefited greatly from your insights. Thank you to John Donohue and Ashley Moore of Westchester Publishing Services, whose editing improved the quality of the manuscript. And a huge thank-you to Jolyon Thomas for extensive, incisive, and formative feedback on an early draft, and for cheering on this project for years.

I am so grateful to my mentors at the University of Toronto, who pushed me to tell this story in a way that would be a pleasurable read while also contributing to conversations in the study of religion. Many parts that I am most pleased with result from your provocations to deepen my analysis and to clarify my prose. Pamela Klassen not only supported this research but included me in countless opportunities for scholarly development and inspired my writing by modeling how scholarship can provoke readers' hearts along with their intellects. I am also indebted to Simon Coleman, Kevin O'Neill, and Mark Rowe for their patience and generosity in (re)reading chapter drafts and meeting to talk through ideas; to Takashi Fujitani for providing incisive feedback as a respondent and internal reader; and to Wendy Cadge for serving as an external examiner and pushing me to further ideas addressed in the conclusion.

My mentors during my master's program at the University of Hawaiʻi at Mānoa helped shape my capacity to think, research, and write about religion (and Reiki) like an academic: thank you to Helen Baroni, Michel Mohr, George Tanabe, Lee Siegel, Kristin Bloomer, and Christine Yano. A special thank-you to my departed friend and mentor Patricia Lee Masters, who started me down the path of studying Japanese religions twenty years ago and always inspired me with her wit, warmth, and wisdom.

Thanks to the many archivists and librarians who helped facilitate this research. Masafumi Honda of the Hawaii Japanese Center was of particular help organizing interviews with elderly Nisei in Hilo, and Malina Pereza and Helen Wong Smith at the Kauai Historical Society; Chris Faye at the Kauai Museum; Joan Hori, Dore Minatodani, and Sherman Seki at the University of Hawaiʻi at Mānoa Library; Gary McDougall at the Penticton Museum Archives; and Yamaguchi Maki at the Doshisha Global Archives all helped me access invaluable archival sources. Thank you also to Christine Kirk-Kuwaye and Lori Pierce for introducing me to the Romanzo Adams Social Research Laboratory Student Papers Archive. A special thanks to Munazza Mansoor for helping code nearly three hundred of Hawayo Takata's letters.

This book benefited from feedback I received at many workshops and conferences, including meetings of the American Academy of Religion, the Association for Asian Studies, the European Association for Japanese Studies, and the International Association for the History of Religions; the Nanzan Seminar at the Nanzan Institute for Religion and Culture; the Centre for Studies in Religion and Society at the University of Victoria; workshops on the 150th anniversary of Usui Mikao's birth and for the *Routledge Handbook of Religion, Medicine, and Health;* and graduate student conferences at the Chao Center for Asian Studies at Rice University, the Department of Religious Studies at Northwestern University, and the Departments of Religion and of East Asian Languages and Cultures at Columbia University. Thank you to the organizers of those events (including Okuyama Michiaki, Paul Swanson, Paul Bramadat, Oliver Klatt, Dorothea Lüddeckens, Elizabeth Rodwell, Matthew John Cressler, and Laura McTighe), my copanelists, and the discussants (including Thomas Tweed, Robert Orsi, Brett Esaki, Victor Sōgen Hori, and Helen Hardacre) for their guidance and encouragement.

Others with whom I had helpful conversations during the research and writing of this book include Matt McMullen, Ioannis Gaitanidis, Erik Schicketanz, Kurita Hidehiko, Moriya Tomoe, Erica Baffelli, Ian Reader,

Birgit Staemmler, Levi McLaughlin, Jessica Main, Jesse LeFebvre, Rebecca Mendelson, Richard Jaffe, Paride Stortini, Orion Klatau, Daniel Friedrich, Philip Deslippe, Torang Asadi, Pierce Salguero, Kin Cheung, Lucas Carmichael, Holly Gayley, Amanda Lucia, David McMahan, Shreena Gandhi, Ira Helderman, Melissa Borja, Dusty Hoesly, Matthew King, Rebecca Bartel, Ashley Vaughan, Takashi Miura, Pamela Runestad, Matt Mitchell, Christine Walters, Zach Anderson, Julia Pyryeskina, Harshita Yalamarty, Diane Domondon, Kimberly Thomas, Dan White, and Katsuno Hirofumi. Hirofumi, Satomi Fukutomi-Kurban, Miki Ōmori Yoneyama, and Lisa Sumiyoshi assisted with Japanese-language materials and presentations. Thank you all and many others for your good cheer and great feedback.

The initial research (including conference travel) was supported with funding from the American Academy of Religion, the Canadian Corporation for the Study of Religion, the Centre for the Study of the United States at the University of Toronto, the German Academic Exchange Service, the Japan Student Services Organization, the Religion and Diversity Project, the University of Toronto School for Graduate Studies, and the University of Victoria Centre for Studies in Religion and Society. Further research and revision were made possible by the Japan Society for the Promotion of Science (JSPS) Postdoctoral Research Fellowship #P17745 and the Kwantlen Polytechnic University (KPU) 0.6% Faculty Professional Development Fund. Special thanks to Mark Rowe for encouraging me to apply for the JSPS, Ōtani Eiichi-sensei for supervising my fellowship, and Kamala Nayar and Jack Hayes for helping me apply for the KPU funds. Phyllis Lei Furumoto helped defray my travel to work on the Hawayo Takata Archive. Monies from the Nippon Foundation, Fred and Ann Notehelfer, and the Sumitomo Mitsui Banking Corporation (SMBC) Global Foundation funded ten months at the Inter-University Center for Japanese Language Studies (IUC); I am particularly grateful to Ōhashi Makiko of the IUC for her great assistance and encouragement.

My deepest gratitude is reserved for my parents, Zack and Vicky; my sister, Lizzie; my wife, Kristin; and my in-laws, Ken and Margaret. One could not ask for a more loving family, and I would never have completed this journey without your encouragement and support. There's a Japanese expression that "fortune comes to a house that laughs," and I have been so fortunate to laugh deeply and often with each of you. Thank you.

Abbreviations

A/C	alternating current
AIA	American Indian Association
AICT	American Indian Church Temple
AMORC	Ancient Mystical Order Rosae Crucis
AOG	Assemblies of God
APM	Academy of Parapsychology and Medicine
CIC	Counter Intelligence Corps of the US Army
FBI	Federal Bureau of Investigation
IAA	Indian Association of America
JACL	Japanese American Citizens League
LPC	Lihue Plantation Company
SACJAK	Society of American Citizens of Japanese Ancestry of Kauai
SAI	Society of American Indians
SFF	Spiritual Frontiers Fellowship
SHY	Spiritual Human Yoga
SRF	Self-Realization Fellowship
TM	Transcendental Meditation
TOA	Tipi Order of America
UCM	Universal Church of the Master
UHM	University of Hawaiʻi at Mānoa
URRI	Usui Reiki Ryoho International
YMBA	Young Men's Buddhist Association

Notes on Orthography and Translation

The names of Japanese people are written in the Japanese style, with the family name first, followed by the given name. The names of Japanese Americans, including first-generation immigrants, are written in the Western style, with the given name first, followed by the family name. Unless otherwise noted, translations of Japanese-language sources are mine.

Romanization of Japanese terms follows the modified Hepburn system, with the exceptions of omitting diacritics for words and names in common use in English (e.g., "judo" instead of *"judō"*; "Tokyo" instead of "Tōkyō") and terms that commonly use older forms of Romanization in Hawai'i (e.g., "Hongwanji" instead of "Honganji"). A glossary contains the characters for all Japanese names and terms.

The *okina* (') and other diacritics are generally used in Hawaiian-language words and names, except in quotations where they were omitted in the original.

"Black" and "White" are capitalized when used in reference to racioethnic identity.

Introduction

On Friday, October 10, 1980, at the start of Canada's Thanksgiving Day weekend, dozens of tree planters, farmers, and "back-to-the-land hippie draft dodgers" journeyed from around the southern British Columbia interior to Gray Creek Hall, a large log building on the forested shore of Kootenay Lake.[1] Those who had come from hours away set up teepees and tents and got settled for the long weekend. Many brought fresh homegrown produce for a potluck feast. Some brought their kids. One couple brought their goats, which needed daily milking. All had come to receive teachings and initiations from a seventy-nine-year-old second-generation Japanese American from Hawai'i named Hawayo Takata. For most present, this was the first time they had ever met Takata, but many had firsthand experiences with the healing system she practiced and taught.

The basic practice of this system, called Reiki, involved gently laying hands on oneself or others. Testimonials asserted this practice could dispel an acute pain within minutes and cure chronic problems with regular treatment. Moreover, some patients and practitioners found that, in addition to enhancing physical wellness, Reiki also affected their mental, emotional, and spiritual lives. Some experienced a newfound sense of calm and trust. Some had paranormal experiences, ranging from strange synchronicities to heightened intuitions to powerful visions. Many felt deepened connections to themselves, their loved ones, the emerging community of practice, and "the universe," said to be the source of this healing power and spiritual growth.

Takata had learned Reiki in the 1930s in Japan, where it was developed by a man she called Dr. Usui, although she said it had died out there during the war. She had introduced it to the British Columbia interior in

1

1975, when an old prospector interested in yoga and alternative health read of Takata in a book and invited her to the Okanagan Valley to teach. Over the next five years, hundreds of people in this rural mountainous region, most of whom lived simply and frugally, scrounged up the considerable fee of 125 USD (about $450 in 2022 US dollars) for the First Degree class: four days of instruction, including an initiation ritual each day, that gave anyone the power to heal with their hands. Takata explained that Reiki worked via a "universal life energy" (also called *reiki*) in which we are constantly awash, like radio waves.[2] She likened herself to a radio technician who raised the student's "antenna" through the initiations so that they, too, could channel *reiki* to heal.

About forty students came to Gray Creek Hall for the First Degree class that October, held for two hours every evening over four days, and another fifteen had come for the Second Degree. The latter group had already taken the First Degree with Takata or with one of the four instructors (called Reiki Masters) whom she had trained in the region in the previous two years.[3] The Second Degree was a substantial investment, costing 500 USD (over $1,800 in 2022 dollars), but it represented a major step up in abilities, as Second Degree students receive three symbols that enhance Reiki practice in certain ways.

Second Degree students were trained to trace these symbols with the hand or visualize them in the mind's eye and activate them by quietly reciting a mantra-like phrase three times. One symbol focuses *reiki* in a particular spot, increasing the power of the treatment; a second treats mental or emotional disturbances, as well as bad habits; and a third empowers the "distance treatment" of people not physically present, or "sending *reiki*" to a situation. These symbols were not to be revealed to the uninitiated or even written down; Takata said Reiki was an oral tradition and generally prohibited note taking in her classes. On that first night in Gray Creek, she gave Second Degree students photocopied handouts of these three symbols, instructing them not to show them to anyone else, to memorize them overnight, and to return the papers to her the following day before she administered the initiation that authorized their use. This was no mean feat, particularly for the "distance symbol," based on Japanese characters, which contains over twenty individual strokes.

When Takata took the front of the room that Friday night to tell the story of Reiki's origin and how she came to find this healing practice, among the sixty-odd people in the crowd, one was particularly grateful. Richard

"Rick" Bockner (b. 1948) was a guitarist, carpenter, and tree planter living off the grid in Argenta, about two hours north of Gray Creek. He had taken his First and Second Degree classes with Takata the prior year and felt the Reiki initiations had set in motion other changes in his life. As he wrote in a letter to Takata in February 1980, he had been "walking a knife edge between despair and hope" after his divorce, but Reiki "saved my life and [gave] me a purpose and task to be done."[4] He wanted to become a Reiki Master and open a healing center and educational facility but did not know how he was going to raise the 10,000 USD to pay for the training. He had made about 8,000 CAD (about 6,800 USD) planting trees that summer, but he and his new wife were living in a teepee and building a house, with a baby on the way. He and Takata worked out a deal where he would give her 5,000 USD and organize a large class for her to teach: she would apply those students' tuition toward his training fee. He mailed seventy-five letters to people he knew, telling them about his remarkable experiences with Takata and Reiki. Fifty-six of them signed up, more than enough to pay his balance, and, together with a few of Takata's Master students, they sat in the log hall that October evening, listening intently to the stories this elderly teacher told in her lilting diction accented with Hawaiian Creole English.[5] One photograph from the event (figure I.1) shows Takata standing outside Gray Creek Hall with three of these Master students: she and her granddaughter Phyllis Furumoto (1948–2019)—whom Takata was training as her successor—stand in the center, framed by Bockner and Wanja Twan (1934–2019).

A second photograph from the event (figure I.2) shows Takata sitting in the center of a triangle of three figures: a young woman on either side and Bockner, who kneels at Takata's feet, seemingly after handing his teacher a bouquet of flowers. Bockner and the woman on the right exhibit conspicuous, yet calm, fixation on their aged master. The way the sunlight streams through the windows of the hall at this moment, illuminating Takata's white hair, it is easy to imagine how these young White students in the mountains of British Columbia saw this elderly Japanese American healer as surrounded by a halo of glowing energy. Indeed, she appears somewhat like a living icon receiving their adoration.

This class, among the largest Takata ever taught, was also among her last. After most of her grateful students returned home, ready to practice their new healing abilities, Takata spent some time in the area teaching and completing Bockner's Master training. In mid-November, Takata traveled to Orcas Island, on the US side of the Salish Sea, which runs between coastal

Figure I.1 (*Left to right*) Rick Bockner, Phyllis Lei Furumoto, Hawayo Takata, and Wanja Twan, Gray Creek, BC, October 1980. Photo by Ametist Homström Summanen.

Figure I.2 Rick Bockner (*kneeling, left*) and other Reiki students surround Hawayo Takata (*center*), Gray Creek, BC, October 1980. Photo by Ametist Homström Summanen.

British Columbia and the Olympic Peninsula. There, her student Helen Haberly (1928–1999) was transcribing audiotapes Takata had dictated as the basis of her autobiography, *Reiki Is God Power,* which she had been eager to publish for years. While in Washington, Takata suffered a heart attack and was hospitalized in Seattle. Once her condition stabilized, she was transferred to Keosauqua, Iowa, where she had been living with her daughter Alice. Takata died there on December 11, 1980, two weeks shy of her eightieth birthday.

About This Book

Alternate Currents examines the development of Reiki in the North Pacific—defined as Japan, Hawai'i, and western North America[6]—from 1922, when Usui Mikao (1865–1926) began teaching Usui Reiki Therapy (Usui Reiki Ryōhō), to the death of Hawayo Takata (1900–1980). It tries to think beyond the essentialist divide between "East" and "West" by focusing on Reiki's circulation within transpacific networks and by arguing that, from its beginning, Reiki developed out of confluences of diverse practices circulating through the North Pacific. It also uses Reiki to illustrate a category I call transnational spiritual therapies: practices designed to promote physical, mental, and spiritual health that are produced out of transnational exchanges and circulate in transnational networks but are strongly identified with a homeland considered the source of their potency.

To structure our pursuit of these somewhat abstract ends, the subsequent chapters follow the life history of Hawayo Takata, the Japanese American woman who, as the first and most prominent figure to adapt Reiki for American audiences, made possible Reiki's global spread in subsequent decades. But this is not Takata's biography. Instead, this book focuses on the interplay between Reiki's performance, its meanings, and its circulation in a transpacific network of practitioners, patients, instructors, and students, in which Takata served as the chief hub. Takata's network connected Japanese American laborers on Hawaiian plantations to elites in Tokyo and Hollywood; midwives in Japanese cities; housewives in American suburbs; and off-the-grid tree planters in the mountains of British Columbia. To explain the dynamics of her diverse network and relationships, these pages contextualize her lifework in the changing structural conditions of the twentieth-century North Pacific, particularly the ongoing rearticulation of her racialized and gendered social position at the juncture of the Japanese and American empires.[7]

Alternate Currents is part of a wave of scholarship about religion in modern Japan that focuses on the impact of cultural exchange with the United States, implicitly or explicitly calling into question the exceptionalist discourses that can be said to characterize much of the study of religion in both countries.[8] By focusing on Takata's role in Reiki's development, it also contributes to the scholarship on Japanese American religion, which also tends to be well attuned to transnational connections.[9] This book's multisited, North Pacific approach responds to calls in religious studies and Japanese American studies to take part in a broader refiguring of area studies around transoceanic connections.[10] By demonstrating the ties between Reiki's decades-long evolution and its movement within emplaced networks, this book also contributes to broader conversations on the relationship between cultural production and cultural circulation. One such contribution is the metaphor of the title—*Alternate Currents*—meant to evoke five interconnected points about how spiritual practices develop and circulate.

Alternate Currents

Currents

First, the term "currents" evokes the movement of water and, as such, has been frequently used to describe the movement or "flow" of cultural practices, particularly overseas.[11] Part of what I find appealing about this aquatic metaphor is its potential nod to the Heraclitean wisdom that "one never steps in the same river twice," suggesting that the very process of circulation transforms the substance (or practice, idea, artifact, etc.) that is circulating.[12]

Of course, "currents" refers to not only flowing water but also other fluids, such as air, and even charged particles, as in electricity. This is a linguistic remnant of nineteenth-century science, which considered electricity a kind of "subtle fluid," akin to the vital force thought to course through living beings. Reiki practitioners often similarly describe "*reiki* energy" in terms of flow. During a Reiki treatment, we are told, the practitioner's fingertips emit what might be considered microflows of *reiki* into the recipient's body on a cellular level. At the mesolevel of social relations, the Japanese character *ryū*, which denotes flowing water, can also denote transmission lineages, in which initiations, teachings, and even authority can "flow" from masters to disciples.[13] On a macro level, *reiki* is thought to flow from "the universe" to practitioners around the planet, so that by practicing or receiving Reiki, one enters a cosmic current that can heal all ills.

Alternation

My description of Reiki's currents as "alternate" is also meant to evoke alternating current (A/C)—that is, an electrical current that regularly reverses its direction. While *reiki* flow is often visualized as unidirectional, flowing from the cosmos through the practitioner into the recipient, some early accounts of Reiki's operation described *reiki* flowing back and forth between the practitioner and recipient, using the same Japanese word (*kōryū*) used for A/C.[14] This idea of "alternation" in the sense of bidirectional influence is helpful when thinking of how the transmission of practices is interactive and can affect the person transmitting as well as the person receiving. This theme helps keep our attention on how the flows between Takata and her students and clients were bidirectional: as she touched them in her treatments and initiations, sometimes changing the course of their lives, they also touched her, influencing how she practiced and taught.

For example, chapters 3–5 detail several ways Takata changed Reiki based on needs she perceived in her students. She instituted some of these changes, such as explicit instructions on how to honor Reiki as an "oral tradition," a new "Reiki ideal" regarding respecting authority, and an influential parable regarding the importance of reciprocity, to instill her American students with values that she considered essential for effective practice. Thus, not only did the practices she taught change her students' lives, but her students' lives changed the practices that she taught. With "alternate currents," I hope to promote attention to this interactive dimension, often overlooked in discussion of flows or transmission. However, just as actual A/C ultimately flows from power plants to end users despite periodic reversals, generally teachers influence their students more than vice versa; I do not mean to imply that the strength of bidirectional influence is symmetric, but these "reversals" should not be overlooked.

Adaptation

This leads to another key concept for alternate currents: *adaptation.* To travel across distances, A/C is transmitted at high voltages, but it is transformed to a lower, safer voltage for use. Similarly, when we travel overseas, we sometimes need to bring a converter to be able to use our everyday devices in a new environment. Thomas Csordas has said that religions "travel well" when they have "portable practices,"[15] but I would like to add that these practices are often adapted for local needs to make them more useful in their new environment.

Not all transformations are adaptations. Transmitting cultural practices is a kind of reproduction. As in the reproduction of genetic information or digital data, transmission events are susceptible to additions, deletions, and substitutions. Often minor changes go unnoticed, but sometimes a particular change can affect that information's ability to be reproduced again in a particular environment, a quality evolutionary biology calls fitness. A sufficiently deleterious impact on fitness might lead to a particular change not being passed on. However, occasionally changes improve fitness, in which case they are called adaptations. Through processes of selection, populations that possess adaptations proliferate relative to those that do not. It is crucial to note that this process is ateleological and context sensitive; in contrast to popular notions of "survival of the fittest," adaptations do not make an organism or cultural practice better in any absolute sense, but rather *better at* reproducing in a particular environment. Some of the changes Takata (and others) made to Reiki might be considered adaptations, in the sense that they made this practice more appealing to new audiences, and many of these adaptations had to do with adjustments to Reiki's *alterity*—that is, the degree to which its practices were considered different from other practices in its environment.

Alterity

Another meaning of "alternate" is "alternative," which gestures toward Reiki and other spiritual therapies being positioned in distinction to "orthodox" or "mainstream" religious and medical institutions as a kind of cultural critique. This position is frequently described in terms of "alternative spirituality" and "alternative medicine," two interrelated modes of creating meaning, connection, and healing.[16] Of course, just because many consider these fields outside the mainstream (although they have become more and more mainstream in recent decades) does not mean they are unaffected by mainstream values, capitalist ideology, or popular culture.[17]

Alterity or difference is at the heart of change. It can be framed as opportunity or crisis, restoration or decline. It is a kind of double-edged blade: a value so honed that it is capable of surgery as well as violence. Michael Taussig describes how Indigenous people of the northern Amazon consider the darker-skinned people of the south to be "inferior," "savages," even "not people," but at the same time regard them as "gifted sorcerers" possessing powerful healing magic. European colonists exhibited similar ambivalence toward Indigenous Amazonians, wantonly murdering them while also seeking out their shamans for healing, and Taussig concludes, "Going to the Indians for their healing power and killing them for their wildness . . . are not only intertwined but are codependent."[18]

This ambivalent power of otherness can be seen in the mixed reception Reiki has received throughout its history. A text attributed to Usui Mikao contrasts his Reiki Therapy with biomedicine, Sino-Japanese medicine (*kanpō*), and other therapies, which it implies are inferior in comparison.[19] Such grandiose claims may have attracted some followers out of curiosity or dissatisfaction with other medical systems, but they also provoked skepticism. An anonymous author in 1928 was surprised at the effects they felt from Usui Reiki Therapy, as Usui was "said to be one of Japan's three fraudulent wizards" and they had accordingly assumed Usui's therapy was a scam.[20]

As Reiki reached North America, its difference continued to mark it as alternately miraculous or fraudulent. A White American woman who received Reiki initiation with her husband from Takata in 1951 wrote an acquaintance about their "strong conviction that an opportunity such as Dr. Takata only comes once in a life time [*sic*]. She is surely a messenger to humanity." This sentiment eventually inverted; in 1965, her husband wrote a memoir-like "testimony" in which he repented for having ever practiced Reiki, saying that "the Lord [opened their] eyes to how foolish we had been . . . as the power Dr. Takato [*sic*] used was not covered by the Blood of Jesus, but an evil power which had a strange way of drawing people to her."[21] In light of the Pentecostal faith to which this couple had converted in the intervening years, Reiki went from a godsend to an intolerable kind of otherness.

Takata's claims of Reiki's Buddhist origins and potential for spiritual transformation gave it authority and appeal for certain audiences and made it off-limits to others. Some are drawn to Reiki as a "Buddhist secret" or because of an indistinct "spiritual component."[22] At the same time, however, the United States Conference of Catholic Bishops' Committee on Doctrine cited those exact qualities when it recommended in 2009 that Reiki be barred from Catholic institutions such as hospitals and retreat centers.[23] In the aftermath of that statement, a Catholic exorcist accused Reiki Masters of having no connection "with the true God" and claimed instead that their "esoteric 'spirit guides' . . . are demons disguised as 'angels of the light.'"[24] Like Taussig's Amazonians, Reiki's alterity is tied up with its potential to be both therapeutic and dangerous.

Oscillation

One final meaning of "alternate" that I want to evoke is how practitioners of Reiki and other spiritual therapies frequently *oscillate* between different vocabularies, employing a discursive style characterized by claims to harmonize disparate spheres of knowledge. The most common of these is their tendency to fluctuate between religious, medical, and scientific idioms. For example, one of Usui's contemporaries, Matsumoto Chiwaki (1872–1942), described mental and physical health as regulated by a kind of "radioactivity" that "is the equivalent of what ancient Indian Brahmans and yoga sutras called prana, Chinese Daoists and medical doctors termed qi, and what [Franz] Mesmer of Austria named animal magnetism"; he continued to say that contemporary science suggests this energy equates "either to alpha waves radiating from radioactive elements or to the anode rays inside radio valves," and his experiments indicate it can be used to heal disease.[25] Similarly, Takata wrote in 1948 that *reiki* is "One Supreme Being . . . an unseen spiritual power that vibrates and all other powers fade into insignificance beside it"; she also described it as "a radionic wave like radio" and "a universal force from the Great Divine Spirit," which promotes "physical health and mental balance" when applied to the body's organs.[26]

This oscillation between religious, scientific, and medical registers has a universalizing effect, suggesting that spiritual therapists around the world tap into a common power that underlies religious and medical phenomena and is on the verge of being understood scientifically. The book's final chapters also demonstrate how Takata—like transnational spiritual therapists more generally—also oscillated between universalist and particularist claims. While Reiki's healing power is accessible to anyone, regardless of nationality or religion, she posited, the best way to access it is through the initiations and symbols, which are rooted in Japanese culture.

"Alternate currents" thus highlights that (1) the process of Reiki's *circulation* around the North Pacific caused it to undergo transformative changes; (2) these changes were *multidirectional,* as Reiki Masters, their students, and the practice of Reiki itself were all transformed through their mutual encounters; (3) some of the ways Reiki changed can be considered *adaptations* for particular audiences or settings; (4) part of Reiki's appeal was that it *differed* from mainstream religious and medical practice, although Hawayo Takata made use of institutional affiliations and appeals to institutional authority in her networking and teaching practices; and (5) Takata's frequent *switching* between religious, medical, and scientific vernaculars tied Reiki to a broader project of integrating aspects of these ostensibly distinct fields.

Transnational Spiritual Therapies

This book also theorizes Reiki as a form of *spiritual therapy,* a category that emphasizes how lived practices often transcend the distinction between religion and medicine. I adopted the term "spiritual therapy" from a "Japanmade English" (*wasei eigo*) term that arose in the late 1990s to describe a range of healing practices that could also be described as "New Age," including Reiki, past-life regression, and channeling.[27] In Japan, scholars and practitioners both use the term "spiritual therapy" (*supirichuaru serapii*) to refer to a broad scope of practice, including energy healing; communication with or channeling of metaphysical entities, such as ancestor spirits, one's "higher self," one's guardian spirit (*shugorei*), deities, or angels; and mental healing (i.e., the use of intention, visualization, and affirmations to improve one's life).[28]

In this book, I use "spiritual therapy" as an analytic category to talk about a broader range of activity that also includes many of these emic uses. I define "spiritual therapy" as the diagnosis, treatment, and prevention of illness and the promotion of well-being (both considered holistic phenomena including, but not limited to, the mind and body) through ritualized practices, generally understood by practitioners to be guided by transpersonal intelligences. As such, spiritual therapies include a wide range of modern practices that are related to (but not necessarily circumscribed by) various religions, from forms of "energy healing" like Reiki, Therapeutic Touch, Healing Touch, and Pranic Healing, to forms of yoga and meditation, to forms of healing prayer and Indigenous ceremony. It should be noted that not all practitioners whom I group under this analytical category would self-identify as "spiritual therapists," but I believe their similarities warrant their inclusion.

Spiritual therapies challenge secularist projects, which conceive of religiosity as an easily recognizable attribute that can be segregated from public, ostensibly secular spaces, such as hospitals, schools, or the halls of statecraft. They also call our attention to how difficult it can be in practice to distinguish between attending to illness and attending to the soul. Spiritual therapists often position themselves in an ambiguous relationship to institutional religion and biomedicine. They draw on the authority of these fields, making strategic use of religious and medical discourses, while simultaneously leveling antimodern criticisms of religion and medicine as dogmatic and fragmented. They tend to assert that their therapy (or something like it) was used in antiquity, prior to religion's and medicine's differentiation, and that it is also key to these fields' future redemption.[29] As such, they position their therapies as not contradicting but complementing religion and medicine. Thus, like the related terms "spirituality" and "spiritual healing," "spiritual therapy" can be employed as a kind of tactical "from below" rhetorical alternative to the "third terms" (such as "magic," "occultism," or "superstition") that authorities "from above" use to strategically exclude certain types of knowledge or practice from either the religious or the secular and scientific.[30]

Reiki and other modern spiritual therapies are inherently transnational in their roots, their fruits, and (often) their self-identities. The Asian teachers who developed Reiki, postural yoga, and the meditation movements that gained global audiences in the twentieth century were all influenced by Euro-American ideas and practices that circulated in their home societies and consciously constructed practices that would appeal to modern cosmopolitans and address modern ills.[31] International interest in these practices, along with their continued spiritualization and therapeuticization overseas, has helped spur interest in them in their ostensible homelands.[32] Similarly, practitioners of "Black Atlantic religion," such as Candomblé and Santeriá, have creatively combined influences from circum-Atlantic locales and exerted influence in many communities of practice, including in West Africa, considered the spiritual source of their practices.[33] Transnational spiritual therapies are transnational not only in their influences and their influence but also in their self-identification, as practitioners often frame their practice's efficacy as rooted in particular national cultures, while also being suitable for use by practitioners around the world. Chapters 4 and 5 delineate the productive tensions between particularism and universalism at work in Reiki, and the conclusion draws out implications for this field more broadly.

The North Pacific Intersystem

This book follows Reiki's development over a period of decades from interactions among Japanese, Japanese Americans, and White Americans in Japan, Hawai'i, and the western United States and Canada. As Japan and America are not homogeneous, bounded, static entities, and as claims to "Japaneseness" and "Americanness" are not "natural kinds" but rather "interactive kinds" that powerfully transform the realities they ostensibly represent,

I try to avoid reifying cultural practices and values as essentially Japanese or American.[34] Rather, I attempt to untether culture from nationality by approaching the North Pacific as an "intersystem" whose national-cultural identities (such as "Japanese culture") are political, historical, and contested "purifications" of messy grays into clearer blacks and whites.[35] Of course, the North Pacific is a heuristic whose components were also embedded in other intersystems. Modern Japanese defined their identities in relation to other nations and (in the prewar period) their colonies, whereas American identities formed in relation to Europe and, during the Cold War, the Soviet Union. This book brackets those other relations to focus on a particular community of practice that spanned the "intertwined worlds" and "intimacies" of the two great Pacific empires.[36]

What Is Reiki?

Today, "reiki" is a common term in the intersecting worlds of spirituality and healing in the Americas, Europe, and elsewhere. Internet search trends from the 2010s suggest recent epicenters of popular interest in "reiki" were in the Spanish- and Portuguese-speaking world, followed by other parts of Europe, Canada, Australia, New Zealand, the United States, South Africa, the former Soviet Union, and Japan.[37] However, "reiki" *sensu lato* has become something of a "floating" or "empty signifier," denoting varied phenomena ranging from bodywork practices to belief in the power of "energy," intention, or destiny, similar to how "zen" has gone from identifying a particular Buddhist school to describing a vaguely defined sense of calm and simplicity with a dose of Asian exoticism.[38] To define "Reiki" *sensu stricto,* I offer a core set of "family resemblances" shared by most practitioners.

First, throughout Reiki's history, its core practice has arguably been using one's hands to heal oneself and others. The most detailed surviving text by Reiki's founder Usui describes treating disease through "gazing, breathing, stroking, laying-on-of-hands, and light patting."[39] Over time, the practices involving the gaze, breath, and more vigorous forms of touch have been de-emphasized, making light touch so at the heart of what Reiki practitioners "do" that it is often how they themselves represent their practice. For example, the US-based International Center for Reiki Training offers a "multimedia toolkit" called *The Reiki Touch,* and the UK-based Reiki Association's quarterly magazine is called *Touch.* Japanese scholarship considers Usui Reiki Therapy a paradigmatic example of "hands-on therapy" (*teate ryōhō*) or "healing with the palms" (*tenohira ni yoru ryōhō*).[40] This said, growing numbers of practitioners hold their hands an inch or two above recipients' bodies, which authoritative sources are starting to reflect. An article on healing and medicine in the *Encyclopedia of Religion* says, "Reiki healing is a good example of nonphysical touch," "done on the astral or energetic level rather than through direct contact with the patient's skin,"[41] and the US National Center for Complementary and Integrative Health webpage on Reiki shows a practitioner's hands about two inches above the recipient's body.[42]

Another core practice, performed by more-advanced practitioners, is the use of symbols, often considered "sacred" and not to be shared with the uninitiated. As mentioned earlier, the Second Degree (or *okuden*) class teaches students to trace these symbols with a hand or visualize them for various purposes: to enhance the efficacy of an in-person treatment; for "mental/emotional treatments" to help recipients overcome "bad habits" ranging from anxiety to alcoholism; or to perform "distance treatments" (*enkaku ryōhō*) for people who are not present. Distance treatments can use physical proxies (such as a photograph, a doll, or a part of the practitioner's own body) or visualization. Some practitioners also use the distance treatment to help ameliorate situations from the mundane to the profound. For example, in recent years, my interlocutors have encouraged me to "send *reiki*" to my job applications, wildfires, the COVID-19 pandemic, and armed conflicts.

A third common aspect of Reiki is the use of an empowerment ceremony to initiate practitioners or to advance their practice. The ability to perform this ceremony is what distinguishes Reiki Masters (also called *shihan*, Japanese for "instructor") from other practitioners. As discussed later in this chapter and in chapter 2, this ceremony was originally called *reiju* ("wonderful bestowal" or "spiritual bestowal") and performed many times throughout a practitioner's development. Some lineages continue this practice today, but in the Takata-lineage forms of Reiki that spread around the world in the 1980s and 1990s and are the most common today, the empowerment ritual is typically only used to initiate someone to a new "degree" or "level," so that Takata-lineage practitioners, even Masters, often only receive a handful of empowerments throughout their lifetime. That said, some Takata-lineage practitioners seek out initiation in many different Reiki "styles," while others find that practice distasteful, even disrespectful to one's initial Master.

A fourth common practice is to position oneself in a lineage that extends back to Usui Mikao. As part of Reiki training, many practitioners are given lineage charts connecting them, through their initiating Master, in an unbroken chain to Usui (a practice that resembles training or initiation lineages in Buddhism and martial arts). Lineage is related to another common practice—the mythic narration of Reiki's history—in that both link practitioners to Reiki's founding myth: that Usui had a mystical experience while fasting and meditating on Mount Kurama (a sacred mountain near Kyoto) that left him able to heal with *reiki* and to awaken that ability in others. In one sense, the instructor performing the *reiju*/initiation ceremony is a proxy for Usui, and generations of instructors have retold his story in their own image.[43] Simultaneously, the ceremony also ritually reenacts Usui's experience on Kurama: the student assumes Usui's role, sitting erect with head bowed, eyes closed, and hands in prayer position (*gasshō*), while the instructor connects them to the cosmic source of *reiki,* bestowing the student with the ability to channel *reiki* themselves.[44]

One final common Reiki practice is practitioners' internalization of five principles to guide their behavior. In Japanese, these are called Reiki's "doctrine" (*kyōgi*) or "five precepts" (*gokai*); in English they are often called "the Reiki Principles" or "Ideals." These principles and the various ways Takata translated and transformed them are discussed in the following chapters, but in general they are a commitment to, "just for today," refrain from anger and worry while cultivating gratitude, kindness, and diligence (later, professional integrity).

Diverse Practices

Reiki began to diversify in the years between 1922, when Usui founded his first training center, and 1935, when Takata began her training in Tokyo. It continued to diversify over the forty-five years of Takata's teaching career, as she adapted it for students in Hawai'i and North America, and it has continued to diversify in the decades since her death. In the 1980s and 1990s, as the Masters whom Takata trained initiated others, Takata-lineage Reiki spread around the world, and the number of Reiki practitioners multiplied from thousands in the North Pacific into possibly millions in over one hundred nations.[45] Yet tremendously diverse forms are taught under the name "Reiki." Some—such as Usui Shiki Ryoho, promoted by The Reiki Alliance, and The Radiance Technique / Real Reiki, promoted by The Radiance Technique International Association—claim to preserve the system exactly as Takata taught it. Others make no such attempt, openly adding to the teachings they had received or abandoning aspects as they see fit. Common additions include new symbols, use of crystals, visualization techniques, and metaphysical concepts and entities such as chakras, angels, spirit guides, and "the higher self." Some of these changes integrate aspects of other healing modalities, while others are based on channeled information. The latter are sometimes coupled with allegations that Takata and Usui themselves did not have the complete system of Reiki, as practiced in ancient Japan, Tibet, or Atlantis, or only now being revealed to humanity.

Among the nations where forms of Takata-lineage Reiki traveled in the 1980s was Japan, where it "returned" (in its adapted form) as a "re-imported" (*gyaku-yunyū*) practice that appealed to a growing New Age or "spiritual world" (*seishin sekai*) subculture.[46] In the 1990s, growing transnational interest in "traditional Japanese Reiki" led to the emergence of several Reiki lineages that purport to maintain the system of Usui Reiki Therapy practiced in prewar Japan, before Takata adapted it for American audiences. The basic practices described earlier—hands-on healing, symbols, distance treatments, initiation/empowerment ceremonies, lineages traced to Usui, and the five principles—are common to all forms of Reiki *sensu stricto,* but (as described in subsequent chapters) Takata de-emphasized practices that these "traditional Japanese" lineages consider central, such as chanting, meditation, and *reiju,* while adding new ones herself.[47] At the time of this writing, Takata-lineage Reiki continues to be the most widespread form worldwide, but even among that lineage, interest is growing in those aspects of Reiki practice that could be said to have been "lost in translation" during Takata's lifetime and in the transmission of Takata's teachings by subsequent generations.

Since Takata's death, representatives of various lineages have disputed the authenticity of other lineages and practices. In the twenty-first century, these disputes include a tendency to divide Reiki into "traditional Japanese" lineages that bypass Takata and "Western" lineages that derive from her lifework.[48] This book's North Pacific approach troubles this binary by demonstrating how practices with American origins influenced even the earliest forms of Usui Reiki Therapy. Moreover, as several of the adaptations Takata introduced for North American audiences were arguably intended to codify aspects of Japanese culture that she considered to be foundational for proper practice, they can be understood as her attempt to "Japanize" Reiki. Finally, as even detractors of "Western Reiki" acknowledge, Takata's labor to transmit and promote Reiki abroad was essential to its revival in Japan so, without her successful adaptation of Reiki for American audiences, Usui Reiki Therapy would have simply been one of hundreds of similar spiritual therapies that attracted followings in early twentieth-century Japan but largely died out by the postwar period.[49]

My Position as a Scholar-Practitioner

As a practitioner of Reiki as well as a scholar of its historical development, I inhabit what Duncan Ryūken Williams describes as "the middle position of a scholar-practitioner" who bridges the worlds of insiders and outsiders. Focusing on the role of Buddhist educators working in secular Buddhist studies, Williams writes that those who occupy this position must balance *sympathetic understanding* (that is, depicting the lived experience of insiders) with *critical perspective* (that is, representing one's own tradition as an object of study with diachronic and synchronic complexity), while avoiding apologetics or proselytization.[50] Several landmark works on new religious movements and spiritual therapies have been composed by scholars who write themselves (and, often, their own spiritual practices) into the text rather than dissemble their own commitments.[51] I hope this book earns a place on the shelf alongside other scholar-practitioners' self-reflexive studies.

I have practiced Reiki and related spiritual therapies for over two decades—essentially my entire adult life—and have researched them from an academic perspective for nearly as long. So many things have led me to this path—my mother's longtime practice of Transcendental Meditation; our family's friendship with and regular patronage of a spiritual therapist; my long-standing ambivalent interest in and skepticism of the paranormal— but one place this story begins is in a dark field in suburban New York in the summer of 1999, when a high school classmate asked if I had ever heard of chakras. We were home from university, working summer jobs and smoking a considerable amount of cannabis. When I replied that I had not, he told me his older brother was teaching a healing practice called Spiritual Human Yoga (SHY) that I might be interested in. About a week later, I was in the living room of their childhood home having my chakras "opened." I closed my eyes, and his brother lightly held his fingertips against various spots on my body for a few minutes: the crown, the "third eye," and four spots along the spine. I do not recall feeling much, but he asserted that my newly opened chakras enabled me to channel "universal energy." Daily meditation practice would enhance my capacity as a channel, and I could begin to diagnose others' chakra function and heal various ailments with my fingertips.

I began experimenting with this practice and began having unusual experiences that seemed profound. During meditation and the healing practice, I had preternatural sensations that I interpreted as the chakras opening and spinning. Treating a friend with chronic sinusitis, I would lightly touch three fingertips to the back of his neck (a spot correlated with the throat chakra, which governs the respiratory system) and his sinuses would emit loud popping noises and mucous would stream from his nose. During treatment, recipients and I often experienced sensations of heat and sweat would drip from our bodies. Sometimes recipients of my healing practice (again, simply a gentle laying of the fingertips on the spine) would have brief convulsions that we interpreted as the effects of "energy" coursing through us.

I attended a second course at my new teacher's home before borrowing hundreds of dollars from my parents to travel with him and some of his other students to Saint Louis to attend a SHY workshop held by the founder, Luong Minh Dang (1942–2007). Being in the presence of Master Dang, as he was typically called, I felt uncomfortable and grew convinced the group was a "cult." At the height of the workshop, Dang performed a mass initiation that he said opened up pyramid-shaped structures in our brains that awakened psychic powers. He told us that if we ever needed guidance, we should listen carefully to a still, small voice within us, and that was his voice, helping us along our paths. I wondered how to balance the profound experiences that my friends and I had while meditating and channeling cosmic power for healing with what seemed like an exploitative, profit-oriented organization.[52]

Over the next few years, I began my training in the academic study of religion and in participant-observation fieldwork. On an experiential Buddhist studies program in Japan, I practiced forms of meditation including *zazen* and esoteric (*mikkyō*) practices such as mantra recitation, *gachirinkan* (full moon meditation), and *ajikan* (meditation on the syllable "a"). To enhance our esoteric practices, we received a Buddhist initiation (*kechien kanjō*) in which we were blindfolded and performed a ritual that we were told linked us to Dainichi Nyorai, the cosmic Buddha. During esoteric practice, I experienced sensations and visions that I found exhilarating but also somewhat frightening, something akin to a psychedelic experience. Some classmates and I also had strange experiences while spending a week at a temple of Agonshū, a Japanese Buddhist "new religion." We felt manic, filled with energy, our heads buzzing, engaged in exciting conversations, laughing until tears streamed down our faces, and sleeping only a few hours a night. When we related our experiences to Agonshū members (through a translator), they assured us that many members felt this way, attributing it to the power of the altars in the building where we were staying, and shared their own remarkable stories of paranormal phenomena they attributed to their ritual practice before their altars in temple and at home.[53] I became interested in the relationship between phenomena associated with religious practice—especially surrounding healing—and commercialized "energy healing" modalities like Reiki and external qigong.

In 2001–2002, I conducted a year of participant-observation fieldwork on this subject thanks to a Thomas J. Watson Fellowship. My original proposal did not include travel to Japan but, in light of post-9/11 travel anxieties, I changed my project to largely examine practices of Japanese origin in countries considered safer for a young American abroad at that volatile time. I researched new religious movements in Japan and Thailand that practiced *jōrei,* a purification method believed to channel "God's light" through a raised hand to dispel pathogenic spiritual "clouds"; related groups in Japan and Australia that practice *okiyome,* a similar practice to exorcise maleficent spirits; and practitioners of Reiki in the United Kingdom, India, and Japan. As part of my research, I was initiated into Sekai Kyūseikyō (the Church of World Messianity, the parent organization of those *jōrei* groups) as well as the First and Second Degrees of (Takata-lineage) Reiki. I spent many hours at the NCC (National Christian Council) Center for the Study of Japanese Religions in Kyoto, familiarizing myself with the scholarly literature on Japanese new religions and trying to figure out how therapies like kundalini yoga, qigong, and Reiki fit alongside those practiced by religious organizations. Like Reiki, *jōrei* and *okiyome* have their roots in the spiritual therapies of 1920s Japan and have spread around the world, although their spread is less extensive and is concentrated in the Global South.[54]

I found that these therapies were meaningful to their practitioners beyond their perceived ability to provide physical healing. Many described bodily healing as one facet of a deeper practice, which they understood as restoring wholeness and balance to their bodies, minds, spirits, societies, and planet. I also found that the Japanese new religions I examined described health and illness in terms of purity and pollution, whereas what I would later call spiritual therapies tended to use the language of balance and imbalance, circulation and congestion.[55]

I wanted to contextualize Reiki vis-à-vis the Japanese new religions that practiced similar healing techniques, but the more I looked into the history of Reiki, by far the most widespread of any of the practices I examined, the more I discovered that much of what circulated was simply hagiography. Until the late 1990s, the only information readily available about Reiki's origins came from the oral history passed down by Takata: an archetypical "hero's journey"[56] about Usui as a Christian minister turned Buddhist monk questing to learn the secret of the healing powers exhibited by Jesus and the Buddhas that seemed roughly equal parts fact and fantasy. Beginning in the 1980s, practitioners ascribed Reiki's origins to ancient civilizations in Egypt and Tibet, the lost civilizations of Atlantis and Lemuria, and possibly extraterrestrials.[57] Many claimed to have uncovered Reiki's true, original forms, including an esoteric Buddhist version purportedly based on historical documents, which attracted prominent supporters until the documents were revealed to be channeled texts.[58]

A German Reiki Master living in Japan named Frank Arjava Petter (b. 1960) laid the foundation for a more empirically verifiable history of Reiki in a series of books that revealed historical information about Reiki prior to its leaving Japan, including translations of early texts by Usui.[59] However, this only spawned a new round of imaginative speculation about Reiki's origins. In the wake of Petter's publications, a group of Reiki Masters from Japan, North America, and Europe met on the nascent web and organized a series of conferences they called Usui Reiki Ryoho International (URRI) between 1999 and 2003. Like Petter, several URRI participants began teaching forms of "traditional Japanese Reiki," which they contrasted favorably with the forms taught by Takata lineages. URRI also promoted new histories based on unverifiable claims of encounters with Usui's surviving elderly students.[60]

The gap between Reiki practitioners' thirst for information about the origins of their practice and the lack of verifiable data about those origins led to my first study of Reiki history, a historiographic analysis of the stories various Reiki Masters told of Usui. I analyzed the text of the memorial that Usui's disciples erected in 1927, the story Takata told her students in the late 1970s, the New Age mythos published in the 1980s, an account of him as an esoteric Buddhist adept in the 1990s, and the "traditional Japanese Reiki" narratives that proliferated in the 2000s. I concluded that these conflicting founder narratives were means for teachers to identify themselves as authentic, authoritative substitutes for the absent original master and to provide mythic maps for their students' journeys to healing.[61] The book you are reading builds on this perspective with another decade-plus of research and the discovery of several troves of data, representing the most complete telling to date of Reiki's first sixty years.

Primary Sources

Alternate Currents is based on several groups of materials I assembled between 2012 and 2023. The first is a collection of over twenty oral histories I conducted with individuals who studied with Takata over the course of her teaching career, from Nisei (second-generation Japanese Americans) who learned Reiki in 1930s Hawai'i to attendees of the class at Gray Creek Hall in 1980. In cases in which Takata's students were deceased or suffered from cognitive decline, I interviewed their families.

While conducting these interviews, I also spent time in the archives at the University of Hawai'i at Mānoa (UHM) and the Kaua'i Historical Society to gather material about Takata's early life, her family, and the sugar planter families that employed them. I read Japanese-language publications from the 1920s and 1930s that described early versions of Reiki in Japan and Hawai'i, including a spate of articles in the *Hawaii Hochi,* one of Honolulu's chief Japanese-language newspapers. I collected publications and unpublished correspondence and testimonials that described Reiki's circulation and practice in the postwar decades. I also found archived assignments written about Reiki for UHM sociology classes in the 1940s by students who knew of Takata, often because of family or acquaintances who had studied under her. In Japan, I found more sources, both in libraries and through speaking with elder members of the organization founded by Usui in 1922, the Usui Reiki Therapy Study Association for Improving Mind and Body (Shinshin Kaizen Usui Reiki Ryōhō Gakkai, hereafter the Usui Association). Very recently, my colleague Olaf Böhm acquired and made available a trove of prewar Usui Association materials that have helped inform my analysis of that period.

Some of the most important sources for this book, the personal papers of Takata, were not yet archived when I began this research. They had been kept in storage for three decades by Takata's granddaughter, Phyllis Furumoto, and had never before been comprehensively examined or organized. Starting in 2014, Furumoto and I worked with a few others (mentioned in the acknowledgments) to organize, catalog, and digitize these photographs, correspondence, certificates, audio recordings, and other materials, which Furumoto subsequently donated to the American Religions Collection of the University of California, Santa Barbara, where they were opened to the public in 2018 as the Hawayo Takata Papers.[62]

I have also performed years of participant-observation research on Reiki in North America and Japan, participating in well over one hundred events where practitioners gather to trade treatments and discuss experiences with Reiki, called "Reiki shares," "study meetings" (*kenkyūkai*), or "exchange meetings" (*kōryūkai*, again using that same Japanese term used for "alternating current"). My status as a Second Degree practitioner has given me access to interviews and materials that would have been unavailable for a nonpractitioner, particularly regarding the symbols, which many practitioners believe should not be shown or even described to individuals who have not been initiated to the Second Degree. At the same time, I am neither a Master nor a professional practitioner. This provides some limitations, as Masters decline to discuss certain topics with me (such as the initiation rituals), but also engenders a certain trust among my interlocutors, who recognize that my research is an end in itself rather than a means to promote my own commercial practice.

Writing This Book

I could have written any number of books based on these materials. I could have looked at how Reiki's development and spread in the postwar United States coincided with and was shaped by the development of the rise of self-identification as "spiritual but not religious" in North America.[63] I could have used the materials in Takata's personal papers to examine how Takata and those she treated and taught learned to tell particular types of stories about illness and healing, a subject common to religious studies and medical anthropology, among other fields.[64] As Reiki's earliest organizations were male dominated but the therapy became predominantly practiced by women by the late 1930s (despite the disproportionate number of men among the most visible teachers), I could have done more extensive analysis of gender in Reiki's history to complement the ethnographic work that has been done on Reiki and gender.[65] Of course, I could have written Takata's biography, whether a hagiography of her remarkable accomplishments or a critical appraisal of her entrepreneurial dealings.

While I touch on all of those concerns in these pages, this book primarily focuses on how Reiki's twentieth-century North Pacific networks shaped its development and circulation; what Reiki's appeal and transformation tell us about that time and place; how spiritual therapies draw on religious, medical, and scientific authority while also critiquing those fields as incomplete; and how transnational spiritual therapies evoke their purported homelands while transcending national boundaries for their influences and in their reach. It addresses how twentieth-century practitioners in Japan, Hawaiʻi, and North America repeatedly reshaped Reiki in relation to their lived experiences of multiple authorities, including religion, medicine, and the ongoing rearticulation of gender and racial difference. The social, cultural, political, economic, and spiritual dimensions of these experiences cannot be fully teased apart, but this study attempts to understand how these forces combined to drive Reiki's development.

In writing this book, I neither was concerned with establishing any given aspect of Reiki practice as more or less authentic or authoritative nor aspired for this to be the only authoritative version of this period of Reiki's history. This is but one telling of that story, and it doubtless contains some inaccuracies and many omissions. Its incompleteness illustrates the fragility inherent to human endeavor. Put poetically by historian Jill Lepore, "History's written from what can be found; what isn't saved is lost, sunken and rotted, eaten by earth."[66] For every story I have salvaged, countless others are irretrievable.

At many points during my research, I felt the regret of being informed that the materials I sought had recently been lost, whether consigned to landfills or to the ravages of amnesia. After several unsuccessful attempts to reach the daughter of one of North America's first Reiki Masters, I finally got her on the phone only to be told, "Oh, I just cleaned out Mom's stuff last year." Even Furumoto, who dutifully retained a dozen boxes of her grandmother's papers and possessions for decades, remembered throwing out a box of her grandmother's letters long ago. As sometimes a single letter led to important revelations, I have often dreamed of what testimonies and research leads that box contained. These losses occur on the mental plane in addition to the physical one. When interviewing elderly Reiki practitioners in Hilo, Hawaiʻi, I was frequently told, "If you came a few years ago, I would remember more." Other historic practitioners whom I contacted were beyond the point of remembering anything. This telling is thus circumscribed by the limits of memory and mortality, the impressions that remain in elders' recollections and dusty boxes retained in storage.

Secrecy

As with anyone writing about a tradition marked by conventions of secrecy, I have had to face difficult decisions about how much to say about the details of Reiki practice.[67] Many Reiki practitioners, like those of other initiation-based organizations, intentionally limit what they reveal in print.[68] This prohibition is sometimes enforced formally, as when, in the spring of 2014, on becoming a member of the aforementioned Usui Association, I had to sign a nondisclosure agreement not to describe its practices to nonmembers. This organization has employed this sort of contract since the 1920s, which resembles a much older practice of written pledges (*kishōmon*) not to betray secret teachings in Japanese initiation-based organizations.[69] It is more often enforced structurally, through practices of omission. For example, while that organization gave me permission to include translated excerpts of its handbook, the text includes little information about how to perform Usui Reiki Therapy, emphasizing the importance of a direct master-student relationship. In places, this balance between disclosure and self-censorship limits the scope of my analysis, but this is among the balancing acts of research ethics.

Amid a proliferation of books about Reiki, many practitioners express distaste, even rancor, for books and websites that reproduce the symbols that are not taught until one is initiated to the advanced levels.[70] A common discourse says disseminating these symbols to uninitiated eyes desacralizes them, reducing their power or efficacy. One practitioner in Hawai'i criticized my regrettable decision to include the symbols in my master's thesis (which at the time I thought was defensible given their proliferation on the internet and their potential interest to religious studies) as "gut-wrenching," "beyond disrespectful," and analogous to "digging up the bones of your ancestors," a powerful comparison to make in a place where the disinterment of ancestral remains is a potent issue.[71] I have since internalized these secrecy practices in an embodied fashion: while conducting fieldwork in the summer of 2016, I was on a public bus with one of Takata's students whom I wanted to show a document that contained the symbols in Takata's hand; as the file opened on my laptop, we both instinctively flinched and reached to tilt the screen to make sure others could not see. Out of respect for this culture, I have intentionally left out crucial information intended for initiates, such as the exact forms of the Reiki symbols and the procedures by which initiations are performed.

Lineage

As a practitioner-scholar, I stand at the intersection of two initiation lineages, two fictive kinships, that each train me to mediate between the embodied and the intangible. My *Doktormutter* (a term for doctoral supervisor that connotes lineage) and doctoral committee pushed me to move more adeptly between data and theory in the study of religion; my training under various Reiki Masters has urged me to tune into subtle bodily sensations. The one connects me to legendary anthropologists, sociologists, and historians; the other to Reiki's so-called spiritual lineage of Grand Masters. Over the decade-plus that I worked on this material, I spent so much time with these figures they began to feel almost like family members. Other scholars also report this air of kin-like proximity with historical subjects and ethnographic interlocutors, and the experience of feeling familial bonds to the initiation lineage is also common in the Reiki world. My interlocutors sometimes refer to the Masters who initiated them as their Reiki parents and others who received initiations from the same Master as their Reiki brothers or sisters. This phenomenon follows the same fictive kinship structure of the Buddhist monastic communities that developed the ceremonies on which the Reiki initiations are patterned.[72] As in more traditional forms of Japanese religion, a practitioner's lineage determines not only their training but also their social status.[73]

This feeling of familial relation adds an uncanny dimension to my genealogical work. The fact that I spent a few exquisite years in Hawai'i contributes to the faux nostalgia I feel when poring over photographs of Reiki classes held in Buddhist churches in the prewar Islands, an imagined connection to a time I never knew, somewhat akin to the feeling of seeing photos of my grandparents as young folks in prewar New York. Yet I know that being a White male accords me privileges denied to Takata and her predominantly female, Japanese American students in the patriarchal, White supremacist society of Territorial Hawai'i, particularly in the war-time years, when their ancestry placed them under threat of incarceration. Complicating matters, the same Orientalist forces that reinforced Takata's authority in teaching "a Japanese healing art" in the postwar decades, when interest rose in religious and medical practices of Asian descent, also helped structure my initial interest in Buddhism and Reiki. Takata's gendered position as a widow, combined with the elder status she possessed near the end of her career, posed other limitations but also structured her authority in complex ways. These factors leave me with a pronounced and peculiar sense of being both insider and outsider in the narration of Takata's life and Reiki's history. My Japanese language abilities and my years of studying Reiki's origins in Japan and Hawai'i lend me authority that can feel uneasy when talking with elders who became Reiki Masters before I was even born.

This unease was particularly pronounced when working with Furumoto, Takata's granddaughter, and I found myself teaching her about aspects of her own family's history.

The authority of the scholar-practitioner's "middle position" is particularly noticeable when I speak to practitioner audiences. While I encounter occasional resistance to my findings or analysis, I am generally overwhelmed by expressions of gratitude from my audiences, who are awed to hear a fellow practitioner offering scholarly analysis of our practice's historical development; I am invariably asked, "When is the book coming out?" These experiences make me conscious of the role my research plays in Reiki's ongoing circulation as communities become aware of the processes behind their own formation. With emic audiences, I often explicitly state that it is not my intention to authorize or discredit any particular forms of practice, and the fact that I have training in both Takata-lineage and "traditional Japanese" Reiki (in addition to the previously mentioned facts that I am neither a Reiki Master nor a professional practitioner) helps substantiate that I do not have my own particular form of practice to promote.

Chapter Outlines

Each chapter examines different "currents" in Reiki's North Pacific circulation. These currents flowed into and alongside each other, yet each had its own characteristics resulting from its time and place, as well as varied ripples formed by those who swam in them.

Chapter 1, "Seeds of a Transpacific Network: A Young Woman on Kaua'i, 1900–1930," describes Takata's early life, from her birth to the untimely death of her husband. It provides context about the creation of the US Territory of Hawai'i and the history of Nikkei settlers (i.e., those of Japanese descent) there. Using archival information collected in Kaua'i and O'ahu and a series of autobiographical recordings Takata made in 1979, it provides a sense of Takata's life before Reiki training. To establish themes sustained in the following chapters, particular attention is paid to Takata's early religious views and her relative social mobility in light of Nikkei's racial formation in early twentieth-century Hawai'i.

Chapter 2, "Drawn into the Current: Encountering Usui Reiki Therapy's Japanese Circulation, 1922–1937," uses Takata's training in 1935 as a springboard to dive into the early circulation of Usui Reiki Therapy in 1920s and 1930s Japan. It provides sociocultural context for the wave of spiritual therapies that crested in Japan in this period, including Japan's rapid mod-

ernization in the late nineteenth and early twentieth centuries and competing trends of Westernization and nativism. It also provides information about
Reiki's founder Usui Mikao, his disciple Hayashi Chūjirō, and the changes
Reiki had already undergone at the time of Takata's training. This chapter
draws on the few documents about Reiki from this time (including Takata's diary), as well as Takata's later recorded recollections. It demonstrates
that, even prior to leaving Japan, Reiki was formed at a confluence of local
and foreign influences; that its promoters alternated between religious, medical, and scientific frequencies; and that Hayashi had adapted Usui's method
to help it reach new audiences.

Chapter 3, "Healing at the Hub of the Transwar Pacific: Adapting
Reiki for Nikkei Hawai'i, 1937–1960," follows Usui Reiki Therapy's circulation in Hawai'i, largely among Nikkei Buddhists, during the transwar
period from the late 1930s through the 1950s. It describes how Takata
adapted its practices in this period in response to her training in naturopathy, massage, and other therapies; the wartime criminalization of Japanese
Buddhism; and the increased professionalization of medical care in the
midcentury United States. This chapter draws on oral histories conducted
in Hawai'i with students of Takata from this period (and their families),
archival materials, and Takata's autobiographical writings and recordings.
It presents tensions between how Takata's predominantly Nikkei Buddhist
students understood their practice and her increasing professionalization of
the practice she began simply calling Reiki.

Chapter 4, "Building Authority in the Cold War United States: Networks, Esotericism, and Alterity in White America, 1948–1972," examines how Takata built networks of (chiefly White Christian) clients and
students on the US mainland in the immediate postwar period, as well as
the bidirectional influences between her and these students. It examines
Takata's involvement with students of varied class backgrounds, from
working-class immigrants to Hollywood stars; the impact of her membership in esoteric fraternal organizations on Reiki; and how Nikkei's racial
rearticulation in the postwar United States affected her teaching practice.
This chapter describes a period of Reiki's history about which little was
previously known, and its data largely comes from Takata's personal papers, especially correspondence with her students, as well as phone interviews with the surviving families of these students. This period saw the
beginning of Takata's coupling of two currents ("Orientalization" and
"universalization") that would increase in power in the 1970s.

Chapter 5, "Coupling Universalism and 'Japanese' Values: Making North American Masters, 1972–1980," looks at how Takata systematized Reiki over the last eight years of her life, the most prolific period teaching in her long career, and the period that would shape the following decades of Reiki's global circulation. It examines Takata's use of print media and religious networks while constructing new narratives and practices that built on Orientalist and perennialist trends prevalent within the communities where she taught. It pays particular attention to three networks that formed the core of her teaching activities in these years—the suburbs of San Francisco and Chicago, and the rural interior of British Columbia—as she trained the next generation of Reiki Masters. It also considers how Takata's authority grew in these years as she became a charismatic elder seen in light of cultural tropes about aged Asian spiritual masters. The data for this chapter is based on archival material—including letters, class logs, receipt books, and publications, memoirs, and other accounts written by Takata's students—as well as original oral histories. It emphasizes that Takata's attempts to socialize her students with certain "Japanese" values that she saw as essential for Reiki's efficacy resulted in a kind of "particular universalism" that combines perennialist and Orientalist themes to attribute Asian origins to this transnational spiritual therapy to bolster its authority. It also examines how students negotiate the relationship between Reiki's commodification and its spirituality, concluding that its potential as a professional vocation actually helped practitioners consider it capable of providing spiritual fulfillment while being independent from (while not unrelated to) institutional religion.

The conclusion highlights the salience of the dynamics of Reiki's development for broader trends in the North Pacific and beyond. It clarifies how this study of Reiki's circulation helps make sense of other phenomena, particularly other spiritual therapies that circulate in transnational networks, including yoga, meditation, and Indigenous ceremony. It reflects on the tension between the particularism that ties these practices and their practitioners to the lands of these therapies' origin, which they imbue with spiritual potency, and the universalism that makes these practices available to global, cosmopolitan audiences. It also remarks on how practitioners negotiate tensions between these therapies' spiritual and commercial dimensions, as well as tensions between structure and agency in their circulation.

CHAPTER 1

Seeds of a Transpacific Network
A Young Woman on Kaua'i, 1900–1930

In July 2014, about a month before her sixty-sixth birthday, I helped Phyllis Lei Furumoto move a dozen boxes from her storage unit into the back of her late-model red SUV. As Phyllis lived in southern Arizona, about forty miles north of the Mexican border, we started early in anticipation of the desert heat. Phyllis' mother, Alice Takata Furumoto, had packed these boxes roughly three decades earlier with the papers and possessions of Phyllis' grandmother, Hawayo Hiromi Kawamura Takata—the woman who transmitted Reiki from Japan to Hawai'i and North America, adapting it along the way to make this spiritual therapy intelligible to non-Japanese—but Phyllis had never been sure what to do with them. My research on Takata's lifework happened to coincide with a time when Phyllis wanted to relieve herself of the responsibility of safeguarding these materials. After a few years of her living with cancer in remission, her doctors had found metastases. With an acute sense of her mortality, Phyllis sought to create a home for these materials where successive generations of Reiki students could access them.

As a first step, the two of us unpacked and organized the boxes' contents in a three-room casita that Phyllis had rented for that purpose. As we opened these dusty boxes and began to spread out and group their contents on ten large folding tables, we repeatedly felt overwhelmed, not only by the sheer quantity of materials but also by the powerful stories these artifacts told of Takata and her interlocutors. Some of these stories were contained in letters or other texts, others were evoked by photographs, and others still silently resonated in objects that held echoes of events long past. In the main room, we propped up some large, framed black-and-white photos of Takata with her teacher and their students, further imbuing the space with their presence.

Among Takata's correspondence, photographs, and personal effects (from Buddhist memorial tablets to golf trophies) was a small cardboard box containing eleven numbered cassette tapes. When we inserted the first tape into a player and pressed play, we heard Takata's voice, a little unsteady, suggesting her advanced age (they were recorded a fortnight before her seventy-ninth birthday), declaring that she will speak about Reiki, which she learned forty-four years prior in Japan. As she continues, her voice gains vitality and exhibits remarkable endurance while she recounts her early years in Kaua'i, her travel to Japan and training, and abundant testimonials of Reiki's power to heal body, mind, and spirit. Takata's compelling elocution of powerful, often unbelievable stories frequently gave me "chicken skin."[1] These tapes were recorded over the course of a week in December 1979 by Takata's student Barbara Weber and were to form the basis of her autobiography, *Reiki Is God-Power,* which she had recruited Weber to ghostwrite. This repository of over seventeen hours of storytelling (seemingly without notes, with only two stories repeated) testifies to Takata's near half century of experience repeating these stories to students and clients, and it is filled with examples of how Takata portrayed her undeniably remarkable life as a mythos that helped establish her spiritual authority for receptive audiences.

The first story on the tape, that of her own birth, exudes this kind of mythic quality, honed through many iterations. As she tells it, the sun was just rising over the rippled hills of eastern Kaua'i on December 24, 1900, when Hatsu Kawamura (1873–1944) gave birth to her third child, a girl, in the plantation shack where she lived with her husband, Otogorō (1866–1953), and their three-year-old son, Kazuo (1897–1920). Hatsu and Otogorō's firstborn, a girl they named Kawayo, after the island where the Kawamuras worked in the cane fields, had died after only ten days. In a plea for their second daughter to have the strength to survive, they named her Hawayo, after the Big Island of Hawai'i, hoping this name would imbue her with the considerable power of that island: the archipelago's largest, home of the active volcano Kilauea, and the namesake of the US Territory of Hawai'i established earlier that year. As Takata reminisced nearly eight decades later, Kawayo's name "was too small, that is why she did not live long," and her parents transferred the high expectations they had for Kawayo's success onto her. Her mother told the midwife, "Please, give her a bath, wrap her on a new blanket, and face her the sun [*sic*]. And then I want you to initiate her by putting your hand on top of her head and say, 'I name you Hawayo.' And say it three times. And after that, she said 'success.' 'Success and success.' . . . So, this was my initiation to the world."[2]

The core elements of this version of her birth story resemble those of another version she told a reporter for the *Honolulu Advertiser* five years prior, in which the attending midwife patted her newborn head three times and "predicted she would be a success."[3] Both emphasize her receiving a ritualized initiation immediately following her birth. The hand on her head and threefold repetition are common elements of ritual that appear in the Reiki initiations and the use of the Reiki symbols. Holding up a newborn child in the rays of the rising sun not only is cinematic but also evokes iconography associated with Japan (the land of the rising sun), popular understandings of Shinto (and its sun goddess Amaterasu), and Reiki's cosmic source. She and her students also consciously foreshadow her spiritual calling by emphasizing her birth on Christmas Eve.[4] Despite being a lifelong Buddhist, Takata's comfort with and predilection for Christian references served her later in life as she built connections to White Christians, who would ultimately make up the majority of her Reiki students.

Her birth story also emphasizes how her life was shaped by Hawai'i and its colonization by the United States. Her parents migrated to Kaua'i to work on a sugar plantation owned by wealthy Americans, where they met and settled.[5] For decades, the plantation was the (direct or indirect) employer for her family and community. Her strong identification with the US annexation of Hawai'i is audible in this recording, when she boasts of having been born "the year Hawaii became a [US] Territory . . . not knowing that in many, many later years [*sic*], we would ever become a state."[6] The most intimate details of Takata's life bear the imprint of the culture that formed in Hawai'i under settler colonial capitalism: her given name is a Japanization of the name of the recently overthrown kingdom, and her English-language pronunciation and intonation are influenced by the Hawaiian Creole English that developed as a common language for diverse settlers from North America, Europe, and Asia to communicate with each other and with Native Hawaiians.[7]

This chapter examines the first three decades of Hawayo Takata's life in Kaua'i to contextualize dimensions of her socialization—particularly regarding her religious life, her ethnoracialization as "Japanese," and her relative social mobility—that later proved crucial to her career as a practitioner and teacher of a spiritual therapy attributed to Japan. It briefly describes the sugar industry that shaped both Hawai'i's colonization and her early life; the position of Nikkei (people of Japanese descent) and Nisei (second-generation Nikkei) in Hawai'i; and her and her husband Saichi's professional advancement and community involvement, which facilitated her ability to gain White patrons in later decades.

Nikkei Labor and the Kaua'i Sugar Industry

The Kawamuras' social status in the nascent Territory of Hawai'i was linked to broader developments in the North Pacific. At the time of Hawayo's birth, sugar dominated the Hawaiian economy: approximately 20 percent of Kaua'i's landmass—the vast majority of its arable land—was planted with cane in 1900.[8] The vast majority of these fields had been planted in the last fifty years as investments by American capitalists, and it was their desire to ensure the profitability of those investments that led to America's colonization of the Kingdom of Hawai'i.

The Kawamura home in Hanama'ulu where Hawayo was born was owned by the Lihue Plantation Company (LPC). Founded in 1849 by three White American investors who would each play an important role in the late years of the Kingdom of Hawai'i, within thirty years the LPC would become the Kingdom's "best financed, most modern, and most costly" plantation.[9] The rise of the American-owned sugar industry occurred in the wake of devastating epidemics that had killed as much as 90 percent of the Native Hawaiian population since the first arrival of Europeans in 1778.[10] In 1810, Kaua'i joined the Hawaiian Kingdom of Kamehameha I (ca. 1736–1819), and Kaikio'ewa (1765–1839), a cousin of Kamehameha, was named its governor in 1825. In 1835, Kaikio'ewa oversaw the beginning of the Hawaiian sugar industry, leasing nearly one thousand acres in Kōloa, on the south shore, to three White Americans who founded the first plantation in the archipelago. Soon thereafter, Kaikio'ewa established the town of Līhu'e (named after his former residence in west O'ahu) as his new residence, planning to grow sugarcane himself, but he died unexpectedly of mumps.[11] Then, in 1848, a massive land redistribution called the Māhele (division) allowed White elites, such as the LPC founders, to acquire large tracts of land at the expense of the surviving Native Hawaiians.[12]

The LPC (then called Henry A. Peirce & Co.) built a large mill in Līhu'e in 1851, helping establish this town as Kaua'i's center of industry, and five years later completed the ten-mile irrigation ditch that allowed the expansion of operations to Hanama'ulu in the northeast.[13] The foundation for the mill there was built in 1855 using stones from a large abandoned *heiau* (temple) named Kalauokamanu, known for its many human sacrifices.[14] Improved irrigation made the plantation profitable, and it expanded further when the plantation manager purchased the entire Hanamaʻulu *ahupuaʻa* (a traditional Hawaiian land division roughly corresponding to a watershed) following the death of its *aliʻi* (chief) in 1870. The LPC further expanded its production in Hanamaʻulu with the construction of a second mill in 1877.[15] During the period of the LPC's expansion, the Reciprocity Treaty of 1875 gave planters in Hawaiʻi free access to US markets—the final factor marking the shift of the Kingdom's chief industry from whaling to sugar—and over the next two decades, sugar production in Hawaiʻi increased twentyfold.[16]

In order to expand planting and production, American investors in Hawaiian sugar required imported labor. They first looked to China, bringing in the first 500 laborers on five-year contracts in 1865. Two decades later, over 22 percent of the Kingdom's population was Chinese.[17] Labor recruiters illegally gave contracts to 150 Japanese in the port city of Yokohama in 1868 (the first year of the Meiji state, which rapidly modernized and internationalized Japan) and smuggled them to the Hawaiian Islands; disagreements over working conditions led many of them to quickly return to Japan.[18] As Chinese residents of Hawaiʻi began to establish their own commercial establishments and demand higher wages, the Kingdom began negotiating with Japan to officially sponsor contract labor immigration and undercut local Chinese labor interests.

Beginning in 1885, when Japan lifted its ban on such migration, Robert Irwin, the Kingdom of Hawaiʻi's acting consul general in Japan, privately organized shiploads of migrant laborers to the Kingdom, each bearing roughly one thousand Japanese. Unlike the failed 1868 experiment, which employed laborers with no farming experience from urban Yokohama, Irwin largely recruited farmers from four rural prefectures (Hiroshima, Yamaguchi, Kumamoto, and Fukuoka) in western Japan. These prefectures had all suffered greatly from the Meiji land reforms that privatized land ownership, setting the stage for the institution of a cash-based taxation system and the development of a capitalist economy. As mortgage foreclosures seized vast areas of farmland and imported cotton depressed the value of silk textiles, peasant riots over land taxes were rampant. Labor migration to Hawaiʻi not only was a source of agricultural labor for American planters but was also seen by Japanese politicians as a way to deal with overpopulation, a lack of domestic resources, and domestic unrest in the impoverished western region.[19]

The Kawamuras were part of this labor diaspora from western Japan to the Hawaiian Islands. Hawayo's father, Otogorō, emigrated from Kumage (Yamaguchi Prefecture) in 1892, and her mother, Hatsu Tamashima, came from Aki (Hiroshima Prefecture) in 1894.[20] American-funded importation of agricultural labor from western Japan developed transpacific social networks linking this region to Territorial Hawai'i and, eventually, the US mainland, so these prefectures continued to be the main sites for Japanese American immigration into the first decade of the twentieth century.[21] At the time of the Immigration Act of 1924, which virtually prohibited further Asian immigration to the United States and its territories, nearly 90 percent of Hawai'i's Nikkei population traced their ancestry to these four western provinces plus Okinawa, an archipelago in Japan's southwest that the Meiji state annexed in the 1870s.[22]

In January 1893, about a year after Otogorō Kamamura arrived and a few months before the Japanese government sent their first state-sponsored ships of contract laborers to the Kingdom of Hawai'i, a group called the Citizen's Committee of Public Safety overthrew the Hawaiian monarchy. The thirteen men who made up this committee were largely US nationals and naturalized Hawaiian citizens of US background, they received US military support, and they plotted this overthrow as a step toward the full US annexation of the Islands. A large part of their motivation was to benefit the local sugar industry. The McKinley Tariff of 1890, effectively a subsidy for beet sugar grown on the US mainland, had caused the value of Hawaiian sugar to drop by nearly half; annexation, the argument went, would eliminate the tariff for Hawaiian sugar in the American market and make it competitive again. The 1898 annexation ultimately had varied effects on the Hawaiian sugar industry, though. When Hawai'i became a US territory, its sugar planters received federal subsidies, but the Hawaiian Organic Act of 1900 also extended US laws to the Islands, putting an end to the contract system and causing labor costs to rise accordingly.[23]

These developments in Hawai'i's political economy led to dramatic changes in its demographics. In the five years leading up to 1890, Nikkei went from being hardly present in the Islands to becoming over 42 percent of Hawai'i's plantation workforce. In 1902, four years after the United States annexed the Islands, over 73 percent of plantation workers were Nikkei.[24] In January 1902, the Hanama'ulu payroll of the LPC was roughly 70 percent

Nikkei, including Otogorō Kawamura, although within a few decades, most of these workers would be replaced by cheaper laborers from the Philippines, also colonized by the United States at the turn of the century.[25] Laborers emigrating from China, Japan, Korea, and the Philippines to Territorial Hawai'i in the late nineteenth and early twentieth centuries generally assumed they would return to their lands of origin after making money working in the profitable US sugar industry, but for a variety of reasons, enough ended up staying and raising families that the population of the Territory of Hawai'i became over half of Chinese or Japanese descent by 1910 and nearly two-thirds of Asian descent (38 percent Nikkei) by 1930.[26]

These immigrants and their children were subjects of America's White supremacist colonial capitalism, which extended its frontier to the Pacific under Presidents William McKinley and Theodore Roosevelt, but they were also settlers participating in the colonization of a recently sovereign nation.[27] They lived in a society economically and culturally dominated by Whites, but the second-generation Nisei achieved "considerable educational and occupational mobility . . . rearticulating dominant concepts and values to assert their identities as simultaneously 'Japanese' *and* 'American.'"[28] However, as their Issei (first-generation) parents were denied the right to naturalize as American citizens, their families lived "between two empires," as many supported the expansion of Imperial Japan, and even subsequent generations were subject to Japanese military conscription.[29] The Nisei Hawayo Kawamura left school after the sixth grade to help provide for her family, but she exhibited social ambition even as a young woman and, in her adult life, would make use of her dual identity to achieve remarkable social mobility.

Childhood

Like some 90 percent of Nisei children in the Territory at the time, Hawayo attended both Japanese school at a religious institution and the so-called normal school, taught in English. This dual education system ensured that she would learn the fundamentals of both the Japanese and English languages, but it was also used in the "Americanization" campaigns of the 1920s to argue that Nisei were being indoctrinated into worship of the Japanese emperor and would never be loyal Americans.[30] Such xenophobic concerns notwithstanding, Hawayo (nicknamed Hawa) was such a good student in the Hanama'ulu Normal School that, in grade six, she won an essay contest to have her composition about a class trip to the seashore published in the local English-language paper.[31] However, in the relative backwaters of Kaua'i, she was not exposed to the same "finishing school" mentality that tied Nisei femininity and social uplift to developing Standard English oratory that prevailed in Honolulu.[32] As a result, she spoke what linguists call "Hawaiian near-standard English," which exhibits some of the phonology, grammar, and intonation of Hawaiian Creole English. To mainland ears, it had "the acoustic effect of a 'foreign accent,'" but locally it marked her as of lower-class origins.[33]

The Kawamuras were Honpa Hongwanji (a.k.a. Nishi Honganji, one of the two largest branches of Jōdo Shinshū—also called Shin—Buddhism), so Hawayo probably first attended Japanese school at the Lihue Hongwanji Mission (founded 1900) near the Hanama'ulu plantation, and, after they moved to the Keālia plantation a few miles to the northeast, at the Kealia Hongwanji Mission (founded 1910). However, Hawayo seems to have also felt at ease with religious traditions outside of her Shin Buddhist upbringing from an early age.

Later in those 1979 recordings, Takata recalled how, as a petite twelve-year-old who suffered through her first summer cutting cane seedlings in Keālia, at the end of the final day, before getting on the train that took them out of the fields, she got on her knees and prayed that God might provide her better things to do with her hands than that strenuous and dangerous job, bowing three times and kissing the ground. For this show of piety, her schoolmates teased, "Oh, you just prayed to Allah. And so you believe in Allah. Allah is your God. Alright, your name shall be Allah from now on," and she recounts that they made this her new nickname.[34] By relating how foreign her prostrations seemed to her classmates, Takata set herself apart from her peers as someone devoutly dedicated to a world beyond the physical, and her reference to "doing better things with my hands" foreshadows her work with Reiki healing in mythic fashion. The strangeness of her religious expression to her ostensibly Nikkei classmates is remarkable given the general acceptance of "multiple religious belonging" in Japanese culture, as well as the existence of prostration in Japanese Buddhist practice.[35]

Takata's late-life recollections of her childhood project the image of an early religious devotion not bounded by her Buddhist education, a kind of liberal eclecticism that may have informed her later perennialism. Her usage of the word "God" in describing her childhood religious beliefs and her memories of her unusual nickname "Allah" suggest an early relationship with non-Buddhist traditions. It is difficult to say where children growing up on a sugar plantation in 1913 Kauaʻi would have encountered descriptions of Islam, but some of her Nisei peers were likely Christians.[36] A small number of Issei were already Christians before immigrating to Hawaiʻi, some converted after immigration and raised their children Christian, and some Nisei were converted because their parents sent them to Japanese Christian church schools to keep them "away from bad company" or as an active means of assimilation.[37] As will be described in chapter 5, Takata employed Christian practices later in life and was ordained in a metaphysical church in the 1970s. However, her continued relationship with Buddhist institutions from the 1930s into the 1970s and her lifelong maintenance of a Buddhist home altar (*butsudan*) suggest that she maintained a Buddhist identity in her private life. Her description of her childhood prayers to "God" may have been a way to translate to her White Christian biographer a devotion to conceptions of deities (*kami-sama*) her parents or priests brought from Japan, or it may reveal monotheistic influences in her childhood. Either way, Takata's anomalous story of her schoolmates teasing her as "Allah" for her prostrations, doubly exoticized as both non-Japanese and non-Christian, expresses to her audience that a fervent religiosity set her apart at an early age.

Early Work Experience

Hawayo's slight build precluded her from being a productive field hand, but she needed to contribute to the household, so she moved out of her parents' home at age thirteen (after finishing grade six) and into a "church boarding school" (most likely the Kealia Hongwanji Church, where she had attended Japanese school), where she worked as a substitute first-grade teacher. This paid her keep plus a little extra, which she gave to her family. The following year, she got a second job at the soda fountain at the Lihue Store, a fancy department store known as Kauai's Emporium that opened to great fanfare in late 1913 because of its elevator, high ceilings, and spacious cold-storage department.[38] So, she recalled, after she finished her school duties at eight o'clock in the morning, when her students left for the English-language normal school, fourteen-year-old Hawayo walked the seven miles from Keālia to Līhuʻe to wash dishes and serve ice cream.[39] She eventually took on a third job in her "spare time" doing paperwork in the store's office.[40] Her working multiple jobs in her early teenage years indicates her diligence, working-class status, and social ambition. Service industry positions like those in education, retail, and domestic labor were among the only professional opportunities available for Nisei women, and wherever she worked, young Hawayo seems to have dedicated herself, networked, and progressively taken on greater responsibilities.

Working at this prestigious department store also provided her new opportunities. While working at the Lihue Store, Hawayo developed a relationship with a regular customer named Julia Makee Spalding (1876–1949), whom she called "the Countess."[41] For decades, the Spalding family had owned the Makee Sugar Company, where Hawayo's father worked at the time, and Julia's brother James Makee Spalding (1880–1954) continued to be the company president and manager of their Keālia plantation even after the family sold a controlling interest to the LPC in 1910.[42] At sixteen, Hawayo joined the household staff of the Valley House, the Spalding family's sumptuous Victorian estate atop the Keālia ridge that slopes down to the Pacific Ocean, carpeted at that time with Makee Sugar cane fields.[43]

At the Valley House, Hawayo served the Spaldings and worked her way up from waitress to pantry girl to head housekeeper, eventually supervising twenty-one servants and managing their payroll using the bookkeeping skills she acquired at the Emporium. While working there, she wore an "elegant" kimono and obi provided by Julia Spalding, who apparently enjoyed having her Nikkei staff dressed in Japanese style.[44] One of Takata's students remembers her saying that the outfit she wore at work "made her look like a living Japanese doll."[45] This aestheticization of Takata's racialized body was part of the Spaldings' broader Orientalist aesthetic, evident in their collection of Egyptian-influenced décor and their hosting of sumptuous Oriental-themed parties (figure 1.1).[46]

Despite the "feudal character" of relations between mistresses and female domestic workers in this period,[47] Julia Spalding seems to have come to see Hawayo as more than just "a living Japanese doll" or even an employee in the roughly two decades that she worked for her. Julia, divorced and childless, later financed Hawayo's enrollment in naturopathy classes on the mainland (see chapter 3), suggesting that she took on the role of patron, even adopted mother, and Hawayo seems to have remembered her fondly. As a young Nikkei woman, Hawayo would have been in demand for domestic work due to Hawai'i's "scarcity of subordinate-group women," causing the majority of domestic workers to be men until the late 1920s, a unique situation in early twentieth-century America.[48] Even at an early age, Hawayo may have begun to see how a strategic framing of her positionality as a "Japanese" woman could help her achieve some level of social advancement,

Figure 1.1   Spalding family costume party, Valley House, Keālia, HI, ca. 1920s.

while also posing limitations in the White supremacist, patriarchal society of Territorial Hawai'i.

Social Aspirations

Not long after Hawayo began working at the Valley House, Julia introduced her to Saichi Takata (1895–1930), a Makee Sugar employee who attained an unusually high status for a Nikkei of his generation in Territorial Hawai'i. Hawayo married Saichi on March 10, 1917, about one year after she began working for the Spaldings, and they would have two daughters, Julia Sayako (1918–1970) and Alice Emiko (1925–2013). Julia was named after Julia Spalding, who was delighted when Takata's firstborn was born on her own birthday.[49] Takata remembered Saichi to her students as the plantation's bookkeeper, but he worked most of his adult life at the plantation store that stood at the intersection of the plantation's main road and the coastal highway, working his way up from the entry-level position of clerk to the store's bookkeeper before being promoted to "superintendent of the company's general supply warehouse" in 1928.[50] As men of European descent disproportionately held these types of superintendencies, Saichi's promotion is a testament to his diligence, intelligence, and ability to cultivate relationships.[51]

These positions also demanded that Saichi be able to mediate between English and Japanese in professional settings and have a strong command of written English.[52]

In addition to his work for Makee Sugar, Saichi was active in business and in his community from an early age. By age twenty-two, he was on the executive board of the Kealia Young Men's Buddhist Association (YMBA) and the Board of Education of the Makee School (a Japanese language school at the Kealia Hongwanji Mission).[53] Before he turned thirty, he became the founding president of the Society of American Citizens of Japanese Ancestry of Kauai (SACJAK).[54] Although he passed away before his thirty-fifth birthday, his obituary called him a "well known citizen" and outlined his work in the private and public sectors, as a stock agent for a local brokerage,[55] as an auditor for an ice and soda works, and in an appointed position to read meters and collect bills for the Kawaihau District Waterworks. "Due to his untiring community spirit," it added, the territorial governor, Wallace Farrington, appointed Saichi to the county child welfare board.[56] As such, he was among the first to represent Hawaiʻi's large Nikkei demographic in local government.[57] Hawayo remembers him as "the first Oriental to be appointed by the governor to be on the welfare [board] . . . and so therefore he was a very liked man in the community." She recalls him negotiating with the local plantation managers to pay the wages of the Buddhist priests who ministered to their workers, which decreased the financial burden on the Nikkei workers and increased the regard for plantation administration in their eyes.[58] These accounts portray Saichi as one of the early Nisei to negotiate between the demands of Nikkei labor and those of the White elites.

His involvement in Nikkei social organizations gives some hints to his political leanings. In the 1920s, the YMBA had a reputation for labor activism due to its involvement in the 1919 higher-wage movement of plantation workers, which led to the formation of the Federation of Japanese Labor, a major player in the strike of 1920, and "yellow peril"–style anti-Buddhist rhetoric by White supremacist politicians and newspaper editorials.[59] However, it is doubtful Saichi was such an agitator. The SACJAK that Saichi organized and led was likely similar to California's Japanese American Citizens League (JACL), which Paul Spickard describes as "an institutional expression of the cultural imperatives of the Nisei: conservative, hardworking, devotedly pro-American, doggedly accepting of whatever crumbs White America offered, quietly persevering in the attempt to win a place for the Nisei in the United States."[60] Yuji Ichioka adds that JACL leaders "tended to be Republicans" (like Saichi) and were largely "urban, college-educated, self-employed professionals . . . hostile to the New Deal and organized labor."[61]

Saichi's government appointment by Governor Farrington is telling: Farrington's governance is synonymous with White suspicion of Nikkei demographic preponderance after the 1920 strike. In a public letter in 1922, Farrington wrote that Hawai'i's "racial elements are out of balance and are seriously in need of adjustment" to ensure "permanent American strength in the future," and the following year he gave a speech to a joint session of the territorial legislature on "the Japanese problem," in which he characterized Nikkei labor activism as "an alien element . . . directed against our American plan of progress" and called for "a military dictatorship" in Hawai'i rather than respect the democratic will of its non-White citizens.[62] The fact that Saichi received an appointment from Farrington in a period when the federal Hawaii Emergency Labor Commission concluded, "*The necessity to curtail the domination of the alien Japanese in every phase of the Hawaiian life is more important than all the other* [labor] *problems combined*," suggests that White elites probably considered Saichi to be a token who would placate a push for Nikkei representation in politics without threatening their own interests.[63]

In another indicator of Saichi's ability to enter White elite social settings, a 1921 newspaper article lists him as winning second place at the inaugural golf tournament at Wailua Golf Club.[64] Out of the eleven competitors, Saichi was the only one without a European surname. The fact that he received a handicap of eighteen strokes while four other competitors had handicaps of twenty-four indicates that he had sufficiently improved at the game to not be considered a complete beginner. The other competitors included the Wailua Golf Course's four founders, among them the plantation manager James Spalding.[65] Saichi's success on the links is another index of his relative social mobility and recognition by the ruling elite.

Despite Saichi's relative prestige for a Nikkei man in 1920s Hawai'i, the Makee Sugar Company payroll registers list him as a "store boy," and while he was compensated more than the Nikkei clerks in the same office, it was a fraction of the earnings of employees with European surnames.[66] While a small number of second-generation immigrants of color were able to attain a certain level of social privilege in the racial hierarchy of the colonial Territory, White elites largely controlled its wealth and politics. Still, the Takatas accrued sufficient financial capital to become homeowners, buying a house in Kawaihau (an upland, or *mauka,* section of the town of Kapaʻa) from a Portuguese couple for $1,500 in 1927 (about $26,000 in 2022 dollars), beginning Hawayo's lifelong investment in real estate.[67]

Hawayo joined her husband in gaining patronage positions. Likely through Saichi's influence, she became active in the Republican Party and, after his untimely death in 1930, she received his appointment as meter reader and bill collector for the local waterworks.[68] Hawayo's pride in her appointment is legible in the archive; in the ship's manifest for her first voyage to mainland North America (a 1932 trip to California to attend a Buddhist youth group conference), under "occupation," she listed her part-time job as "water collector" rather than her full-time position of housekeeper.[69] Her appointment lasted until 1934, when Democratic president Franklin D. Roosevelt appointed a new governor who shuffled the political appointments to reward Democrats. Having lost her second job, she picked up side work collecting money for *Star-Bulletin* newspaper subscriptions and working as a "sub-agent" for an insurance company.[70] As the Republicans had been the party of the White elite and dominated territorial politics since the overthrow of the monarchy, though the Democratic Party became the unofficial party of Hawaiʻi's Nikkei population, the Takatas' politics were closer to those of the White planters than those of their working-class parents and neighbors.[71]

Saichi and Hawayo Takata experienced some of the complex of issues that Japanese Americans in the prewar period described as "the Nisei problem." The circumstances of their birth granted them the American citizenship denied their parents, but they faced a glass ceiling limiting their professional and social advancement as White supremacist structures kept them from attaining the education, training, and opportunities to join the professional classes. Sociologists of the period, following the groundbreaking ethnicity theorist Robert Park, framed the Nisei problem in terms of incomplete assimilation, but this ignored the racial exclusion experienced by Nikkei Americans.[72] The Takatas arguably took on "middleman minority" roles in their petit bourgeois supervisory positions that mediated between White power and working-class people of color, but their closeness to White elites did not fit the model of "social separateness" in the "ethnic economy" that sociologists described as typical of Nisei enterprise.[73] Rather, they networked within White-dominated power structures, working with local stockbrokers to recruit investors, becoming proficient at golf, actively participating in the Republican Party, and even receiving positions of political patronage. Hawayo Takata's ability to develop relationships with

White elites despite her racialization and unpolished diction would serve her in her career as a practitioner and teacher of spiritual therapy.

Saichi's "Transition"

The Takatas had relatively important roles working for the Spalding family and in the community at large, but they were given time off to attend to Saichi's poor health. He suffered from a lung condition, diagnosed as pleurisy. Nikkei in Hawai'i at that time had limited access to medical care, and the petits bourgeois often traveled to Japan for advanced care. In 1923, Hawayo and Saichi took what was likely their first trip to their parents' homeland; they probably left four-year-old Julia with her parents, took a ferry to Honolulu, a steamer to Yokohama, and then a train to Tokyo. There, Saichi had two ribs removed by the prestigious doctor Maeda Tomosuke (1887–1975), who taught orthopedic surgery at Keio University Medical School (figure 1.2).[74] In his early thirties, Saichi and Hawayo made two more trips to Japan, in 1928 and 1929, to receive further treatment at Maeda's new clinic in Akasaka, Tokyo.[75] Despite their best efforts, Saichi died at home in Keālia on October 8, 1930, at the age of thirty-four.[76]

Figure 1.2 Photo album page showing Saichi and Hawayo Takata's 1923 trip to Maeda Tomosuke's clinic; handwritten captions by Alice Takata Furumoto.

As mentioned previously, in the more than seventeen hours of tapes Takata recorded to recount her life story for a biography, she only repeated two stories. One of them was the story of Saichi's final days. Three days before Saichi "went into transition," she said, he spoke to her about how to deal with the event of his death. In the first version, he says,

> "When we are born, this is a universal law. You are a church-going [Buddhist] woman and I am, too, and we have to understand that everything that is born and mature [*sic*]. . . . There will come a time of great change which we call 'transition.' And transition, some people say death, but in our religion we do not say death and this is the end. No. With the law of evolution . . . everything goes through a change, and in the human life . . . when the time comes, no one can stop and we are going. Only whether you go first or I go first . . . we do not know. And so therefore . . . when I go, which I think will be soon," he said, "please, do not grieve over it. And I do not want to be buried here in Keālia. So there shall be no grave." Then I said, "What shall I do?" He said, "wrap it up in a clean sheet, take it over the pier, dump it in the ocean, and the sharks will enjoy it, but I am not there. . . . The minute you think I am gone . . . look up and smile." And he said, "if you look up and smile, then I will understand that you, also, understood religion."[77]

This story was recorded nearly fifty years after the actual event, and it is unclear to what degree elements of its telling changed over the years, but it presents a vision of the impermanence of physical forms and the persistence of the spirit. This vision, informed by the Takatas' Shin Buddhist socialization in their families and at the Kealia Hongwanji Church, would also affect Hawayo's teaching career in the second half of her life.

Saichi's farewell words suggest human life is part of a grander reality that does not end at the limits of the human body but, rather, what we know as death is actually a "transition" to another state of existence. This concept, expressed by Hawayo Takata, has left a lasting impression on Reiki culture; many (if not most) Reiki communities continue to use this language of "making one's transition" when speaking of death.[78] In relating this story, Takata affirmed her husband's claim that recognition of humanity's extraphysical nature is the essence of religion. By tying this inevitable transition from life to "the law of evolution," they switch between religious and scientific registers, drawing on scientific authority to validate their spiritual assertions. Further research would be needed to know to what degree Buddhist priests in Hawai'i made use of evolutionist thought, but such rhetoric was a major trend in the Buddhist modernism of the turn of the twentieth century, and Japanese Buddhist intellectuals in this period ultimately affirmed Darwinism as confirming the Dharma (hō).[79]

In discussing Reiki, Hawayo Takata often related this concept of universal law to the concept of "cause and effect." Reiki, she would say, treated the cause of illness; "remove the cause and there shall be no effect."[80] For someone who attended and taught at Kealia Hongwanji Church and was involved with Shin Buddhist activities into her adult life, these concepts of universal law and cause and effect would have resonated with the concepts of Dharma and karma (gō).[81] Saichi and Hawayo were likely familiar with these basic concepts of Shin Buddhism, so when Saichi says in the second version of the story, "the law of the universe is change," he seems to invoke the Buddha-dharma of the impermanence of all things.[82] Similarly, Buddhist modernists in this period commonly considered karma a universal law of causation to portray Buddhist doctrine as rational and scientific.[83]

The idea that the interconnected world of matter and spirit obeys a universal law of flux, which guarantees both our mortality and our "transition" into another state of being, also resembles aspects of ancestor veneration as practiced in Japan and Japanese diasporas. The practice of daily prayer at a *butsudan* is an act of memorializing and pacifying the spirits of departed relatives, and it is likely that part of the reason Hawayo kept a Buddhist altar throughout her life was to have an anchor for Saichi's spirit.[84] This recognition of his presence appears in the second version of the story when Saichi tells her to "leave one chair open" at his memorial dinner because "I will be there."[85]

Yet while he assures Hawayo his spirit will survive his physical death, he specifically tells her to feed his body to the sharks, so nothing will tie her to Keālia. "If there is a grave here," he says, "you would be stuck, and you are very young, and . . . the world is yours [sic]. . . . Since you are born on this earth plane . . . [it] is yours to walk and to travel and to work and also to improve yourself and to live. . . . And you make your own life and not worry about the grave in that hill or that piece of dirt."[86] Here, Saichi evokes the words of Shinran (1173–1263), the founder of Shin Buddhism, who told his followers to feed his body to the fish in the Kamo River rather than building him a mausoleum, a story with which Saichi and Hawayo would have been familiar from their Shin education.[87] Yet this story not only links Saichi to the virtue of Shinran but also represents his giving his blessing to Hawayo's taking on a peripatetic life, which would be necessary to dedicate herself to spreading Reiki. Wanja Twan, a Master student of Takata's in the 1970s, told me that when she informed Takata that she and her husband were breaking up, Takata replied by saying something like, "Good, you can't travel to teach Reiki with a husband."[88] While losing Saichi was heartbreaking for Hawayo, she recognized that her loss created a space in her life that she would dedicate to her healing and teaching. If he had recovered and lived a longer life, Reiki would likely not have taken the path it did, possibly not becoming the global phenomenon that it has.

Finally, Takata emphasized that Saichi gave her guidance and inspiration throughout her life. After he said his piece, she replied,

> "When you go . . . I need your help. I need you every single minute. I want you by my side and teach me. Give me guidance, give me courage, and I shall not fail." And so he said, "Yes, it is possible. Nothing is impossible and I know you will try very hard." And I said yes, and I kept my word. I tried very hard so that I would be financially able and capable of taking care of my family, and then I was never, never lazy. But he was by my side whenever I needed him so badly, when I was stuck against the wall, such as illness.[89]

Here, she provides an interactive view of how Saichi provided for her in the period following his death. On the one hand, she says he was always there for her in her times of need, but on the other, she suggests that his presence also relied on her own persistent hard work. This implies that at least part of the way in which Saichi's spirit aided her was by inspiring her to be diligent. Yet in the second version, she added,

> After his transition, I heard his voice whenever I had to make a crucial decision or if I felt I could not decide. If I meditated, I always got the answer. Therefore, [when] . . . I have been led to the proper road to find, it was through his guidance. He showed me the way and all the years after that, when I needed help and I could not turn to any other source, I sit [sic] in deep meditation and he gave me the answer, for which I was very fortunate. And therefore, I believe that meditation is very important, and also to have faith in your religion. I found out the more experience I have had, the Reiki is not only for physical but also for spiritual [sic].[90]

In this version, which she told Barbara Weber to use for the biography's preface, she asserted that Saichi's presence was a more external force, but one that she accessed by quieting her inner world. She explicitly tied this access to religious faith and to the spiritual benefits of practicing both meditation and Reiki. We shall see in the next chapter that disembodied voices spoke to her at two crucial junctures leading her to Reiki, and although she did not say so when telling those parts of the story, this passage implies that she attributed those voices to her departed husband. Thus, when she told a newspaper reporter, "I owe my good fortune to my late husband, Saichi, who was a guiding light until his death in 1930,"[91] she omitted that she actually considered him to guide her for many years afterward, including by bringing her to the practice of Reiki.

Conclusion

The circumstances leading to Hawayo Kawamura Takata's birth in Hanama'ulu are entangled with broad geopolitical and economic trends at the turn of the twentieth century. America's empire expanded into the Pacific contemporaneously with Japan's rapid modernization, and the Hawaiian Islands became tied to both developments. The Kingdom of Hawai'i became a site of settler colonial capitalism, as Americans built profitable industries on Indigenous land using migrant laborers from Asia. These capitalists then overthrew the Hawaiian monarchy, establishing the short-lived Republic of Hawai'i, followed by US annexation. Under a racist logic that reserved the right of naturalization for immigrants of European descent, the state denied migrant laborers in the new US territory the possibility of American naturalization. However, the laborers' children were American citizens by jus soli—that is, for having been born on land the United States had seized from its sovereign rulers. As such, from the moment the midwife held infant Hawayo's body up to the rays of the sun rising over Kālepa ridge—at whose base an American-owned mill stood on the stones of an ancient Hawaiian temple, grinding sugarcane picked by Japanese labor—she was already caught in complex North Pacific currents.

Thirty years later (and about forty-five minutes into her narration on the first cassette), she was the widowed mother of two daughters and the head housekeeper for a wealthy plantation family's opulent estate. Her late husband had been a Nisei community leader who, it seems, did his best to negotiate between the interests of Nikkei labor and White employers and was reportedly responsible for a historic agreement to have plantation capital fund Buddhist institutions. He seems to have been a religious Shin Buddhist, perhaps partly because, as a gravely ill young man, he sought the reassurance that there was something beyond this earthly existence. Despite being sickly since age twenty-eight and passing away at thirty-four, he did well for himself financially, owning his own home and stock in several local companies.[92]

Hawayo tried to follow in his footsteps by remaining industrious in a number of fields. She worked long hours at the Valley House and in other jobs, continuing to build relationships with White elites and participate in the Republican Party. She also cultivated her spiritual dimension through meditation so that, even though Saichi was physically gone, he could remain her "guiding light." All of these factors helped shape the contours of the next fifty years of her professional and religious life and, by extension, the circulation and development of the spiritual therapy she would soon encounter.

CHAPTER 2

Drawn into the Current

Encountering Usui Reiki Therapy's Japanese
Circulation, 1922–1937

In early October 1935, Hawayo Takata boarded a ferry in Kaua'i's Nawili-wili Harbor. She was gravely ill, with severe abdominal pains, and local doctors dared not operate for fear of killing her. The ferry took her and her younger daughter, nine-year-old Alice, to Honolulu; there, they transferred to the Asama Maru ocean steamer, on which they traveled third class for the eight-day voyage to Yokohama.[1] Hawayo carried the ashes of her late husband, Saichi, who had traveled to Japan three times for medical treatment to no avail. He died at thirty-four, the same age she was at this time. She must have wondered if she would survive the trip and, if not, what would become of her two daughters.

One year later, she was back in Kaua'i in perfect health, operating a clinic where she treated patients with a method called Usui Reiki Therapy (Usui Reiki Ryōhō). She advertised this therapy in the local English-language newspaper as "ABSOLUTELY DRUGLESS" with "Special Treatments for Stomach and Internal Ailments; Nervous Diseases and General Debility" (figure 2.1). This ad explicitly contrasted Reiki Therapy with biomedicine and claimed efficacy for disorders that biomedicine had difficulty treating, as she could testify from personal experience.

This chapter examines how Takata was drawn into the current of Usui Reiki Therapy in Japan through her treatment and subsequent training, while also contextualizing her encounter with attention to this therapy's development in Japan before her training. It describes factors in early twentieth-century Japan that led to a boom in novel spiritual therapies; the life and works of Usui Mikao (1865–1926), creator of his eponymous Reiki

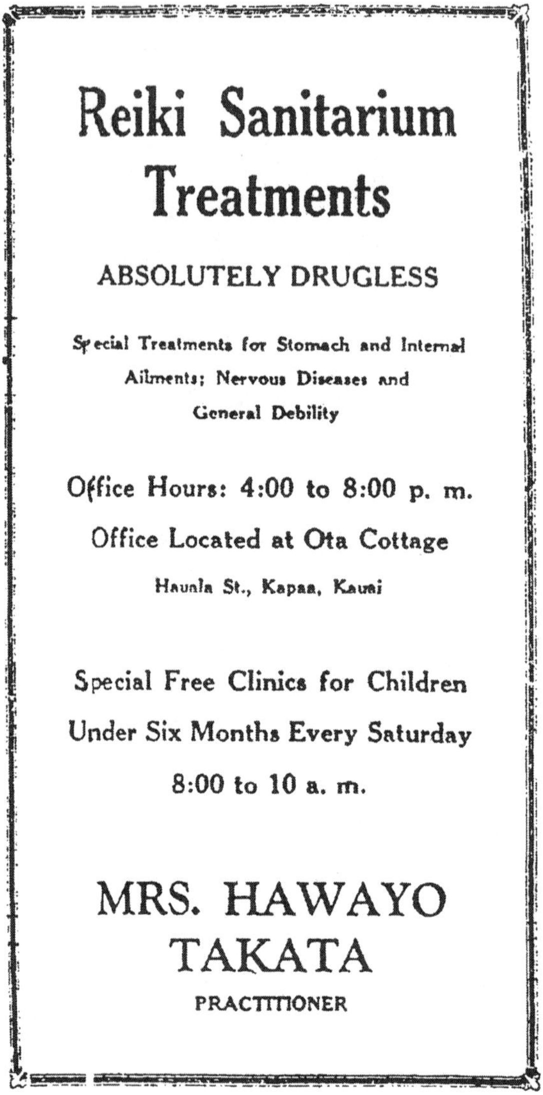

> # Reiki Sanitarium Treatments
>
> ## ABSOLUTELY DRUGLESS
>
> Special Treatments for Stomach and Internal
> Ailments; Nervous Diseases and
> General Debility
>
> Office Hours: 4:00 to 8:00 p. m.
>
> Office Located at Ota Cottage
>
> Haunla St., Kapaa, Kauai
>
> Special Free Clinics for Children
> Under Six Months Every Saturday
> 8:00 to 10 a. m.
>
> # MRS. HAWAYO TAKATA
>
> PRACTITIONER

Figure 2.1 Advertisement for Takata's Kapa'a clinic, *The Garden Island*, October 13, 1936.

Therapy; and adaptations that Usui's disciple Hayashi Chūjirō (1880–1940) made prior to Takata's arrival at his clinic in 1935. These sections establish that Usui Reiki Therapy was a transnational spiritual therapy that fulfilled my five criteria of an *alternate current* before its leaving Japan. Usui developed his Reiki Therapy by creatively combining elements from several practices *circulating* in Japan at the time, some with long East Asian pedigrees and others that were recent imports from the United States, *adapted* for

Japanese audiences in the early twentieth century. Japanese teachers of Usui Reiki Therapy, including Takata's teacher Hayashi, were already adapting Usui's therapy prior to Takata's encounter with the practice, setting up the further adaptations Takata made for American audiences in the decades to come. As Usui and Hayashi adapted their practices based on students' needs, they demonstrate the *bidirectional* relationships between masters and disciples. Additionally, Usui Reiki Therapy, like its contemporary spiritual therapies, was developed as an *alternative* to institutional religion and mainstream medicine, and from the beginning, its promoters *oscillated* regularly between religious, medical, and scientific idioms.

Guided to Hayashi's Clinic

In the early 1930s, the widowed Hawayo Takata continued working as the housekeeper of the Valley House, supervising the estate for Julia Spalding, who traveled from Keālia to California to care for her dying father.[2] She also continued her side jobs working for the waterworks and selling newspaper subscriptions and insurance policies. Putting in long hours to support her two children, Takata suffered serious depression following Saichi's death. She later recounted, "they [i.e., her children] alone kept me from suicide."[3]

One other outlet seems to have been her engagement with the Young Men's Buddhist Association (YMBA). Saichi had long served on the executive board of Keālia's chapter, and Takata continued his legacy when she became the first woman elected secretary of this mostly male organization in 1934.[4] Shin Buddhist youth groups in the 1930s were not just local social organizations but transnational North Pacific networks.[5] In July 1932, Takata was named one of three Kaua'i delegates to the First Canada-Hawaii-American Young Buddhists' Conference, held in San Francisco, where she chaired a roundtable on "religious problems and their solutions."[6] In her five weeks of travel to California, she enjoyed the maiden voyage of the luxury liner SS *Monterey*; traveled to sites across the state, including Yosemite National Park, Santa Barbara, and Los Angeles (where she attended events in the Summer Olympics); and made connections with Nikkei Buddhists from Hawai'i, California, and British Columbia. The camaraderie and pleasure of this tour is palpable in her photographs and her souvenir autograph book, but the fact that she and her travel companions were racialized second-class American citizens is visible in the ship manifest, which lists the permits they were issued in Honolulu in order to travel between the Islands and the US mainland.[7]

In 1935, Takata was alone with Alice. She had sent her older daughter, Julia, to attend high school in Japan, a fairly common practice for petty bourgeois Nikkei Americans at the time, facilitated by the steep decline of the yen relative to the US dollar in the early 1930s.[8] After forty years of working in Kauaian cane fields, her parents had taken a one-year sabbatical to return to the Kawamura family home in Yamaguchi Prefecture. As mentioned in chapter 1, she had lost her second job as the meter reader and bill collector for the local waterworks due to the appointment of a new territorial governor, so she picked up extra hours, probably partly to help pay the tuition of Julia's boarding school. Takata recalls that her overwork caused her to suffer nervous breakdowns, terrible abdominal pains, and terrible difficulties breathing. She sought medical attention, but local doctors said they could not treat her.

Around this time, Takata's younger sister, Fusae, died from tetanus, adding to her desperation. In her autobiographical recordings, she said she began nightly meditations in which she prayed to God for guidance. As noted in chapter 1, it is difficult to know whether she prayed to a Christian-inflected God or whether this was how she translated whatever concept of divinity she received in her Nikkei Buddhist socialization (such as Amida Buddha or the *kami*) to her White Christian ghostwriter. Either way, she recalled,

> Through this meditation one night when it was so dark . . . I heard out of the clear sky a voice [that said,] the first thing for you to do is to have health. . . . If you have health, you shall have wealth, because you can work and you can earn. But if you have poor health, you shall have poverty and you shall have worries, and therefore nothing but sorrows and sorrows [*sic*] and unhappiness.[9]

She elsewhere attributed this voice to Saichi, but this telling of the story suggests God answered her prayers by telling her to attend to her health. This story, which she sometimes included in her free lectures to promote Reiki, reinforced to potential clients and students that the substantial fees for Reiki treatments or courses were money well spent, as the dividends from investing in health are priceless.

Based on this (divine?) message, Takata took leave of her jobs and traveled to Japan with nine-year-old Alice to check into the Maeda Surgical Clinic, where she had accompanied Saichi. She never says as much in her autobiographical materials, but the trip to Japan and her treatment at the Maeda clinic must have been a tremendous financial burden for this woman who was, after all, a domestic servant. The journey to Japan required first traveling to Honolulu, where she and Alice boarded the *Asama Maru* on October 8 for the voyage to Yokohama. Takata's first destination in Japan was rural Yamaguchi, hundreds of miles to the west, where she would inform her parents of Fusae's death and leave Alice in their care while she pursued medical treatment.[10] Unfamiliar with the logistics of journeying to Yamaguchi, Hawayo traveled with her sister-in-law Katsuyo Takata, who had immigrated to Hawai'i from the adjacent Hiroshima Prefecture, and two of Katsuyo's children.[11]

The final member of her entourage was Saichi, whose ashes Hawayo brought on the ship to Japan. Despite his instructions to feed his body to the sharks, she cremated it in the typical Japanese Buddhist fashion. She had hoped "when I was able and I had the means" to make arrangements for "a second funeral" for him at "the Ōtani temple" in Kyoto and inter his ashes there.[12] Fortuitously, on the boat to Yokohama she met a priest returning from Kona to the sect headquarters in Kyoto. They arranged for him to bring Saichi's ashes to Kyoto, where they would hold a funeral the following March. Hawayo, Katsuyo, and the children spent time with the Kawamuras in Yamaguchi, held a memorial service for Fusae at the family temple, visited Hawayo's maternal grandmother in Hiroshima, and relaxed at the spas of Beppu. Takata then left Alice with her parents and traveled to Tokyo, where she was admitted to the Maeda Surgical Clinic.[13]

Before Dr. Maeda Tomosuke would examine her, she recalled, he insisted she have three weeks' bed rest to relax and gain some weight on a diet prescribed by the clinic's dietician, his older sister, Mrs. Shimura.[14] After three weeks, Takata had gained a few pounds and her breathing had improved. Maeda conducted an examination, including a series of X-rays. He diagnosed Takata with a uterine tumor, gallstones, and appendicitis, and scheduled her for surgery the following morning.[15] What follows is the turning point in the narrative she told in her introductory classes, and thus a story she honed over hundreds of repetitions to thousands of students.

As she lay on the operating table, a disembodied voice spoke to her, echoing the one she had heard in Keālia telling her to take care of her health. It told her the surgery was unnecessary and urged her to ask Maeda for an alternative. Maeda asked how long she could stay in Japan; she replied that she had years if necessary. Pleased, he sent Takata with Shimura to "a studio where they were taking people to give them drugless and bloodless treatments," where Shimura herself had experienced a miraculous recovery from a dysentery-induced coma some years prior.[16] This "studio" was the headquarters of the Hayashi Reiki Research Association (Hayashi Reiki Kenkyūkai), where they practiced something called Usui Reiki Therapy.

Spiritual Therapies in Prewar Japan

In 1920s and 1930s Japan, Usui Reiki Therapy was one of hundreds of spiritual therapies taught by tens of thousands of practitioners, largely among the new urban middle class.[17] These therapies, contemporaneously called *seishin ryōhō* (psycho-spiritual therapies) or *reijutsu* (marvelous arts or spiritual techniques), occupied a space between the religious and the medical/psychological at a time in Japan when modern categories like the "mental" and "spiritual" were still being worked out.[18] In the early twentieth century, *seishin* and *rei* were used somewhat interchangeably to denote the invisible dimensions of humanity, similar to the word "psyche," which can refer to the mind, spirit, or soul. As in American "metaphysical religion" (which powerfully influenced these therapies), Japanese spiritual therapists considered the visible world (matter) and the invisible (mind) to be intimately intertwined, even "made of the same 'stuff'[:] . . . a stream of energy flowing from [the macrocosm] above to [the microcosm] below . . . is a healing salve for all . . . ills."[19] Thus, while *seishin ryōhō* largely came to denote secularized and medicalized forms of psychotherapy by the postwar period, in prewar Japan it included a broader range of therapies—including ritual practices for healing or spiritual development—and was understood in distinction from "material therapies" like biomedicine, acupuncture, moxibustion, and herbalism.[20]

The popularity of spiritual therapies in Japan rose and fell over the first half of the twentieth century, peaking in the 1920s.[21] Their "boom" in this period can be attributed to a number of factors. First, it must be said that many of them were modernized adaptations of Japanese practices with longstanding popularity. While the Meiji (1868–1912) and Taishō (1912–1926) periods undoubtedly saw dramatic changes in many facets of Japanese life, interest in self-cultivation (*shūyō* or *shūshin*) is a point of continuity with the early modern Tokugawa period (1603–1867). Japanese self-cultivation culture tends toward holistic assertions that one's physical, mental, and spiritual lives are inseparable. Thus, like my category of spiritual therapies, it includes practices that are difficult to classify as strictly religious or medical.[22]

Mid-nineteenth-century self-cultivation drew on earlier "nourishing life" (*yōjō*) practices thought to promote longevity by cultivating *ki* (vital force) and calming the spirit through proper diet, abstinence from sex and alcohol, breathing exercises to cultivate the concentration of *ki* in the lower abdomen, meditation, and prayer.[23] Healing meditations to cultivate the lower abdomen (*hara*) described by the Rinzai Zen monk Hakuin (1686–1769) were particularly influential (and continued to be in the twentieth century).[24]

In addition to these self-cultivation practices, other healing rituals proliferated in the late Tokugawa period. New regulations of Shugendō, an ascetic tradition influenced by esoteric Buddhism and mountain worship, resulted in their practitioners largely becoming healing ritual specialists for paying clients. The most sought-after ritual in this period was *yorigitō*, derived from an earlier esoteric Buddhist practice, in which a medium (often a young woman called a *miko*) would enter a state of spirit possession in order for a male ascetic (*yamabushi*) to interrogate that spirit before exorcising it. *Yorigitō* was used for a variety of purposes, including divination, but healing was the most common.[25] Another popular ritual with esoteric Buddhist origins performed by a range of Tokugawa-period practitioners was *kaji kitō* (empowered prayer), considered "especially efficacious in the treatment of illnesses."[26] Despite (or perhaps due to) the popularity of these practices, they were criticized by neo-Confucian elites who considered folk medicine harmful to the body politic, as well as by promoters of new religious movements that offered alternatives to (often expensive) professional ritual specialists.[27]

Throughout the Meiji period's modernization campaigns, a series of edicts, revisions of the criminal code, and antisuperstition campaigns banned many religious therapies, including *yorigitō* and *kaji kitō*, as well as other types of divination, mediumship, incantation, and the production of talismans and "healing water." The first such edicts in the 1870s were intended to purify Shinto shrines from the divinatory and healing practices that had long flourished there—which state officials (following Tokugawa-era critiques by neo-Confucian and Kokugaku scholars) considered "superstitions"—but their scope and enforcement were expanded to promote a strong nation through biopolitical policies promoting hygiene.[28] Such policies continued through the prewar and wartime period. In 1921, the state took up a related crusade against Ōmoto, a new religious movement that had drawn millions of followers due to its *chinkon kishin* (pacify spirits, return the gods) possession ritual, often used for healing purposes, which could be considered a democratized form of *yorigitō*.[29] In the following decades, the police repeatedly harassed Okada Mokichi (1882–1955)—an Ōmoto branch leader who left to found his own spiritual hand-healing practice— for practicing medicine without a license.[30]

In the late Meiji period (roughly 1887–1912), Japan saw not only a rise in Western-style spiritualism (adapted for Japanese audiences), which helped fuel Ōmoto's rise, but also intense interest in hypnotism.[31] Japan's early hypnotists based their practices on translated texts from the United States and Europe but soon developed original discourses that integrated aspects derived from Asian philosophies.[32] Hypnotherapists helped fill a niche for ritual therapies while, following the period's modernist trends, asserting that hypnotism was a Western import that rationally and scientifically explained folk magic and religious miracles as results of the limitless power of the mind's energies. Thus, hypnotists promoted an "alternate current" by distinguishing themselves from the popular religions and materialist medicine of their time, while switching between religious, medical, and scientific registers as befit their ends. Some hypnotists chose to call themselves "spiritual therapists" (*seishin ryōhōka* or *reijutsuka*) rather than "hypnotists" (*saiminjutsu-shi*), and this became more common after lobbyists for regulating hypnotism (including physicians and some prominent hypnotists) inspired a 1908 law against hypnotism's "abuse."[33] The hypnotism boom popularized the idea that treating the *seishin* (the psyche) could cure the body, helping to prime Japanese publics to be open to the claims of the next generation of spiritual therapists.[34]

Taishō-era spiritual therapies also benefited from a broader trend of increasing concern with interiority. As cosmopolitan elites fused local self-cultivation discourses with imported trends adapted for local contexts, such as German Idealism and Romanticism, modernist literature, and scientific psychology, the growing middle class developed unprecedented attention to their subjectivity.[35] The self (and its relation to different forms of collectivity) was often described in terms of *seishin,* which could refer to the psychologist's "mind" or G. W. F. Hegel's *Geist* (including derivatives like the *Volksgeist,* or "national spirit"), as well as an omnipotent, omnipresent healing power (the universal "Mind"). Social classes awash in influences emphasizing the inner world's importance were culturally predisposed toward spiritual therapies that reinforced those messages.

The Japanese public was also driven to spiritual therapies in the early twentieth century because biomedicine was unable to address public health needs.[36] Meiji-era policies inadvertently set up conditions for devastating epidemics. Regulations that limited medical practice to graduates of government-certified institutions reduced public access to medical care.[37] New land taxes provided revenue for ambitious public works, but also had the unintended consequence of producing widespread poverty and rapid urbanization (as well as the overseas labor migration described in chapter 1). At the same time that destitute migrants rushed to Japan's swelling port cities for work, growing numbers of foreign sailors brought pathogens along with overseas goods. Crowded dormitories for the new factories and inadequate waste treatment accelerated devastating outbreaks of cholera, dysentery, smallpox, tuberculosis, and typhoid.[38]

Improvements in public hygiene helped curb cholera and dysentery by the end of the nineteenth century, but even those able to receive biomedical care experienced unsatisfying results against the diseases that ravaged Japan well into the twentieth century. Starting in the 1910s, tuberculosis killed over one million Japanese in every decade in the first half of the twentieth century, and the ongoing search for a remedy for its choking scourge may have contributed to the popularity of healing methods emphasizing breathing techniques in this period.[39] Infant mortality rates actually rose from the Meiji into the Taishō periods, not declining until the mid-1920s.[40] On top of these perennial killers, the Spanish influenza outbreak of 1918–1920 killed roughly 400,000–500,000 Japanese, nearly 1 percent of the national population. These epidemics caused the "Taishō mortality crisis," in which the mortality rate surpassed the birthrate in many Japanese cities.[41] In addition to contagious disease, eastern Japan suffered one of the greatest natural disasters of the twentieth century: the Great Kantō Earthquake of 1923, which caused firestorms that swept through the capital region, killing nearly 130,000, injuring many more, and leaving about 60 percent of Tokyo and 90 percent of Yokohama homeless. For those unable to access or find relief in biomedicine, spiritual therapies—along with other "alternative" health products and practices—were a natural place to turn.[42]

The same modernist biases that led to the Meiji state's prohibiting "superstitious" therapies and promoting biomedicine over long-standing medical traditions pushed spiritual therapists to couch their practices in scientific language in support of their claims to rationality.[43] Their tendency to oscillate between scientific and religious registers was imported from the West alongside various spiritual therapies. As previously mentioned, Euro-American forms of spiritualism and hypnotism—often understood in terms of electricity, magnetism, and other scientific principles—became popular in the late Meiji period, and Japanese therapists often cited Western scientists to lend authority to their practices. In Taishō, practices like abdominal breathing, autonomic movement, visualization, affirmation, and the laying on of hands came into vogue (partly due to translated texts from the United States, as described later in this chapter), and new scientific theories including particle physics and radiation were used to explain them.[44] Deguchi Onisaburō (1871–1948), Ōmoto's charismatic leader from the 1910s to the 1940s, echoed Western spiritualists when he said that mediums were like electrical conductors, passively carrying "currents" from deities.[45] Reiki therapists would similarly say that they were not healers but conduits for a healing power from the cosmos, a frequency they could "tune into" like a radio transmission.

These therapies were modern not only due to their appropriation of scientific vocabulary but also because of their claims to treat modern ills. Many touted their effectiveness in treating neurasthenia, "a disease of exhaustion resulting from modern civilization making excessive demands on the brain or nervous energy" that plagued Japan at the turn of the twentieth century no less than Europe and North America.[46] Modernity was not just physically exhausting but also a source of moral pollution. Moral crusaders considered cities breeding grounds for "viral" criminal and barbarous elements capable of infecting society at large, and urban culture as fostering decadence and laxity in habits like drinking, smoking, consumerism, and pursuit of new fashions imported from the West. These vices were decried as degrading Japan's national spirit and traditional values.[47] Promoters of spiritual therapies emphasized they not only promoted physical healing but were also ways to "correct the vices" of modernity, benefiting both individuals and the nation.[48] Thus, spiritual therapists in early twentieth-century Japan were in continuity with early modern self-cultivation movements that represented bodies as sites of moral development, but they were also responses to the alienation of modern urban life.[49]

While many came to spiritual therapies to heal disease or to assuage modernity's ills, others likely engaged with them as novel curiosities. Meiji-era education reforms brought unprecedentedly high literacy rates, fueling an explosion in Japan's publishing industry.[50] Print media facilitated interest in hypnotism in the first decade of the twentieth century, and many spiritual therapies in subsequent decades similarly spread through inexpensive pamphlets and volumes.[51] Undoubtedly, some readers of these texts never directly experienced the therapies they described but nevertheless enjoyed pondering their possibilities. While certain spiritual therapies developed more mass appeal, the trend as a whole seems to have predominantly appealed to Japan's growing class of educated, white-collar urbanites.[52] This was partly because learning these methods could be expensive, but also because some texts contained complex philosophies in abstruse prose, requiring the equivalent of a university education to be read and understood. Again, the flourishing of translated texts in this period allowed the creators of spiritual therapies to draw on similar practices from distant lands.[53]

Spiritual therapies and other ideas from "the West" in this period were not uncritically celebrated but were rather received in ways entangled with the Occidentalism of their age. Occidentalism, like its counterpart Orientalism, is based on a binary division between "East" and "West," both understood in essentialist, monolithic terms. Occidentalism and Orientalism are both products of an age in which Western colonial power and material superiority affected all international affairs and in which modernization was generally equated with Westernization. They both are examples "of a larger process of self-definition through opposition with the alien."[54] In early twentieth-century Japan, Occidentalism helped Japanese counter the West's material superiority by critiquing Occidental culture as "juvenile, abrasive, tactless, and materialistic and therefore not as (or un-)civilized" compared with Oriental (typified by Japanese) culture, which was "pure, sagacious, old, and civilized."[55]

Spiritual therapists of the time drew on Occidentalism when they argued that their therapies contained curative Oriental powers absent from Occidental biomedicine, proving "the superiority of Japanese culture over the materialist Western one"; such claims were often tied to the period's growing nationalism and imperial veneration.[56] Their Occidentalist rhetoric resembled that of contemporaneous Japanese Buddhist modernists such as Shaku Sōen (1860–1919) and his student Suzuki Daisetsu Teitarō (a.k.a. D. T. Suzuki, 1870–1966), who strategically appropriated American interest in Buddhism to advance their own agendas.[57] Spiritual therapists and Buddhist modernists alike insisted that their practices were entirely modern, scientific, and empirical, while also attributing their efficacy to their descent from Japan's "Eastern" wisdom traditions.

Thus, the success of Japanese spiritual therapists in the early twentieth century can be understood as truly modern, linked to turn-of-the-century trends in epidemiology, technology, morality, education, print culture, leisure, transnationalism, and imperialism. Their students often sought "spiritual self-cultivation" (*seishin shūyō*) as a means to acquire worldly benefits—from health and prosperity to improving at martial arts and strengthening the Japanese nation—a trend that is in line with dominant currents in Japanese religion.[58] At the same time, these therapies tended to circulate in "alternate currents," as their promoters distinguished themselves from mainstream religion and medicine, while appropriating religious and medical authority to justify their practices. By linking the vocabularies, worldviews, and practices of local traditions with those adapted from foreign practices like mesmerism and New Thought, they created novel spiritual therapies in a tenuous "third space" between proscribed or persecuted religious therapies and inaccessible or ineffective medical ones.[59] This is the context in which Usui Mikao developed and taught his eponymous Reiki Therapy.

Usui Mikao (1865–1926)

Usui was born just before the Meiji Restoration that rapidly modernized Japan. His home village, Taniai, Yamagata District, Gifu Prefecture, is in the mountains of central Honshu. His father, Uzaemon, was a successful merchant and the village headman, and his grandfather had owned a *sake* brewery.[60] The unusual first character of Usui's given name signifies an earthen jar, suggesting that, as the oldest son, his family may have intended him to take over his grandfather's brewery. Like the other youths of his village born to nonfarming families, Usui probably attended the temple school at the local Pure Land (Jōdo) temple Zendōji for part of his childhood. However, in 1872, when Usui was about seven years old, the state issued the Educational System Order abolishing temple schools in favor of Western-style public schools. Rural Japanese communities resisted these new elementary schools and the disruption they presented to traditional social patterns, but it is likely that at some point Usui's education transitioned from Buddhist to public administration.[61]

The grand memorial stele posthumously erected by Usui's students in Tokyo describes him as a man of unusual diligence and broad interests, traveling to China and the West to deepen his studies, which included medicine, psychology, physiognomy, history, Christian and Buddhist scripture, Daoist geomancy, incantation, and divination.[62] Usui seems to have worked a variety of jobs. One (disputed) text claims he worked as a missionary, a Buddhist prison chaplain, a public servant, and a private businessman.[63] A former president of the Usui Reiki Therapy Study Association for Improving Mind and Body (Shinshin Kaizen Usui Reiki Ryōhō Gakkai, hereafter Usui Association) reportedly said that Usui worked as "a journalist . . . a prison counselor, a social worker, a company employee, and as a Shinto missionary," as well as the private secretary of the Meiji statesman Gotō Shinpei (1857–1929).[64] Connections with a man of Gotō's stature in Japan's expanding empire would support claims of Usui's privilege to study and travel internationally and reports of the state's recognition of Usui's service in the aftermath of the Great Kantō Earthquake.[65] However, searches of Gotō's papers have found no mention of Usui's name.[66]

The story of Usui's life related on his memorial stele and in other sources follows several conventions from the lives of founders of new religious movements and other spiritual therapies. For one, it recounts that he endured a period of poverty that hardened his resolve to train his body and mind.[67] Around 1919, Usui seems to have suffered from the failure of his business and taken up devout spiritual practice in Kyoto; he is said to have "entered the gate of Zen," suggesting a semimonastic practice.[68] Photos of Usui from the mid-1920s invariably show him in dark, simple robes, possibly evoking this period of Buddhist practice, and photos of him with his male students suggest that many of them emulated their master's style of dress, at least in the dojo (training facility).[69]

Another founder narrative convention that appears in Usui's life story is the emphasis that Usui received his healing system as a result of spiritual practice on a sacred mountain. Usui went to Mount Kurama, northeast of Kyoto, to perform "severe austerities and difficult training," including fasting.[70] As Kurama has long been associated with ascetics performing practices such as meditating under bone-chilling waterfalls to attain spiritual power, it is possible he engaged in similar practices there. Usui and his followers consider this experience to be the source of his therapy and its potency. According to his memorial, after twenty-one days of practice on Kurama, Usui "suddenly felt a great *reiki* overhead and instantly acquired Reiki Therapy."[71] In the longest surviving text by Usui—a document called *Public Explanation of Instruction* (*Kōkai denju setsumeisho,* hereafter *Public Explanation*), mostly written in question-and-answer format, which was first published as a standalone booklet and later reproduced in an expanded Usui Association handbook—he explained that he acquired his healing powers when "mysteriously inspired after being touched by the ether (*taiki*) during a fast"; thus, "although I am the founder of this method, even I cannot clearly explain [its operations]."[72] Usui's comfort in allowing the operation of his therapy to remain a relative mystery stands in contrast with the stance of many of his contemporary therapists, who published copious pamphlets and volumes detailing the origins, operations, and applications of their therapies. Still, Usui's story—his midlife problems, his persistence in overcoming them through eclectic studies and ascetic practice on a sacred mountain, and his return with a ritual boon for humanity to be shared through a social organization—follows conventions shared with the hagiographies of founders of healing-oriented new religions. As with other founder narratives, stories of Usui's life establish his charisma and provide models of behavior to which followers might aspire.[73]

The Usui Association

Numerous sources, including the memorial and *Public Explanation,* emphasize that, after acquiring Reiki Therapy on Kurama, Usui developed a method to pass it to others because he was compelled to not keep it a private treasure within his own family, but to share it with the broader world.[74] The memorial recounts that Usui traveled to Harajuku, Tokyo, in April 1922, where he founded his first dojo. His organization, the Usui Association, opened branches across Japan. The memorial states that Usui taught his Reiki Therapy to over two thousand students and healed countless more in the approximately four years between the establishment of his association and his untimely death in March 1926. It recounts how the entrance to Usui's main dojo was constantly filled with the shoes of the patients and students inside. He was particularly active in the aftermath of the Great Kantō Earthquake, and the memorial implies his relief efforts in this time helped him to gain national renown.[75] The association continued expanding in the years after Usui's death, including, in the 1930s, to Japan's overseas colonies.[76]

A photo dated January 16, 1926, less than two months before Usui's death, suggests he trained twenty students to be instructors (*shihan*).[77] These top students were all men and at least six were high-ranking military officers, including at least four from the Imperial Navy: Rear Admiral Ushida Jūzaburō (1865–1935), who succeeded Usui as the association's second president; Rear Admiral Taketomi Kan'ichi (1878–1960), the third president; Wanami Hōichi (1883–1975), the fifth president, who was a captain during Usui's lifetime but retired in 1935 as a vice admiral; and Captain Hayashi Chūjirō (1880–1940), who founded the Hayashi Reiki Research Association (Hayashi Reiki Kenkyūkai), described later. In the years following Usui's death, several other high-ranking naval officers became *shi-han,* and they dominated the Usui Association's leadership.[78] Several high-profile Japanese Reiki instructors have reflected on this connection between Usui Reiki Therapy and the navy. Koyama Kimiko (1906–1999), the sixth Usui Association president, who studied under Taketomi, said naval officers found it "convenient" to be able to treat sailors on their warships with Reiki.[79] The son of a student of Hayashi wrote, "The Navy adopted Reiki because it was useful on long voyages. On warships space was very limited so they used Reiki instead of other more cumbersome medical equipment."[80] It is possible naval officers became interested in Usui Reiki Therapy through the aforementioned new religion Ōmoto, which had a significant naval following, offered somewhat similar healing practices, and suffered state suppression the year before Usui founded his association.[81] However, prominent military officers at the time were widely known to be involved with spiritual therapies, including Major General Kaetsu Satoshi (1870–1944) and Major General Ishii Tsunezō (1875–d.u.), who founded his own Life Force Self-Strengthening Therapy (Seiki Jikyō Ryōhō).[82] Contemporaneous descriptions of Usui Reiki Therapy commented on this phenomenon, with one author even opining that military personnel seem to have special abilities in the realm of psychic affairs.[83]

In addition to the naval officers who led the Usui Association, Usui's other top disciples were disproportionately social elites, including military officers, artists, and businessmen. These included a "high official in the imperial army," another "high military official," a scientist, a professional musician, and a master of tea ceremony.[84] Another *shihan* Usui trained was the fertilizer magnate Tomabechi Gizō (1880–1959), who became a prominent politician after the war and wrote about his experiences with Usui and Usui Reiki Therapy in his 1951 memoir.[85] These members' high status meant that their patients also tended to be social elites: Shibusawa Eiichi, the so-called father of Japanese capitalism, received treatment for some chronic ailment in 1925 from Usui's disciple Ushida Jūzaburō, the rear admiral who would succeed Usui as the association's second president; Shibusawa was introduced to Ushida by his nephew, Tanaka Eihachirō (1863–1941), himself president of several corporations.[86]

The Usui Association's elite membership may have been partly due to the organization's recruitment through word of mouth in social networks, which tends to follow the sociological principle of homophily: that is, the more similar two people are when compared with their surrounding populations, the more likely they are to make a connection. This "birds of a feather" principle enables individuals to form connections with others who share values, attitudes, and status, either "ascribed (e.g., age, race, sex) or acquired (e.g., marital status, education, occupation)."[87] However, we must also consider other factors. The organization charged high fees for membership and advancement, causing a bias for those who could afford it.[88] Usui and his *shihan* may also have advanced elites to the top ranks more quickly than people of lower social status, whether as a strategic means to promote the organization among elite circles or as an unconscious "halo effect," where positive evaluations of one aspect of an individual can affect how their other attributes are assessed.[89] In this case, the aura of these individuals' success in their respective fields may have affected perceptions of their therapeutic abilities.

Despite the social prestige of Usui Reiki Therapy practitioners, segments of the public perceived it as fraudulent and Usui as a quack. In an extended testimonial, an anonymous journalist wrote in 1928 of the cognitive dissonance they felt when they experienced unexpected results from an Usui Reiki Therapy treatment given jointly by three practitioners: "From under the piled hands, my stomach grumbled like ice needles melting and crumbling. . . . At that time, I recalled the founder of this therapy, said to be one of Japan's three fraudulent wizards."[90] This author's impressions of Usui and his followers were quite negative before experiencing Usui Reiki Therapy, but their experience led them to tentatively rethink their skepticism. Thus, Usui Mikao seems to have become widely known, at least among a certain social class, in 1920s Japan but was largely forgotten within a few years of his passing. However, Usui Reiki Therapy, in adapted forms, has attracted millions of advocates around the world, while those of his more renowned contemporaries largely faded away.

Usui Reiki Therapy in the Context of Religious and Healing Traditions

Usui Reiki Therapy was one of a number of therapies in prewar Japan that purported to manipulate or channel a force that pervades the cosmos and governs health. Many of these therapies appealed to the latest science in describing this force: Tanaka Morihei (1884–1928), founder of the largest spiritual therapy of its time, Taireidō, called this force *reishi* (spirit particles), and Matsumoto Chiwaki (1872–1942) taught Human Body Radioactivity Therapy (Jintai Hōshanō Ryōhō).[91] Usui and some of his contemporaries called this force by the name *reiki* (spiritual *ki* or wonderful *ki*), which draws more on East Asian religious and medical traditions than modern science; that said, the term *reiki* was popularized in modern spiritual therapy culture in the writings of an agricultural scientist named Tamari Kizō (1856–1931), who recast this traditional concept in a more scientific-seeming way.[92] Of course, even the most scientist of these therapies resemble some elements of spiritual therapies with a longer history in East Asia, such as medical qigong and the aforementioned *kaji kitō*.[93]

Usui distinguished his eponymous Reiki Therapy from other *reiki* therapies in Taishō-era Japan—such as Kawakami Mataji's Reiki Therapy (Reiki Ryōhō), Takagi Hidesuke's Human Aura Reiki Techniques (Jintai Aura Reiki-jutsu), and Matsubara Kōgetsu's Heart-Mind-Cleaning-Style Psychic Healing Techniques (Senshin-ryū Shinrei Chiryō-jutsu)—by applying his name to it.[94] However, we can also distinguish Usui Reiki Therapy from similar spiritual therapies due to Usui's use of three distinctive practices adapted from local religious traditions.

The first is the empowerment ceremony called *reiju* (spirit bestowal or wonderful bestowal), which connects practitioners to *reiki*'s cosmic source and authorizes Reiki practice. *Reiju* is derived from esoteric Buddhist initiations (J. *kanjō;* Skt. *abhiṣekha*) that Usui may have learned in connection to his practice on Mount Kurama.[95] In both *reiju* and *kanjō,* recipients sit with palms together in front of the chest, eyes closed, while the facilitators use light touch and forceful, directed breath on their heads and hands.[96] *Kanjō* links initiates to a Buddha, generally the cosmic Buddha (Dainichi Nyorai), whereas *reiju* links them to the cosmos, the source of *reiki,* enhancing their abilities to practice Usui Reiki Therapy.

Reiju essentially reenacts Usui's experience on Mount Kurama in which he was "mysteriously inspired after being touched by the ether during a fast" and received the "wonderful ability to heal."[97] Usui had a single transformative experience, but members of the Usui Association repeatedly received *reiju* at meetings called *reijukai* (*reiju* meetings), held regularly at branches around Japan. The first four ranks of the system—moving up from *roku-tō* (sixth-grade, the lowest) to *san-tō* (third-grade)—were collectively called *shoden* (first transmissions). Each *reijukai* a *shoden* practitioner attended made them eligible to move up a level, so conceivably one could reach *san-tō* after four meetings.[98] These advancements were tracked through certificates bearing the signatures and seals of the *shihan* administering *reiju*.[99] After ten months at *san-tō,* students became eligible for initiation into *okuden* (inner transmissions) and were selected based on their abilities, possibly on a practical examination.[100] Eventually, *okuden* practitioners could become eligible for *shinpiden* (mystery transmissions), learn to perform *reiju* themselves, and become a *shihan*. Above *shihan* was a level called *dai-shihan* (great teacher), thought to have been the level at which one was authorized to train other *shihan*.[101]

This pedagogical style—in which students progress through a series of levels, each marked with an initiation, and are gradually entrusted with teachings not to be shared with the uninitiated—is known in Japan as "secret transmission" (*hiden*) or "oral transmission" (*kuden*). This practice is historically rooted in esoteric Buddhism but has been a common element of Japanese arts and commercial trades from poetry to carpentry since the medieval period (twelfth to sixteenth century), as well as in Shinto.[102] Jacqueline Stone even calls secret transmission "the normative mode of transmitting knowledge in premodern Japan."[103] That said, it was especially prevalent in systems of "somatic knowledge," such as theater and swordsmanship.[104] Initiations and transmissions, sometimes dependent on passing practical examinations, incorporate initiates into a hierarchical familial lineage (*ryūha*), authorize their practice, and define their organizational status.[105] Initiates made written pledges (*kishōmon*) not to betray the secret teachings, a practice that the Usui Association also employed.[106]

Organizations employing secret transmission vary in terms of how many within the organization are authorized to know or teach the complete system, a factor related to the relative concentration of authority in the leaders. At one extreme are lineages in which a single master, known as the *iemoto* or *sōke,* has a monopoly on the complete system until they choose to transmit it to a successor, often a son (whether biological or adopted), who will become the next *iemoto*. In this system, the *iemoto* oversees subordinate instructors (*natori*), who pay licensing fees for the right to teach lower-level students; however, the *iemoto* controls who may teach what to whom and restricts "access to the most advanced lore, to which [he or she] alone was privy."[107] At the other extreme is the "complete transmission" (*kanzen sōden*) system, common in martial arts, in which the mentor "transmits not only the teachings but also the right and mechanism for further transmission" to multiple disciples, known as *shihan*.[108] These *shihan* were often able to teach the complete system—sometimes slightly changed from their teacher's—at their own dojos and could, in turn, authorize their own students as *shihan*.[109]

The Usui Association operated somewhere between these two models. Like the "complete transmission" model, *shihan* (or *dai-shihan*) could learn the entire system. On the other hand, somewhat like *natori,* the heads of the Usui Association's regional branches do seem to have had to defer to the Tokyo headquarters' authority. Usui Association documents such as certificates and the "*reiju* regulations" (*reiju kitei*) refer to the leaders as *sōke,* and most extant certificates were signed and sealed by the president.[110] That said, the existence of executive boards of *shihan* and *dai-shihan* suggests that a body of leaders made decisions collectively rather than one *iemoto*-like figure exerting complete authority.[111]

Usui's use of the secret transmission model helped legitimate his innovative Reiki Therapy and its practitioners by connecting them to traditional modes of knowledge transmission based on hierarchical authority. The secret transmission model also helped limit imitative forms by demanding intensive investments of time, money, and practice before one learned the full system. This may be why therapies derived from Usui Reiki Therapy, like Eguchi Toshihiro's Palm Healing (Tenohira Ryōji) and Tomita Kaiji's Tomita-style Hands-on Therapy (Tomita-ryū Teate Ryōhō), did not employ methods only taught to the most-senior practitioners, like *reiju.* The performance of *reiju* by *shihan* on junior practitioners, who themselves could someday become *shihan,* reproduced the hierarchical esoteric Buddhist lineages that were the traditional context for *kanjō.* At the same time, as "worldly" laypeople were performing an empowerment ceremony similar to those normally limited to religious professionals, in a sense, *reiju* (and other *hiden* initiations) can be understood as democratizing esoteric ritual for modern, urban audiences. This tension between broadening access to rituals once controlled by institutional monopolies and reproducing institutional hierarchies reflects broader trends in Japan's healing-focused new religions.[112]

The second practice that distinguishes Usui Reiki Therapy from other similar *reiki* therapies is its use of sacred symbols. Upon reaching *okuden,* students learn three graphic symbols, not to be revealed to noninitiates, used to enhance one's healing practice, to treat bad habits (*seiheki chiryō*), and to send "distance treatments" (*enkaku chiryō*).[113] Each of these symbols is to be traced with the hand or visualized during the practice while invoking a corresponding short phrase to activate it. This practice resembles elements of the esoteric Buddhist practice of *kaji* (Skt. *adhiṣṭhāna*), a form of deity yoga that Jason Josephson describes as "the pinnacle of a mutual relationship between the Cosmic Buddha (*Dainichi Nyorai*) and the devotee, when the compassion of the Buddha merges with the devotion of the practitioner, producing a sympathetic resonance" that manifests "buddhahood in this very body."[114] This mystical merging of the practitioner with the Buddha (*nyūga ga'nyū*) can be considered a kind of "alternating current": an energetic exchange between the practitioner and the cosmic Buddha. *Kaji*, like *kanjō*, was also adapted for settings outside of institutional Buddhism, including by Shinto priests and "quasi-lay practitioners, including mountain ascetics and other shamanic figures."[115] In some forms, practitioners merged with and embodied *kami* or even the emperor.[116]

Like *kaji*, the use of symbols by advanced Usui Reiki Therapy practitioners combines the "three mysteries" (*sanmitsu*) of body, speech, and mind by physically tracing the symbols and activating them with ritualized enunciations and visualizations. Also, like *kaji* practitioners, Reiki practitioners claim that they are not "healers" themselves but conduits for a greater power. The hands-on-healing techniques (*teate ryōhō*) taught to beginners share some of *kaji*'s functions, such as diagnosing and healing illness as well as empowering objects or spaces, but the symbols are said to enhance these abilities. This progression resembles how esoteric Buddhism considers exoteric healing rites a necessary step toward the more efficacious esoteric ones.[117]

Reiki's first symbol is a somewhat generic form that appears in cultures around the world,[118] but the second symbol, used for treating mental disorders or curing bad habits, and the third symbol, used for distance treatments, both have specific precedents in Japanese religion. The second symbol is a simplified form of *kiriku* (Skt. *hrīḥ*), a Sanskrit syllable (*bonji*) that represents Amida Butsu (Skt. Amitābha) and Kannon Bosatsu (Skt. Avalokiteśvara), so Usui's usage of this symbol probably invokes one of these two Buddhist figures. Usui grew up in the Jōdo-shū sect of Buddhism, centered on Amida, so such devotion would have come naturally to him, but devotion to both Amida and Kannon was practiced on Mount Kurama, where Usui had his formative experience.[119] Either way, Usui likely learned to write Sanskrit syllables through instruction in esoteric Buddhism or Shugendō, which incorporates aspects of esoteric Buddhist practice.

The third symbol condenses five characters in a talismanic form inherited from Chinese traditions and used by religious professionals in many forms of Japanese religion, but prominently in esoteric Buddhism. Its characters roughly mean "our original nature is right mindfulness," with "right mindfulness" (*shōnen*) being the penultimate step on the Eightfold Path taught by the historical Buddha. This message of returning to one's original Buddha-nature resonates with the merging of self with the Buddha in *kaji* practice. This particular five-character talisman appears as part of a larger talisman used in ninjutsu to connect to the target of a spell.[120]

Some members of the Usui Association seem aware of the connections between the symbols of Usui Reiki Therapy and older forms of Japanese religious practice. In an interview, Usui Association member Ogawa Fumio recognized the second symbol as a Sanskrit character (associated with esoteric Buddhism) and called the third symbol "a shortened conglomeration of five characters, a *jumon* (magic formula)."[121] Such connections undermine claims that Usui "instantly acquired Reiki Therapy" as a result of his austerities on Mount Kurama, without having received instruction from anyone or studied anything to gain "the wondrous ability to heal."[122]

The third practice differentiating Usui Reiki Therapy from the *reiki* therapies of his contemporaries is the recitation of *waka* poetry by the late Meiji Emperor (1852–1912). These poems, called *gyosei,* were likely recited while kneeling with hands held in front of the chest, palms pressed together (*seiza gasshō*).[123] The Usui Association published a collection of 100 *gyosei* during Usui's lifetime, and later Usui Association handbooks include 125 *gyosei.*[124] In addition to poems on themes of self-cultivation ("If our behavior is not correct, it is difficult to teach others") and perseverance ("Although things may not transpire as we wish, our hearts must be calm"), any of the poems in the original collection resonate with nationalist and Shintoist themes, such as, "Persevering through all difficulty: this is the Japanese spirit of our land," or, "The teachings of the ancestral *kami* keep the hearts of the Japanese people unified."[125] Ritualized recitation of the Meiji Emperor's writings was an ingrained element of Japanese life in this period. Schoolchildren recited the Imperial Rescript on Education daily, and military personnel were required to have memorized the much longer Rescript to Soldiers and Sailors. Both were treated with great reverence (with failure to do so bearing legal consequences) and powerfully influenced early twentieth-century Japanese ideology and practices.[126] But *gyosei* recitation's meaning for Usui Association members exceeded reverence or even spiritual inspiration.

Tomita Kaiji—an Usui Association member who left to form his own spiritual therapy based on Usui's teachings—calls *gyosei* recitation a "heart-mind purification method" (*jōshin-hō*) that works by allowing the emperor's heart-mind, expressed in the *gyosei,* to "illuminate and correct" one's own heart-mind.[127] Similarly, the man who may have inspired the use of *gyosei* in Usui Reiki Therapy—the nationalist author, activist, and spiritual therapist Mitsui Kōshi—writes that reciting *gyosei* essentially replaces one's own heart-mind with that of a *kami,* which corrects the heart-mind and body and strengthens one's power to heal others.[128] Like *kaji,* then, *gyosei* recitation can be considered a form of "deity yoga," as the practitioner takes on the desired attributes of a superhuman being—in this case, the deified Meiji Emperor, who was enshrined in Tokyo's Meiji Jingu in 1920, just two years before Usui opened his dojo in nearby Harajuku.

In addition to Usui and his students' earnestness in reciting *gyosei,* it was surely also politically expedient for them to emphasize imperial veneration in an age of state persecution of nonmedical healers and new religions that performed healing.[129] Indeed, state efforts to repress an "evil cult" called Hitonomichi Kyōdan in the 1930s were stymied by the fact that the group's creed "dutifully quoted" the Rescript on Education.[130] Similarly, *gyosei* recitation would have imbued *reijukai* and Usui Reiki Therapy more broadly with a patriotic air.

Usui Reiki Therapy as a Transnational Spiritual Therapy

Reiki practitioners today look back at the Usui Reiki Therapy of 1920s Japan as the template for "traditional Japanese Reiki," emphasizing its continuity with premodern Japanese practices.[131] Despite this impulse to essentialize it as distinctly Japanese, Usui created his Reiki Therapy by combining elements of traditions with long histories in Japan with elements of practices recently imported from the United States and adapted for Japanese audiences. Thus, before Reiki was ever practiced beyond Japanese borders, it could be considered a transnational spiritual therapy.

The spiritual therapies of early twentieth-century Japan were largely created by people like Usui who read widely and were interested in foreign practices like mesmerism and yoga in addition to local traditions. They commonly claimed that their therapies utilized the same force used by therapies in ancient India and China, which also underlay recent findings in Western science, from animal magnetism to modern physics.[132] These claims drew on strains of universalism and perennialism that were hallmarks of modernism in early twentieth-century Japan in fields from philosophy to religion to fine art.[133] As with many other universalists, the liberalism of these practitioners was often not egalitarian but rather a style that Josephson has called "hierarchical inclusion," which interprets difference as an inferior type of similarity.[134] While their therapies may resemble those of ancient Eastern civilizations and those of modern Western mesmerists, theirs alone have uniquely bridged East and West, religion and science, to achieve therapeutics' apogee.

This discourse, while prevalent in early twentieth-century Japan, did not originate there. While some of Usui Reiki Therapy's most distinctive practices drew on local precedents like *kanjō* and *kaji,* many of the discursive and bodily practices it shared with other contemporaneous spiritual therapies closely resemble those described in the books of Yogi Ramacharaka, one of several pen names used by the prolific American author William Walker Atkinson (1862–1932). The thirteen Ramacharaka books released by Atkinson's Chicago-based Yogi Publication Society combined aspects of "physical culture" with concepts of subtle energies and the power of the mind from mesmerism, theosophy, New Thought, and medical hypnotism.[135] Several of these books, such as *The Hindi-Yoga Science of Breath* (1904) and *The Science of Psychic Healing* (1906), gained transnational audiences through translation into many languages, including Japanese.[136] Well-known Japanese authors such as Nukariya Kaiten (1867–1934), a Sōtō Zen priest and founding president of Komazawa University, and Nakamura Tempū (1876–1968), founder of Shinshin Tōitsu-dō (The Way of Mind-Body Unification), an influential spiritual therapy also known as "Japanese yoga," cited Ramacharaka as an authoritative source on yoga.[137] Several more spiritual therapists, including Usui, appear to have incorporated techniques from Ramacharaka's translated texts into their own therapies without attribution.

Hirano Naoko has argued that the strong resemblances between Ramacharaka's "pranic healing" practices and those of Usui Reiki Therapy, Kawakami Mataji's aforementioned Reiki Therapy, Takagi Hidesuke's aforementioned Human Aura Reiki Techniques, and the Prana Therapy (Purana Ryōhō) of pioneering Japanese osteopath Yamada Shin'ichi imply that these Japanese therapies were localized versions of Ramacharaka's practices.[138] Ramacharaka's most influential book in this regard was *The Science of Psychic Healing* (1906), translated into Japanese as *The Latest Spiritual Therapy* (*Saishin seishin ryōhō,* 1916).[139] The similarities Hirano identified include discourse about a force called prana or *reiki* that fills the universe and governs physical and mental health through its proper circulation; ways to channel prana/*reiki* through touch, breath, and gaze; distance treatment methods; and meditations to cultivate prana/*reiki* in the abdomen and distribute it throughout the body.[140] This last one is a particularly strong connection: Ramacharaka's Prana Distributing meditation is described, with slight changes, in Yamada's 1920 volume as Purification Breathing (*seijō kokyū-hō*), and the Usui Association practices a similar meditation under the name Heart-Mind Purification Breathing (*jōshin kokyū-hō*).[141] Like *kaji* and *gyosei* recitation, this meditation can also be considered to employ the logic of deity yoga, in that it promotes visualizing the gradual fusion of the meditator with ultimate reality, but in place of a specific deity, the practitioner becomes one (or "not-two") with the cosmos, following the "I am the universe" (*ware soku uchū*) cosmology common in twentieth-century North Pacific spiritual therapies.[142]

The (perhaps indirect) influence of Ramacharaka's books on Usui exceeds even what Hirano indicates.[143] For example, Ramacharaka describes a technique to use the index and middle fingers to stroke the muscles on either side of the spine downward from the neck to the tailbone; he says to "always conclude" pranic treatments with stroking, which "equalizes the circulation."[144] In Usui Reiki Therapy, this technique is called the Blood Exchange Method (*ketsueki kōkan-hō*) and is used to conclude treatments; as the name suggests, it is also associated with circulation.[145] Ramacharaka also discusses finding particular areas that require extra treatment through cultivating intuition and paying attention to sensations of cold and heat in the hands, methods that resemble Usui's "mysterious signs method" (*reiji-hō*) and his scanning diagnostic technique called *byōsen*.[146] Even the phrase "*reiki* of the universe" (*uchū no reiki*), which Usui's memorial says is the basis for his therapy, appears in *The Latest Spiritual Therapy*.[147] Ramacharaka's influence on Usui and other early twentieth-century Japanese spiritual therapists is one example of how their therapies are better understood as the products of transpacific circulation than purely Japanese traditions.

Some of these Japanese spiritual therapies share another technique that also appears to have been adapted from America: a recitation of a short text believed to—like the *gyosei*—purify the heart-mind and enhance one's ability to work with *reiki*. Usui was one of several therapists who taught this method of reciting a short series of affirmations that Usui called "the Usui Reiki Therapy doctrine" and his followers called the *gokai,* a term that ordinarily refers to the five precepts that guide the conduct of Buddhist laypeople. Usui's version of the text reads, "The secret method to summon good fortune, the wonder drug for all disease: just for today, do not anger, do not worry, be grateful, fulfill duty, be kind to people. Morning and evening, put hands in prayer, recite these words in your heart-mind and with your mouth."[148] Usui's memorial states that it is the simplicity and efficacy of this recitation practice that made so many seek out Usui's excellent method (*reihō*): "It is not difficult: sit quietly with palms pressed together, meditating and chanting [the precepts], and you will cultivate a pure, healthy heart-mind."[149]

The text of the five precepts, written in Usui's calligraphic hand, likely hung alongside his portrait in Usui Association dojos.[150] The association reproduced it in the opening pages of its publications and on the large memorial stone it erected for him at a Buddhist temple in Tokyo. However, its basic form seems to predate Usui. Both Usui and his contemporary *reiki* therapist Takagi Hidesuke appear to have based their recitation of these five precepts on a passage from a 1914 book by Suzuki Bizan, a spiritual therapist deeply influenced by Christian Science.[151] Suzuki's Health Philosophy (Kenzen Tetsugaku) claimed to cure physical disease by correcting the heart-mind, synthesizing self-cultivation practices prevalent in nineteenth-century Japan with American teachings about the power of the mind and practices like affirmation and visualization, which he learned while studying philosophy in the United States. Due to his widespread newspaper advertisements and numerous publications, Suzuki was among the best-known spiritual therapists of the time, and the public considered his therapy a localized form of Christian Science.[152]

Given these American influences on the spiritual therapies of Usui and his contemporaries, they cannot be understood as distinctively Japanese, but rather were created at a particular juncture of North Pacific influences. The diverse influences Usui synthesized in his Reiki Therapy demonstrate his broad studies and his genius for creative combination. He united currents from varied streams: esoteric Buddhism, nationalistic recitation of imperial poetry, and practices like mesmeric healing and mind cure that were developed in the United States and translated for Japanese audiences. Nearly a century after his death, Reiki practitioners still revere Usui as the founder of their practice and try to recover his original teachings, but within a decade of his passing, several of his disciples had already adapted his practices for different audiences, introducing new methods of training and treatment.

Hayashi Chūjirō (1880–1940) and the Hayashi Reiki Research Association

One of Usui's chief disciples, Hayashi Chūjirō, was a retired naval captain. It is said Hayashi received medical training in the navy and Usui asked him to open a clinic to research, practice, and teach Usui Reiki Therapy from a more biomedical perspective.[153] A 1932 profile of Hayashi says that he was such an accomplished practitioner that Usui asked him to manage the Nakano dojo (the Usui Association headquarters).[154] His inclusion in the January 1926 group photograph of "all those authorized to perform *reiju*" indicates he had already reached the rank of *shihan* by that time, and a 1928 directory lists Hayashi as one of three Usui Association directors under President Ushida.[155] However, perhaps as early as 1927, Hayashi founded his own Hayashi Reiki Research Association (hereafter the Hayashi Association) and left the Usui Association.[156]

The Hayashi Association taught Usui Reiki Therapy largely as its founder had learned it from his master. They performed *reiju* and taught students *gyosei* and *gokai* recitation; Heart-Mind Purification Breathing; the *byōsen* scanning technique to find areas in need of *reiki;* the channeling of *reiki* with the hands, breath, and eyes; use of the symbols to treat bad habits and perform distance treatments; and how to finish treatments with the Blood Exchange Method.[157] However, in the decade between Usui's death in 1926 and Takata's arrival at the Hayashi Association's Tokyo headquarters in 1935, Hayashi also seems to have adapted the practice for his students.

In place of the system by which students gradually advanced through the ranks of the Usui Association, Hayashi introduced an intensive training course to allow students to rapidly progress to the *okuden* level, at which the symbols are taught. This course followed the Usui Association's precedent of holding five-day *reijukai*—Frank Petter cites an account of one in 1925 headed by Usui himself—but, as previously described, Usui Association regulations required students to wait ten months after reaching *san-tō* (the highest level of *shoden*) before being allowed to take *okuden*.[158] In contrast, at the completion of the five-day Hayashi Association course, students received certificates attesting to their completion of both *shoden* and *okuden*.

According to Yamaguchi Chiyoko (1921–2003), who took a five-day course in Daishōji, Ishikawa Prefecture (present-day Kaga City) in 1938, Hayashi developed these combined *shoden* and *okuden* courses for outlying regions without local *shihan* to oversee students' progress. She recalls the course consisting of instruction in the various recitation, meditation, and healing practices, including practical training in which the students experienced giving and receiving treatments, as well as receiving daily *reiju*.[159] The course was very expensive: Yamaguchi remembers it costing fifty yen, roughly a month's salary for an average worker.[160] Thus, members of the Daishōji branch of the Hayashi Association "were wealthy. There were business people, housewives (from wealthy families) and midwives."[161] Matsui Shōō (1870–1933), a playwright who studied Usui Reiki Therapy under Hayashi in Tokyo, corroborates this point, as his introduction to the Hayashi Association was through a successful businessman who had studied in the United Kingdom and whose father was a former president of Japan's national bank. He suggests that he would have likely laughed off the suggestion to study this therapy if it had not had such a high-class endorsement.[162] The upper-class composition of the Hayashi Association is a point of similarity with the Usui Association, but Hayashi's accelerated training course appears to have a major innovation.

In the Hayashi Association training course, students received treatment manuals called *Therapy Guidelines* (*Ryōho shishin*) that contain a list of ailments and suggested hand positions to treat these ailments.[163] Compared with a similar text published by the Usui Association in 1928 (later incorporated into its handbook), the Hayashi manual uses more specialized anatomical vocabulary, suggesting the Hayashi Association's training courses included basic instruction in anatomy.[164] Takata and another Nikkei student who studied with Hayashi's wife both returned to Hawai'i with Japanese-language anatomical charts, suggesting they received them during their study, and an 1937 edition of the manual designed for teaching in Hawai'i contained a bilingual chart identifying twenty-six organs.[165] An account of a treatment by Hayashi's student Matsui describes a medicalized intake procedure, in which the patient undressed and had his blood pressure checked and heart examined, that does not appear to have been practiced by the Usui Association.[166] Hayashi's treatments for losing consciousness and drowning also include a technique called *katsu* (resuscitation), taken from martial arts, which does not appear in the Usui Association handbook.[167] Thus, Hayashi seems to have introduced a more anatomically informed approach to treatment and introduced new techniques.

By the late 1930s, the Hayashi Association had branches around the country and had an estimated four to five thousand members.[168] Its main branch was in Shinanomachi, Tokyo, close to the renowned Keio University Hospital, which had opened in 1920. That Takata remarked on this proximity throughout her career suggests it held significance for Hayashi and his students.[169] This location may have lent Hayashi's clinic some of the authority of that esteemed biomedical center, but Hayashi and his students were also sometimes called to treat patients at Keio, some of whom (like

Shimura, Maeda's sister) later became members of the Hayashi Association based on their healing experiences.[170] This proximity meant it was also near Maeda's clinic—where a disembodied voice urged Takata to seek an alternative to the surgery she awaited—as Maeda had opened his clinic near the Keio Medical School, where he taught surgery.[171]

The Hayashi Association headquarters hosted a morning clinic, where Hayashi and his students paired up to treat patients; with eight beds, up to sixteen practitioners could treat at once. These beds, reportedly elevated like hospital beds, were another innovation, as the Usui Association typically treated patients on tatami mats, either sitting up or lying on futons.[172] In the afternoon, Hayashi, aided by his wife, Chie, and other top disciples, met with some students while others went out to treat patients who were hospitalized or required home visits. This morning clinic is where Shimura brought Takata that morning in late 1935.

Getting Treated at Hayashi's Clinic

Takata lay on a bed while Hayashi's students examined her. Simply placing their hands on her body and feeling "vibrations," they were able to make the same diagnoses as Maeda had from his X-rays. Skeptical of the intense heat and vibrations she felt coming from their hands, Takata inspected their sleeves for hidden wires or mechanisms. This made them laugh, attracting Hayashi's attention. When he inquired what was so funny, she said she was looking for a machine, as "the hands, they were working, and I could feel the vibration [sic]. They were not ordinary hands, but I said he must have some kind of connection with some kind of a force or power." Hayashi explained to her that this power was "not any kind of electricity" but *reiki*.[173] He said that he had learned English in preparation for his numerous travels to the United States and Australia as a naval cadet, and that "in English, [*reiki*] is called 'Universal Life Energy'":

> He said it comes from the sun, from the space, from the moon . . . this is universal . . . and he said the only thing that is different between you and me: we [sic] have the contact, you don't. . . . [My students] are filling your body with life energy. And this is too, too big. We cannot measure it. Too, too deep. Deeper than the ocean. We cannot fathom it. Therefore, in Japanese, we call it *reiki*. . . . You don't know how [radio works] because you are not a radio technician, nor am I, but the principles are the same. It goes through space without wire. Therefore, he said, you

have to accept that this great force can be contacted. And when you have the contact, then it is automatic, universal . . . limitless, unlimited power, when you have the switch on. And when you want to stop, all you have to do is take your hands off. Hands off, he says, and it just stops. So therefore it is very simple.[174]

Naturally, this 1979 recollection is an amalgam of memory and countless iterations of cultural translation and storytelling to Euro-American audiences, but it resembles what we know of the teachings of the Usui Association where Hayashi studied. He presents *reiki*'s origins as mysterious, although it follows certain natural laws, which fits with 1920s depictions of the origins and operations of *reiki* and Usui Reiki Therapy as mysterious. While Takata's translation of *reiki* as "universal life energy" effaces the literal meaning of the prefix *rei-* as either "spirit" or "wonderful," and her explanation elsewhere that *rei* literally means "universal" is positively misleading, it does evoke Usui Reiki Therapy's historical emphasis on "the universe" (*uchū*).

Usui's few extant teachings make frequent use of the term, as when he says that Reiki Therapy is "based on a mysterious [or spiritual] ability (*reinō*) that permeates the universe," and the similar statement on Usui's memorial stone that his "method of improving mind and body is based on the *reiki* of the universe."[175] These connections between macrocosm and microcosm resemble not only the doctrines of Usui's contemporary spiritual therapists in Japan who emphasized the limitless power of mind or spirit but also the doctrines of correspondence and influx that characterize American metaphysical religion.[176] As with Japanese therapists' use of the word *reiki* to translate foreign terms like "vital energy" and "prana," imported from the United States through translated texts, explaining *reiki* with the English phrase "universal life energy" is a kind of "reverse translation" of a Japanese term used to localize a nebulous, translocal concept.[177]

Whereas Usui claimed that modern science does not yet understand *reiki*, "though it is certain that it will accord with science in a coming age,"[178] Hayashi implied that this day had already come. He marshalled scientific authority when he explained to Takata that Reiki followed universal, verging on mechanistic, principles. Takata's class notes and diary from the period suggest that Hayashi's training described it in terms of "energy" (*enerugii*), which has a much more scientific connotation than *ki* (often glossed as "vital force"), inherited from the Sino-Japanese medicine (*kanpō*).[179] First, on December 10, 1935, her first day of training, she wrote of the "'Leiki' Energy within oneself," situated a couple of inches below the navel.[180] Then, in a diary entry from May 1936, near the end of her time in Tokyo, she wrote that Hayashi would soon teach her "the utmost secret in the Energy Science," suggesting that, by the mid-1930s, Hayashi used a similar Japanese phrase to explicitly frame Usui Reiki Therapy as an esoteric "energy science."[181] This scientific discourse implies that the nature and operations of *reiki* are presently understood, which somewhat contradicts Usui's location of such knowledge in a future time and Takata's recollection that Hayashi taught that *reiki* is immeasurable and its operations are mysterious.

These tensions between present and future, scientific measurability and spiritual boundlessness, are characteristic of early twentieth-century North Pacific spiritual therapists. In North America, spiritualists, mesmerists, and theosophists all used the language of "spiritual science" to describe their practices, and many of them described "animal magnetism" and "human electricity" as limited manifestations of a limitless sea of divine energy.[182] Meanwhile in Japan, Usui's contemporary spiritual therapists also made ample use of scientific terminologies to describe the powerful energies underlying their healing practices, as in Tanaka Morihei's Spirit Particle Technique (Reishijutsu) and Matsumoto Chiwaki's Human Body Radioactivity Therapy (Jintai Hōshanō Ryōhō). Thus, Takata's recollection of Hayashi's use of mechanistic metaphors—explaining *reiki* traveling like radio waves and the touch of an Usui Reiki Therapy practitioner's hand functioning like flipping a switch to close a circuit—despite the infiniteness and unknowability of these healing powers' cosmic source, befits the era.

After three further weeks of resting at the Maeda clinic while receiving daily Reiki treatments, both at Hayashi Association headquarters, where she went every day after breakfast, and from Shimura, who was an Usui Reiki Therapy practitioner herself, Takata's ailments healed completely.[183] Amazed by her recovery, she felt that she had "found [her] life" in Usui Reiki Therapy and was determined to learn the practice and bring it back to Hawai'i. Unfortunately, Shimura told her, it was simply impossible, as Takata was not Japanese. "She said, 'We have given many, many cultures to the outside world. We have given kendo, judo, karate, tea arrangement [*sic*], flower arrangement, these are all cultures. But Reiki, no. We guarding [*sic*] it with a fence around it and it shall not get out of Japan.'"[184] This narrative frames Usui Reiki Therapy as an essentially "Japanese" art akin to other cultural practices that had gained international renown, but also sets it apart as something precious and inaccessible to the outside world.

The exact objection to teaching Reiki to foreigners is unclear. It may be tied to a cultural chauvinism that resisted instructing foreigners in a practice that they would be unable to properly learn, because there is something essentially Japanese in the practice of Reiki. The mystical abilities to sense vibrations in the patient's body with the hands in order to diagnose the issue and then channel invisible cosmic energies to heal could easily have been tied to a nationalist "theory of the Japanese people" (*nihonjinron*) that set the Japanese apart as uniquely capable of intuiting spiritual truths. For example, the nationalist therapist Mitsui Kōshi described *gyosei* recitation as, "for us Japanese, a rite of our national religion," which endowed them with healing powers; he likely believed it would not work for foreigners, even Japanese Americans.[185] Alternatively, there could also have been practical concerns about teaching Usui Reiki Therapy to someone who primarily resided outside Japan. Even with Hayashi's training course, Hayashi Association members regularly attended *reijukai* where one could receive *reiju* and obtain feedback on the quality of one's practice. This sort of long-term social relationship to one's teacher and to other practitioners would be difficult, if not impossible, to maintain overseas.

Shimura's refusal may also be linked specifically to Takata's identity as an American. Earlier, she had chastised Takata for her inquisitiveness in searching the practitioners' kimonos for an electrical device, prompting Hayashi to explain the nature of Reiki to Takata. Afterward, Takata relates,

> [Hayashi] told his practitioners, "Mrs. Takata is an American. She looks Japanese, has a Japanese name, but is an American, born in Hawaii [as an] American citizen, and therefore what she have [*sic*] just expressed is democracy. That's how all Americans are: very open, very frank. And so, in Hawaii, this is nothing strange or not even rude. But in Japan, the ladies are very silent and they restrain from expressing themselves, and the law of the Japanese philosophy is ladies do not display emotions in the public. . . . [A Japanese lady] will not dare come here and open her mouth. . . . So therefore you find a difference between a Japanese and the Americans. . . . They express their opinion: they want to know, they say it."[186]

While Takata was pleased that Hayashi understood her inquisitive nature and explained it to his students, Shimura told her, "If you have any questions about Reiki . . . please do not open your mouth there, but keep it to yourself," as she would answer all of Takata's questions in private.[187] Shimura's remark may stem from female avoidance of assertiveness in Japan's public sphere (Shimura herself seems to have been rather frank in private) but also provides potential insight into the reluctance to teach Reiki to an American. Usui Reiki Therapy was taught in a hierarchical structure based on initiation, seniority, and formalized assessment. The leadership of the Hayashi Association may have considered "democratic" Americans unfit to learn such a practice.

Moreover, Nisei Americans (i.e., second-generation Japanese Americans) who traveled to their parents' homeland were often viewed contemptuously, partly due to class bias. As Japanese immigrants to America generally came from Japan's lower class, Nisei, "referred to pejoratively as *imin no ko,* or children of immigrants, were considered no better" by educated Japanese, such as the Hayashi Association members.[188] Gender socialization was another issue. Contemporary accounts said Japanese American women in 1930s Japan "registered as shamelessly arrogant and demanding" because they had not been brought up with "the strict standards of social etiquette for Japanese women."[189] Thus, Takata, like her Nisei peers who traveled to Japan, would have experienced a kind of "triple consciousness," seeing herself not only through her own eyes but also as an outsider in both the United States and Japan, as members of the dominant ethnicities in both places projected varied meanings onto her.[190]

After much meditation and prayer, Takata recalled, she petitioned Maeda as "the greatest humanitarian" to help convince Hayashi to take her on and allow her to bring Usui Reiki Therapy back to Hawaiʻi for her family and her community, which had suffered much from disease and untimely deaths.[191] She said she would sell her house to raise the money for her training. Impressed by her commitment, he composed a handwritten letter to Hayashi on a calligraphic scroll. Upon receiving this letter from the great doctor, Hayashi and his disciples agreed to take on Takata as an "honorary member."[192]

Takata's Initial Training and Practice

Takata's notes in the back of her Hayashi Association manual and her certificates suggest she took a four-day training course with Hayashi at the

Hayashi Association headquarters, from December 10 to December 13, 1935, which constituted both *shoden* and *okuden*.[193] If true, this would contradict her recollection to her biographer that she initially only took the "first degree" class, offered monthly, as well as the recollection of Hayashi's student Yamaguchi Chiyoko that Hayashi only gave (five-day) *shoden/okuden* seminars in outlying regions without local instructors, as his main centers in Tokyo and Osaka practiced the same mode of gradual advancement through multiple ranks as the Usui Association.[194]

Takata recuperated at the Maeda Surgical Clinic until late March 1936, when she traveled to Kyoto for Saichi's memorial service at the Ōtani Honbyō, the mausoleum of Shinran (1173–1253), founder of Jōdo Shinshū. In her journal, she mentions "curing" a family member's child during her Kyoto trip as well as a fellow traveler at her hotel. Upon her return to Tokyo, and after her parents and her daughter Alice left for Kaua'i in early April, the Hayashis invited Takata and her older daughter, Julia, to move in with them.[195] As such, Takata became an "inner disciple" (*uchideshi*), a great honor traditionally reserved for students of great potential, potentially the successor to the master.[196] Her diary reflects this transition, as an entry dated April 2 states, "This must have been my real lucky day as I come to think, I have gained so much knowledge in line of my treatments that I found myself taking patients naturally [*sic*]."[197] Takata's words reflect her pride in receiving recognition from her master Hayashi and in the advancement she saw in her treatment abilities.

In the months that followed, Takata increased the frequency of her treatments. A subsequent diary entry dated in May states, "Went to cure the 2 girls of Baron Taku 2 days and they were cured, Mrs Hanazawa at Keio Hospital, every night at 7:30 P.M.—Treatment for after operation—finds it very good and fast recovery. At the home office patients began to increase ever since I came to to [*sic*] them, it makes me feel good & very encouraging—today is the 21st and it reached to 20 patients."[198] She recalls Hayashi later revealing that this period of apprenticeship was a kind of examination, as he timed how long it took her to travel to and from her patient and followed up with the patient to see how long she treated, in order to see whether she got lost or whether Reiki would guide her. "You did not know Tokyo," he said, "but you never came back one time and said you lost direction. You see, you were following Reiki. Reiki gave you the lead."[199] His pleasure with her progress overjoyed her. She wrote in her diary,

Mr. Hayashi has granted to bestow upon me the secret of ShinpeDen [*sic*]. . . . Know one [*sic*] can imagine my happiness to think that I have the honor & respect to be trusted with this gift—a gift of a life time [*sic*] & I promised within me to do my utmost in regard to this beautiful & wonderful teaching that I just received—I shall promise to do what is right thru sincereness & kindness and shall regard and respect the teaching and its teacher with utmost reverence and respect.[200]

After receiving the *shinpiden* that authorized her to give *reiju* and teach Usui Reiki Therapy, Takata returned to Hawai'i, sailing out of Yokohama on June 2, 1936, and arriving in Honolulu eight days later.[201] From there, she returned home to Keālia, likely the first Reiki Master outside of the Japanese Empire.[202]

In Kaua'i, Takata began treating patients and initiating her first students.[203] Her October 1936 ad mentioned earlier (see figure 2.1) says she practiced from 4:00 p.m. to 8:00 p.m. daily in Kapa'a, the town just south of Keālia. Her office was in "Ota Cottage," likely a small, freestanding structure on the property of an Ota family. The ad also states that she held a free weekly clinic for infants on Saturday mornings. That she held office hours in the late afternoon and evening on weekdays and in the morning on Saturdays suggests that her clientele could not take off work to receive treatments, or that she could not take time off from her main job to provide them. The likelihood that this was her second job, in addition to her responsibilities as head housekeeper at the palatial Valley House, is supported by a recollection by Rufus P. Spalding Jr. (1910–ca. 1995), a nephew of Julia Spalding, as told to a chronicler of the family:

> There was a young Japanese, spotted by Rufus' Aunt Dudu [Julia Makee Spalding] as a barefoot girl on the plantation; seeing that she was very bright, Dudu installed her as "majordomo" at Valley House, and later helped her to get to the Mainland for medical training, so that she became a doctor. When Rufus was first married, he wanted to bring his bride out to Valley House, which had been unoccupied for some time. He called, or wrote to this Japanese doctor, and she arranged everything— opened up the place, installed cook and servants, saw that everything was clean and tidy. Before leaving, they held the last of many luaus at Valley House. The dining room table alone seated 30 to 40 people. . . . They had houseguests, and all the neighbors came. It was a great feast, and they had "music, of course. . . ." This was in 1936.[204]

While Takata did not actually become a doctor (the reference to her mainland training probably refers to naturopathy classes she took in Chicago in 1938, detailed in chapter 3), this fascinating reference establishes that Takata continued to work for the Spaldings after returning from Japan, and provides insight into Julia Spalding's perspective as her benefactor. While Takata's story emphasizes her labor to cultivate a relationship with an important customer of the esteemed Lihue Store, where she worked front of house while also doing basic bookkeeping, Rufus Spalding's take reinforces Julia's benevolence in plucking up this "barefoot girl" and giving her professional opportunities, first as the head of her domestic staff and then as a medical professional. The slippage between the two accounts attests to the Islands' gross racial inequality at the time, as well as to Spalding's seeing Takata as both a charity case and quite capable.

After teaching over fifty students in Kaua'i, Takata returned to Japan in the summer of 1937 to receive further training from Hayashi.[205] At this time, she invited Hayashi to the Hawaiian Islands (as described in the following chapter) to support her efforts to strengthen Usui Reiki Therapy's circulation there.

Conclusion

In late 1935, Hawayo Takata was drawn into the current of Usui Reiki Therapy's Japanese circulation. Its force transformed her from patient to therapist, evoking the archetype that Carl Jung, drawing on Greek mythology, dubbed the wounded physician. "It is his own hurt," Jung wrote, "that gives the measure of his power to heal."[206] The narrative Takata told of her path to Usui Reiki Therapy framed her illness as leading to a professional calling but also, equally importantly, as an opportunity for spiritual growth. As she said regarding her feeling that Saichi guided her to this practice from beyond the grave, "I found out the more experience I have had, the Reiki is not only for the physical but also for spiritual [sic]."[207] Such stories, which Takata frequently told to her clients and students, helped shape their understanding of Reiki and their expectations of what it would provide for them.[208] They also served Takata's establishment of her spiritual authority by highlighting how her own life story followed mythic conventions in addition to the archetypal hero's quest she would develop about the founder Usui, putting her on a path toward becoming a "charismatic entrepreneur."[209] The (often female) founders of many healing-oriented Japanese new religions similarly experienced their own health crises before undergoing miraculous healings and receiving the ability to heal others. This pattern follows earlier models of (again, often female) Japanese shamans.[210]

Takata's encounter with Usui Reiki Therapy in Tokyo could easily be understood as her initiation into a Japanese healing art in the vein of premodern folk therapies, but it also demonstrates that medicine in prewar Japan was a complex system awash in influences from the American side of the North Pacific, including both biomedicine and spiritual therapies. Sickly patients in 1930s Tokyo consulted practitioners of biomedicine, Sino-Japanese medicine, folk therapies (some of which were officially proscribed), healing-focused new religions, and innovative spiritual therapies that combined democratized "reinventions" of older Japanese therapeutics with practices recently imported from North America and adapted for Japanese audiences. Many of these therapies were alternate currents. As they and their healing energies circulated between instructors and students, practitioners and patients, influences alternated back and forth among these parties, and therapists adapted their therapies for use by different audiences. Spiritual therapists highlighted their therapies' alterity as they contrasted them with orthodox forms like biomedicine and *kanpō* (as well as with rival spiritual therapies), yet they also drew on the authority of conventional medicine, science, and religion as they oscillated between their vocabularies and concepts.

Many turned to spiritual therapies after other forms of medicine proved ineffective. Hayashi's student Matsui Shōō listed numerous examples of patients he healed with Usui Reiki Therapy after biomedical doctors pronounced them incurable.[211] Matsui's claims that Usui Reiki Therapy's diagnostic technique could detect physiological sources of disease invisible to biomedical practitioners illustrate how spiritual therapies were promoted as "no less, and perhaps even more, scientific and empirical than the orthodox medical treatments."[212] Usui also said as much when he cited "well-known European medical doctors" who "severely criticized medicine" and named Japanese doctors who decried biomedical ignorance of the psyche, castigated "the narrow-mindedness" of colleagues who rejected the potentials of spiritual therapy, and foretold a coming "great revolution" of medicine by those with "spiritual knowledge" (*reichi*). Usui concluded this section by saying, "Clearly, medical doctors, pharmacists, etc., are acknowledging the efficacy [of spiritual therapies such as Reiki Therapy] and are learning them for themselves."[213] His implication that Usui Reiki Therapy provides therapeutic benefits that biomedicine cannot continues today in the rhetoric of integrative medicine.

Usui's followers attributed the efficacy of his therapy (and its superiority to material medicine) to elements closely tied with Japanese identity, such as *gyosei* recitations while in *seiza gasshō*. Such discourse was tied up with the Occidentalism of its time, in which Asian nationalists inverted Orientalist claims for their own purposes. For example, in a kind of judo, they reversed the Orientalist attack that Asians have yet to reach the highest levels of civilization because they are overly "traditional" and "culture-bound," saying that, in fact, it is the cultural (as opposed to the material) that is "the real and vital base of civilization."[214] The case of Japanese adaptations of the pranic therapies of America's Yogi Ramacharaka is a striking example of Occidentalism's "hall-of-mirrors" effect, where Asians reflect Euro-Americans' representations of Asians.

Despite engaging in discourse that the Orient and Occident are essentially discrete and opposed, Usui and his contemporary spiritual therapists (as well as Buddhist modernists) were embedded in transpacific currents that blur boundaries between East and West. We have seen how Usui and his contemporaries employed elements of spiritual therapies imported from the United States such as pranic therapy and forms of New Thought affirmation, whether directly or through contemporary localizations of these practices. Usui can be said to have employed a particularly "domesticating" translation strategy that emphasized continuities with local practices, in contrast to others who "foreignized" their practices by deliberately retaining Occidental or Indian elements that broke with local conventions.[215] These complementary translation strategies would have appealed to different audiences in search of healing.

Usui's use of practices derived from esoteric Buddhism—the *reiju* ceremony derived from *kanjō* initiations; the pedagogical system of secret transmission; and the use of symbol, incantation, and visualization derived from *kaji* empowerments—as well as his promotion of mystical union with the Meiji Emperor all embedded Usui, his teachings, and his students in the authority of local traditions (despite claims of his therapy's originality). Recitation practices meant to purify the heart-mind and dispel disease, performed while kneeling on the floor, hands in prayer position, focused on the lower abdomen, creatively adapted aspects of the translocal New Thought movement by imprinting them with aspects of local praxis.

The interplay between Usui Reiki Therapy's "Japanization" and its transnational identity influenced its subsequent uptake in Hawai'i, North America, and beyond. In wartime Hawai'i, when being a Nikkei religious professional was means for incarceration, Takata excised elements with explicitly Japanese cultural markers, such as the meditations with hands in prayer position and the Japanese-language recitation practices. Yet in the Cold War United States, when Japan attained new status as an ally in the fight to contain Asian Communism, framing Reiki as a "Japanese art" dovetailed with Orientalist interest in Japanese spiritual practices, particularly Zen. At the same time, its North Pacific character helped mediate its uptake by North American audiences, as students' familiarity with vitalistic worldviews and laying-on-of-hands practices harmonized with the perennialism that marked the liberal religious sensibilities shared by suburban housewives and youth countercultures. Reiki's esoteric initiation structure also facilitated its postwar success overseas. Just as Usui's use of secret transmission helped legitimize Usui Reiki Therapy for his followers while also slowing its early growth and limiting the printed materials about the practice, part of Reiki's appeal to Takata's students in postwar North America was that its initiations linked them into a lineage stretching back to Usui, an authentic Japanese master. Through Takata's involvement in initiation-based fraternal organizations on the US mainland, Reiki's esotericism took on new meanings as it was introduced to and practiced within new communities.

Thus, in multiple ways—Usui's engagement in Occidentalism; his fusion of elements derived from New Thought and those derived from esoteric Buddhism; and the changing significance of Usui Reiki Therapy's initiation lineage and other practices that can denote "Asianness"— linkages between Usui Reiki Therapy's movement and its evolution illustrate how it is a product of North Pacific circulation. As an alternate current, the introduction of Usui Reiki Therapy to new audiences was tied to the repeated refiguring of its practices and their meanings through multidirectional influences. Its identity (as well as the identities of its practitioners and recipients) was defined in relation to but also in contradistinction from religion and medicine.

The circulation of Reiki and other spiritual therapies influenced their development but also transformed the networks in which they circulated. Social ties took on new meanings, as friends, family members, and acquaintances became masters and students, practitioners and patients. The social networks of new students and recipients of treatment then became new potential audiences for transmission, opening up new networks in turn. Furthermore, some touched by *reiki* also experienced transformations of other values, particularly a spiritualization of their embodied experiences and aspects of Japanese culture.

This chapter examined the earliest examples of Usui Reiki Therapy students projecting spiritual potency onto Usui Mikao, his disciples, and their practices, from the *reiju* ceremony that awakened their healing powers, to Usui's spiritual awakening on Mount Kurama, to the recitation of *gyosei* to correct their heart-minds through mystical union with the Meiji Emperor. As these practices entered other North Pacific currents, they and the meanings assigned to them continued to transform, and they in turn transformed those who encountered them.

CHAPTER 3

Healing at the Hub of the Transwar Pacific
Adapting Reiki for Nikkei Hawai'i, 1937–1960

On Sunday, February 20, 1938, the retired naval captain Hayashi Chūjirō addressed a grand luncheon of approximately two hundred people who filled the second floor of Shunchōrō, a large teahouse in Honolulu's Alewa Heights with harbor views (figure 3.1). KGMB-AM simultaneously broadcast this address, delivered in Hayashi's native Japanese, and the Japanese-language newspaper the *Hawaii Hochi* would publish a full transcript. The attendees had studied Usui Reiki Therapy under Hayashi and his disciple, Kaua'i-born Hawayo Takata, and they sat facing heaping plates bearing leftover lobsters and *makizushi* (sushi rolls) as the great master of this therapy recounted how, since his arrival in October, he and Takata had trained approximately 350 people in fourteen courses. At each course, he said, "many new members attended, they understood [the teachings] well, and, of course, they painlessly healed the diseases of their close relatives and were grateful for the happiness of health."[1] Hayashi's grateful students sent him home with four hundred pounds of Hawaiian sugar and other local specialties including Kona coffee; koa-wood bowls; cases of oranges, pineapples, and olives; and so many leis he could not wear them all (figure 3.2).[2] As Hayashi could not legally work in the United States at a time of rising tension between these two Pacific empires, these lavish gifts may have been in place of cash payments.[3]

Three years later, in 1941, a spy for the Japanese navy spent long hours in the very same teahouse, using a telescope to monitor the comings and goings of ships at the US naval base of Pearl Harbor, six miles to the west; this intelligence helped plan the bombardment of Pearl Harbor

Figure 3.1 Farewell banquet for Hayashi Chūjirō (*standing, far left*), Shunchōrō Teahouse, Honolulu, February 20, 1938.

Figure 3.2 Departure of Hayashi Chūjirō and Kiyoe (wearing leis), Tatsuta Maru, Honolulu Harbor, February 22, 1938.

that December in one of several simultaneous offensives that launched the Pacific War.[4] For roughly the next three years, the US Territory of Hawai'i was under martial law. The Counter Intelligence Corps of the US Army (CIC) and the Federal Bureau of Investigation (FBI) immediately began arresting hundreds of Nikkei community leaders on FBI lists and commenced further investigations of other Nikkei residing in Hawai'i as potential threats to national security.[5] Roughly half of the ten thousand individuals under investigation were *kibei,* or local Nikkei whose parents sent them to Japan for schooling, so it is likely that the CIC investigated Takata's family.[6]

Takata's decision to have her elder daughter, Julia, educated in her parents' homeland was not the only reason she may have been under suspicion in wartime Hawai'i. She herself traveled to Japan five times in the 1920s and 1930s: three times to accompany her dying husband as he received medical treatment and two longer trips during which she studied Usui Reiki Therapy under Hayashi. Several of the numerous newspaper articles about Hayashi and Takata's collaborative teaching of Usui Reiki Therapy described him as a naval officer, which could also have endangered Takata if American military intelligence monitored local Japanese-language media. Moreover, many of the Nikkei incarcerated in Hawai'i were leaders of religious organizations, considered to foster Japanese nationalism; almost all Buddhist priests were incarcerated, including hundreds arrested the day after the Pearl Harbor attacks.[7] If the CIC knew that a chief practice of Reiki had been the reverential recitation of the Meiji Emperor's poetry, Takata would likely have joined them.

While Takata was not incarcerated during the war, her fear of being suspected of ties with Japan is plainly legible in the sign that hung outside her home clinic in Hilo (figure 3.3). Its palimpsestic layers illustrate the changing times of 1940s Hawai'i. The main text, from top to bottom, originally read, "REIKI MASSAGE / SWEDISH MASSAGE / [illegible] / H. TAKATA." Below that were Japanese characters advertising the Takata Reiki Treatment Center (Takata Reiki Chiryōin), and on the right-hand side it vertically spelled out Takata's name in Japanese style. Her decision to paint over this sign, removing the Japanese characters, decreasing the size of her Japanese name, and replacing "Reiki" with "NERVE • GLAND • SHORT WAVE TREATMENTS," reflects anxieties about appearing too Japanese in a time when it was a liability.

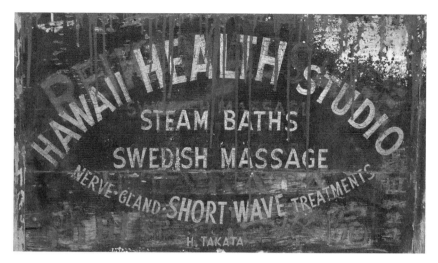

Figure 3.3   English-language sign for Takata's Hilo clinic with older writing (in both English and Japanese) that has been painted over, ca. 1940s.

This chapter examines the networks through which Usui Reiki Therapy circulated as an alternate current in Territorial Hawai'i's Nikkei community during the transwar period from the late 1930s to the late 1950s. It pays particular attention to how Takata adapted Reiki as she trained in naturopathy, massage, and radionics, as well as to how Hawai'i's Nikkei, who made up the vast majority of Reiki practitioners outside Japan prior to the mid-1970s, assigned varied meanings to Reiki practice. Examining this period spanning the Pacific War reveals continuities that are occluded when one chooses the war's outbreak or its completion as an endpoint.[8]

This is not to say that the war did not present an important break in the lives of Hawai'i's Nikkei. Wartime discrimination built on earlier "yellow peril" rhetoric regarding Nikkei Americans' unassimilability and the presumption that their loyalties were divided between the United States and Japan, but wartime propaganda newly cast these US residents and citizens as unprecedented alien threats to American sovereignty, and the imposition of martial law in the Territory made suspicion sufficient cause for incarceration. On the other hand, the bravery of Nisei who served on the front lines in Europe would be held up in the immediate postwar period as a symbol of Japanese Americans' patriotism and assimilation.[9] This chapter balances sensitivity to these wartime discontinuities with attention to other continuities in Reiki's circulation in transwar Hawai'i's Nikkei community. As the first of three chapters to focus on Takata's teaching, it (like the two that follow) profiles a few of Takata's students to help illustrate who was swept up in Reiki's currents in this place and time. It considers the bidirectional influences between Takata and her interlocutors, especially the forms of alternative medicine and spirituality she encountered in these years. It also documents the beginning of Takata's professionalization of Reiki practice and examines tensions within this early Reiki community about commodifying this spiritual therapy.

Hayashi and Takata's Teaching Tour

One marked difference between Usui Reiki Therapy's circulation in Japan and in Hawai'i began even prior to Hayashi's arrival in Honolulu. In September 1937, Takata left Yokohama one week before Hayashi, and she began promoting his visit as soon as she hit Hawaiian shores. The *Hawaii Hochi*, one of Honolulu's major Japanese-language daily newspapers, ran an article announcing Hayashi's imminent arrival two days before his landing, and the day he arrived they ran a second article with a photo of him and his daughter Kiyoe, his traveling companion during the five months he was in the Islands.[10] Takata's media savvy undoubtedly helped draw the crowd of over two hundred people who attended Hayashi's public lecture on Reiki Therapy one rainy Wednesday night in November 1937.[11] She also undoubtedly helped arrange the space for this talk: the Young Men's Buddhist Association (YMBA) Hall of the enormous Honpa Hongwanji Hawaii Betsuin, the sect headquarters for most Japanese Buddhists in the Territory.[12]

This media coverage of Hayashi's teaching likely helped Reiki Therapy's initial momentum in Hawai'i, but it sharply contrasted with Usui Mikao and Hayashi's policies in Japan, which discouraged publicity or advertising. The most extensive prewar practitioner accounts of Usui Reiki Therapy are those of a playwright named Matsui Shōō, who (as mentioned in chapter 2) studied under Hayashi and described the therapy in newspapers and magazines. In a 1928 newspaper article, Matsui wrote, "For some reason, Usui especially disliked making [his therapy] public, so those trained in his schools also still avoid advertising." Matsui continued by saying that he knew others in the Hayashi Reiki Kenkyūkai (Hayashi Reiki Research Association, hereafter the Hayashi Association) opposed his publicizing Usui Reiki Therapy, but he replied, "If any truth contributes to human happiness, isn't our duty to humanity to promote it?"[13] The reasons behind Usui's aversion to promotion are unknown but are probably linked to factors described in chapter 2, including his use of "secret transmission" (*hiden*) and possible caution about attracting state suspicion in a time when other organizations promoting spiritual therapies were suppressed, notably in the 1921 Ōmoto incident. Takata clearly did not share these concerns in 1937 Hawai'i, and Hayashi at least tacitly agreed to the press coverage, as it continued consistently throughout his stay.

Takata and Hayashi traveled together to Kaua'i for a brief visit, teaching two classes before settling in Honolulu with their respective daughters, Julia and Kiyoe, who were about the same age and had grown friendly in Japan. After some initial difficulty at a couple of hotels downtown, they resided in two "cottages" at a boarding house called the Grove Hotel at 1633 Nuuanu Avenue, just *mauka* (mountain-ward) of School Street. The Grove was on the quiet *mauka* edge of the Honolulu neighborhood then called Chūō Rengō (Central Business District), dominated by Nikkei commercial activity, and was about one block from the Honpa Hongwanji Hawaii Betsuin and its YMBA Hall.[14]

A visitor to Chūō Rengō in the 1930s could have the impression that Hawai'i's thriving Nikkei community was an extension of Japan's growing empire, and US agencies closely monitored Hawai'i's "Japanese problem." Anti-Japanese bias and "Americanization" campaigns were issues in Hawai'i and the US mainland throughout the early twentieth century, largely due to White anxieties over Japanese Americans' "unassimilability."[15] Related concerns were the second and third generations' rising political power (as American citizens, they had voting rights) and the question of whether the Territory's large Nikkei demographic would be loyal to the United States in case of war with Japan. These concerns intensified in the 1920s and 1930s following several incidents: the 1920 plantation strikes organized by the Japanese Labor Federation; two well-publicized cases with Japanese defendants (the 1928–1929 Fukunaga case and the 1932 Massie case); and Japan's aggression on the Asian mainland, beginning with the 1931 invasion of Manchuria. Federal agencies and commissions, including the Department of Justice and the House Committee on Immigration and Naturalization, wrote reports addressing alleged threats that Nikkei posed to American rule in Hawai'i and national security more broadly. Prominent figures, including Territorial governor Charles McCrary and Rear Admiral Yates Stirling Jr. (commandant of the Fourteenth Naval District and Pearl Harbor), asked for the Territory's self-rule to be revoked and it placed under control of a federal commission to prevent Nikkei Americans from dominating democratic elections.[16]

Takata recalled using political connections to help navigate this adverse environment. In her autobiographical recordings, she described difficulties with Hayashi's immigration status after a local Nikkei woman reported him to the police as a Japanese national conducting business without proper paperwork, but Takata's Republican Party ties saved the day. As "immigration is federal," she said, the investigation ultimately extended to Washington, DC, where she contacted Hawai'i's congressional delegate, Samuel Wilder King (1886–1959). Reportedly, he took an interest in the dispute and, at its resolution, personally informed her via phone and telegram, "Takata won the case," allowing Hayashi to stay without incident.[17] Whether or not the story is true, it situates Takata as a connected Nikkei entrepreneur who rose from humble roots on the periphery of the American empire to gain influence that extended to the center of American state power.

Hayashi and Takata's fourteen training courses (kōshūkai) on Oʻahu, mostly held at the Grove Hotel, averaged between fifteen and twenty students.[18] As these courses were each held over five consecutive weekday evenings, from 7:00 to 9:00, they likely resembled Hayashi's five-day courses in Japan, which contained both the "first transmissions" (shoden) and "inner transmissions" (okuden), so that students completing the course would know the symbols used in advanced techniques, including distance treatment. Hayashi recounted that these courses included "whites, Hawaiians, and Chinese who understand absolutely no Japanese language," but courses were likely taught in Japanese.[19] Surviving photos and other records suggest these early students were almost entirely Nikkei and mostly Issei, who generally spoke limited English. Moreover, despite Hayashi's apparent instruction in English as a naval cadet (see chapter 2), his fluency was probably insufficient to teach in English. In the story Takata told of Hayashi's interview with US immigration officials, she insisted on the presence of an interpreter to avoid misunderstandings.[20] Teaching in Japanese would not have significantly limited their class sizes: in 1930, the Nikkei population was approximately 140,000, nearly 40 percent of the Territory's population,[21] and due to the limited English spoken by most Issei, their Nisei children tended to be conversationally proficient in casual Japanese even if their literacy was limited.

An album of students from Hayashi's trip, with handwritten captions indicating the students' names, their addresses, and which of the fourteen

Figure 3.4   Photo album page showing students from the eighth (December 1937) and ninth (January 1938) classes taught by Hayashi and Takata.

classes they attended, contains eighty portraits (figure 3.4).[22] All the students in this album have Japanese surnames, and all save one have their names written in Japanese characters; the one exception, Samuel Osamu Inouye (1915–2004) of Ewa, seems to have had a non-Nikkei, possibly Native Hawaiian, mother. Some photos in this album show their subjects in bucolic settings, but most of these early students seem to have been from the upper segments of Honolulu's urban Nikkei society. The cost of these classes remains unclear, but (as established in chapter 2) the fees Hayashi charged in Japan were roughly a month's salary for the average worker, and Takata charged similar prices a few years later on the island of Hawai'i.[23] One *Hawaii Hochi* article extols Hayashi for "devoting all his energies bringing the health preservation therapy to men and women of all ages and every social class," but then boasts how among them are "doctors, soldiers, high-ranking officials, the very wealthy, and scholars."[24] Another contemporary article told its readers, "the first seminar charge is—do not be shocked—fifty dollars," and that, due to that price, those who enrolled were "managers at banks and corporations."[25] From what we know of those who became involved in

Honolulu, a disproportionate number were in the Nikkei community's petit bourgeois class sociologists have called "middleman minorities."[26]

Reiki's Early Supporters in Honolulu

One important early supporter of Reiki in Honolulu was Alice Sae Teshima Noda (1894–1964), who, along with her husband, Steere Gikaku Noda (1892–1986), was among the Hawaiian Nikkei community's most prominent and successful figures. Alice came to Hawaiʻi at age five, the eldest daughter of two immigrants who were able to accumulate sufficient capital working in Oʻahu's plantations that they could buy land in Wahiawa and start their own pineapple plantation.[27] At age eighteen, Alice married Steere, a local baseball star who went into law and became the first Nikkei to work in Hawaiʻi's courts; after the war he became a successful politician. After raising four children, Alice first went into dental hygiene, becoming head of the local dental hygiene college and president of the local hygienists' association, and then into "beauty culture," studying on the mainland and becoming an examiner for the territorial board and president of the local hairdresser and cosmetology associations. She built a chain of salons, with four on Oʻahu and one in Tokyo's posh Ginza shopping district, and wrote a column on beauty and Western etiquette that became syndicated in Japanese-language newspapers and magazines in Hawaiʻi and Japan. For Japanese and Nikkei women in the North Pacific, Alice Noda represented the heights of class and glamour to which they too might rise with proper attention to beauty and etiquette.

Noda seems to have greatly helped Reiki in its early days in Hawaiʻi. She and Takata took the same steamship from Yokohama to Honolulu in September 1937, which may be where they met.[28] A week after returning home to Honolulu, the Nodas accompanied Takata to the harbor to meet the Hayashis when they arrived October 2, and they all went together to the offices of the *Hawaii Hochi,* where the Hayashis had their photo taken for the newspaper to promote the upcoming classes.[29] Alice then accompanied Takata and the Hayashis to Kauaʻi a few days later (her first trip to that island), possibly enrolling in one of the courses they held there.[30] By the end of the month, ads for Hayashi's first Honolulu course listed Noda's name as a contact for registration, along with the address and phone number of her Cherry Beauty Salon; prior to Hayashi's departure in February 1938, Noda's salons advertised free Reiki treatments, offering separate spaces for men and women.[31]

The combination of the strength of Noda's renown in the Nikkei community and the publicization of her early support for an unknown therapy in a popular newspaper must have helped draw students to Hayashi and Takata. Furthermore, the association of Reiki with Noda probably played into its disproportionate appeal to women.[32] Not only was Noda's name synonymous with beauty culture in Hawai'i's prewar Nikkei community, but the ad for free treatments in her Honolulu salons framed Reiki as both "the new therapy to restore one's health" and "the latest technique to return one's beauty to the way it was formerly."[33] Noda also promoted Reiki to women's groups alongside beauty tips; in a talk at the April 1940 meeting of the Japanese Housewives Club (Shufu-no-kai) at the Honolulu YWCA, she spoke on "'Personal Appearance' and the 'Reiki Treatment and its Effect.'"[34] This was probably an infrequent occurrence, as Noda does not seem to have mentioned Reiki in her regular beauty column. Moreover, when I spoke with Noda's daughter Lillian Yajima (b. 1920), she did not remember her mother giving many treatments in the salons, so this too was probably a short-term development; Yajima did say, however, that her mother became known for the quality of her Reiki treatments and was often asked to make house calls, even to travel to the "neighbor islands" to treat friends and acquaintances who were unwell.[35] Such travels must have inspired an article that credits Mr. and Mrs. Noda's Reiki practice for making Maui residents think, "if they received a treatment from their teacher Mrs. Takata, the blind would see and the mute would begin to sing."[36] Thus, while Reiki's appearance in Alice Noda's salons may have been brief, the visibility of her early support for this novel therapy probably helped establish it in the Islands, and her continued practice helped introduce Takata and Reiki to many more for years to come.[37]

Another example of an early petit bourgeois supporter of Reiki in Honolulu is the owner of the Grove Hotel, Bunki Aoyama (1885–unknown), who became Takata's second-in-command after Hayashi's departure.[38] Aoyama moved to Hawai'i in 1906 from Kumamoto and quickly raised sufficient funds to invest in a succession of small businesses, including dyeing textiles and owning a laundry and a restaurant, before becoming a landlord in 1937.[39] He traveled frequently between Hawai'i and Japan, making at least five such trips between his emigration and the beginning of the Pacific War. Aoyama was also an enthusiastic host of the Japanese Imperial Navy when they visited Hawai'i; he served as head of the committee that gave Japanese sailors a tour of O'ahu, which a local publication called the most important aspect of the navy's visit to the island.[40] Their connections to the Imperial Navy likely helped Aoyama and Hayashi bond, and before the Hayashis' departure, they visited a Japanese naval cemetery in Honolulu's Makiki Valley with Aoyama and Takata; the *Hawaii Hochi* ran two articles on this, one of which included a photo of the four of them bowing to the Japanese sailors' graves.[41]

Aoyama was noted for his adaptability, intellect, enthusiasm, and throaty voice, all of which made him a skilled master of ceremonies at fleet receptions (though he was somewhat taciturn in his everyday life); this experience seems to have led to him emceeing the meetings of the Hawai'i chapter of the Hayashi Association and Hayashi's farewell banquet.[42] By the time of Hayashi's farewell, Aoyama had become Takata's right hand: he was included in a number of photo opportunities with her and the Hayashis, Hayashi's farewell address urged listeners "who want instruction or are troubled by illness [to] please consult Mrs. Takata or the treatment manager Bunki Aoyama," and Aoyama continued to go by the titles "treatment manager" (*chiryō shunin*) and "executive secretary" (*kanji,* a term that could also mean "emcee") in descriptions of the Hayashi Association's Hawai'i branch after Hayashi's departure.[43]

Having her landlord invested in her organization was clearly helpful for Takata, as Aoyama may have provided her and Hayashi with reduced rates for the spaces where they treated clients and held classes, but Aoyama must also have been a dedicated practitioner to have been named the branch's treatment manager after only a few months of practice. His enthusiasm for the Japanese military, seen in his volunteer work with the visiting Imperial Navy and in his eldest son's enlistment in Japan's Imperial Army,[44] may have influenced his dedication to this therapy, which had a significant military following in Japan (particularly the navy). Thus, Noda and Aoyama show how Usui Reiki Therapy's meaning was flexible enough to appeal to opposite gendered ideals in Hawai'i's Nikkei community, from the hyperfeminine beautician to the hypermasculine military buff.

After Hayashi's departure in February 1938, Takata continued operating a Reiki clinic at the Grove Hotel for about two months. She held four more weekly training courses there and at the large YMBA Hall nearby. Under Takata's leadership, the Hawai'i branch of the Hayashi Association continued holding monthly meetings at the YMBA Hall into June, and the early meetings are recorded as drawing about 150 people.[45]

However, Takata would miss the May meeting, which fell during her seven-week trip to the US mainland. She had been invited by the bishop of the Jōdo Mission of Hawai'i, Kyokujō Kubokawa (1874–unknown), to interpret for him and a group of priests on a trip to California.[46] She had also received invitations from multiple White women in California—a pianist and writer from Los Angeles whom she met in Kyoto and a French baroness living in San Francisco who wrote her three times, asking her to come and teach Reiki—so this allowed her to see them, as well as enrolling in classes at a naturopathy college in Chicago.[47] Thus, in mid-April, she set sail for Los Angeles, leaving the Hayashi Association's Hawai'i branch under the supervision of her "beloved daughter" Julia and her clinic to six of her advanced students, who continued treating and holding seminars in her absence.[48] This trip may have included the first Reiki classes on the US mainland, as Takata seems to have been asked for instruction everywhere she went, from the California ladies with whom she was in correspondence to "two schools" of people in Chicago who wanted initiation.[49] But the classes she may have taught made less of an impact on Reiki's development and circulation than the classes she took, which contributed to Reiki's gradual professionalization, as detailed in the next section.

Adapting Reiki in Transwar Hawai'i

The bombing of Pearl Harbor and immediately subsequent incarceration of Japanese Buddhist clergy and other Nikkei community leaders ruptured the everyday lives of Hawai'i's Nikkei community, including how Reiki was taught and practiced. However, as Takata had begun altering what she learned from Hayashi shortly after returning from Japan to Kaua'i in 1936, the rupture of wartime was just one of several factors affecting Reiki's circulation in the 1930s and 1940s. This section examines how Takata adapted Reiki in these years, including adding methods she learned in Chicago, making changes to professionalize and standardize treatments, (re)instituting a more pronounced gradation of training by removing the advanced techniques from the initial training, shifting from a "group membership" model to a "certified practitioner" model, and removing techniques that could be read as "Japanese religion" at a time when that category was imbued with danger.

Naturopathy

Around May 1938, after touring California with the Jōdo priests, Takata traveled to Chicago, where she took classes at the National College of Drugless Physicians, part of the National College of Chiropractic. Takata told her biographer that she had been accepted to this naturopathy program even before Bishop Kubokawa asked her to join his group, and that, prior to leaving Hawai'i, she told Fred Makino, publisher of the *Hawaii Hochi,* that the classes would "improve my technique and myself."[50] In this phrase, Takata demonstrates an experimentalist, progressivist ethos that considers the potential that what she received from her teacher is able to be improved. In much the same way that Hayashi may have incorporated elements of Sino-Japanese medicine into the hand positions he taught to treat certain ailments,[51] Takata was determined to make her own contributions to Usui Reiki Therapy to make it as efficacious as possible.

In Chicago, Takata reports having studied Swedish massage, colonics, hydrotherapy, electrotherapy, and other forms of naturopathic medicine.[52] She felt her naturopathy coursework complemented her experiences with Reiki. "I came back with confidence," she said, as she felt her courses would "help me to get more established much better because now I [knew] much more about the physical and the technical of the human body [*sic*]."[53] In other words, Takata felt that learning physiology and allied therapies helped her establish herself as a health professional in Hawai'i and improved the quality of her treatments. It also helped establish her authority: Michiko Kitagawa studied Reiki in 1945 with her family and, despite her skepticism of Reiki's efficacy, she considered Takata an intelligent woman, in part because she was "familiar with the physiological make up of the human body and its functions."[54] Takata's time in Chicago may have impressed on her the importance of the endocrine system and Reiki's ability to treat it, as she began to stress Reiki's value for "glandular ailments" in her interviews and advertisements.[55] A chiropractor from Chicago named Ruth Hart, whom Takata likely met during her naturopathy coursework, also traveled to Hawai'i and worked with her briefly in 1939 when she established her first Hilo clinic.[56]

One direct contribution of Takata's naturopathy training to her work as a health professional is that it led her to promote the value of fresh fruit and vegetable juices for over forty years. Most of those with whom I spoke who studied Reiki in transwar Hawai'i (or had parents or grandparents who did) purchased expensive blenders on Takata's advice, and to the end of her life Takata promoted "Reiki juice," made from vegetables including beets, carrots, and celery. For cases as diverse as arthritis, tuberculosis, and leukemia, she prescribed a fresh vegetable juice of watercress, carrots, beets, and celery that she called "an excellent blood builder which energized the whole body."[57] In the 1970s, Takata claimed this practice came from Hayashi's clinic, where she was prescribed "special diets" including "red beet juice," but as "table beets" (as opposed to sugar beets) remain uncommon in Japan even with today's globalized food industry, it is much more likely that she encountered juicing in Chicago.[58]

Takata seems to have been familiar with some variety of naturopathy in Territorial Hawai'i prior to her Chicago trip. The text of her English-language Reiki Master certificate, signed by Hayashi and notarized in Honolulu just before his departure in February 1938, describes Reiki as "the Usui Reiki system of drugless healing."[59] This phrase is not a direct translation of any known Japanese description of Reiki, suggesting that it was a strategic translation of Reiki into terms that would have been easily understood in the local setting, and it is likely that Takata either wrote or revised the certificate's English text.[60] In the early twentieth-century United States, a number of alternative medical practices, including osteopathy and chiropractic, called themselves "drugless healing," but it became most closely associated with hygeiotherapy: a mix of hydrotherapy, dietary therapy, and massage that became rebranded as naturopathy.[61]

Massage

Takata's training in massage influenced how she practiced and taught Reiki. She may have practiced massage before Chicago; she says that Wilfred Chomatsu Tsukiyama (1897–1966), the Honolulu city and county attorney, gave her a massage license in the fall of 1937 to "frame it and put it in the room for everyone to see."[62] As such official licensure was chiefly a strategic means to avoid legal difficulties, it is unclear how much massage experience she had by this time. Eventually, however, she learned enough to become a "certified massagist" with a license from the Territory of Hawai'i Board of Massage. A number of directory listings and advertisements listed Takata as a massage therapist, and she gave her occupation as "masseur" when traveling.[63]

Takata's precaution to obtain licensure may have helped her escape legal difficulties as she promoted and practiced an unregulated therapy. Harue Kanemitsu (b. 1937), a Yonsei (fourth-generation Nikkei) from Lahaina, Maui, who studied Reiki with Takata in British Columbia in the late 1970s, told me Takata had been "run out" of Maui County for laying hands without a license.[64] Another student remembered Takata recounting that her first massage license had helped her evade trouble with the police in Honolulu following Hayashi's departure.[65] Finally, a 1948 interview with a public health nurse confirms that the Board of Health had investigated taking legal action against Takata while she lived in Hilo, but they had no recourse as she did not prescribe drugs.[66] Some of Takata's 1939 ads and interviews described "Reiki Massage Treatments" and "the Usui Reiki massage treatment," but she later distinguished between the two: an ad she ran in the *Hawaii Tribune-Herald* (Hilo) from November 1939 to February 1940 read, "Reiki health restoring, rejuvenating nerve and glandular treatments. Swedish massage for reducing [blood pressure] and good circulation. All manipulations by hand."[67] Thus, while she came to distinguish Reiki from massage, in the transwar period, massage licensure and Reiki's status as a "drugless" therapy provided some legal protection.

Until the end of her life, Takata advised students to obtain massage licenses in order to avoid any legal difficulties from their Reiki practice, particularly the "blood exchange method" (*ketsueki kōkan-hō,* described in chapter 2), which she redubbed the "nerve stroke." This method, applied at the end of a treatment, involves applying light pressure to the muscles on either side of the spine and rubbing downward from the shoulders to the end of the spinal cord. According to an essay she wrote in 1948, titled "The Art of Healing," to receive a doctor of naturopathy diploma from the Indian Association of America (described in chapter 4), this technique "[adjusts] the circulation," and before performing it, she would "apply on the skin a few drops of sesame oil or any pure vegetable oil."[68] The use of oil appears to have been an innovation and would have required clients to bare their torsos, as in Swedish massage. Additionally, Takata instructed students, before the "nerve stroke," to raise the foot at a right angle, then "massage foot, ankles; rub calf towards heart, down and hard. Make a ring with both hands around the ankle and shake it."[69] Again, this technique seems to be something she added based on her massage training and experience. Thus, Takata considered the therapeutic value of the practices she learned from Hayashi as capable of being enhanced by adding certain massage techniques.

Professionalization

Takata's experience as a massage therapist may have been not only a source of new somatic techniques but also an influence on her decision to standardize Reiki sessions to sixty minutes. Peter Skrivanic describes this "therapeutic hour" as "a widely-observed norm in complementary and alternative medical treatments in North America, in which the provision of a service is confined to prescribed sixty-minute duration as a basis for determining its value."[70] As discussed at more length later, this standardization of treatments can be understood as part of the transactional logic of *commodities*, in which a therapist's services are assigned a set monetary value, in contrast with the reciprocal logic of *gifts*, where the act of giving establishes ongoing social relations.[71]

In addition to these apparent influences from her training in naturopathy, especially massage, Takata, like her master Hayashi, physically positioned her practice in close proximity to a major biomedical center. After returning to Honolulu from the mainland in June 1938, Takata moved her clinic from the Grove Hotel to a new location; her advertisement for the new clinic mentioned that it was half a block from Queen's Hospital.[72] The possibility that she was inspired to pick this location for its proximity to this prestigious hospital, the largest in the Islands, is strengthened by the fact that Hayashi's clinic in Tokyo was close to Keio University Hospital. These locales had practical and symbolic benefits: they were conveniently located for treating the hospital's patients, and they may have acquired authority by being within the "aura" of these well-regarded medical centers.

After Takata established her new Honolulu clinic, she seems to have curtailed the weekly teaching practice that she had continued directly following Hayashi's departure, though she taught a handful of classes in Buddhist "churches" in plantation communities around Kaua'i, O'ahu, and Hawai'i between October 1938 and her move to Hilo in May 1939.[73] In December 1940, she established a new clinic with an *onsen* (literally "hot spring," but possibly just a bath), suggesting she offered hydrotherapy there, and "cabinet baths," a kind of personal sauna (figure 3.5).[74] Takata gradually standardized her treatments over a period of years, and she made exceptions for particular cases that needed longer treatments, but she seems to have set standard treatment times at sixty minutes by the time she established her Hilo clinic.

Commoditization

Takata's standardization and professionalization of Reiki were also tied to her charging set fees for treatments. When I spoke to the now-elderly Nisei children of Takata's Issei students, they told me their parents had viewed these developments as contrary to the spirit of the practice. Tatsuji Nagao (1892–1988) attended Takata's very first class on the island of Hawai'i, at the Kurtistown Jodo Mission outside Hilo in December 1938 (figure 3.6).

間時療治

ごあいさつ

皆さま、ごぶさたいたして居ります

お變りは御座いませんか、姿こと、今同日本及び米大陸の研究から歸りまして左記の場所に土地と建物を求めまして治療院を開きました、『溫泉』もあります

ので持に皆樣にお目にかけたいと存じますが、御多忙の事と存じますが、治療院と溫泉を御見物かた〴〵お遊びにお出で下さいませ、尚講習會は隨時希望者に對し

講習、研究會は毎月一回第一月曜日午前八時よりと午后七時より開催し、中食の用意も致します。

先はごあいさつと御案内まで

一九四◯年十二月七日

ヒロ市キラウエア街二◯七◯
（ハートマン氏邸宅跡）

臼井式靈氣療養院（電話 二九六四）

高田布哇與

『溫泉』

毎日午前七時より十一時迄
午后一時より六時迄

但し每週月曜は休みます

Figure 3.5 Japanese-language announcement for Takata's new Reiki clinic and monthly *kenkyūkai* (study meetings) in Hilo, dated December 7, 1940.

Nagao had learned tinsmithery before emigrating from Hiroshima Prefecture to Hawai'i in 1910, and he earned enough money making metal containers to buy his own cane fields.[75] Nagao was no stranger to alternate currents, having studied other hand-healing therapies before meeting Takata, but he became a renowned healer for his Reiki practice, which took

Figure 3.6 "Usui-shiki Reiki Ryōhō class, Kurtistown, December 26, 1940," Tatsuji Nagao (*standing, far left*) and Hawayo Takata (*standing, sixth from left*).

several hours per treatment, sometimes focused on a single spot. It is possible Nagao's practice was influenced by his prior knowledge of other spiritual therapies or by his continued study of Usui Reiki Therapy with Hayashi's widow in Tokyo after the war. However, resemblances between Nagao's practice and that of Kino Yuda (1902–2002), another Hilo practitioner who "got Reiki" from Takata circa 1939 and became well known locally, suggest that Takata made significant adaptations during the 1940s, between teaching Nagao and Yuda and writing the "Art of Healing" essay in 1948, which describes a standardized "foundation treatment."[76]

The oral histories I collected suggest some early students on Hawai'i Island resisted and resented Reiki's standardization and commoditization. When I met Nagao's eldest daughter, Yoshie Kimura (1920–2015), in June 2012 at Hilo Meishoin, a Jōdo church just a mile from Takata's old home clinic, she was very grateful to Takata for Reiki, which she had been practicing nearly daily for about seventy years, but was critical of her professional approach to treating patients. "Mrs. Takata," she told me, "that was her business, so one hour, each patient, and she stops already. But my father, sometimes for hours he'd stay with the patient."[77] When I met with Yuda's family, including her elderly daughter and her grandchildren, in Hilo in June 2013, they expressed similar negative opinions about contemporary Reiki practitioners, whom they considered as "commercial—one hour and they're done."[78]

In contrast, Takata's students in Hawai'i from this period, such as Nagao and Yuda, treated for hours at a time without charge. Ruth Fujimoto (1918–2012), who also learned under Takata circa 1939, told me she used Reiki "as a friend," and her memoirs recall her shock when a friend of hers, after giving her a treatment, asked for seventy-five dollars in payment.[79] Similarly, Yoshie Kimura laughed when I told her that Takata instructed her students in the 1970s that Reiki would not work if the practitioner treated for free (a narrative analyzed in chapter 5); she said, "That's something— my father used to say that if he charges, it's not going to work," recounting a Japanese saying of his, "If they hang a sign, it doesn't work" (Kanban ka-ketara, kikanai). Kimura and her younger brother Robert Nagao (b. 1939) both recalled how, during the sugarcane's growing season, when their family had more free time, their father accepted inpatients who would come from all over the island and stay with the family for weeks while receiving care. While he did not charge, his patients, almost entirely Nikkei, customarily recipro-cated with presents of gratitude called *orei:* sometimes things they had grown, such as fruits and flowers, other times commercial goods they pur-chased. Robert said some grateful patients continued to bring his father *orei* for years; "Sometimes my father would say, 'Enough already!'"[80]

In anthropological terms, these Hilo Nikkei resented the commoditi-zation of Reiki treatment because they considered treatment to be a *gift* whose bestowal was a moral act that created an "obligation to reciprocate" and established social relationships that endured after the kindness was re-paid.[81] This gift exchange model seems to more closely resemble earlier forms of Reiki practice, both in Japan and in Honolulu in 1937–1938. Hayashi's immigration case in Hawai'i hinged on whether he charged for his treat-ments and his workshops, which he was not allowed to do on a tourist visa; Takata's political connections notwithstanding, he was reportedly let off because he charged nothing for treatments.[82] Alice Noda's Honolulu salons also advertised "free treatments" (*seryō*) in 1938.[83] Thus, Takata's fee-for-service model for treatments may have been an innovation in the Hayashi lineage. However, at least some Usui Reiki Ryōhō Gakkai (Usui Reiki Study Association, hereafter Usui Association) branches had set fees for treatments, although they provided discounts or possibly even free treatments for the poor.[84]

Takata's model dates to the time of her first clinic in Kapaʻa in 1936. Her advertisement of "special free clinics for children under six months" for two hours on Saturday mornings implies she charged for other treatments. Her commoditization of Reiki practice in the late 1930s can be understood in terms of her vision of Reiki as both a professional and a spiritual calling. She was largely unable to successfully express this vision to her students until the 1970s, but this did not hinder her professional success: less than a year after establishing the Kapaʻa clinic, she left her job at the Valley House and became a full-time practitioner and teacher of Reiki, which led to her financial independence. This must be understood in the context of her as a young widow with a multigenerational family to support; part of her excitement about the large house where she moved on the outskirts of Hilo in 1940 was because it had room for her aging parents as well as her Reiki clinic.[85]

Practicing and teaching Reiki soon generated Takata some degree of wealth. In 1948, a university student originally from Hilo called her "a good businesswoman" and "definitely financially well off," citing her frequent travel between Hilo and Honolulu and her recent sale of her share of the Waimea Hotel, a property in "upcountry" Hawaiʻi in which she had invested.[86] Takata also invested in property on Oʻahu during the transwar period, purchasing approximately a half acre of land just across the Ala Wai Canal from Waikiki in 1939, and building a ten-unit apartment building there in 1946. She furnished the apartments and collected rental income for decades; the property generated significant income in the 1960s, when a twelve-story condominium with roughly eighty units was also built on this land.[87] Also in late 1946, Takata opened a short-lived health food store with a Hawaiʻi-born White partner (also widowed) named Sophie Bergau (1886–1969).[88] Thus, Reiki was but one of Takata's professional pursuits as she invested her income from teaching and treatments in real estate and natural health; she later combined these interests in repeated attempts to open a health resort or healing center.[89]

Standardization

As Takata established set fees for sixty-minute treatments, at some point in the 1940s she also created a standardized series of hand positions she called "the foundation treatment." This treatment somewhat undermined the emphasis that had been placed on practitioners developing sensitivity in their hands to "vibrations" (*hibiki*) that allowed them to detect problem locations in the body. Usui's and Hayashi's students in Japan called these locations the "sick glands" (*byōsen*) or "source of sickness" (*byōgen*), while Takata's early students in Hawai'i also called them the "root" of the fever, illness, or pain.[90] Gaining facility in locating these points was essential to becoming an effective practitioner, as these "sources" or "roots" of illness were sometimes at a point distant from the most evident symptoms and, as Takata often told her students, one had to remove the cause to dispel the effects.

In addition to developing sensitivity with the hands, Usui, Hayashi, and Takata each also taught other modes of diagnosis for treatment. Usui's and Hayashi's handbooks prescribed specific series of hand positions for hundreds of specific ailments. Takata's 1948 essay "The Art of Healing" includes many of the treatments in Hayashi's handbook in abbreviated, adapted forms, but it also presents the series of hand positions she called "the foundation treatment," which provides a comprehensive treatment of the head, torso, and back; over time this developed into a standard series of twelve to fifteen hand positions to serve as initial treatments for any condition.[91] This treatment became tied to an ethic of holism, as one of her students recalls her saying, "The body is a complete unit, so whenever possible, treat it completely."[92]

This is not to say that Takata excised the earlier teaching about developing sensitivity to find the cause of disease with one's hands. In "The Art of Healing," she wrote, "During the treatment, trust in your hands. Listen to the vibrations or reaction," distinguishing between the vibrations given off by chronic and acute ailments.[93] Her later students similarly remember her teaching them to "listen" to their hands and one student wrote (in all capital letters) in her class notes, "YOU WILL GET VIBRATION OR FEELING ONLY THROUGH PRACTICE."[94] However, Takata's foundation treatment gradually became formalized into twelve positions held for five minutes each, tying it to the "therapeutic hour."[95] It was thus another innovation that contributed to the standardization of Reiki practice and the professionalization of the Reiki therapist, likely influenced by her massage training.

(Re)establishing Degrees of Training

In addition to the inclusion of naturopathic techniques and the standardization of treatment, another apparent change after Hayashi's departure was Takata's separation of the "first transmissions" (*shoden*) and "inner transmissions" (*okuden*) initiations into two classes. She continued to call them by their Japanese names at this time but eventually called them "First Degree" and "Second Degree," respectively. The First Degree class focused on hands-on treatment (*teate ryōhō*) and was held over four days, with an initiation (the *reiju* ceremony described in chapter 2) performed each day. The night before a four-day class, Takata often gave a free informational lecture about Reiki and its origins and demonstrations of Reiki on some of the attendees: a means to attract students to the paid class. This could explain why Takata's classes often remained five days, whereas Hayashi's five-day course included the Second Degree class, with the three sacred symbols used to perform advanced techniques, including distance treatments.

This change appears to have occurred shortly after Hayashi's departure. When I met with Yuda's family, they told me she had studied under Takata in the late 1930s, but when I asked them about the distance treatment, they associated it with *jōrei*, another Japanese spiritual healing practice that came to Hawai'i in the 1950s, suggesting that it was not included in Yuda's training. A series of archived papers written by Nikkei undergraduate students from Hilo for University of Hawai'i at Mānoa (UHM) sociology classes confirm that Takata taught the beginner and intermediate classes separately and suggest she experimented with different ways to teach the introductory class. A report by an anonymous Sansei (third-generation Nikkei American) whose mother and grandparents were plantation laborers who "acquired" Reiki in the 1940s said Takata charged fifty dollars for the introductory course and "she can also endow people with Okuden, but for a much larger fee."[96] Another student took Reiki with seven other members of her family in 1945; it cost fifty dollars per person for the five-day class.[97] A third student, writing based on interviews with friends regarding classes likely held in the late 1940s, said Takata transferred the "leiki" in sessions that cost twenty-five dollars per person, per day, "and since there were at least fifteen to twenty people who attended the three night sessions she made a nice sum of money."[98] This last account is an outlier in terms of both duration and cost, but my oral histories also provide other examples of experimental class formats.

Most of Takata's prewar courses had approximately twenty students and ran four or five days, resembling Hayashi's training courses, but I spoke with one woman whom Takata taught in a two-person class in a private home in Hilo in 1948. I met "Mrs. B" (b. 1930), who asked to remain anonymous, in June 2013 at a Sunday service at Honpa Hongwanji Hilo Betsuin, the head Nishi Hongwanji institution on Hawai'i Island and, as the church

Takata attended while living in Hilo from roughly 1940 to 1950, a key site for her networking. As a high school student, B. received Reiki treatments from a neighbor to ease the pain of severe menstrual cramps, and once she was accepted to a mainland university, her mother thought it would be best for her to learn Reiki herself. Takata initiated B. and another woman in a one-day "crash course" that, to the best of B.'s memory, included little instruction, basically just saying, "Put your hands where it hurts." "After that," B. recalls, "whenever I had any stomachache or any other muscle ache, I pressed my hands on the affected area. I could feel the heat coming from my hands and the pain went away."[99] This is a radically condensed form of Usui Reiki Therapy, but even students who took Takata's full five-day class did not learn several practices that a prior generation had considered central.

Eliminating Practices Resembling "Japanese Religion"

It is unclear whether Hayashi and Takata taught the earliest students in Hawai'i to recite the poetry of the Meiji Emperor called *gyosei* to purify the heart-mind. As described in chapter 2, this had been a fundamental practice of the Usui Association, and the Hayashi Association also distributed booklets with one hundred *gyosei* for use at *reijukai* (*reiju* meetings).[100] If Takata received one of these booklets in her 1935–1937 training, she may have destroyed it to avoid charges of being a "Mikadoist" (i.e., one who worships the Japanese emperor) during the war, as many Nikkei Americans destroyed Buddhist literature and other Japanese-language materials after the bombing of Pearl Harbor. Either way, I have found no evidence that Takata or her students ever engaged in *gyosei* recitation.

During the late 1930s or 1940s, Takata stopped teaching what had been another key component of Usui Reiki Therapy in Japan: the morning and evening meditation (described in chapter 2) in which practitioners place their palms together and recite the "five precepts" (*gokai*), which Takata later called the Reiki Ideals. None of my interlocutors remembered learning this practice, although the photographs of Takata's prewar classes prominently depict a hanging scroll with the precepts written by Hayashi, so they were clearly an important part of instruction (see figure 3.6).

One of Takata's students, Tatsuji Nagao, hung a scroll of the Reiki precepts (also written by Hayashi) beside his Buddhist family altar (*butsudan*). Every morning and evening, his son remembers, he knelt before the altar with his hands in prayer position (*seiza gasshō*) and "mentally" recited the precepts. His daughter included a photo of Nagao kneeling before the *butsudan* in an unpublished essay about her father, writing, "He lived with heart and soul, morning and evening before the altar, by the rules of reiki," echoing her translation of Nagao's *gokai* scroll, which ends, "Every morning and evening, join your hands in prayer."[101] It is unclear whether Nagao learned this practice from Takata, as he also traveled to Tokyo after the war and received further training under Hayashi's widow, Chie, but at least some Reiki practitioners in Hawai'i engaged in *gokai* recitation.[102]

Mrs. Sawami Koshiyama (1903–2001) studied under Takata in 1940s Hilo, and her class apparently included a form of *seiza gasshō* meditation. An essay written by her son-in-law says: "She sat on the floor with her legs underneath her, placed her palms together above her heart and sat there for 45 minutes everyday [*sic*] for a week. At the end of the seventh day her hands started to vibrate gently and then so violently that she practically 'bounced all over the floor.'"[103] This meditation practice was meant to awaken the healing power in one's hands, resembling some contemporaneous Japanese accounts of Reiki practice.[104] Yet Takata discontinued teaching this meditation and the *gokai* recitation practice.

As recitation of Japanese texts while kneeling in *gasshō* before a hanging scroll could easily be seen as a Japanese religious practice, Takata's omission of these practices was likely a strategic move at a time when being a religious leader in her community was cause for persecution by state authorities. Among the Nikkei religious leaders arrested shortly after the bombing of Pearl Harbor was a Hawai'i-born Buddhist nun who trained in Japan and had a reputation for her healing abilities.[105] Making Reiki less overtly religious and Japanese could only have helped Takata's odds of not arousing state suspicion, a tactic writ large on the palimpsestic sign posted outside Takata's home clinic described in this chapter's opening (see figure 3.3). That she repainted this sign in reaction to wartime anti-Japanese sentiment is supported by the fact that, in a classified ad from the *Hilo Tribune-Herald*, she was comfortable openly publicizing her Reiki treatments under the Japanese name just nine months prior to the bombing of Pearl Harbor.[106]

Moreover, Takata explicitly tied Reiki to Japanese religion before the war. A July 1938 *Hawaii Hochi* article recounting her trip to Chicago described how a religious group there had relentlessly asked her for Reiki instruction, as they felt that the *reiki* she channeled was identical to the "energy wave" that was at the heart of their teaching.[107] This group was likely the Saint Germain Foundation (a.k.a. the I Am Movement), based in the Chicago suburb of Schaumburg. Takata called it the "Voice of [the] I

Am," which was the name of that organization's monthly journal.[108] She told the *Hochi* reporter she declined to teach them Reiki because there was a fundamental difference between their beliefs, which she believed to be founded on Christian Science, and Reiki, which originated in Japan and was thus rooted in Buddhist thought.[109] Takata apparently told them they could not learn Reiki "unless they started fresh" (*denaosaneba*) with Japanese Buddhist thought, Indian philosophy, and so on, and to that end she gave them an English book about Zen. She was very moved to learn that, by the time she was leaving the mainland, they were eagerly practicing *zazen* (Zen meditation), but even then, it does not seem that she took them on as students.[110] As we shall see in the following chapters, Takata would curtail this cultural essentialism that requires familiarity with Japanese Buddhism to practice Reiki, but she would make other changes to the practice to enculturate her students with values she considered Japanese.

Eliminating Group Membership

As previously mentioned, Takata was named the president of the Hawai'i branch of the Hayashi Association in January 1938, and her Japanese-language announcement of her new clinic in Hilo in December 1940 mentions a schedule for monthly association meetings. This implies that she was continuing the practice of the Usui Association and the Hayashi Association of giving regular *reiju* to her students to aid them in their development as practitioners. She likely suspended this "group membership" model due to the outbreak of the Pacific War in December 1941 and the incarceration of Nikkei leaders. While she continued offering classes during the war, attending a workshop that produced "licensed practitioners" was likely considered safer than being a dues-paying member of an organization that practiced spiritual healing at regular meetings. However, Takata does not seem to have reinstated monthly *reijukai* after the war, instead telling her students that their initiations would last a lifetime with proper conduct.[111] Rather than being repeatedly reconnected to *reiki*'s cosmic source through regular *reiju* empowerments, her students were encouraged to practice daily self-treatments to "recharge their battery."[112]

This adaptation would end up being crucial to Reiki's circulation in North America and beyond. As mentioned in chapter 2, one possible objection to Takata's membership in the Hayashi Association was that she would be unable to regularly attend meetings and receive *reiju* after returning to Hawai'i. Changing Reiki's pedagogy from one that requires continued oversight by an instructor (*shihan*) to one where certified practitioners can independently deepen their connection to *reiki*'s cosmic source on their own surely facilitated Reiki's spread in subsequent decades. The idea that a certificate indicating one had completed a workshop was all one needed to be a Reiki practitioner, rather than a skill one deepened under a master's watchful supervision, might also be considered a shift from an approach more resembling other Japanese arts (from karate to ikebana) to the kind of licensure model that other American unorthodox medical practices (such as naturopathy) had adopted by 1940.[113]

Radionics

One of the most unconventional (and seemingly short-lived) changes Takata incorporated into her practice in the prewar period is the use of radionics, which she advertised as "short-wave treatment." Radionics is a therapy developed by Albert Abrams (1864–1924) in the early twentieth century based on the idea that all human tissue emits vibrations, which can be measured to diagnose disease; he also created electronic equipment to alter these vibrations and thus cure any disease. In December 1940, when Takata opened her new Hilo clinic, she advertised having an Oscilloclast, a machine leased out by the San Francisco–based Electronic Medical Foundation, founded by Abrams. The Oscilloclast allegedly measured the vibrations of diseased tissue and transmitted the same frequencies back to neutralize them and "clear" the patient of disease.[114]

Takata likely first encountered radionics in Chicago in 1938. In the interview she gave upon her return to Hawai'i, she described not only her encounter with the "Voice of I Am" but also an encounter with a group of "medical scientists" (*igakusha*) led by a Dr. A. R. Williamson. This group researched diagnosing and treating patients using "the vital force of the cosmos (*uchū no seiki*), called ether," which they put in a "can" using scientific methods.[115] Williamson became interested in Takata upon hearing about Reiki, and they held a day-long demonstration of their therapies. Takata was asked to treat a World War I veteran's war wound, and Williamson was so impressed by the impact of a single Reiki treatment that he said, "If I could learn this therapy, our [research institute] would become unnecessary." However, Takata declined to initiate him at that time, saying she was too busy, and he agreed to come to Hawai'i in the future for training.

Takata's stories of these religious and medical groups being willing to give up their own practices to follow her Reiki adhere to a trope common in religious and healing groups of a "showdown" between different practices. From the biblical story of Aaron's staff becoming a serpent that devours those created by Egyptian magicians to modern spiritual therapists' stories of diagnosing and curing diseases that baffle physicians, showdown narratives are powerful testimonials to the efficacy of the storyteller's practice, even its superiority over others.[116] Despite Williamson's apparent proclamation that Reiki made radionics redundant, Takata's leasing of an expensive Oscilloclast machine demonstrates that she also saw value in this technological approach to energy healing, highlighting the bidirectional flow of her "alternate current." Moreover, the I Am Movement, radionics, and Reiki all oscillated between different vocabularies, but Takata's "showdown" narratives set hers as including and superior to the others in the "hierarchical inclusion" approach to alterity described in chapter 2.

Adapting Reiki for Nikkei Hawai'i

Takata changed Reiki in a number of ways between 1936, when she completed her apprenticeship at the Hayashi Association's Tokyo headquarters, and 1948, when she penned the "Art of Healing" essay to get membership in a mainland organization. In these momentous years spanning the Pacific War, she adopted naturopathic methods, professionalized and standardized treatments, separated the beginner and intermediate classes, and removed meditative and recitation techniques whose content and bodily forms could be read as markers of Japanese religiosity.

These moves betray multiple motives. Her additions of nutritional and massage techniques reveal a progressivist approach that ventured to improve on the system she received from her teacher, as he did before her. Both with these additions and with her development of the foundation treatment and a fee-for-service model, she absorbed elements of other health-care systems to help build Reiki's credibility and make a good living. Her students criticized her for commoditizing a practice they considered a gift, and skeptics considered her a quack, as had Usui's critics in 1920s Japan. Even her supporters who emphasized her generosity saw the fifty-dollar training fee as somewhat shocking.[117]

One could easily depict her as an opportunist who used Reiki to gain economic success. Takata generated sufficient income in this period to invest in multiple properties, including one in Honolulu that would eventually make her financially stable for the rest of her life. If one wanted to establish a simple dichotomy between Reiki as a practice of spiritual cultivation and Reiki as a professional opportunity, one could interpret Takata's elimination of precept recitation as recasting Reiki as more of a physical therapy than a means for moral and spiritual development. However, as will become clear in the following chapters, Takata herself increasingly linked Reiki's potential as a professional calling to its potential for spiritual transformation, though few of her students in transwar Hawai'i (particularly her Nikkei students) made the same connection. Instead, they primarily considered Reiki to grow out of one's spiritual values (tied to one's religious practice) rather than to be a source of spiritual instruction and inspiration.

Reiki and Religion in Transwar Hawai'i

Japanese American Buddhism

Takata linked Reiki to Zen Buddhism for mainland Whites, but her Reiki students in 1930s to 1940s Hawai'i were overwhelmingly Jōdo Shinshū (hereafter Shin) Buddhists, reflecting the preponderance of this sect affiliation among Hawai'i's Nikkei population more broadly. The uptake of a healing practice that draws on a mystical power transmitted through the hands contradicts official Shin doctrine, which rejects practices oriented toward "worldly benefits," such as healing and prosperity, as superstitious.[118] In fact, the highly influential Shin leader Rennyo (1415–1499) specifically prohibited the *kaji kitō* healing empowerments (described in chapter 2) that seem to have inspired aspects of Reiki practice.[119] Prior scholarship has emphasized that Shin immigrants to Hawai'i conspicuously rejected their countrymen's "miscellaneous practices" (*zasshu*)—including New Year's celebrations, shrine visitations, the calculation of lucky dates, and *kaji kitō* and other healing rites—as superstitions.[120] However, the fact that Takata and Hayashi's students were predominantly Shin Buddhists supports the idea that Shin laypeople often seek worldly benefits through "folk" religious practices, including spiritual healing, despite official prohibition.[121]

What is more surprising is that Reiki was taught and practiced in Shin Buddhist institutional spaces, from the large YMBA Hall near downtown Honolulu to the prayer halls of clapboard plantation churches (where priests posed in the class photos), and that a Shin Buddhist priest was an early leader in the Hawai'i branch of the Hayashi Association.[122] It is unclear how Takata became connected to Hōun Tamayose (1881–1955)—possibly through her involvement in the YMBA in the early 1930s—but he was another important early supporter of Reiki in Hawai'i. A native of Naha (Okinawa),

Tamayose graduated from Ōtani University in Kyoto in 1907, immigrated to Hawai'i as a missionary circa 1919, and founded a church in 1922 that eventually became McCully Higashi Hongwanji Church, where he served as head priest (*jūshoku*) for over thirty years.[123] Tamayose sponsored Hayashi's large public lecture at the YMBA Hall in November 1937, which drew over two hundred people, and he likely became a practitioner: two months later he became secretary of the Hayashi Association's Hawai'i branch.[124] The class photos Takata took with the head priests of other Shin and Jōdo (Pure Land) temples also suggest that other Buddhist clergy in Hawai'i also became members of the local Hayashi Association chapter, something that does not seem to have occurred in Japan.[125]

Not only did Buddhist clergy practice Reiki, but they may have even integrated it into their ministry. A typed transcription of one of Takata's classes (part of an early autobiography draft) tells of a student of hers who was a "country minister . . . of the Jodo Buddhist sect" with "a small church with less than 200 members." She continued, "he was very, very good in REIKI [and] has cured or helped many, many non-members of the church." She told a story that this minister had related to her of "a total cripple—unable to walk" who came to his church. The man had no religious background, saying, "I don't know how to pray." The minister replied, "I am a priest and my work is to help people spiritually and physically if I can. And now I feel that I can help with both." The story suggests that the minister leading the man in prayer and giving him Reiki treatments and massages made the man able to walk after three days. Takata finished this story by saying that the minister's one hundredth successful Reiki patient was his own wife, whom he treated for difficulties breastfeeding after giving birth, for which he was so grateful that he hosted a "testimonial dinner" for Takata at a teahouse with "16 of the [Jodo] sect priests."[126]

The Reiki practiced by Takata's early students was tied up with Buddhist elements. Tatsuji Nagao, Kino Yuda, and Sawami Koshiyama (three aforementioned Hilo-area practitioners) were all devout Shin Buddhists who regularly affirmed their gratitude to Amida Buddha (Skt. Amitābha) through recitations of his name (*nenbutsu*) and performed ancestor veneration at their *butsudan*. Their families attribute some of their efficacy as Reiki practitioners to their regular Buddhist practice. Nagao's daughter Yoshie told me that the key to Reiki, as in Shin Buddhism, is "gratitude for everything," and his son Robert indirectly related the Reiki precept of "do not anger" to the Buddhist ideal of right speech. He also said that he and his father would perform *"shashin Reiki"* (i.e., distance Reiki using a photograph) while kneeling in front of the *butsudan,* with the photo between his hands in prayer position, suggesting Tatsuji Nagao himself connected his veneration of Amida and ancestors at the *butsudan* to the efficacy of his treatment. Yuda's family similarly attributed the strength of her Reiki treatments to her Buddhist spirituality, manifested in her frequent chanting, charity work, and combination of selflessness and self-confidence. They told me that her Reiki practice, along with frequent donations of food and handmade crafts to the temple, epitomized the virtue of *danna* (generosity; Skt. *dāna*), as she gave so much to others without expecting anything in return. Koshiyama's granddaughter also recounted that her grandmother's Reiki practice was an extension of her strong faith and beliefs, including the importance of compassion and helping others with their suffering.[127]

Even through the "dark valley" of the war years, in which Nikkei Buddhist churches were shut down and their leaders incarcerated,[128] Buddhist communities provided important resources for Reiki's circulation in Hawai'i. While Takata does not appear to have taught at Buddhist churches after the bombing of Pearl Harbor, Buddhist spaces continued to facilitate the word-of-mouth networks on which Reiki's spread depended. Social networks formed through social organizations, including Buddhist churches, women's groups (*fujinkai*), prefectural associations (*kenjinkai*), and other voluntary mutual aid societies (*kumiai*), helped structure the word-of-mouth by which Takata recruited students. One UHM student writes that she "first became acquainted with Reiki during the early part of the war years," through her grandmother, who "was a fervent Buddhist, and . . . learned of Reiki through her church friends."[129] And Yuda's granddaughter told me "all the Reiki ladies" were Buddhist and they formed a kind of "support group," telling Buddhist stories to the patient and to each other during practice to reinforce moral values.[130] Thus, Buddhist communities, particularly networks of Buddhist women, helped provide frameworks both for the social relationships that helped Reiki spread and for the meaning-making entangled with the confrontation of illness and the process of healing.[131]

Traditional and Folk Therapies

Nikkei Reiki practitioners in transwar Hawai'i combined their Reiki practice with other therapies. Out of the Hilo-area practitioners whose stories I encountered, two used the ability they learned in Reiki to locate the "source of disease" by sensing "vibrations" with their hands to improve the efficacy of their moxibustion (*yaito*) treatments. Moxibustion is among the chief techniques of *kanpō* (Sino-Japanese medicine) and traditionally involves burning a small cone of dried mugwort leaves on a vital spot (*tsubo*) on the body to stimulate *ki*. As in acupuncture, determining where to apply treatment is "the most important step" in moxibustion.[132] While a trained practitioner would know hundreds of different spots to treat specific diagnoses, folk practitioners might know a handful of common ones, and others might use unorthodox means (like intuition or sensitivity to *ki*) to locate treatment positions. Mrs. Yuda's family told me that she used a matchstick like a miniature dowsing rod to help amplify the vibrations and pinpoint the spot to treat, whereas Mrs. Koshiyama's granddaughter said that she used her thumb to identify the spots. Mrs. Koshiyama also frequently used Reiki to treat the *sanri* point below the kneecap, a very common spot for moxibustion and acupressure.[133] Finally, Mrs. Koshiyama was also a dedicated practitioner of Nishi-shiki Kenkō-hō (Nishi-style Health Methods), a system of health practices including hydrotherapy and physical exercise developed in 1927 by Nishi Katsuzō (1884–1959), an engineer and aikido teacher.[134]

Other Spiritual Therapies

During the war, Reiki was one of several spiritual therapies that Hawai'i's Nikkei employed to support family and friends fighting in the segregated 100th Infantry Battalion and 442nd Infantry Regiment of the US Army, famed for their heroic frontline combat against the Germans in France and Italy. In her autobiographical recordings, Takata recounts sitting with a family who had all taken the Second Degree and collectively sending a distance treatment to their son, a member of the 100th, who had badly injured his arm in the Battle of Anzio. As Takata tells the story, their treatments helped stop the bleeding, eased his pain, and prevented infection; although the arm was eventually amputated, the treatments made the doctors "very happy" and hastened his recovery.[135] It is likely that Takata used this story to encourage people to enroll in the (expensive) Second Degree course so that they too could support the overseas troops from the comfort of their own home.

Takata was just one of several Nikkei women on the home front using spiritual therapies to support the Nisei men in battle in Europe. Like the "photograph Reiki" distance treatments, these therapies typically used soldiers' photographs in rituals to treat or protect people at a distance. The leader of a Honolulu chapter of Seichō no Ie (literally, "House of Growth";

a Japanese new religion described in the following section) reported performing rites on nearly 1,300 different photographs (often in members' homes) to protect Nisei soldiers and claimed that, "owing to her ministrations and the faith of the parents, none of them were killed."[136] Kiyo Myōsei Matsumoto (1884–1959), the cofounder and second leader of Honolulu's Palolo Kwannon Temple (affiliated with the Tendai sect), also performed rituals for distance healing and protection over the photographs of Nikkei soldiers. One soldier in the 442nd over whom Matsumoto prayed saw an apparition of her during battle, which led him away from a bomb that would have killed him.[137] In contrast to these rituals performed by religious professionals, anyone could learn Reiki's distance treatments (for a considerable fee), illustrating the "democratizing" trend described in chapter 2.

New Thought

Takata's few non-Nikkei clients and students in the Hawaiian Islands also associated Reiki with spiritual potency. In 1943, a Pacific Islander nurse at Honolulu's Queen's Hospital named Esther Kekela (1908–1985) mailed Takata a letter along with a money order to finish paying for her class.[138] She wrote,

> I would like to thank you a million times for your kokua [assistance]. It certainly helped me. I have been promoted, & with a raise in salary next month. Every thing has turned out for the best. Have pressed on Kujoko and a few of my friends outside the Hospital. Of course, am continuing the treatment on myself.
>
> Gee! Mrs. Takata, I am sure grateful—to think that there is such a wonderful thing as Leiki.[139]

As it is unlikely Kekela attributed her promotion to her successful Reiki treatment of colleagues or patients at the hospital, the most prestigious in the Pacific, it seems her gratitude is related to Takata's claim that daily Reiki practice can help one fulfill one's life goals. For example, in her 1948 "Art of Healing" essay, Takata wrote,

> God gave us this body, a place to dwell, and our daily bread. We were put into this world for some purpose, therefore, we should have health and happiness. It was God's plan so he provides us with everything. He gave us hands to use them to apply and heal, to retain physical health

and mental balance, to free ourselves from ignorance, and live in an enlightened world, to live in harmony with yourself and others, to love all
beings. When these rules are applied daily, the body shall respond and
all we wish and desire to attain in this world is within our reach. Health,
happiness and [handwritten note: security] the road to longevity, which
we all seek—I call this Perfection.[140]

Takata's words reflect ideas that in postwar Christianity came to be known
as prosperity theology: namely, that God wishes the devout to be healthy,
happy, and successful. This is not because she was an evangelical Christian
but rather because she and early US prosperity evangelists like Kenneth E.
Hagin (1917–2003) and Granville Oral Roberts (1918–2009) were all heirs
to the legacy of New Thought mind power.[141]

Unlike Hagin or Roberts, however, Takata may have been introduced
to New Thought during her time in Japan. Some of this came through the
influence of New Thought affirmation and Christian Science idealism on
some Usui Reiki Therapy practices described in chapter 2, such as the *gokai*
recitation, but she also seems to have been exposed to two New Thought–
inflected Japanese new religions while she was training at Hayashi's clinic.

The one with stronger New Thought ties is Seichō no Ie. Takata's diary
contains a handwritten note with the name of Taniguchi Masaharu (1893–
1985), Seichō no Ie's founder, alongside the name and address of his Tokyo
publishing house, directly under a note with a Buddhist proverb.[142] Taniguchi had been involved in spiritual healing and spiritualism as a member
of Ōmoto when he became interested in New Thought.[143] After translating
two books by the American New Thought author Fenwicke Holmes (1883–
1973),[144] Taniguchi had a series of religious experiences that he described in
his magazine *Seichō no ie*, which he later codified in a series of books called
Seimei no jissō (Truth of life).[145] Taniguchi engaged in the type of Occidentalist universalism described in chapter 2, claiming to unify all religions (especially Buddhism, Confucianism, and Christianity), along with modern
science and psychology. Like other spiritual therapists of his time, Taniguchi emphasized cultivating a positive mind, characterized by gratitude. This
message would have resonated with Takata, due to Hayashi's teaching of
the power of gratitude as part of the five precepts, and Takata's English translation of that precept evokes some of Taniguchi's language.[146]

Takata's diary also contains notes from a series of lectures she attended
in January 1936 (about one month after joining the Hayashi Association) at

a Tokyo group called Moralogy (a.k.a. Morality Science [Jp. Dōtoku Kagaku]), which combined New Thought teachings with elements of Buddhism and Confucianism. Her notes say that a Professor Hiroike gave an "explanation of Moralogy—Ameterasu Kami, Confucius, Shaka [Shakyamuni Buddha], Christ, & Socrates, combined." Another lecturer, a Mr. Kagawa, combined prosperity language with the Buddhist "middle path." She recorded, "One must practice supreme 'Truth' in order to gain and to attain success. . . . It is the supreme 'Truth' & the middle path and when put into practice, one will attain success and happiness."[147] In a later passage, Takata wrote, "In order to have a peaceful world, one must possess a peacefull [sic] mind," below which someone wrote a Chinese saying from the Confucian scholar Mencius: "If one cultivates the nobility of heaven, the nobility of humans will naturally follow."[148] These teachings synthesized elements from across the North Pacific regarding the power of the mind to harmonize the microcosm and the macrocosm for personal success.[149]

As both Seichō no Ie and Moralogy became associated with Japanese right-wing politics, perhaps elements of their political or economic philosophy matched the values Takata held in association with her Republican Party affiliation in 1930s Hawai'i. New Thought in the early twentieth-century United States was largely associated with progressivism and socialism, but New Thought teachings, like those of prosperity theology, can explain (and justify) socioeconomic inequalities with recourse to individual virtue rather than structural causes.[150]

Takata's work as a cultural translator, mediating Reiki for local audiences in Hawai'i and North America, was thus not a simple matter of adapting the performance and meaning of Japanese practices for American audiences. The currents she encountered in Japan, including Usui Reiki Therapy and the doctrines of new religious movements like Seichō no Ie and Moralogy, were not themselves purely Japanese but rather products of North Pacific circulation. Her diary entries suggest Takata received New Thought philosophy regarding the material benefits of mental clarity and affirmation practice in much the same way that she received elements of mesmerism: in Japan, through localized receptions of practices originally developed in her native United States. Then, she unwittingly completed their North Pacific circuit by bringing Reiki, inflected with elements of mesmerism and New Thought, to American audiences as the teachings of the spiritual East. As such, Takata is an intriguing example of what Wendy Cadge calls a "reverse messenger"—an American who travels to Asia and

returns with teachings—as her teachings, portrayed as Asian, are more ac-
curately understood as the products of a Japanese hub in a broader North
Pacific network.[151]

Conclusion

In June 1948, eight UHM undergraduate students wrote a joint report, *Faith
Healing in Hawaii,* for their final project in Social Disorganization, a sociology class.[152] The Reiki (or "Leiki") practiced by Takata and her students
appears prominently in this report—two of the twelve chapters are dedicated
to it, and it makes appearances in two others as well—alongside a litany of
other spiritual and religious therapies, including Native Hawaiian "Kahu-
naism," healing prayers of Chinese and Japanese Buddhists, Shinto purification rites, the holy water of Portuguese Catholics, and practices of "faith
healing cults" such as Christian Science and Seichō no Ie, as well as more
physical remedies such as moxibustion, herbal medicine, and bloodletting.
Reiki's prevalence in the minds of this report's authors and their twenty-
five interviewees is in tension with one author's assertion that "the fad for
[Reiki] declined during the post-war period," after having "swept most of
the Japanese population's interest" in the wartime years.[153] This hypothesis
fit the "social disorganization theory" around which this course was
centered—the idea that social movements, such as "healing cults," form at
times of social unrest, such as the stresses of migration or war—and likely
pleased the professor.

Takata's teaching activity may have peaked among Hilo's Nikkei population in the wartime years—one of my oral history interviewees told me
it was "the talk of the town" in the early 1940s[154]—and, like the rising popularity of Seichō no Ie in this period, this was certainly influenced by the
war, which "removed the normal religious supports of the Japanese community and created new and pressing spiritual needs."[155] However, Reiki did
not die out in the postwar years but rather continued to be practiced by figures like Tatsuji Nagao and Kino Yuda, while also shifting to other social
circles, including ones quite different from the racialized, lower-class subjects of most studies utilizing social disorganization theory. As another UHM
sociology student, writing in 1953, put it, "You will be surprised to see that
haoles—the most 'high-class' haoles believe in it, even teachers and nurses."[156]
As the next chapter explores, Takata had local "haole" (White) patients
and students in the transwar years and taught White students on the US
mainland by 1951. Naturally, Reiki underwent further adaptations as she

introduced it to majority White Christian communities, and its status as an alternate current took on new meanings as it circulated among students and clients who saw Takata as a racialized Other. But she had already begun adapting Usui Reiki Therapy for American audiences while her students and clientele were predominantly Hawaiian Nikkei.

In the years immediately after Hayashi's departure in early 1938, Takata began making changes to the training she had received at the Hayashi Association. She maintained Hayashi's method of administering *reiju* on successive days as a form of initiation, but she separated the material into two separate classes, making the price for a First Degree class roughly comparable to the fees Hayashi charged for his course (about a month's salary for many workers), while charging a substantially higher fee for the intermediate *okuden* class with advanced techniques. She stopped holding regular meetings of the Hawai'i branch of the Hayashi Association, shifting from a "group membership" to a "certified practitioner" model. This may have been due to wartime exigencies, but she did not reinstitute *reijukai* when peace was restored. She integrated elements from her naturopathy training, employing massage techniques and prescribing fruit and vegetable juices, while also offering radionic "short-wave" treatments. In a gesture toward professionalization, she standardized her Reiki treatments and charged set fees for hourlong sessions at her Hilo clinic, while her earlier Hilo students like Nagao and Yuda continued treating as Hayashi's students seem to have done in Japan: for hours on end, until the "fever" broke or the vibrations stopped, for no set fee. This was the beginning of Reiki's transformation from a "folk medical system" into a "partially professionalized heterodox therapeutic system" and—as in homeopathy and other modalities to undergo it—this change faced some resistance.[157]

Maintaining similarly high fees for training as those charged in Japan effectively limited Reiki practice to the elites of Hawai'i's Nikkei community, but Takata's students differed greatly from the military officers, intellectuals, and business magnates who studied with Usui and the wealthy housewives who studied with Hayashi. The relatively well-off Nikkei who studied Reiki with Takata in transwar Hawai'i generally made their money through entrepreneurial activities that supplemented their wages as plantation workers and, after years of working a double shift, invested their surplus in land or commercial enterprises. Tatsuji Nagao was a tinsmith who made bento boxes, lanterns, and containers for water and molasses for farmers and farm laborers; Kino Yuda and her husband grew vegetables they sold from a cart; and others I spoke with ran import businesses. Although Hawai'i's racial hierarchy limited their professional opportunities, particularly during the war years, these immigrants and their children aspired to climb the social ladder. They typically charged nothing for their treatments, but their roles as healers helped them acquire social capital, evidenced by the countless *orei* heaped on them by grateful former patients. Reiki's setting in a largely agricultural community is evident when one reads through Takata's healing stories from this time, which include many accounts of treating injuries sustained on farms as well as Reiki's benefits for crops and livestock.

But these "middleman minorities" who established businesses within the local "ethnic economy" resented Takata's treating patients on a fee-for-service model.[158] Their attitude that Reiki treatments were not amenable to commoditization reflects a perennial tension in Reiki communities. However, at the same time that they criticized Takata for charging money for treatments, they seem not to have considered Reiki capable of producing spiritual transformation on its own; rather, it was a healing technique that complemented and benefited from their Buddhist practice. My interviews indicate Nikkei Buddhists who learned Reiki in the 1930s and 1940s believed it operated via an "invisible power" that could produce dramatic healings, clairvoyance, and other paranormal phenomena, and they considered the Reiki precepts to be valuable lessons that fit their religious morals about the value of controlling one's emotions and cultivating gratitude, diligence, and kindness.[159] This is also seen in the story of the Buddhist minister who considered Reiki treatments to complement Buddhist prayer in his commitment to "help people spiritually and physically."[160] In contrast, the letter from Esther Kekela attributing her raise at work to her Reiki practice is more indicative of the kind of faith in Reiki's power to transform every aspect of one's life, including material prosperity, which became more prominent in Reiki in later decades, particularly as the possibility of being a Reiki professional became more tenable in the mid-1970s when Takata began initiating other Masters.

Takata's role as the singular agent by which Usui Reiki Therapy entered Territorial Hawai'i, where it took on the abbreviated name Reiki, is at a nexus of agency, structure (at multiple scales), and considerable contingency. Certainly, Reiki's proliferation in Hawai'i in the decade between Hayashi's farewell speech and the writing of *Faith Healing in Hawaii* testifies to Takata's determination as the sole authorized teacher in the Territory. Yet her status as the only Reiki Master in a majority-Nikkei US territory was also made possible by the exclusivity of both Japanese organizations and American immigration policies. As an unusually upwardly mobile Nisei, Takata possessed an uncommon set of attributes allowing her to generate sufficient financial and social capital (both in Hawai'i and in Japan) to enable transoceanic travel, acquire permission to study an exclusively elitist practice, and spend the better part of a year apprenticing with her master. This intersectional position, combined with her great efforts, allowed her to become the first Reiki Master outside Japan, but the prohibition of Asian immigration to the United States from 1924 to 1965, the rupture in Japan-US cultural exchange following Pearl Harbor, the Usui Association's postwar insularity, and the Hayashi Association's postwar decline are among the factors that made it unlikely that anyone could follow in her footsteps.

The adaptations Takata made in the period after Hayashi's 1937–1938 visit—the three-step training system, one-time initiations, standardized hand positions, and one-hour treatments—were all present by the time she began teaching widely on the North American mainland around 1951. In these new settings, examined in chapters 4 and 5, she used the same strategy of interfacing with religious organizations that valued spiritual therapy as she had in Hawai'i, but on the mainland, Takata's Japaneseness became a point of difference, not commonality, between her and the majority of her students. Thus, she found herself in a situation where she had to further adapt Reiki to transmit this "Japanese healing art" to non-Nikkei students socialized with quite different values. In 1938 Chicago, she had refused to teach the followers of the I Am Movement because they lacked the Japanese Buddhist worldview that she considered essential to properly understand and practice Reiki. As detailed in the following chapter, Takata began teaching White-majority classes in Hawai'i by the early 1940s and had a wide-ranging tour of the US mainland in 1951, where she had no problem teaching White Christian students without insisting on their learning Buddhism. Her eventual success on the postwar mainland depended on her ability to negotiate between the cultural hegemony of Whiteness and Christianity and the "Japaneseness" of Reiki and herself. She ultimately achieved this by adapting Reiki's discourses to include a type of discourse that oscillated between universalism and particularism, as well as elements of Occidentalism and Orientalism, that became prevalent in the mid-twentieth-century North Pacific.

CHAPTER 4

Building Authority in the Cold War United States

Networks, Esotericism, and Alterity in White America, 1948–1972

In our Arizona casita in July 2014, Phyllis Furumoto and I were unpacking the boxes of Hawayo Takata's papers we had pulled out of storage when we came across two nondescript, sandy brown, imitation leather folding cases containing 7" × 8.5" gelatin-silver prints (figure 4.1). One case contained photographs of the three Japanese-language certificates Takata received from the Tokyo-based Hayashi Reiki Kenkyūkai (Hayashi Reiki Research Association, hereafter the Hayashi Association) in the 1930s. These certificates, bearing the signature and seal of her master, Hayashi Chūjirō, authorized Takata as a practitioner and an instructor of Usui Reiki Therapy for Improving Mind and Body (Shinshin Kaizen Usui Reiki Ryōhō). Of these three, two briefer certificates, both dated December 13, Shōwa 10 (1935), recognize Takata as having received the introductory and advanced ranks (*shoden* and *okuden,* respectively). Although the text on them resembles handwritten calligraphy, these certificates were generic templates on which Hayashi wrote Takata's name, the date, and his own name as the one who performed the initiations (*reijusha*) before stamping the certificate with two seals: one for his own name and one for his organization. The third certificate is rather different. Dated October 1, Shōwa 11 (1936), it is a handwritten account by Hayashi that recognizes Takata as having reached the organization's highest level (*shinpiden*), with a personal account of Takata's rapid progress in the Reiki Therapy system, her efficacy in diagnosis and treatment, and his decision to make her what would later be called a Reiki Master.[1]

The second case contained photographs of two English-language documents. The first reads,

Figure 4.1   Hawayo Takata's folding travel certificate cases, photographed in Green Valley, AZ.

TO THE FRIENDS AND PATRONS OF SCIENCE AND TO WHOM IT MAY CONCERN: GREETINGS:

BE IT KNOWN THAT Hawayo Kawamura Takata-Wild Flower-Na-do-na,

having completed the prescribed Course of Study in Nature Healing and Herbology, given by The Indian Association of America, Inc., and having satisfactorily passed the required Examination, is hereby awarded the Degree of

DOCTOR OF NATUROPATHY-NATURE HEALER, N. D.

and Granted This Diploma: With all rights, privileges, and immunities thereunto pertaining. Given at Shawnee, State of Oklahoma, U.S.A., in the Season of Beaver Moon—21—SUNS—1948—GREAT SUNS, November 21st 1948 A.D.

It is typeset in a variety of fonts, with Takata's name and the date handwritten on lines provided. It also bears various Native American–themed icons, including a bison, a thunderbird, a peace pipe, and a Native man wearing a feathered headdress. The second document, a typewritten page on the letterhead of the "American Indian Church Temple and Indian Missions in communion with Ecumenical Eastern Orthodox Churches," declares,

IN THE NAME OF THE FATHER, THE SON, AND THE HOLY SPIRIT, AMEN!

TO ALL THE FAITHFUL IN CHRIST JESUS—APOSTOLIC BENEDICATION [*sic*]

THIS IS TO CERTIFY THAT:—

REVEREND HAWAYO KAWAMURA TAKATA—WILD FLOW
[*sic*]—NA-DO-NA

IS AN ordained Licentiate Minister of the American Indian Mayan Church and Indian Missions, having the right to Christian [*sic*], perform Marriages, to Teach, to pray for the sick, and Divine Healing, and to buried [*sic*] the Departed, and hold Services, and to hold classes for Spiritual Science in the Art of Nature Healing.

Both documents are dated November 21, 1948, stamped with embossed golden seals (rendered nearly black in the monochromatic photographs), and signed by the Venerable Reverend Barnabas Sa-Hiuhushu (Red Fox), PhD, DD, ND: great sachem and chief executive of the Indian Association of America (IAA) and apostolic administrator of the American Indian Church Temple (AICT). Furumoto and I knew nothing about these organizations when we first came across these certificates, but she associated them with a story her grandmother had told of demonstrating her healing powers to a conference of "Indian chiefs" who recognized Reiki as being a powerful application of the healing force also employed by their healers.[2]

Two years later, I was back in Arizona doing a final inventory and some last documentation of Takata's materials before sending the originals to be archived at the American Religions Collection at the University of California, Santa Barbara. In our discussion of which of her grandmother's materials to digitize and photograph, Furumoto questioned my interest in these two folding document cases. She argued that photographing the cases and scanning the photographic prints they contained would redundantly reproduce mere reproductions, as we had already photographed the original certificates, which she had removed from the boxes and framed years earlier. Reflecting on this conversation, I sympathize with her perspective that the value of the original certificate rendered documenting the print unnecessary. She echoed Walter Benjamin's famous argument that reproductions reduce the aura of the originals.[3] Indeed, the very materials of the traveling cases themselves, textured imitation leather and warped vinyl, register as ersatz and disposable. Yet, I replied, although these portfolios may hold mechanical reproductions, they were themselves powerful objects that provide insight into Takata's early teaching tours, about which little was previously known.

Although these cases appeared entirely unremarkable from the outside, their contents must have held great potency for Takata as an itinerant practitioner and teacher of an unorthodox, practically unknown spiritual therapy on the US mainland. She traveled alone through a land that had, just a few years prior, mass incarcerated its citizens who shared her ancestry. As she went from city to city, teaching Reiki in private homes and at spa retreats, these photographs of her certificates materialized her training, her lineage, and her authority as a spiritual therapist. Even to those for whom the Japanese was illegible, Hayashi's certificates supported Takata's claim of being the only living disciple of her Japanese master. The IAA and AICT certificates proclaiming her to be a naturopathic doctor and licentiate minister could only have strengthened her claims to be able to diagnose illness and lay hands. Although their issuing organizations were likely as unknown to their viewers as the Reiki method Takata practiced and promoted, they tied Takata to naturopathy, Christianity, and Native American tradition, bolstering her authority by connecting her to traditions both familiar and exotic to audiences in the mainland United States.

Moreover, the certificates reproduced in these cases, like the "massage license" given her by Honolulu's sympathetic city attorney in 1937 for her to frame and hang in her clinic "for everyone to see" (described in chapter 3), performed the kind of bureaucratic authority that Max Weber described as being "at the root of the modern Western state" and essential to the operations of modern capitalism.[4] Their potency relies on the viewer's trust in the authority of the powers that produced their stamps and embossed seals. However, the professional identities performed by these pieces of paper must also have been haunted by the possibility that they were issued by suspect organizations, particularly the IAA and AICT licenses, which (it turns out) Takata received by mail order from an obscure organization. To adopt a phrase from David Chidester, these latter licenses were "authentic fakes," objects of suspect pedigree whose authority depended on how convinced an audience was by their performance.[5] That Takata carried these dubious licenses alongside those that verified her training under Hayashi speaks volumes about the precariousness of her authority on the US mainland in the early postwar period.

This chapter analyzes a quarter century of Takata's work to extend Reiki's circulation on the US mainland by building a network of (largely) White Christian patients and students, as well as the impact that her interactions with these audiences had on Reiki's practice and meanings. It has been long assumed that she never taught in North America until the 1970s, as almost nothing has been known about Reiki in North America until that decade.[6] However, the early Cold War era was a crucial period in her career when she brought Reiki to mainland audiences socialized with quite different cultural values from those prevalent during her training in interwar Tokyo and her early teaching career in transwar Hawai'i. Thus, this chapter examines how Takata built bridges in this period through social and institutional networks; considers the impact of structural forces, especially race, on Takata's social position; and looks at how Reiki took on new meanings as it circulated among new audiences.

As substantiated in her traveling certificate cases, Takata's authority for mainland students stood at the intersection of different social fields, including an initiation lineage extending to prewar Japan and attempts to establish relationships with religious and medical organizations in postwar America. Her authority as a practitioner and teacher of a spiritual therapy was also tied to cultural meanings assigned to her position as a late-midlife Nikkei widow from Hawai'i. The contours of her authority, which grew with age and life experience, dovetailed with new meanings of Japaneseness (and Asianness more broadly) in the Cold War United States. Shortly after the end of the Pacific War, popular depictions of Japanese Americans radically changed, from threats to national security to emblems of the American Dream, just as America's burgeoning political engagements in Asia helped give rise to new forms of Orientalism, including interest in Zen Buddhism. However, White supremacist sentiments and policies generally continued to actively exclude people of color from many social spaces throughout the period, reinforcing social tendencies toward self-segregation. As a result of these trends, Takata's racialized difference could have been either burden or boon, depending on her audience.

To some extent, Takata mitigated negative impacts of her racialization by cultivating "weak ties" of social acquaintances to form "local bridges" connecting otherwise-distant parts of social networks.[7] Once she recruited a new client or student, that social connection could transform into a strengthened, asymmetrical, spiritualized relationship between healer and healed or master and disciple. This kind of snowball effect allowed her to quickly cultivate relationships across vast swaths of the country, as seen in a far-reaching 1951 mainland tour in which she treated and taught from Puget Sound to the Rio Grande Valley to New York City. These new clients and students were clustered in two class-segregated subnetworks: one of elite socialites and another of middle-class and working-class individuals. Word of mouth helped Takata recruit clients and students without advertising or print media appearances, which she had used to great effect in prewar Hawai'i. However, one limiting factor on Reiki's spread was that Takata told students in this period to maintain an ethic of secrecy about their Reiki practice. Likely a holdover from wartime precautions, this could also be related to an affinity between Reiki's initiation structure and those of esoteric fraternal orders (like the IAA) that she joined in the late 1940s.

Takata's Class-Segregated Networking on the Postwar Mainland

Takata initially brought Reiki to the US mainland through word-of-mouth references. As seen in the last chapter, before the bombing of Pearl Harbor, she had advertised her clinic and courses in Japanese- and English-language print media in Hawai'i. She also promoted Reiki in media appearances during her 1938 Chicago trip. While enrolled at the National College of Drugless Physicians, she was interviewed by newspaper and magazine reporters "because she is a teacher of Reiki Therapy," and she spoke about "the greatness of Reiki" in a WLS radio interview about the manners, customs, and national characteristics of the Japanese.[8] Takata wore a formal kimono for her interview, in which she "made efforts to clear up White people's misunderstandings about 'the China incident'" (*shina jihen;* i.e., Japan's ongoing invasion of China), for which a Hawaiian Japanese-language magazine called her "a heroine."[9] Thus, in the late 1930s, she happily used media to promote Reiki, even going so far as apologizing for Japanese militarism in an effort to make Japanese Americans and their cultural practices more sympathetic to White audiences.

However, once Nikkei Americans faced incarceration under martial law, Takata stopped using print (and broadcast) media to promote her practice and moved her courses from Buddhist spaces into private homes. These changes inadvertently restored the aversion to advertising that had been a hallmark of Usui Reiki Therapy in prewar Japan.[10] At the same time, Hilo Nisei told me Reiki had been "the talk of the town" in the war years, and an archival source asserted that Reiki's popularity in Hilo peaked at that time,[11] so Reiki could be said to have been something of an "open secret." This ambivalence toward secrecy continued as Reiki moved to the mainland. Takata told students not to tell others about their Reiki practice; however, as an itinerant healer and teacher, she relied on social encounters and word-of-mouth introductions to recruit clients and students in new locales.

Two of Takata's initial ties to the mainland were through White women whom she met in Hawai'i in the early 1940s and with whom she would maintain communication for the rest of her life: the wealthy heiress Doris Duke, who introduced Takata to a network of celebrities and socialites centered in Los Angeles, and the middle-class housewife Esther Vento, who introduced Takata to a network of her friends and family centered in Bremerton, Washington, a navy port near Seattle. This class divide between Takata's networks persisted as she moved eastward on her 1951 tour, which is her first documented trip treating and teaching across the United States.

Doris Duke and Takata's Early Elite Network on the US Mainland

Doris Duke (1912–1993) came to the Hawaiian Islands around the same time Takata returned from Japan with Reiki, and she was likely among the first White Reiki practitioners. Duke was the only child of James Buchanan Duke (1856–1925), owner of the American Tobacco Company, and inherited his vast fortune as a young woman. She fell in love with Hawai'i while honeymooning there with her first husband in 1935, and in 1937 she began constructing an Islamic-themed estate, Shangri La, on Diamond Head's dramatic coastline.[12] As Duke became estranged from her husband, Shangri La became her prime residence. She conceived a child, probably with her lover and surfing instructor, the Honolulu sheriff and Olympic gold medal swimmer Duke Kahanamoku (1890–1968), but went into labor three months prematurely, giving birth to a baby girl at Honolulu's Queens Hospital on July 11, 1940. A friend reported that, when the infant died a day later, Doris desperately tried to lay hands on the baby to heal her, but hospital staff prevented her from doing so.[13] This suggests Takata may have already initiated Duke by that time.[14]

Duke was certainly a Reiki student by April 1952, when she wrote to Takata to politely defer funding a project, calling the proposal "a bit unformulated." Duke ended the letter saying, "I am looking forward to seeing you this summer and taking my second degree."[15] Despite Duke's initial reluctance to back Takata's project, three years later she invested $75,000 in a resort Takata planned to open in La Quinta, California (near Palm

Springs).[16] Takata received Duke's largesse again in 1957 when she accompanied Duke on an extensive trip to Asia. As Takata told the story two decades later, Takata was giving Duke daily treatments for a broken wrist when Duke, bored in Honolulu, proposed a "shopping trip" to the Philippines, Hong Kong, Thailand, Ceylon, India, Burma, and Japan, probably to acquire Asian art, which she avidly collected.[17] They traveled together for about ten weeks, and upon arriving in Japan, Takata won a wager that Duke's wrist would be fully healed by this time; as a reward, Duke paid for Takata's "one month's bonus" stay, during which she visited Hayashi's widow, Chie.[18]

Duke not only was Takata's patron and friend but also provided her access to elite social contacts that would have otherwise been difficult or impossible to access due to social tendencies to associate with people of the same race, ethnicity, and class, which reinforce racist and classist structures.[19] Through Duke, Takata became friendly with Barbara Hutton (1912–1979), heiress to the Woolworth fortune, whom the popular press often paired with Duke as "the Gold Dust Twins"; treated Rosanna Seaborn Todd (1912–2009), a Montreal stage actress and producer who had been friends with Duke since finishing school; and reportedly initiated Aldous Huxley (1894–1963), the famous British author who lived in Southern California, whom Duke likely knew through their mutual interest in yogic meditation and parapsychology.[20] Such introductions helped Takata establish a clientele of other elites. For example, in a 1961 letter, Sylvia Fine Kaye—songwriter, producer, and manager of her actor husband, Danny Kaye—offered to pay for Takata's travel to California so that she could receive treatments "for a few weeks" in her Beverly Hills home. She told Takata she had also given her contact information to *Vogue*'s features editor, Allene Talmey Plaut, who was in New York recovering from a fall. Moreover, she said she had persuaded musician Eddie Fisher to have Takata come and treat his wife, actress Elizabeth Taylor, but Taylor remained resistant to the idea.[21] It seems that Duke's initial introductions to Los Angeles–area elites snowballed into a network of clients and students that helped support Takata financially in this period.

In addition to the financial capital represented by wealthy socialites and Hollywood actors, Takata name-dropped her connections with these elites to build social capital for herself and for Reiki.[22] Name-dropping can establish trust with strangers by demonstrating one's social and cultural capital, as well as one's social position.[23] By recounting her connections to well-known celebrities like Doris Duke and Danny Kaye, Takata motioned to prospective clients and students that she was trustworthy and that Reiki was effective. This strategy would have been effective among people from all walks of life, who (for a considerable fee) could occupy the same relational position (patient or student) to Takata as these figures from newspaper headlines and movie screens. Wealthy and influential clients such as Duke and Kaye helped Takata develop symbolic and financial capital, making possible mainland trips to teach the middle-class students who would ultimately be her largest clientele.

Esther Opsata Vento and Takata's Initial Middle-Class Network on the US Mainland

Aside from possibly teaching a handful of students in the summer of 1938, Takata's first mainland teaching trip seems to have been a 1951 tour that began with a class in Bremerton, Washington, composed of the friends and family of another White woman she knew from Hawai'i, Esther Opsata Vento (1910–1987). Esther and her son Ted (b. 1932) were possibly the first Reiki practitioners in North America. Esther was born in Tennessee of Norwegian immigrants. Her family relocated to the Seattle area and, at nineteen, she married James Joseph Vento (1903–1972), a sailor stationed at the navy yard in Bremerton. A few years later James was transferred to Virginia, where Ted was born, and in 1937 he was transferred again to Pearl Harbor, where the Ventos had a second son, Steven.

In early December 1941, James was at sea on the heavy cruiser USS *Pensacola* when Esther left Ted with a neighbor to travel with two-year-old Steven to Hilo on the Big Island of Hawai'i. They stayed with a friend who had told her about Takata's miraculous Reiki treatments. Esther had been recently diagnosed with leukemia and required weekly blood transfusions. Following the bombing of Pearl Harbor, interisland ferries were interrupted and Esther could not return to O'ahu for some weeks. Takata closed her office, probably to maintain a low profile as a prominent member of Hilo's Nikkei community, and Esther received her full attention. Takata wrote that, with daily Reiki treatments, she "[began] to improve, even though she had no transfusions," and she probably encouraged Esther to take the First Degree class so she could continue treating herself. After the ferries began running again around the New Year, Esther returned home and helped organize a January 1942 class at the Honolulu home of her Swiss friend Elizabeth Abplanalp (1904–1994); Esther and Ted were among the forty-two students there who took Takata's five-day course and received their Reiki initiations.

Takata reported that, following the class, "[Esther's] friends worked on her daily for six weeks, after which she was completely well."[24] In March, with the United States going to total war, Esther got passage for herself and her two children to California, and they returned to Bremerton to live near her family.

During the war years, Ted remembers, they lived in a beachside cabin where Esther, "alone and isolated like that . . . really got into her Reiki stuff and other spiritual thoughts."[25] He assisted his mother with treatments, and word of the Ventos' healing practice inspired demand for Reiki instruction in Esther's social network. Letters from Esther to Takata in 1942 reported successful treatments, particularly on her aging parents; asked for advice on chronic ailments; and encouraged Takata to travel to the mainland to teach classes once Japanese Americans regained the right to freely travel. In one letter Esther recounted,

> We are kept quite busy giving treatments and the results have made so many people interested in your classes. There are even people back East now who have written me about it. Of course such things will have to wait for the duration—but I want you to know that we are all waiting to see you when. . . . The other day I had a letter from a woman in Tennessee who said she would like to write you. Her interest is very intense and no doubt you could tell her better about this than I.[26]

This initial demand for Reiki on the US mainland occurred contemporaneously with the incarceration of approximately 120,000 Japanese Americans and the promulgation of virulent depictions of Japanese in both state-sponsored and commercial propaganda. Yet Vento's letters suggest that the desire for Reiki within her social network transcended any mistrust of Takata due to her background; even James, fighting the Japanese in the Pacific, "want[ed] lessons too of course as soon as possible."[27] These letters illustrate how proximate social connections allowed some mainland Whites to transcend the distancing effects of anti-Japanese sentiment and express interest in learning a spiritual therapy attributed to Japan from a Japanese American teacher, even during the Pacific War.

Their first chance came in 1951, when Takata taught a First Degree class at Esther's home in Bremerton to Esther's family and friends, including her parents, her brothers, and their wives. In a book of thank-yous that commemorates this trip, many express their eager anticipation of this visit and report being profoundly affected by their initiations. In one example, Esther's sister-in-law Neva Opsata (1905–1996) wrote, "Since the time Esther first came home and told us about your wonderful work, I have hoped and prayed that someday, somehow, I would be able to meet you and take the lessons. Now that it has come to pass, I count this as the greatest experience of my life. I hope I shall be worthy of it."[28] Thus, Takata's initial connection with Esther Vento in Hilo, made via the contingencies of her husband James' naval assignment, Esther's illness, and a word-of-mouth reference, led to cultivating powerful connections with mainland Whites and their initiation into a spiritual lineage that spanned the same North Pacific that James Vento had patrolled a few years prior.

Spiritual Authority and the Strength of Weak Ties

The way social connections enabled Takata's students to overcome vicious anti-Japanese propaganda and find meaning in Reiki illustrates the "strength of weak ties." This classic insight of network theory states that acquaintances (in contrast to friends and family) create "low-density networks" that "bridge" otherwise-distant parts of social networks.[29] Such bridges are essential to the spread of ideas and practices between subnetworks "separated by race, ethnicity, geography, or other characteristics."[30] Esther Vento's initial introduction to Reiki in 1941 came through the reference of a friend who likely knew of Takata through word of mouth in Hilo. The weak ties linking Vento and Takata mirror the introductions by the Honolulu Japanese Chamber of Commerce that convinced Takata to treat certain servicemen during the war; the chamber of commerce vouched for the trustworthiness of these military personnel not to report this Japanese American spiritual therapist to their superiors.[31] Conversely, the weak ties that connected Esther to Takata allowed Esther to build trust in her healer and teacher, subsequently helping her friends and family, and even her husband, who was actively fighting the Japanese, overcome wartime prejudices and seek out Reiki treatment and instruction.

Esther's bridge was consequential for the introduction of Reiki to mainland communities as Takata used a kind of "snowball effect" to accrue financial as well as social capital. The income Takata gained from her first Reiki class in Bremerton, attended by roughly a dozen people, helped finance further travels in the summer and fall of 1951 to Texas, Pennsylvania, Ohio, and New York. The fees for the Bremerton class are unclear, but by September, Takata charged $150 per person for the First Degree class, her standard fee for decades to come. Even considering that Takata often taught the elderly for free or at a discounted rate in her Hawai'i classes, it is likely she made $1,500 on the Bremerton class, a sum worth more than eleven times that amount in 2022 dollars.

In addition to collecting fees for treatments and courses, Takata also fundraised for a real estate project, likely a health resort where she could practice and teach Reiki. She sought out investors of diverse backgrounds, from the extravagantly wealthy Doris Duke to middle-class Americans. Thomas Mackler (1898–1973), head of an insurance agency, and his wife, Clara (1897–1980), a teacher, met Takata in the summer of 1951 at an Adventist service held at a Pennsylvania health resort they called "the Ranch." Impressed by the results Takata claimed in treating doctors and successful businesspeople, the Macklers invited her to their home in Canton, Ohio, so they and Clara's sister could receive the First Degree initiations. In a document titled "Testimony" written some fifteen years later, after converting to the Pentecostal church Assemblies of God (AOG), Thomas denounced Takata and Reiki. He recounted how Takata's authority convinced him to invest "over $10,000.00 cold cash" in a real estate project, but he later "found that Dr. Takato [*sic*] went all over the country more or less mystifying people to supply her financial needs abundantly." His confession of having succumbed to Takata's Reiki, "an evil power which had a strange way of drawing people to her," suggested that their desire to heal was mixed up with a desire to make money. He later felt this desire was sinful because, although "God wants us to be shrewd in business . . . best He will provide the need." Mackler attributes this experience to God's working "in mysterious ways to get us to come to Him," as their repentance for following Takata led them to AOG.[32] This unique document shows that some White Christians on the mainland were as troubled by Takata's commoditization of this spiritual therapy as were the Nikkei Buddhists of Hawai'i described in chapter 3, but it also testifies to Takata's ability to inspire middle-class Americans to invest huge sums in her projects.

Part of the trust that Takata inspired in her students was due to the spiritual status she held in the asymmetrical bonds of lineage. Reiki initiations follow para-genealogical connections, strengthening her authority as a parental figure. These asymmetrical bonds of transmission from master to disciple are modeled on other initiatory practices, notably those of Buddhist monasticism, which "draw on the affective powers of sibling and parental relationships to maintain communal bonds."[33] Entering late middle age doubtless facilitated Takata's ability to fulfill this role for students. Even when the housewives she taught were only a few years younger than herself, being a widow in her fifties with adult daughters gave Takata a matronly air that bolstered her teaching authority. As discussed later in this chapter, Takata's racialization and Orientalist trends also benefited her spiritual authority. Moreover, by 1951, the pedagogical and rhetorical strategies she had developed over fifteen years' experience with Reiki also informed her authority. She illustrated her explanations of Reiki practice with liberal examples from her training in Japan and her experience as a healer in Hawai'i. Thus, through a combination of weak ties and spiritual authority, established in part through reference to her experiences in exotic, far-off lands, Takata gained sufficient trust from relative strangers to motivate them to invest significant funds to undergo training in an unknown therapy and even to invest in her real estate ventures.

Cross-Country, Class-Segregated Networks

Takata attracted clients, students, and financial backers across class divides, but her New York contacts from her 1951 trip illustrate how her social networks clustered into separate groups of elites and nonelites. Prospective clients and students hoping to meet Takata while she was in New York wrote to her care of (at least) two individuals: Hugh S. Gibson (1883–1954), an American diplomat working to avert famine in postwar Europe, and Elsa Kane (1897–1996), a Hungarian immigrant who sewed clothes for designer Elizabeth Arden. At Gibson's prestigious Midtown Manhattan address, Takata received a letter from Isabel Carden Griffin (ca. 1892–1954), daughter of a Dallas banker and wife of a wealthy businessman and philanthropist. On stationery from her room at the Plaza Hotel, one of New York's most luxurious addresses, Griffin said she had heard of Takata through a Mrs. Obermer and requested treatment for her insomnia, providing dates when she would be in Manhattan and when she would be at her New Jersey farm.[34] Mrs. Obermer is likely Ernestine "Nesta" Sawyer Obermer (1893–1984) of Honolulu, wife of a wealthy British playwright and philanthropist nearly three decades her elder.[35] As with Doris Duke's Hollywood ties, the connections between Takata, Obermer, Gibson, and Griffin show how Honolulu elites introduced Takata to elite contacts on the mainland.

In contrast, Takata received correspondence from nonelites at another address, far uptown: the Hungarian seamstress Elsa Kane's apartment in Hamilton Heights, a West Harlem neighborhood that had become predominantly African American in the 1930s and 1940s.[36] Kane's daughter told me her mother "didn't have much faith in doctors" and, like Duke, was a lifelong advocate of unorthodox medical practices. "She believed our bodies could heal ourselves" and was fond of fresh vegetable and fruit juices, one of Takata's top recommendations.[37] Takata may have met the working-class Kane over the summer at the same Pennsylvania health resort where she met the middle-class Macklers, as, shortly afterward, Clara Mackler wrote Elsa about their mutual connection: "Am only writing to you because of our strong conviction that an opportunity such as Dr. Takata only comes once in a life time [sic]. She is surely a messenger to humanity."[38] Takata received mail from other middle-class Americans at Kane's address, like a letter marked "very urgent!!" from Mae Thompson Pool (1898–1973), a devout Mormon and middle-class housewife who had recently hosted Takata at her home in McAllen, Texas (on the Mexican border at the southern tip of the state). Pool's letter said she and her husband were driving the nearly two thousand miles to New York with another couple who had been impressed by Takata, and they all hoped to try and "take the lectures while there."[39] Again, Takata had an ability to inspire Americans from all walks of life, all over the country, to make great sacrifices to learn Reiki.

In New York, Gibson and Kane served as hubs linking Takata to networks of others of similar race, age, class, and social status, a trend that sociologists call homophily (previously discussed in chapter 2). Idiomatically known as the principle that "birds of a feather flock together," homophily helped and hampered Takata in different ways. On the one hand, homophilic social networks helped ensure her contacts knew others with common interests in "alternate currents," which allowed them to organize classes with a sufficient number of students and finance Takata's teaching travel. Duke had connections with many other wealthy European Americans with interests in Asia, spiritual development, paranormal ability, and unorthodox medicine, and Kane's interest in unorthodox medicine drew her to the alternative health retreat where she met Takata and Mackler. Takata's racialization and accented English probably lent her authority for students with an interest in Asian spiritual therapies, who would have seen her as foreign and exotic. However, Takata's working-class background, racialization, diction, and accent could also make forging connections in middle- and upper-class White American social networks something of an uphill struggle. A 2001 article on homophily in social networks concludes that "race and ethnicity are clearly the biggest divide in social networks today in the United States," a trend that was doubtless even stronger a half century earlier.[40] Christine Yano notes that, for Nikkei women in Hawai'i, speaking "standard English" was considered essential for upward mobility.[41] Yet Takata overcame this divide by cultivating relationships with a small number of White students in Hawai'i who became hubs for her mainland networks. Furthermore, Takata snowballed weak ties into local bridges in new locales, such as Gibson and Kane in New York. It is unclear exactly how she made all of these connections, but some were likely through her involvement with esoteric fraternal orders.

Hawayo Takata and Esoteric Fraternal Orders on the US Mainland

Formalized institutions, increasingly racially integrated in the postwar United States, helped strengthen, supplement, and structure Takata's informal social networks. People who identify as "spiritual but not religious" tend to emphasize their freedom from institutions, but spiritual practitioners and teachers often gain legitimacy through institutional interactions, which also help shape and circulate their ostensibly individualized practices, ideas, and experiences.[42] From the beginning of her career in the mid-1930s, Takata depended on institutions to legitimize and promote Reiki, including the Hayashi Association in Tokyo, the naturopathy college she attended in Chicago, and the Buddhist churches where she taught in Hawai'i. Wartime exigencies demanded she and other Nikkei withdraw from public or community organizations in Hawai'i in the early 1940s. However, in the postwar decades, as Whites grew less discriminatory toward Japanese Americans, Takata joined some majority-White organizations. Two of these were fraternal orders in which members progressively learned teachings and rituals as they advanced through a series of ranks. Such esoteric organizations were mainstays of American culture in the nineteenth and early twentieth centuries, when they were largely segregated by race, ethnicity, gender, and religion, but Takata's acceptance into such organizations in the late 1940s testifies to their growing integration.

In one of the traveling certificate cases described at the chapter's start, Takata carried documents issued by the IAA that certified her as a minister and a naturopathic doctor, which she hoped would bolster her legitimacy for potential students and authorities alike. The prime signatory of these documents was the IAA's founder and "Great Sachem" (i.e., chief executive), an enigmatic figure named Red Fox (ca. 1890–ca. 1950).[43] Red Fox founded the IAA in the mid-1930s as an amalgamation of two intertwined organizations he had previously cofounded: an esoteric fraternal order called the Tipi Order of America (TOA, also Tepee Order of America, active 1915–1927) and an organization focused on promoting Native American culture and rights called the American Indian Association (AIA, active 1922–ca. 1935).[44] The TOA and AIA initially included prominent elder Native activists like Sherman Coolidge (1862–1932), who served as the first chief executive of both organizations, and Charles Eastman (1858–1939), who helped compose the TOA's degrees and rituals. However, they also developed substantial White memberships whose perhaps genuine sympathy for Native causes was tied up with their appropriation of Native identities by donning TOA "Indian names" and performing "Indian occult rituals" resembling Masonic rites in Native trappings.[45] In this way, the TOA can be considered to be a more integrated version of the much larger fraternal organization the Improved Order of Red Men, which was only open to Whites, whereas the TOA also encouraged Native membership.[46]

Takata likely discovered Red Fox and his IAA through their mutual involvement in another fraternal society called the Ancient Mystical Order Rosae Crucis (AMORC). Their initial correspondence in October 1948 suggests Takata was already an AMORC member by that time. While AMORC was a majority-White organization, roughly one-fifth of the attendees posing with Takata in a group photo of AMORC's annual international convention held at its Supreme Temple in San Jose, California, in July 1951 appear to be people of color. If this is accurate, it means this convention was about twice as racially diverse as the United States as a whole at that time (figure 4.2).[47]

AMORC developed in the early twentieth century as a Rosicrucian fraternal order teaching a Christian-inflected perennial philosophy ascribed to "Eastern mystery schools," particularly from Egypt, that contains teachings about reincarnation and karma influenced by theosophy and anthroposophy.[48] AMORC members study these secret teachings to advance through a series of levels, as mastery of one level qualifies one for initiation into the next. After the death of the founder, H. Spencer Lewis (1883–1939), his son Ralph M. Lewis (1904–1987) became AMORC's second imperator (ritual leader) and oversaw an expansion of the organization fueled by a correspondence system of study, advertised in the pages of national magazines.[49] As AMORC directories from this period include no lodges or chapters in

Figure 4.2 AMORC convention photo (cropped), San Jose, CA, July 1951, with Hawayo Takata (*seated, second row from bottom, second from right*).

Hawai'i and there is no evidence that Takata traveled to the mainland between 1938 and 1951, she likely joined via distance initiation sometime before October 1948.

Red Fox himself had strong connections to Rosicrucian organizations since at least 1925, when George Winslow Plummer (1876–1944), imperator and supreme magus of the Societus Rosicruciana in America, ordained him a deacon of the Anglican Universal Church of Christ, a church Plummer led and cofounded.[50] Red Fox also cultivated relations with AMORC's top leadership. In response to an inquiry from Takata about IAA membership, he wrote, "We have a great many Rosicrucians who are members," adding, "P.S. Mr. Ralph M. Lewis & wife have been members of our Association for past *10 years.* The late Dr. H. Spencer Lewis was a member also." Red Fox's name-dropping of the Lewises and his assurance of the commonness of Rosicrucian membership among IAA members imply Takata mentioned her AMORC membership in her initial letter inquiring about IAA membership.[51]

Networking through Esoteric Fraternal Orders

Takata used the AMORC and the IAA to expand her social networks, a crucial activity for gaining new clients and students. By midcentury, American membership in fraternal orders had declined from a few decades earlier, when an estimated 40 to 50 percent of US adults belonged to at least one order, but these organizations remained important social institutions and valuable ways to meet new people.[52] Many of the contacts that fill the address book Takata used on her 1951 trip may have been people she met at the AMORC conference in San Jose or contacts given her by fellow attendees. This book contains addresses and phone numbers of people from across North America, including prominent figures like the spiritualist Arthur Ford (1896–1971) and Columbia University professor Ryusaku Tsunoda (1877–1964). It includes Dr. Charles Benson of Los Angeles, the dietician with whom Takata would plan to open the Duke-funded health resort, as well as the names of a number of health resorts in the Los Angeles area, possible sites for her practice or teaching. It also lists Margaret Holder of Brooklyn, New York, beneath whose address and telephone number Takata wrote, "colored people met at Rosicr. wants to know about class." Thus, while AMORC was a majority-White institution and the conference was likely disproportionally attended by Californians, it offered Takata opportunities to form weak ties with racially and geographically diverse contacts.

Takata also used her IAA certification as a "doctor of naturopathy" and "licentiate minister of the American Indian Mayan Church and Indian Missions" to legitimize her authority to audiences for whom her Japanese-language certificates from the Hayashi Reiki Research Society would have been unintelligible, even damning. Moreover, she told students in the 1970s that she received an "Indian name" and a certificate saying she was "a Medicine Woman" by passing a test held by a group of five Indian chiefs to verify that she had the "same energy" as "the Indian healers called Medicine Men." This test, she said, was held in a Los Angeles hotel, although the medicine men flew in from the East Coast. She "[sent] the energy from my room to their quarters" using distance treatment, "which was like tuning into a short wave [radio]." Afterward she "received very complimentary words from the Indian Chief," whom she treated for a month, after which "all his ailments disappeared, so he went home completely whole." He seems to have learned Reiki, as from then on, Takata said, she visited him every time she was in New York or New Jersey and "he was using [Reiki] with very good results."[53]

This story contradicts that told by Takata's archived correspondence with Red Fox, which suggests she received her Indian name and certificates by submitting an application form, $12 ($2 for the entrance fee and four years' of membership fees at $2.50/year), and a two-thousand-word essay before the two ever met in person,[54] but it may combine multiple actual events to make a more compelling story. Her students and clients in the Los Angeles area and Red Fox's connections with the California-based AMORC add to the plausibility of the story that she met him (or other IAA leadership) in Los Angeles. His initial letter to her in Honolulu in October 1948 is a reply to an airmail letter she addressed to him in Los Angeles; in it, he says he is about to return to New York, evidence that he frequently traveled between these two cities. Of course, if she did test her powers for IAA leaders, a number of these "Indian chiefs" would likely have been White men "playing" at being Native Americans.[55]

Regardless of the veracity of Takata's story, the idea that a group of Indian chiefs verified that *reiki* was identical to the power used by their medicine men would have appealed to North American Whites interested in the spiritual therapies of racialized Others, considered to possess authenticity and the potential for their physical and spiritual rehabilitation. Takata's "playing Indian" by taking on a Native name not only had the dimensions of romanticizing and appropriating Native culture, but, as Valerie Matsumoto writes regarding the affinity for Native names among Nisei groups in transwar Los Angeles, it also reflects "the desire to claim American identity by identifying with an incontestably native group that shares the Japanese Americans' non-white status."[56] Finally, this story's suggestion that Native American and Japanese spiritual therapies used the same power to heal evokes the perennialism employed by both the IAA and AMORC, one of several ways that Takata's membership in these esoteric fraternal orders may have influenced Reiki practice.

Possible Influences of Esoteric Fraternal Orders on Reiki

Takata's membership in AMORC and the IAA left lasting impressions on how she presented Reiki to her students in the postwar period. First, AMORC's emphasis on secrecy may have encouraged her to frame Reiki similarly. Phyllis and Sidney Krystal, who studied with Takata in 1950s Los Angeles, recalled, "Students at this time were told never to tell anyone that they had Reiki. This was sacred knowledge that Takata felt must be kept secret; she felt the time was not yet right for the world to know about Reiki."[57]

Takata's secrecy may also have been related to lingering anti-Japanese discrimination in the immediate postwar period. When I asked Ted Vento (who was initiated with his mother, Esther, in Honolulu in 1942 and attended the course in Bremerton in 1951) about anti-Japanese sentiment in postwar Washington State, where the Japanese population had been dispossessed and incarcerated just a few years prior, he told me, "There was none in my family . . . [but] it wasn't like [Takata] was out in the public. Her marketing was very personal, with friends and their family. . . . [Reiki] wasn't something you just talked about, and I never have, only with people who are close."[58] This hesitance to discuss Reiki contrasts strongly with it being "the talk of the town" in prewar Hilo, where Takata hung a sign advertising Reiki treatment outside her home clinic and promoted her practice in the newspaper's classified section. Thus, while AMORC may not have been the only influence on Takata's secrecy practices, the idea of being initiated into a lineage that "wasn't something you just talked about" is a point of convergence between esoteric fraternal orders and Reiki on the postwar mainland.

AMORC's self-identification as a perennial philosophy that synthesized religion, medicine, and science may also have influenced how Takata presented Reiki. The two most detailed texts containing Takata's descriptions of Reiki from this period—her 1948 "Art of Healing" essay and a 1961 testimony before a congressional subcommittee in Hilo—make use of language similar to that found in Rosicrucian publications.[59] In both she refers to *reiki* as a "cosmic wave" or "cosmic energy," and AMORC's teachings at this time similarly reference cosmic healing vibrations.[60] Both texts also compare *reiki* to a "radionic wave." The same radionics Takata encountered in 1938 Chicago, leading to her leasing a radionic device for her clinic, was discussed in AMORC publications. An article on "electronic medicine," prominently featuring radionics, appeared in the May 1948 *Rosicrucian Digest,* which Takata may have read shortly before writing the "Art of Healing" essay for Red Fox that autumn.[61]

Takata's "Art of Healing" essay implies that *reiki* is universal not only in the sense that it comes from the cosmos but also in the sense that it is known to peoples from around the world under different names and is available to all.[62] "Being a universal force from the Great Divine Spirit," she writes, "it belongs to all who seek and a [*sic*] desire to learn the art of healing. It knows no color, nor creed, old or young."[63] Takata's repeated use of "Great Spirit" in this essay for admission to the IAA appeals to the sensibilities of an organization that based its teachings on Native American culture while claiming a universalist ethos. The IAA and AMORC were by no means the only places Takata might have encountered the perennial philosophy, but it was a common creed for these overlapping groups. For example, the October 1949 issue of *Rosicrucian Digest,* AMORC's monthly magazine, contains an article by the IAA's national councilor on the Golden Rule in the "world's religions," concluding, "There exists an underlying brotherhood of religions . . . religious oneness and universality."[64] The circumstances of the "Art of Healing" essay's authorship and its juxtaposition of the cosmic-universal and the perennial-universal make it likely that Takata's involvement with AMORC and the IAA helped shape her discourse about Reiki.

AMORC may also have introduced Takata to narratives she incorporated into her telling of the story of Reiki. For example, she said that Usui found his disciples by walking up and down in busy marketplaces in midday with a lit torch, and when people would approach him to ask why he had a torch in broad daylight, he would reply, "I am searching for people that need this light to brighten their hearts and to take away their depression, and strengthen their character and their mind and body."[65] The trope of a torch (or lantern) being carried in a marketplace in broad daylight as a means to engage with strangers dates to the Cynic philosopher Diogenes of Sinope. At the time of Takata's AMORC membership, *Rosicrucian Digest* ran a regular ad for their fraternal ring that compared the ring to Diogenes' lantern, so this may be how she first encountered this story, which continues to circulate within Reiki communities.

These fraternal organizations influenced Takata's practices materially as well as discursively. It is not clear when Takata began issuing Reiki certificates to her students on the North American mainland, but when she did, they more closely resembled those of the IAA than those of her Reiki teacher. In contrast with the intimacy of Hayashi's handwritten certificates, particularly the highly personalized Master (*shinpiden*) certificate, the IAA and AICT certificates bear institutional and legal trappings. Each is professionally formatted with graphic symbols of iconic Native American themes; each bears an embossed gold seal; each references its respective organization as being "life chartered under the laws" of a particular US state; and each bears the names of four executive officers, with both English and "Indian" initiation names as well as professional titles.

The certificates Takata eventually issued in the 1970s draw on elements of both Hayashi's and Red Fox's certificates (figure 4.3). They bear two *hanko* (Japanese-style seals) in red ink, one with her family name and one for her institution, along with a gold seal embossed with the formal name she adopted for the practice: Usui Shiki Ryoho (Usui-Style Therapy). The cursive font resembles handwriting, somewhat evoking the calligraphy of Hayashi's Japanese-language blank certificates on which Takata filled in the names of her students in prewar Hawai'i. However, the rest of the formatting, including the typesetting, the formal language, and the embossed gold seal, more closely resembles that of the certificates from Red Fox's organizations.

Finally, similarities between Reiki and esoteric fraternal societies like AMORC could have increased Reiki's appeal to mainland Whites in the postwar period. Like these societies, Reiki offered a series of initiations that conferred sequential degrees of increasing status, in which one gradually learns secret knowledge of universal laws and efficacious techniques based on those laws. AMORC taught healing techniques influenced by similar mesmeric and New Thought practices to those that influenced Usui Reiki Therapy and other spiritual therapies in early twentieth-century Japan (as described in chapter 2). The sixth of AMORC's seven degrees is "devoted . . . [to maintaining] health through applying techniques that promote proper

Figure 4.3   Blank certificate for Takata's First Degree class, 1970s.

breathing, harness 'the healing Forces of the Universe' and cause 'rapid changes in serious conditions.'"[66] Like the spiritual therapies of Taishō Japan, AMORC was an alternate current in the senses of alterity and oscillation. As with other American fraternal societies, including Freemasonry and the Shriners, AMORC ascribed its esoteric lore and rituals to the mystic East, strengthening (for its members) Takata's authority as an "authentic Oriental" offering direct transmissions from Japan. It also claimed that its teachings were based in universal laws known to ancient Rosicrucian mystics that modern science had not yet discovered.[67] Even for nonmembers, knowledge of these societies may have helped some feel more familiar with some of Reiki's practices, including the idea of undergoing an initiation to receive their Reiki "degree" and the secrecy practices that accompanied it.

In some ways, Reiki's Japaneseness functioned something like the IAA's Indianness in the setting of the postwar US mainland. Takata, like Red Fox, offered White Christian Americans an opportunity to consume alterity through ritualized practices. Through initiations, they both mediated connections to ostensibly ancient traditions containing timeless wisdom capable of eradicating the problems that plagued modern Americans. Ironically, despite the resonance of such discourses with those of antimodern romanticism, which tends to critique commercial motives,[68] Takata and Red Fox offered initiations for monetized fees. Moreover, as examined in the following section, the rearticulation of racial categories in the midcentury United States brought both Asians and Native Americans closer to the category of Whiteness, as racial categories became consolidated and a new Black-White binary came to dominate White America's racial imagination.[69]

At the same time, popular occultist and scientific writers equated components of Indigenous religion with Asian religions, especially Buddhism, and discussed their therapeutic value. Philip Jenkins has shown how authors in the 1940s like Frank Waters (1902–1995) drew on earlier narratives from theosophists and others to argue that Native American religion was equivalent to Buddhist and yogic practices and that modern medicine and psychology had much to learn from their insights.[70] A few years later, Aldous Huxley (possibly around the same time he received Reiki initiations from Takata) tried mescaline, which he influentially described in *The Doors of Perception* (1954): after waxing poetically about peyote use in the "primitive religion" of Native peoples in North America, he took his dose and among his first thoughts was a Zen koan from an essay by D. T. Suzuki, which was suddenly "clear as day." Under the influence of this synthetic substance meant to approximate a sacred medicine of Native peoples (and he includes an extended reflection on the Native American Church), Huxley read from *The Tibetan Book of the Dead* and pondered, "What those Buddhist monks did for the dying and the dead, might not the modern psychiatrist do for the insane?"[71]

These authors' visions of a common treasury of human wisdom and their earnest hope that White society might benefit from the ancient traditions of racialized Others notwithstanding, there are clearly stark differences between Native American religion, Japanese religion, and (the issue at hand) White appropriation thereof. The mass incarceration and loss of property suffered by Japanese Americans during the Pacific War, while patently violent and unjust, is incomparable to the centuries of physical and cultural genocide enacted against Native Americans. As such, the appropriation of Native American spiritual practice perpetuates colonial patterns and coexists with the continued material disenfranchisement of North America's Indigenous peoples. The IAA was just one example of a tradition of "playing

Indian" that had been a mainstream White American pastime since the colonial era, whereas White American interest in Japanese culture, including Japanese Buddhism, was of more recent provenance and, until the 1950s, more marginal.[72] That said, Red Fox and Takata did both use their racialization as indices of cultural heritage: an asset that authorized their initiation of White Americans into lineages that connected them to exotic landscapes, their instruction of these students in the "authentic" practices of these lands, and the issuance of certificates to substantiate those students' achievements and abilities, all for substantial fees.

Takata's Postwar Positionality

Reiki's success in the postwar United States is inextricably bound up with Takata's intersectional position. Her gender, race, ethnicity, religion, class, age, motherhood, widowhood, and institutional affiliations all informed the relationships she formed with others around the North Pacific. As she entered the second decade of her career as a Reiki Master in the late 1940s, her status changed due to factors including her move toward White Christian mainland audiences, her advancing age and experience, and the protean meanings of Japaneseness in postwar America. On the one hand, as American society privileged (and continues to privilege) Whiteness, maleness, and Christianity in a variety of ways, both implicit and explicit, Takata's position as a Buddhist woman of color was an obstacle to promoting an unorthodox, little-known spiritual healing practice. On the other, new stereotypes about Asia and Asian Americans became assets for Takata in building authority as a healer and teacher of a practice she learned in Japan, a development that would evolve further in the 1970s (chapter 5).

The Changing Meanings of Japanese Heritage in the Postwar United States

Although Takata gradually made inroads with White students like Duke and Vento, the vast majority of her clients and students in transwar Territorial Hawai'i were from the Nikkei community. This was not only due to the social tendency to cultivate relationships with others of the same race, ethnicity, religion, or social status.[73] Anti-Japanese discrimination was not as violent in Territorial Hawai'i as it was on the US mainland, but White supremacist attitudes and policies discouraged or excluded Japanese Americans from White spaces in the prewar and wartime periods.[74] Historian Jonathan Okamura argues, "Japanese Americans were the most despised group in [prewar] Hawaii."[75] Even in the more integrated postwar period, few Nikkei in Hawai'i socialized in majority-White settings; a 1971 survey of 477 Honolulu Nikkei showed that only 2 percent reported belonging to organizations with many members not at least of partly Nikkei descent.[76]

However, as described in chapter 1, Takata's strong drive for upward mobility brought her into successively higher-status positions in White-dominated spaces from an early age. Over the course of her teenage years, she went from field hand to store clerk to head of staff for a palatial estate. Takata may have made the decision to take domestic work in a White household as a tactical means to acculturation, as did other Nisei women in 1920s Hawai'i.[77] Her late husband's social mobility facilitated her involvement in White-dominated social organizations, including the local Republican Party, which helped her achieve unusually high-status positions for a Japanese American woman in prewar Hawai'i. She held a political appointment as the waterworks' bill collector, received funding from her wealthy employer to study naturopathy in Chicago, and learned golf, an overwhelmingly upper-class White sport that she played regularly and that may have proved a helpful activity for networking on the postwar mainland.

During the 1940s, American attitudes toward Japanese and Japanese Americans underwent two radical transformations in quick succession. First, after the bombing of Pearl Harbor in December 1941, popular media and social scientists alike reworked earlier racist portrayals previously applied indiscriminately to people of East Asian descent to cast the Japanese as "a uniquely contemptible and formidable foe who deserved no mercy and virtually demanded extermination."[78] Cartoonists, animators, advertisers, and journalists in wartime America drew on "yellow peril" tropes to portray Japanese as sinister, subhuman, and animalistic; businesses across the country began printing "Jap hunting licenses" and stores hung signs proclaiming "Open Season on Japs."[79] Social scientists described the Japanese "national character" as fanatical, and scientific racism was reproduced in popular media targeting Nikkei Americans.[80] Public opinion quickly turned against Japanese Americans. In December 1942, 97 percent of people polled in the western United States approved of Nikkei internment and a majority expressed they would be unwilling to hire Nikkei servants or frequent Nikkei-owned businesses after the war; in a poll conducted in December 1944, 13 percent favored the extermination of all Japanese people after the war.[81]

This dehumanizing hostility radically softened within a few years of the war's conclusion. In April 1949, 34 percent of Americans polled felt "friendly" toward the Japanese, a number that rose to 50 percent among college-educated respondents.[82] Attitudes toward Japanese Americans continued to change in the Cold War era as, for the first time in US history, Asian immigrants received the same rights as European immigrants.[83] The Immigration and Nationality Act of 1952 abolished racial restrictions to naturalization, in part because of concerns that these racist policies were soft targets for anti-American Communist propaganda, and the subsequent Immigration and Nationality Act of 1965 eliminated the national origins quota system that had virtually prohibited Asian immigration since 1924.[84] As Christina Klein writes, "As the social structures organizing Asian people within the United States changed, the meaning of Asianness did as well."[85] New portrayals of Asian Americans as hardworking immigrants overtook earlier yellow peril motifs in the public consciousness.

This development was tied to broader rearticulations of race in the transwar United States. In the 1920s, the three human races of scientific racism—Caucasian, Negroid, and Mongoloid—became enshrined in court cases such as the 1922 *Ozawa v. United States* (which unanimously defined "free white persons" as "members of the Caucasian race," denying naturalization to Japanese immigrants) and legislation including the Immigration Act of 1924 (which essentially ended non-European immigration to the United States). Thus, scientific racism essentially "consolidated" various groups previously considered distinct.[86] In the postwar period, Asian Americans were used as foils for Blacks and Whites in a racial hierarchy where "the yellow race" approached, but remained distinct from, Whiteness, extending limited improvements to Asian Americans while reinforcing White supremacist hegemony.[87] As David Yoo writes, into the late twentieth century, Asian Americans remained "perpetual foreigners" who provided a proximate Other for "Americans seeking to reinvent themselves through the exotic and mysterious traditions of the Orient."[88] All of these developments formed a background for Takata's entry to mainland White networks, offering her White students a "bridge" to the Reiki practice she learned in Japan.[89]

By the 1950s and 1960s, Takata's racialized difference, which government documents from prewar Hawai'i described in terms of "Japanese nationality" (despite her being a US citizen) and wartime propaganda characterized as sinister or subhuman, began giving way to an exotic ethnic identity that situated her as a hardworking middle-class American with deep ties to a mysterious, profound homeland.[90] This transformation is tied to the rise of two so-called positive stereotypes about Asians and Asian Americans: the "model minority" and the "wise Oriental." These stereotypes that helped facilitate Takata's success with White mainland audiences are entangled with America's postwar rise as a global superpower.

The Myth of the Model Minority

The myth of the model minority was established in the immediate postwar period, as Japanese Americans leaving the concentration camps achieved "rapid social mobility and general acceptance" in cities like Chicago.[91] Indeed, even before the Pacific War ended, a pamphlet issued by the US War Relocation Authority addressing "common misconceptions regarding Americans of Japanese ancestry" claimed, "Probably no other group of immigrants confronted with so many obstacles at outset, has equaled the progress of the Japanese in adapting themselves to the wide scope of American industry and commerce."[92]

The phrase "model minority" came to prominence with a 1966 *New York Times Magazine* article by Berkeley sociologist William Petersen. At the height of the African American civil rights movement, Petersen argued that, as Japanese Americans enjoyed economic and social integration in the United States despite having possibly been "subjected to the most discrimination and the worst injustices" of any ethnic minorities, America was indeed a land of opportunity for those who possessed "achievement orientation." Echoing Robert Bellah, Petersen concluded that Nikkei achievements result from an "almost religious" devotion to diligence and frugality that he compared to Weber's "Protestant ethic." He also extolled Nikkei Americans' "meaningful links with an alien culture," which provided them with "pride in their heritage and shame for any reduction in its only partly legendary glory." In both their work ethic and their ethnic pride, Petersen explicitly contrasted Nikkei Americans' success with Black Americans' struggle.[93]

Petersen's pro-Japanese, anti-Black analysis is an example of what Christina Klein calls "Cold War Orientalism": portrayals of Asians and Asian Americans in the postwar United States that operated "through a logic of affiliation as well as through one of difference," as "the domestic project of integrating Asian and African Americans within the United States was intimately bound up with the international project of integrating the decolonizing nations into the capitalist 'free world' order."[94] The transformation of the role of the Japanese in American imaginations from a sub-human, fanatical race to the United States' most important ally in Asian democracy and capitalism was inseparable from the construction of Japanese Americans as a model minority. As Takashi Fujitani writes, Americans in the postwar decades cast Japanese and Japanese Americans as an "almost, but not quite White" younger sibling, able to modernize and succeed because of cultural values of diligence and frugality, and ultimately "deployed as the new model for aspiring peoples of color throughout the world."[95]

Takata's students drew on elements of the model minority myth to position her as a hardworking ethnic minority trying to provide for her family. I asked Ted Vento about a statement his younger sister had made that their aunt had felt that Takata was "a bit pushy trying to get people to take her class." He responded, "Well, she might have been. If you stop and think about it, she's all alone in the world and this is her business. And if being pushy got her the business . . . you know, Oriental people are inherently, pretty strong, I would use the word strong rather than pushy . . . and I believe that [Takata] *was* a strong person, but she accomplished what she did because of that."[96] This attribution of strength as an inherently "Oriental" trait is linked to the myth of the model minority.

Takata's position as a Hawai'i-born Nisei woman in the postwar period may have benefited from association with mass media portrayals of Hawai'i-born Nisei men who served in the segregated 100th Infantry Battalion and the 442nd Infantry Regiment. As described in chapter 3, Takata and other (chiefly female) spiritual therapists on the homefront sent distance treatments to these "local boys" facing adversity far from home, which likely encouraged some to enroll in the expensive *okuden* course that authorized them to send treatments as well. The heroism of the 100th and the 442nd also captured mainland White Americans' imaginations in the transwar period, as they were portrayed in wartime newsreels, honored with a 1946 reception by President Harry S. Truman, and dramatized in the 1951 film *Go for Broke!* and James Michener's best-selling 1959 novel *Hawaii,* popular cultural works that likely served as reference points for many of Takata's mainland students to conceive of Hawai'i's Nikkei culture. The masculine "model minority" heroism of the Nisei soldier propelled the postwar political success of veterans like Hawai'i senator Daniel Inouye (1924–2012), Representative Spark Matsunaga (1916–1990), and Governor George Ariyoshi (b. 1926). This political success is emblematic of Nikkei's rising social status in Hawai'i, where they became increasingly middle class and eventually one of the dominant groups, with Whites and Chinese Americans, another "model minority."[97]

However, Nikkei women in Hawai'i advanced more slowly both symbolically and materially.[98] Nikkei men were actually overrepresented in Hawai'i's professional classes by 1930 and, despite losing ground during the war years, regained a normal proportion by 1960; Nikkei women, in contrast, show a gradual decade-by-decade increase in professional employment over the course of the twentieth century but were still significantly underrepresented in 1960, especially compared with White and Chinese American women. For both Nisei men and women, teaching was "an important avenue of upward mobility," and the other major profession Nisei women pursued was nursing.[99] Takata's role as a healer and teacher combined the two primary occupations available to upwardly mobile Nisei women at the time she came of age.

Ted Vento's statement about Takata being an accomplished businesswoman who was "all alone in the world" also references her position as a late middle-age widow. Takata was conscious that her widowhood provided the independence she needed to be an itinerant healer and teacher. As mentioned in chapter 1, when one of her Master students from the 1970s told Takata that she and her husband were breaking up, the reply was, "Good, you can't travel to teach Reiki with a husband."[100] The accounts of Takata's students combine stereotypes about powerful women, from the tough-as-nails "iron maiden" or the dangerously seductive "dragon lady" (as in Thomas Mackler's account of her hypnotic power) to the "wise woman" or "crone."[101] Increasingly, the image of Takata as a "wise woman" intersected in the postwar period with a second so-called positive stereotype about Asians and Asian Americans: the wise Oriental.

The Image of the Wise Oriental

Takata's success teaching Reiki in the postwar United States cannot be teased apart from the increasing mediatization of images of "Orientals" as privy to a tradition of ancient spiritual wisdom capable of assuaging modern ills. Jane Iwamura has shown how the "icon of the Oriental Monk," building on earlier Orientalist precedents, became an American popular media trope by the mid-1950s. She traces this icon to mass media portrayals of Zen apologist D. T. Suzuki (1870–1966) that marked "Eastern spirituality as a 'stylized religion' and consumable object." Suzuki became the paradigmatic aged Asian who transmits "oriental wisdom and spiritual insight" to a "bridge figure," a young, Euro-American disciple whose destiny is to preserve this authentic tradition of an East in decline and bring it to the dominant West, where it will prove the salvation to the crisis of alienation.[102] In 1956 and 1957, *Vogue, Time, Newsweek,* the *Saturday Review,* and the *New Yorker* published photo-driven articles about Suzuki and his White students, including John Cage (1912–1992), Alan Watts (1915–1973), and Jack Kerouac (1922–1969). Iwamura argues these mediations, along with publications by figures like Watts and Kerouac, helped create a late-1950s "Zen boom" that still plays out today, from the marketplace for Zen-themed commodities to the popularity of mindfulness practices.[103] This phenomenon followed the rising popularity of other Japanese cultural products in the 1950s, from mass-produced housewares and bonsai to highbrow arthouse cinema.[104]

Takata's career strongly resonates with Iwamura's Oriental Monk icon in certain ways. For example, her claim that Reiki had died out in Japan and only survived in the West echoes the discourse highlighted by Iwamura that presents Eastern religions as no longer practiced authentically in their homelands, requiring Western intervention for their survival.[105] For instance, Watts argued, "The spiritual species [of Zen] could only be saved if transplanted into new soil and cross-fertilized in just the right way."[106] Takata's students must have seen themselves to some degree as preserving this Japanese healing art that their teacher told them had vanished in its land of origin.

However, Takata also complicates Iwamura's icon. As an "iron maiden," even a "dragon lady," she provides a powerful counterexample to Iwamura's claim that the Oriental Monk is recognizable based on "his conformity to general features that are paradigmatically encapsulated in the icon of the Oriental Monk," including "his manner of dress and—most obviously— his peculiar gendered character": an effeminate Asian man in a kimono.[107] This feminization of Japan and Japanese men in American imaginations was not confined to depictions of Japanese religion but propagated in popular texts about Japan more broadly, from the middlebrow *Life* magazine to Ruth Benedict's influential 1946 anthropological study *The Chrysanthemum and the Sword.*[108]

To some extent, Takata projects the Oriental Monk icon onto the mythologized versions of Usui and Hayashi she developed in the postwar decades (presented in chapter 5) and casts herself as a mediating figure between the male Japanese masters and her mostly female White American students. Yet Takata's students had no difficulty recognizing her as a powerful spiritual teacher regardless of her gender or her failure to conform to assumptions of femininity. As many of them commented on the striking contrast between Takata's petite stature (roughly five feet tall and one hundred pounds) and her assertive, commanding presence ("like a drill sergeant," I was told more than once), she troubles the femininity that Iwamura asserts is essential to the Oriental Monk icon. Takata's power (and her age) also distinguished her from "the image of the Oriental woman as . . . sexually available, submissive, obedient, domestic, sweet and passive, etc." that grew increasingly common in the postwar period.[109]

A second way that Takata's case complicates Iwamura's Oriental Monk schema is in her role as an Asian American bridge figure revered by her students. In Iwamura's telling, Asian Americans, particularly Japanese American Buddhists, are invariably relegated to peripheral roles in representations of Asian religion in the United States. They appear, she writes, as "able caretakers providing a comfortable environment for more authentic Buddhist representatives from Asia. . . . In the narrative of the Oriental Monk, the character of the Japanese American will always be relegated to the supporting cast *if* she appears at all."[110] Iwamura genders the Japanese American as female because her specific example is of Mihoko Okamura (b. 1934), Suzuki's personal secretary in the 1950s and 1960s, but also because of her characterization of the Japanese American as a "supporting cast" member to the star monk in patriarchal society. Takata offers a compelling counter-example of a Japanese American woman who, like Suzuki himself, had adoring White students who considered her a spiritual authority and was able to teach across the United States due to their financial support.[111]

These inconsistencies between Iwamura's description of the mediated Oriental Monk figure and Takata's flesh-and-blood case of a successful Asian American spiritual teacher provoke a reconsideration of the interplay between race, gender, and spiritual authority in spiritual practices coded as Asian in the postwar United States. Takata's success could have been partly facilitated by her upbringing in Hawaiʻi. As previously mentioned, her accented English marked her as more "foreign" to her mainland US students than the unaccented speech of a Nisei raised in California or New York. That she was a Hawaiʻi-born Nisei—raised not only between the culture of her Japanese immigrant parents and that of the White elites for whom they worked but also in the distinct space of Hawaiian plantation culture—is an essential factor in considering Takata's ability to inspire mainland Whites' devotion to her and to the Reiki practices she translated so effectively.

Reframing Reiki for White Audiences on the Postwar US Mainland

When Hawayo Takata arrived in Los Angeles in July 1951 to attend AMORC's annual international conference, the United States, particularly Los Angeles, was awash in divine healing energies. A new generation of Christian ministers from Granville Oral Roberts (1918–2009) to Norman Vincent Peale (1898–1993) gained national audiences in the immediate postwar period with radio broadcasts that featured dramatic healings through the influx of God's power, often described in terms of energy. Roberts described the presence of the Holy Spirit as "pure energy . . . an invisible spiritual force that comes upon you and you feel it . . . like electricity," a force he first experienced in 1935 and one he began channeling through the laying on of hands when he began his healing ministry in 1947.[112] And in his 1952 best seller *The Power of Positive Thinking*, Peale promised readers "a never ceasing flow of energy" if they opened up to God, "the source of all energy," and described his experiences healing illness by channeling God's power through his hand.[113]

Broadcast evangelism, crucial to the rise of Peale, Roberts, and others, was established a generation prior by Aimee Semple McPherson (1890–1944), whose ministry in Los Angeles rose to national prominence in the early 1920s due to her performance of dramatic healings through the laying on of hands. McPherson spoke of the healing power of God being like "a shock of electricity . . . [that] flowed through my whole body," and like recipients of Reiki, those she touched reported perspiring from the tremendous heat emitted by her hands.[114] Reiki's promoters generally exhibited more liberal views than charismatic Christians about the nature of their healing energy—the pervasive evangelical and Pentecostal motif of "spiritual warfare" divides the world into a binary of godly and demonic forces, whereas the typical Reiki worldview at this time was much more monistic, stressing the importance of proper circulation—but they shared powerful experiences of divine healing through the laying on of hands, which they experienced and described in terms of heat, electricity, and energy. As noted in chapter 3, Takata, Roberts, and Peale also shared a concept, rooted in the teachings of New Thought authors such as Ralph Waldo Trine, Napoleon Hill, and William Walker Atkinson, that properly flowing energy helped ensure both "health and wealth."[115]

The postwar years also saw growing interest in yogis who expressed divinity in terms of healing energy. Paramahansa Yogananda's (1893–1952)

Autobiography of a Yogi, published in 1946 and in its third edition by the time Takata came to Los Angeles in 1951, brought his devotional Kriya Yoga to broad American audiences. The rise of Yogananda's Self-Realization Fellowship (SRF) occurred alongside that of evangelical Christian healing; his followers built the SRF headquarters on Los Angeles' Mount Washington in 1925, just a few miles to the northeast of the Angelus Temple megachurch McPherson had opened two years prior. Yogananda combined Indian spiritual practices "with an American language of science that circled New Thought and theosophical themes and that coexisted comfortably with liberal versions of Christianity."[116] Like the evangelicals, Yogananda taught in a 1947 lecture in Hollywood that "God's omnipresent divine power" was a "universal life energy" capable of healing all disease, and that those who experience this power are "charged with electric current, life energy, not from food, but from God."[117] Of course, evangelicals would disagree with Yogananda's mystical teachings that Jesus and Krishna were both manifestations of Christ Consciousness who enabled humanity to reach union with God.[118] But Yogananda's combinative perennialism, like that of AMORC, may have been a model for Takata's similar rhetoric, and he engaged in a combination of universalism and Occidentalism that foreshadowed her later rhetoric.[119]

Since at least 1951, Takata was interested in yoga both as a healing tradition from which she could learn and as a more established Asian spiritual therapy that could bolster her authority. Her address book from her 1951 trip contains the titles, authors, and publishing information of several books by prominent names in yogic healing.[120] She may have read *Autobiography of a Yogi* (or had someone relate it to her), as her telling of Hayashi's death seems to include elements of a story Yogananda told about his guru's death.[121] Takata's interest in yoga and Yogananda may have been sparked by her friendship with Doris Duke, an active SRF member who practiced daily meditation at their Los Angeles center in the early 1950s and helped finance their new headquarters shortly before Yogananda's death.[122] Takata recalled seeking out gurus on her 1957 trip to India with Duke, as she had heard of gifted Indian healers and thought she could improve Reiki through learning yoga; unfortunately, she reported, Duke's friends in India told her that the yogis were all up in the mountains until the monsoon season.[123] Regardless, Takata cited having "researched yoga" while in India in an October 1957 talk to the Honolulu Lions Club.[124] Thus, yoga not only possibly inspired Takata but was also a means of strengthening her authority as a spiritual therapist.

Like Yogananda and AMORC leaders, Takata used perennialist language to frame Reiki as but one means to access a universal phenomenon. This is particularly visible in the earliest detailed description of Reiki in the English language: the two-thousand-word essay "The Art of Healing," which Takata wrote in the autumn of 1948 as the "examination" for her doctor of naturopathy diploma from the IAA. Its opening states,

> I believe there exists one Supreme Being—the Absolute Infinite—a Dynamic Force that governs the world and universe. It is an unseen spiritual power that vibrates and all other powers fade into insignificance beside it. So, therefore, it is Absolute. This power is unfathomable, immeasurable, and being a universal life force, it is incomprehensible to man. Yet, every single living being is receiving its blessings daily, awake or asleep. Different teachers and masters call Him The Great Spirit; The Universal Life Force; Life Energy, because when applied it vitalizes the whole system; Ether Wave, because it soothes pain and puts you into deep slumber as if under an anesthetic, and The Cosmic Wave, because it radiates vibrations of exultant feeling and lifts you into harmony. I shall call it "Reiki" because I studied it under that expression.[125]

The perennialist universalism of this essay was deliberate. It was typed in triplicate, as Takata submitted one copy to Red Fox, and Furumoto and I found two copies in the boxes: the original top sheet with some handwritten corrections and a carbon copy on vellum. Its formal diction, impressive for an author who left school after the sixth grade, suggests multiple drafts. Thus, this was a conscious crafting of her ideas, specifically targeting a mainland audience.

The essay's four references to "the Great Spirit," including calling Reiki "the way of the Great Spirit," are explained by the fact that it was written for Red Fox of the IAA, but Takata also made use of a number of Christian markers. Although she avoids the term "God," she refers to the "one Supreme Being" with the masculine pronoun, which would strongly connote the Heavenly Father to Christian Americans. Moreover, near the end of the essay, she translated Usui's five precepts (*gokai*) into distinctly King Jamesian language:

Just for today—Thou Shalt not Anger
Just for today—Thou Shalt not Worry

Thou shall be grateful for thy many blessings
Earn thy livelihood with honest labor
Be kind to thy neighbors.[126]

She would tie Reiki to Christianity more explicitly in the 1970s, describing Usui as a Christian minister in search of the secrets of Jesus' healing powers and calling Reiki "God power," but the 1948 essay represents an early reframing of Reiki in Christian hegemonic language. Her Rosicrucian membership is one possible influence, but her increasing interaction with White Christian students and patients is also likely.

Takata's students and their acquaintances clearly understood Reiki and Takata in terms of their Christian faith. In 1949, Gertrude Kilgore of Bay City, Michigan, wrote to Esther Vento regarding her stories of Reiki:

> I think that what you say about Mrs. Takata is about the most wonderful thing I know. One can read a lot of wonderful things in books about people and what they have done, but to come into this close contact with one of them is another side to the story. I feel in a way that I already know Mrs. Takata and I hope that feeling will truly materialize some day when the Lord is ready for us to meet.
>
> It is the greatest desire of my life to become a healer, one like she is: one that can truly do the healing.[127]

Although Kilgore does not explicitly reference biblical healings, her contrast between reading about miracles and personally experiencing them recalls charismatic Christian rhetoric. Furthermore, she is confident that the opportunity to meet Takata and learn Reiki would be ordained by God and would lead to the fulfillment of her life's purpose. It resembles the earlier-cited example of Clara Mackler's "strong conviction that an opportunity such as Dr. Takata only comes once in a life time [sic]. She is surely a messenger to humanity."[128] Again, while Mackler does not explicitly mention God in this letter, when I shared the letter with her son, he confirmed that his mother's strong Christian faith would have prompted her to understand Takata in those terms.[129]

The way Takata herself conceived the relationship between Reiki, religion, and biomedicine is clarified by another "showdown" story she often told students about a 1954 interaction with the president of the American Medical Association, who was living in Hawai'i. Takata said an acquaintance of hers told her the president "wanted to have a forum" to find out about Reiki, so they set up a dinner with Takata and "this famous doctor, very kind and very noted M.D." The three retired to her friend's fancy suite after dinner, where Takata was shocked to find forty-three of her students and patients sitting on the carpet. They said they had heard of the "forum" and came to provide moral support. Takata calmly answered the doctor's questions for what seemed like a couple of hours, but when she checked her watch it was 1:30 a.m.[130]

She was shocked and tried to excuse herself, but the doctor said he would like to ask two final questions. First, he asked, "Do you think that all the M.D.'s in Honolulu should learn Reiki?" She replied, "Yes, doctor, and not only the doctors but also the ministers." Surprised, he asked, "Why the ministers?" and Takata replied,

> Doctor, I shall be very, very happy if all the M.D.'s understood Reiki and took Reiki and used it to add to their profession. It will be a great service for mankind and community [*sic*]. On the other hand . . . if the ministers did Monday to Friday Reiki, Reiki and helped all their friends and members of the church who were seeking better health, better mental attitudes, with the sermons on Saturdays or Sundays you would make them a complete whole.

According to Takata's reminiscence, the doctor remained quiet for a number of seconds and then rushed Takata and shook her hand, exclaiming, "You have said the truth! This is absolutely truth!" He then asked Takata to find the location of his backaches, which she quickly did by feeling vibrations with her hand. He asked how to treat it and she replied that, as a chronic condition, it required regular treatments, so it would be best to teach his wife Reiki so she could treat him nightly. She was willing, so Takata told her to gather a group of her friends and their friends to create a class.[131]

This story, which Takata related to clients and students for decades, locates Reiki as fulfilling an essential, yet missing, element of both religion and medicine: two spheres of activity that mainstream culture generally considered separate in the ostensibly secular postwar United States.[132] Like other religious healers of the time who employed narratives of the spirit's therapeutic power winning over physicians, Takata had a flair for storytelling that made the most of this showdown.[133] In contrast to the stories she told about being a naïve "country mouse" in Honolulu in the 1930s, Takata comes off as much more sophisticated in this story, down to the orchid corsage she recalls wearing to dinner in the fancy Royal Hawaiian dining room. The doctor's response clearly indicates his respect for Takata and Reiki, and she won him over with her attitude to Reiki's role in both medicine and religion: a prescient emphasis on the rhetoric of interconnectedness that would come to be known as "holistic health" in the 1970s.

Conclusion

When Hawayo Takata arrived on the US mainland in 1951, she occupied a complex, intersectional position in relation to the White Christian Americans who made up the vast majority of her potential clients and students. As a Hawai'i-born Buddhist Nisei widow in her early fifties, she presented as an exotic figure but also as a hardworking fellow American: a proximate Other. Students saw her not only as having spiritual authority as a practitioner and teacher of a ritual healing technique with spiritual elements but also as a "messenger to humanity," inspiring devotion somewhat in line with that inspired by other religious healers of the time, from conservative Christian evangelists to mystical Indian yogis. Her authority was a product of her talent at building social capital through networking as well as the transformation of the cultural capital of Japaneseness in the midcentury United States.

Through her travels in the summer and fall of 1951, which took her across the continental United States, from Puget Sound in the Northwest to a small town at the southern tip of Texas up to Canton, Ohio, and New York City, Takata carried the folding certificate cases described in this chapter's introduction. These two cases each represented a separate bridge Takata built from the Hawaiian Islands and a different form of legitimacy for potential students or clients in the postwar US mainland. Her certificates from the Hayashi Association represented an initiation lineage that extended to the mystical Orient and authorized Takata to initiate others, even White Christian Americans, into that lineage for a considerable fee. Her certificates from the IAA performed her acceptance by mainland institutions, identifying her as a Christian minister and a doctor of naturopathy. While she received these latter certificates through the mail by submitting an application form, twelve dollars, and a two-thousand-word essay, they had the form of professional legitimacy in postwar America: signatories with letters after their names and embossed seals. It is easy to imagine her using these certificates to help win over a prospective student or to get out of a difficult situation during her teaching tours.

Takata's membership in mainland, majority-White social institutions like AMORC and the IAA gave her access to new social connections, strengthened her authority for prospective clients and students, and helped shape the way she presented Reiki in the postwar period. Her networking practices are legible in her address book, where contacts are often annotated to say that he or she is a friend of a prior contact. Even among people to whom she did not have direct social connections, her embeddedness in these networks allowed her to build the trust of strangers through name-dropping, particularly the names of celebrities and medical professionals who received Reiki treatments and initiations. The presentation of Reiki in this period as the Japanese form of a universal practice was influenced by the perennialism of the period, from *The Perennial Philosophy* (1945) by her alleged student Aldous Huxley to the teachings of spiritual leaders like the SRF's Yogananda and AMORC's H. Spencer Lewis. Her reinstatement of Reiki as a "secret" practice and her development of her own certificates were also likely influenced by her membership in these esoteric fraternal orders. Finally, like both AMORC and the IAA, her brand of perennialism took on Christian inflections in this period, which would become even more explicit in the 1970s.

Reiki's circulation on the US mainland not only transformed the practice, but it also developed new social networks to facilitate its circulation and transformed the lives and values of the people embedded in these networks. From the beginning, Takata's students on the North American mainland, and those whom they touched, understood their experiences with Reiki as transformative and pregnant with meaning. Her students exchanged financial capital for spiritual capital, gaining membership in an initiatory lineage that crossed the Pacific. They may have been discouraged from overtly publicizing their Reiki practice, but to themselves and those with whom they shared their healing practice, they became "bridge figures" able to heal the ills of the materialist West by taking on the spiritual practices of the mystic Orient, which had ostensibly died out in their land of origin. Connections to Takata, whether as clients or as students, also connected otherwise strangers, particularly those who served as hubs by receiving her mail or helping her organize classes. Although Takata's weak ties helped her transcend divides of race and ethnicity between herself and her students, homophilic tendencies also created clustered subnetworks on either side of a social class divide between elites and nonelites.

There are not many extant accounts of Reiki in this period, and as with Takata's archived materials more generally, there is a selection bias for the most enthusiastic of her students, but the data that survived is filled with proclamations of the profundity of Reiki initiation. In the same letter in which she proclaimed that Takata was "surely a messenger to humanity," the Ohio schoolteacher Clara Mackler wrote to the Hungarian immigrant seamstress Elsa Kane,

> Since [receiving the Reiki initiations] last summer I am already a en-lightened person and not to boast but feel very confident with my hands. . . . I feel like I did when I was very young that I was put on the earth for a special purpose, now I truly feel that Ive [sic] suffered enough to go thru the channel to meet life's problems an [sic] help folks in the way I should.[134]

Reiki initiations and practice clearly provoked a turning point in this woman's life akin to a conversion experience. Of course, as her husband Thomas' "Testimony" written after their conversion to the AOG attests, some of these profound experiences with Reiki were but one stop on the evolving spiritual paths of Takata's students.

Many of Takata's students made sense of their experiences within the framework of their Christian background, but Reiki practice also turned others to the Orient, such as two California psychiatrists who were "thinking longingly of the pilgrimage we may make with [Takata] to Japan."[135] It is difficult to say definitively without further reports, but learning Reiki most likely inculcated others in this period with broader interest in Japan as a locus of spiritual wisdom, as it would for her students in the 1970s. The middle-class White Americans who were interested in Takata's method in the 1950s were part of what Robert Wuthnow describes as an "underground spiritual economy," in which "rebels" bonded "around exotic rather than normative religious symbols."[136] Their otherwise conventional identities contrast with the assumption that the primary group to be interested in Eastern philosophies and gurus in 1950s America were people like the Beats who visibly protested the "general milieu of conservatism in American society."[137] Takata's middle-class suburbanite students were part of a largely unseen group of people who felt unfulfilled by the era's consumer-ism and conformity, which were somaticized by biomedical hegemony and spiritualized in "the religion of the American Dream."[138]

Reiki's circulation on the postwar mainland changed the lifeworlds of Takata's clients and students and also influenced Takata and how she taught and practiced. Through the strength of weak ties, she developed deep con-nections with Whites of various socioeconomic classes regardless of her having been raised in a plantation camp and only receiving a sixth-grade education. Her upbringing stands in contrast to that of the itinerant yoga teachers in the early twentieth-century United States, whom Philip Deslippe describes as, "nearly to a person," Indians of "well-educated, middle-class to affluent" backgrounds, which he considered a prerequisite "to engage with the middle class students and affluent patrons that comprised the base of their support."[139] Despite Takata's humble beginnings and the rampant de-humanization of Japanese Americans just a few years prior, her ability to network and adapt Reiki inspired mainland Whites to take up a virtually unknown spiritual therapy and enter an initiation lineage linking them to the nation with which they had just been at war. Many understood their new powers in terms of their Christian backgrounds, as Hawaiian Nikkei understood them in Buddhist terms, but for both groups, the belief that Takata's initiations gave them the power to heal others with their touch evoked deep gratitude for this gift, for which they gladly paid what were, at that time, considerable sums. Her ability to induce such trust and devotion only increased in the 1970s, when she attracted thousands of students as she further transformed Reiki.

Takata's adaptations of Reiki based on her growing interaction with stu-dents and patients on the US mainland highlight the bidirectionality of the alternate currents that flowed between them. Her 1948 essay "The Art of Healing" indicates that, by that time, she had already adopted perennialist and Christian language and was comfortable oscillating between religious, medical, and scientific registers. As Takata increasingly taught White Chris-tians, her universalism deepened and Reiki became more Orientalized, a pairing that would intensify in her final decade. As we shall see in chap-ter 5, Takata would make additional changes to Reiki in the 1970s to inculcate her students with "Japanese values," further professionalize the practice, and create a new generation of Reiki Masters.

CHAPTER 5

Coupling Universalism and "Japanese" Values
Making North American Masters, 1972–1980

In 1970s North America, transnational spiritual therapies ascribed Asian origins (including some yogic and meditation movements) were moving from counterculture to mainstream, as their proponents gained some institutional authority.[1] These practices increasingly gained cultural cachet and appeared with more frequency in the public sphere, including popular cultural media and public institutions, where they sometimes appeared alongside and interacted with more homegrown spiritual therapies.

One such setting was a series of symposia at the University of California, Los Angeles, and Stanford University called Dimensions of Healing hosted by the Academy of Parapsychology and Medicine (APM) in the autumn of 1972. Each symposium ran for three days and featured lectures and panel discussions by a variety of spiritual therapists, as well as medical and scientific researchers who investigated unorthodox healing practices. Sally Hammond (1916–1993) was engrossed in the talks. She had taken a leave of absence from the *New York Post,* where she had been a features reporter for fifteen years, to research a book about spiritual healing. Sally's sister Marcelle was hospitalized, receiving treatment for bone cancer, and in terrible pain. Sally was desperate to help her beloved sister and frustrated with conventional medical care. She had previously had some inexplicable experiences with spiritual healers and hoped that, in researching this world, she could find someone who could cure Marcelle.[2] As she later reflected that the APM conference was "designed for physicians and other interested professionals rather than the general public," she had likely hoped it would be more practically oriented.[3] Despite her initial disappointment, an encounter

Sally had at this symposium gave Sally and Marcelle hope for Marcelle's recovery. Moreover, this encounter, articulated in prose and disseminated through far-reaching print media networks, led to countless individuals' discipleship under an elderly Japanese American healer.

One of the many lectures Sally Hammond attended at the APM conference was by Olga Worrall (1906–1985), who performed laying on of hands at the New Life Clinic she directed at Mount Washington Methodist Church in Baltimore.[4] Worrall's lecture addressed a "healing power" that healers around the world had channeled through their hands since ancient Egypt and China; "it flows strictly in accordance with Immutable Law," she said, and "the majority of people call [its] source 'God.'"[5] Hammond recalled that just as Worrall finished,

> I was suddenly aware of a crackling bundle of energy in the seat beside me—a small, black-haired woman, who appeared to be Japanese. . . . Her name was Hawayo Hiromi Takata, and she wore fire-engine red slacks, a tunic splashed with tropical flowers and her hair very short and straight. . . . "She really knows what she is talking about," she said to me, eyes sparkling. Then she quickly mentioned that she, too, was a healer and practiced in Waikiki. I quickly made a date with her for lunch.[6]

Hammond's recollection of her encounter with Takata appears near the end of her best-selling account of her year researching spiritual healing, *We Are All Healers*. After describing dozens of others who perform and teach healing, Hammond presents Takata as uniquely possessing a technique to facilitate her students' development of healing abilities: "I give my pupils the contact with the great universal life force that does the healing—I have the secret of how to tune into it!" Hammond closes this section with the lament, "Since my chance encounter with this dynamic little Hawaiian healer I've wished many times that I had a 'quicker' way of making contact with the healing power, that I knew the old Buddhist secret for speeding up my development as a healer."[7]

Neither Hammond nor Takata saw any conflict between Takata's "Buddhist secret" and Worrall's Christian laying on of hands, and there is no indication they considered the speakers' religious testimonial narratives to conflict with the academic university setting. Rather, Worrall's and Takata's claims to channel a "universal energy" actively effaced such distinctions by suggesting that an empirically verifiable force underlies all healing, a force that supports the fundamental unity of all religions. However, Takata endorsed this universalism while simultaneously distinguishing herself as "the only living master" of a distinctly Japanese system. She told Hammond, "I studied in Japan under a great master . . . the chosen disciple of Mikao Usui, founder of the Usui system. . . . [Reiki] is a method Usui revived from the Buddhist scriptures, a way of tuning into the *reiki*—that's the Japanese word for 'universal force.'"[8]

Here, Takata invokes a discourse that posits one culture has a kind of privileged access to the shared reality toward which all cultures are situated. Bruno Latour coined the phrase "particular universalism" to explain the chauvinistic assumption of Western scientific objectivity, but it works equally well to describe a kind of twentieth-century Orientalism (or Occidentalism) that asserts a liberal universalist paradigm alongside a kind of exceptionalism that considers Asian religious traditions to have uniquely valid insights into the nature of reality.[9] This example of particular universalism appears together with Takata's extolling Reiki's Buddhist roots, reflecting Buddhism's rising stock in the 1970s United States and foreshadowing her "master narrative" of Usui that reached fruition in this decade.[10] The way Takata coupled perennialism and Orientalism was not unique to the 1970s, but it gained a particularly powerful resonance in that decade, as transnational spiritual therapies attributed to Asia became more mainstream, while maintaining their status as "alternative."[11]

The way Hammond recounts Takata's presentation of Reiki encapsulates four interrelated factors that characterized the final years of Takata's career and helped make them her most productive, facilitating her training of thousands of students and at least twenty-two teachers, whom she would call Reiki Masters, allowing the practice to enter a new phase of truly global circulation.[12] First, by the 1970s, Takata had departed from the secrecy she advocated on the 1950s and 1960s mainland, resuming her promotion of Reiki through print media and institutional affiliations as she had in prewar Hawai'i. This allowed her to greatly widen Reiki's spread and also influenced how she framed its practice. Second, the growing popularity of transnational spiritual therapies attributed to Asia primed 1970s North Americans to be open to Reiki and helped pattern how they saw Takata and their practice. Third, by this period, Takata had creatively reshaped Reiki practice to encode it with values she (and her students) understood as specifically linked to Japan, Buddhism, or Asia, while continuing to maintain (as she had since at least 1948) that Reiki was a universal practice open to all, regardless of one's racioethnic background or religious adherence. In other words, Takata "Japanized" Reiki to ensure her students (and, increasingly, their students) held certain attitudes toward their practice that she considered inherent to Reiki's efficacy but deficient in her North American students. At the same time, Takata strategically tempered this "foreignizing translation" by couching Reiki in Christian rhetoric and casting it as a professional (as well as a spiritual) vocation, providing "domestic" points of entry for her mostly White and Christian students.[13] Last, Takata's charisma and spiritual authority grew in this period as she became an elderly master, one or two generations senior to most of her students, telling stories she had honed over decades. Takata's advanced age also increased the urgency to study under her and opened the possibility of training as a Reiki Master, as the transience of her embodied, charismatic presence became increasingly clear in her final years.

These four factors—the promotion of Reiki through print media and institutions, interest in "Asian" spiritual therapies, the "Japanization" of Reiki in Christian and professional contexts, and Takata's increasing age and experience—interplayed in the expansion of Reiki's socio-spiritual networks in the years leading up to Takata's death in 1980. It was in these years that she came closest to Nancy Stalker's "charismatic entrepreneur," who combines spiritual authority with "innovative use of technology and the mass media, and flexible accommodation of social concerns not addressed by the state or mainstream religions."[14] Takata's students in her final years understood Reiki practice as a calling, both in the sense of spiritually transformative and as a professional opportunity, in ways that earlier generations of her students did not, suggesting productive linkages of spiritual and professional identities. Takata's coupling of universalist perennialism and Orientalist valorization of "Japanese" values also produced the four "alternate" features theorized in the introduction. Takata's *adaptation* of Reiki as something both *foreign* and familiar was a product of *bilateral* interactions between her and her students that amplified the frequency of her *oscillation* between several religious and medical idioms. Despite her limited formal education, Takata became highly fluent in the rhetoric of North American spiritual therapies and her stories and teachings inspired thousands to pattern their lives after her example.

Institutional Networking: Print Media, Religious Organizations, and Public Universities

Takata and her students promoted Reiki and expanded their healing and teaching networks through print media, religious organizations, and public universities in the 1970s. Such openness contrasts with Takata's eschewal of publicity in the 1950s and 1960s, when she told students on the US mainland to keep their practice secret because "the time was not yet right for the world to know about Reiki."[15] Her tendency toward secrecy in the immediate postwar period limited the word-of-mouth networking by which she found new clients and students and was probably influenced by her experience in wartime Hawai'i as well as her moving into an unfamiliar environment that had been even more hostile toward Japanese Americans. But in the early 1970s, Takata returned to organizing classes through print media and religious networks, methods she had used effectively in prewar Hawai'i. Furthermore, she used these institutions not only as ways to recruit students but also as ways to imbue herself and Reiki with their authority.

Print Media Networks

Takata's appearance in Hammond's best-selling *We Are All Healers* (1973) was her first in English-language commercial media since the prewar period, and it introduced Takata to thousands of readers in geographically diverse audiences, many of whom sought out Takata's "old Buddhist secret." *Healers* provided no contact information for Takata other than that she lived in Honolulu and practiced in Waikiki, but some readers found her address through directories or writing to Hammond's publisher, while enough others simply wrote to "Hawayo Takata / Waikiki / Honolulu, HI" that the post office began marking them with Takata's address and delivering them to her apartment building, no mean feat in a sizable city.[16] Takata's surviving correspondence contains letters from twenty individuals from across the United States and Canada, and even England and South Africa, who read about her in *Healers* and wanted to travel to Hawai'i to take her class.[17] Many of Takata's students in the 1970s encountered her via this book, and (as described in the pages that follow) these students would introduce Takata to others. Print networks thus supplemented and amplified the word-of-mouth promotion through social networks that served Takata in the wartime and postwar periods.

Hammond's account of her encounter with Takata is enmeshed in a number of institutional networks. Hammond's publication of *Healers* with the major New York publisher Harper and Row (as well as a smaller publisher, Turnstone, in London), which gave her resources for promotional travel, depended on publishers' and editors' belief that market trends (buoyed by the nascent New Age movement) supported a project on spiritual healing.[18] The book's distribution and sales were equally dependent on networks of bookstores and customers willing to devote shelf space, dollars, and leisure time to it. That a few pages near the end of a book inspired readers on at least three continents to contact Takata within a few years of her encounter with Hammond testifies to the potential for print media to mobilize audiences to action. By scaling up demand for Reiki, *Healers* established opportunities for Takata to scale up her teaching as well.

Appearances in print media helped Takata and her students promote Reiki without taking out paid advertisements, a practice Takata continued to avoid and discouraged among her students in the 1970s. This tendency is illustrated in the story of Reiki's spread to Canada, where Takata's teaching was centered in the rural British Columbia Interior. Takata's initial trip there was in 1975, spurred by an old prospector named Hubert "Hugh" Gibbs (1899–1994) living in the Okanagan Valley, who wrote to Takata after reading *Healers*. She told him to organize a class of at least ten students without advertising; unable to find enough local students through word of mouth, Gibbs arranged for the *Penticton Herald* to write an article about Takata's coming visit.[19] Barbara Brown (ca. 1915–2000) was pushed to attend the class by her husband, who had learned about it from the *Herald* article. She was reluctant to attend, especially considering the cost, but she was amazed when, after the first day of the class, a chronic vision problem she had suffered disappeared. Brown went on to organize subsequent classes for Takata, becoming a Reiki Master herself in 1979.[20] Hammond's book and the *Herald* article are links in a causal chain (along with the considerable labors of Takata and her students) responsible for the innumerable Reiki students around the world who trace their lineage to Brown and the four other Masters Takata trained in the British Columbia interior between 1978 and 1980.[21]

As in her in-person networking, Takata ensured her print appearances connected her to other institutional authorities. Hammond's section on Takata derives some of its power from its co-option of biomedical authority. In the setting of an academic conference, Hammond highlighted

Takata's stories of teaching "many doctors and their wives," particularly her "forum" with the American Medical Association president, described in chapter 4.[22] A 1974 front-page article on Takata in the *Maui News* similarly reports her having given a miraculous treatment to "a well-known surgeon," that her upcoming mainland teaching tour will "include associations of doctors," and that "doctors have often been among her students."[23] These stories of prominent physicians recognizing Reiki's potency must have assuaged some readers' doubts about this unknown therapy.

Takata also used print media to publicize her ties to social elites. She told Hammond her students included "a famous American heiress but made me promise to keep it confidential," but shortly thereafter, the *Honolulu Advertiser* reported, "During the 39 years of practicing Reiki in Hawaii, she acquired students from all corners of the globe, including Barbara Hutton and Doris Duke."[24] Takata's face-to-face citation of social connections to doctors and celebrities wielded a certain level of discursive power, but the mediation of the printed page lent these ties new degrees of authority and circulation.

Metaphysical Religious Networks

Takata also employed metaphysical religious organizations to extend her networks to new audiences.[25] Whereas in prewar Hawai'i Takata taught Reiki in the most dominant religious organizations in a marginalized community—Japanese churches of the Jōdo and Jōdo Shinshū denominations—in 1970s North America she taught in marginalized religious organizations of the dominant community: new religious movements with largely White, middle-class Protestant memberships. These organizations gave Takata spaces to teach and advertised her classes in their newsletters. She became involved with four such organizations between late 1973 and mid-1974, suggesting a concerted effort to use them as networking tools. Two of these organizations only led to a handful of classes,[26] but the other two provided social networks that proved crucial to Reiki's eventual circulation throughout the United States and beyond.

The Spiritual Frontiers Fellowship (SFF) mediated Reiki's success in the Chicago area for Takata and for her first two widely recognized Reiki Masters.[27] The SFF was founded in 1956 as a nondenominational group of Protestant ministers interested in spiritualism and psychical research, but it shifted focus in the 1970s to "mystical prayer and spiritual healing."[28] In the mid-1970s, Virginia Samdahl (1918–1994) was well known in the SFF for her healing, psychic, and spirit communication abilities, and she gave courses and certifications under the name the American College of Psychic Studies. As part of a series of psychically foretold events, which included her discovery of Takata in *Healers,* Samdahl enrolled in what may have been Takata's first Midwest class, held in Kewanee, Illinois, in August 1974. The following month, Takata stayed with Samdahl and her family in Park Forest, a prototypical middle-class suburb, while completing Samdahl's twenty-hour seminar on experimental parapsychology and extrasensory development.[29]

Samdahl invited Takata to teach at the SFF's national headquarters, in Evanston, Illinois. The Chicago-area SFF chapters, including the main Evanston one, held their programs, including Takata's visits, in local mainline Protestant churches and advertised them through newsletters and other mailings to the roughly five thousand SFF members in the Chicago metropolitan area.[30] As she did elsewhere, Takata gave free introductory lectures and demonstrations to advertise her four-day First Degree classes. After receiving Reiki initiations, SFF members began charging set fees for healing services, which they had previously performed without charge or by donation.[31] Thus, Reiki training caused the SFF to standardize, professionalize, and commodify its healing practices.

The US bicentennial year of 1976 ushered in a new era of Reiki, as Takata announced the creation of new Reiki Masters: Samdahl and Ethel Lombardi (1923–2009), another Chicago-area spiritual healer associated with the SFF. Out of the dozens, likely hundreds, of Second Degree students Takata initiated in the mid-1970s, Samdahl and Lombardi were among the first who were so motivated to teach Reiki that they agreed to pay Takata $10,000 (over $50,000 in 2022 dollars) to make them Masters.[32] This development was essential to Reiki's continuation beyond Takata's approaching mortality. Multiple Masters, each able to initiate practitioners and (eventually) other Masters, allowed Reiki to grow exponentially to a worldwide phenomenon.[33]

The second religious organization that shaped Reiki's networked circulation in the 1970s was the Trinity Metaphysical Center of Redwood City, California, a suburb in San Francisco's South Bay. Trinity was a chapter of a metaphysical Christian organization called the Universal Church of the Master (UCM) when a new minister, Rev. Beth Gray (1918–2008), took over in November 1973. Spiritual healing was central to the UCM, but it lacked a systematic practice and Beth's husband, John Harvey Gray (1917–

2011), remembered their weekly healing meditations as ineffective and chaotic.[34] In 1974, a number of UCM members, including Beth and John, attended Takata's classes in the home of a local airline pilot who studied under Takata in Honolulu after his wife read about her in *Healers*.[35] Beth saw great potential in Reiki and eventually required participants in Trinity's healing service to have Reiki training, which she found improved the effectiveness of the healing treatments.[36] Trinity eventually established a space that served as the first Reiki clinic in North America (and likely the largest such center in Reiki's history).[37] Trinity seems to not have charged set fees for treatments but, at Takata's suggestion, provided donation envelopes with the words "Thanks to Reiki" printed on them.[38]

Trinity gave Reiki an institutional base in the San Francisco area, a locale strongly attuned to "alternate currents" such as spiritual therapies and Asian imports, providing Takata with resources to promote her teaching in a community that honored her as a great teacher (figure 5.1). The Grays went on to become important promoters of Reiki in the period of its rapid growth in the decades after Takata's death. Takata made John the third publicly recognized Reiki Master in 1976, a few months after Samdahl and Lombardi. In 1979, after quitting his job and separating from Beth, John devoted himself to teaching Reiki full time. In thirty-six years of teaching, he taught over nine hundred courses in forty-eight of the fifty US states; introduced Reiki to New England, where he settled in 1985; and taught about fifteen thousand students.[39] Beth Gray became a Master in 1978, taught Reiki in Northern California for decades, and is credited with introducing Reiki to Australia in the 1980s and initiating thousands there.[40] Takata made a third Master among Trinity's regulars: Fran Brown (1924–2009) of San Mateo, who went on to teach many students and turned the stories Takata told of her life into a short biography.[41] Thus, as with the SFF, Takata's interactions with Trinity formatively affected Reiki's circulation.

Furthermore, Takata's interactions with the UCM (and possibly the SFF) likely influenced how she increasingly described Reiki with Christian language. Before the mid-1970s, Takata does not seem to have spoken much of God or Jesus, even as her clientele became more and more Christian. Sally Okura Lee (b. 1949), along with her parents and three siblings, received Reiki initiation from Takata around 1960 in her home in Honomu, about ten miles up the Hamakua coast from Hilo on the island of Hawai'i. The Okuras were members of Honomu's Church of Jesus Christ of Latter-day Saints, but

Figure 5.1   Beth Gray (*second from left*) with Hawayo Takata (*center*), Trinity Metaphysical Center, Redwood City, CA, ca. 1979.

Sally does not remember Takata using any religious terminology—Buddhist or Christian—in describing Reiki to her family; rather, she simply described it in terms of energy. However, Lee explained,

> I think that if you don't have that spiritual element, and you only try to deal with that energy in the physical sense, that a component would be missing. Like when you're healing somebody, this is a concept I got from my mother . . . you're doing something so good and service-oriented, that you're doing something that would be pleasing to God to do that, that you have to have a component of caring and love.[42]

Lee felt not only that Reiki is an opportunity to cultivate Christian values but also that Reiki employs the same divine energy that Christ used in his healings. "I really believe that Christ had a priesthood: the power of God, given to man. And with the power of the priesthood, he healed people. He healed the blind and the sick, and I believe that is that same energy. . . . You know, that power of the priesthood that heals, it's that same power that's like energy for Reiki."[43] While Lee and her family made sense of Takata and Reiki practice through their Mormon faith, she had no idea that in the 1970s, Takata described Usui as a Christian minister seeking the secret of Jesus' healing powers and, moreover, that she herself became a minister and used the title "reverend." "What?" she exclaimed. "I never linked [Takata] with Christianity. Oh my goodness."[44]

Despite Lee's surprise, by the 1970s Takata described Reiki in explicitly Christian language and, after becoming ordained as a UCM minister in 1975, used the title "reverend" to bolster her authority.[45] In contrast to her prior ministerial license from the Indian Association of America, which she got by mailing a fee to the church's founder, the UCM ordination required an examination. Among Takata's archived papers is an extensive exam that served as a kind of catechism, with 50 short-answer questions and 150 true-or-false questions on the nature of the church, its predecessors (including spiritualism and theosophy), and the spiritual world. The final essay question asked the potential minister to "explain in your own words your relationship with Christ."[46] Thus, despite a lifelong affiliation with Buddhism, expressed in daily veneration at her Buddhist altar (when at home) and her attendance of Buddhist services at the Hilo Honpa Hongwanji Betsuin and the Pearl City Risshō Kōsei-kai (a Japanese Buddhist new religion that Takata appears to have joined in the early 1970s), Takata also learned to express her spiritual beliefs using Christian language late in life.

Takata's training for the UCM ministry influenced her expression of Reiki in increasingly Christian ways. Class notes attributed to a 1975 First Degree workshop read,

> It is advisable, good, and practical for two or more REIKI healers to work together, to heal each other, to strengthen their mutual faith, exchange experiences, and gain confidence. Furthermore "Where two or three are gathered together in my name, there I am in the midst of them." Since "REIKI" means universal power and wisdom, the above quote is applicable. Jesus was not talking of Himself, but of Universal Love and Wisdom, with which He declared Himself to be one.[47]

Records from this period suggest this class was taught at the Grays' home in Woodside, California, strengthening the possibility that her citation of Matthew 18:20 as support for her teaching practice was influenced by her connection to the UCM.[48]

Such Christian translations spoke to some students in ways that Takata's earlier modes of explaining Reiki did not. Paul Mitchell (b. 1946) was teaching religion and working as a youth minister at a Catholic high school when he first studied under Takata in 1978. He recalled, "When [Takata] defined Reiki, she defined it as universal life energy or God-power. And she referred to a Creator or God, often. So, universal life energy didn't connect anyplace with me but God-power did." Mitchell said he felt a "power of presence" in Takata that inspired him to practice daily, although in the first few weeks he could not feel the Reiki energy. "The first time that I had this really clear sensation, what went through my mind was, 'This is divine energy.'" Takata's use of the term "God-power," he clarified, spoke to a "greater reality" that he could "relate easily to the 'greater than' experiences manifested through my practice of Reiki."[49] Thus, Takata's borrowing of Christian language that she learned (at least in part) through her training for the UCM ministry helped Reiki make sense to new audiences. Just as Takata's Shin Buddhist students in transwar Hawai'i connected their Reiki practice to their Buddhist practices and values, Takata's predominantly Christian mainland students made sense of Reiki using resources from their religious worlds.

The SFF and the UCM provided Takata with other resources that helped propagate Reiki to largely White, middle-class audiences in the suburbs of San Francisco and Chicago. J. Gordon Melton (b. 1942), a scholar of religious studies who was the SFF's field director while Takata, Samdahl, and Lombardi taught Reiki in conjunction with that organization, likened the way the SFF provided Reiki Masters with access to preestablished social networks, mailing lists, and spaces for classes (including in mainline Protestant churches) to the ways that the Theosophical Society facilitated the introduction of Indian yogis and other gurus to the United States.[50] Like the Theosophical Society before them, the SFF and the UCM were integral not only in arranging the physical logistics of inviting and lodging instructors, providing venues for their lectures and workshops, and recruiting audiences but also in maintaining the social fields and the discursive and physical spaces that facilitated these audiences' reproduction of those teachers' practices after their departures. Furthermore, they supported Reiki's outreach into their broader local communities, as newspapers in the suburbs around the SFF and Trinity covered Takata's practice and classes.[51]

Public Universities

Religious organizations were not the only institutional settings where Takata taught Reiki in the 1970s. From 1974 to 1976, she taught Reiki through the Bureau of Student Activities at the University of Hawaiʻi at Mānoa in Honolulu. She taught this class at a tremendous discount: First Degree, usually $125 (sometimes $100 or $150) per person, was offered for $20.[52] She may have justified this as a public service to her community, but these classes also paid in prestige, as she and her students consistently mentioned Takata's teaching at the university during interviews, although attendees of her classes there were not necessarily university students.[53]

Another university connection was through George Araki (1932–2006), a biologist at San Francisco State University who was the founding director of the university's Center for Interdisciplinary Science. Araki learned about Takata through a graduate student (and Trinity member) and began studying Reiki in 1978.[54] That spring, Takata began guest lecturing in Araki's seminars on holistic health, where she recruited students for her Reiki classes offered at his home that summer. Paul Mitchell discovered Takata in Araki's class; Paul and his wife, Susan, regularly attended the Thursday-evening "Reiki circle" at the Arakis' home, and Paul and George became Masters the following year.[55] Thus, universities not only helped Takata accrue cultural capital, but her recruitment of students in the classrooms of American public universities, which largely eliminated offering credit for Bible classes over the middle decades of the twentieth century, also demonstrates that her framing of Reiki as a therapeutic practice helped it be considered appropriate for secular educational settings.[56]

Takata strategically used connections to media, religious, and educational institutions to extend her social networks and establish Reiki's legitimacy. Her growing ties to Christian groups gave her and Reiki new types of authority. But religious affiliation could be a double-edged sword. In her media appearances, religious claims like *reiki* "is God, the power he makes available to his children who seek it," were unfailingly paired with the assertion that "it is not a religion," crucial to Reiki's ability to enter secular spaces like the public university classroom.[57] Universities provided Takata with places to recruit and teach but also, perhaps more importantly, affiliations she could cite to gain the trust of new audiences in the same way that she name-dropped connections to medical professionals and celebrities. Print media networks disseminated and amplified these claims to authority at scales of magnitude greater than her word-of-mouth network could in the postwar decades, when she abided by a stronger code of secrecy.

Spiritual Therapies of Asian Descent in 1970s North America

Reiki's growth in the 1970s, when the number of practitioners on the North American mainland went from the dozens to the thousands, benefited from and was partly shaped by broader interest in other spiritual therapies of Asian descent. The final third of the twentieth century saw a tremendous rise in the prevalence and prestige of religious and therapeutic practices in North America ascribed Asian origins, including yoga, meditation, and acupuncture. Their North American presence was not entirely new: religious and medical practices of Asian origin have been in North America since the early nineteenth century, and practices ascribed Asian origins by Orientalist imaginations date to the early days of the American republic.[58] But political and cultural shifts in the 1960s caused an upswell of such practices and their gradual movement from fringe to mainstream.

The Immigration and Naturalization Act of 1965 changed the racist quota system instituted in the early 1920s, which had effectively prohibited Asian immigration, to a system where each nation was assigned an equal quota.[59] Increased numbers of Asian Americans meant increased presence of Asian cultural practices. These political and demographic shifts coincided with a period of social unrest, during which mistrust of dominant medical and religious institutions swelled, a phenomenon that has been called the end of biomedicine's "golden age" and the rise of "a generation of seekers" looking for holistic healing and spiritual fulfillment.[60] The holistic health movement grew out of the late 1960s counterculture and its interest in "alternate currents" including "Eastern philosophy and medicine, and . . . Western heterodox medical systems."[61]

By the 1970s, trends sparked by the 1960s youth counterculture entered the mainstream. The popular television show *Kung Fu* (1972–1975) brought spiritual wisdom and powers attributed to the mystic East, hybridized with the genre conventions of the television Western, into American living rooms every Thursday night.[62] *Kung Fu* was just one of many Orientalist depictions of Asian monks and gurus in the period's mass media, but its vivid portrayal of young Caine's discipleship under his Shaolin masters is particularly relevant to the case of Reiki. Of course, not all of Takata's students in the 1970s were avid viewers of this program, but its popularity meant that the concept of the novice submitting to an aged, enigmatic Asian master would have been stronger in their consciousness than in earlier eras.

Master Kan taught Caine about qi, the Chinese conception of vital force that underlies much of East Asian medical and religious beliefs (in Japanese, it is the *ki* of *reiki*), and Americans in the early 1970s were curious about qi's healing applications. Demand for "Oriental medicine" surged in the United States following a 1971 *New York Times* front-page story in which an American reporter making a historic trip to the People's Republic of China described the efficacy of acupuncture and moxibustion in postoperative care following the emergency removal of his appendix.[63] Inspired by his story and other media coverage of acupuncture during President Richard Nixon's trip to China the following year, busloads of Americans traveled hundreds of miles to urban Chinatowns seeking treatment. During this "acupuncture craze," Chinese Americans traveled to Hong Kong for brief acupuncture courses so they could set up clinics in the United States, where Chinese medicine was unregulated.[64] Americans understood acupuncture and other East Asian health practices like qigong in religious terms. Physicians decried "the acupuncture cult" and suggested that practitioners were akin to "miracle-working gurus or evangelists," while the metaphysically minded read qi in terms of their own religious beliefs about "energy."[65] These alternate currents, like Reiki, were adapted for American audiences, were understood as alternatives to orthodox medicine and religion, and oscillated between the language of physics, physiology, and spirituality.[66]

Media coverage of Takata in the mid-1970s explicitly connected Reiki to the acupuncture boom. A *Maui Times* interview said Takata "credits President Nixon with much of America's present awareness of natural healing powers, because he opened up China where everyone could see millions of people living in health, not because there are so many doctors but because there are other forms of medicine available, acupuncture among them."[67] Another article in a Chicago-area newspaper, "Reiki: Japanese Method of Healing Could Spark Public Interest Similar to Chinese Acupuncture," predicted, "Reiki may prove to create as many problems for the medical profession as the Chinese art of acupuncture."[68] Its author, a Reiki practitioner named Mary Straub (1929–2009), did not explicitly link these two practices as qi phenomena, but rather as imports from East Asia that challenged Western biomedical hegemony through their mysterious efficacy.

Straub (channeling Takata) contrasted Reiki with biomedicine, which holistic health proponents thought overemphasized physical factors while overlooking psychological and spiritual health, by associating Reiki with the profundity of Eastern religion and the potency of cosmic vibrations. "Reiki's origin," she wrote, "is Zen Buddhism, its secret key was gleaned from the Sutras (an Eastern philosophical format) by Buddhist monk, Dr. Usui, its first master [*sic*]." Here, Straub (again, following Takata) drew on American interest in Zen to imply that Reiki students are initiated into a lineage that extends to the Japanese monastery. In calling Reiki a "national art" of Japan, Straub drew a comparison to other Japanese arts, from swordsmanship to tea ceremony, linked to Zen in the postwar period by promoters such as D. T. Suzuki in his popular *Zen and Japanese Culture* (1959). Indeed, Takata often mentioned Reiki in the same breath with other Japanese exports like karate and ikebana flower arrangement.[69]

Straub did not mention qi as such, but quoted Takata calling *reiki* "cosmic energy," continuing, "The diseased organs literally drink up the Reiki that is in the hands of the healer, the vibrations penetrating deep into areas that need it, Mrs. Takata explains. Often we're not even aware of where our trouble actually lies until the reaction is felt beneath the healer's touch." This suggests that Reiki mediates the mystical and the material, revealing and removing the unseen causes of physical ailments in ways unavailable to other medical practices. Based on these factors, Straub concludes, "Reiki could be the importation of the century," again stressing its foreignness, but now also suggesting its superiority over other Asian imports such as acupuncture, martial arts, and Zen, due to the efficacy of its treatments.

While some Reiki practitioners in the 1970s understood Takata and her practice in light of Christian commitments, others came to her out of involvement in other Asia-derived practices like meditation, yoga, and guru devotion. John Harvey Gray discovered Transcendental Meditation (TM) while a systems programmer at the Stanford Research Institute in 1973, and he credited it with saving his life by introducing him to other states of consciousness, leading to him leaving his job and following his "soul path" of a spiritual healer and teacher.[70] His involvement in TM, a Hindu-inspired meditation movement, provided him with resources to make sense of Takata and her stories. For example, Takata told of her teacher Hayashi Chūjirō's foreknowledge of his death date, assembling his students to say goodbye, and naming her as his successor before consciously stopping his heart; Gray interpreted Hayashi's ability to do this as evidence that he was "an enlightened human being," a phrase Takata never used herself in this context.[71] As mentioned previously, the hagiographies of Usui and Hayashi that Takata recounted drew on conventions in miracle stories of other Asian holy men, and her students' familiarity with that genre added to their value. It also became common to describe one's experience with Reiki in terms of the chakra system derived from Indic traditions; one student told Takata in a letter that, in their class, she felt Takata "[sending] charges of electrical energy through the crown chakra and throughout the body . . . a most profound experience."[72]

Others came to Reiki directly through their interest in yoga. In 1978, Rick Bockner (b. 1948), a musician and woodworker, was living a back-to-the-land lifestyle among other conscientious objectors to the Vietnam War in Argenta, a remote, small town in the rural Kootenay region of southeastern British Columbia. Nearly forty years later, sitting in a tranquil forest near the shoreline of British Columbia's Cortes Island, where Bockner currently lives, he told me about how he found Reiki. At a yoga retreat held by Baba Hari Dass (1923–2018), an Indian yogi and early promoter of Ayurveda in North America, Bockner saw an advertisement on the bulletin board for a Reiki healing class and a friend urged him to take the course. He and his wife were interested, as they were having difficulty conceiving a child, but they were unable to connect with Takata on that visit. A year later, they had divorced and Bockner was despondent. A friend told him Takata had returned to teach again and although he was reluctant in his depressed state, she paid his tuition and forced him to attend. He was not fully engaged in the class until a moment when Takata did something that sparked a memory of a "shockingly powerful" dream he had had about four years earlier that had been the basis for a song he wrote.

In the dream, Bockner was in a burned-out forest when he encountered a large grizzly bear; it stood up on its hind legs and terrifyingly reached its paws into the sky, shocking him "with an Oriental human face." Frozen, he was surprised when the bear came down from this stance and led him and about twelve others to a cabin in the forest, where five "subtly powerful" older women gave them tea and cookies. Years later, at the Reiki class in a little house in the woods, he was wondering what he was doing there until Takata suddenly turned to him, reached her hands into the air as the bear had done, and said in a forceful voice, "Reiki very powerful!" "All of a sudden," Bockner recalled,

> my hair started to tingle and my spine started the kundalini reactions
> and, oh man, I knew that this was momentous. . . . If it hadn't been for
> that dream, I wouldn't be here [as a Reiki Master] today . . . because I
> also had a very strong Jewish, middle-class, leftist cynicism about things
> spiritual and things relating to authority, so it was very easy for me to
> put something down and not fully embrace it.[73]

In this dream, Bockner was in the moment of despair when he encountered the power of nature, mediated through a teacher with an Asian countenance. Despite her small stature, Takata conveyed the power of the grizzly, which Bockner experienced in an embodied experience rooted in yogic meditation on the kundalini energy that follows the spine. This experience shocked Bockner out of his skepticism and into a state of devotion to a spiritual teacher. When he told Takata about his experience, she offered to teach him First and Second Degree back-to-back, something Bockner said she reserved for "people she felt were receptive." This mystical example demonstrates how prior experiences with Asia-derived spiritual therapies helped structure the experiences and unconscious minds of Takata's students in the 1970s, making them more amenable to accepting the authority of this Japanese American and her healing art, ascribed to Japan. It also shows how these individuals narrativized their encounters with Takata to help make sense (to themselves and to others) of their discipleship to her and their dedication to Reiki. Such narratives are part of a broader connection between Reiki as a spiritual calling and Reiki as a professional vocation that the next section examines in detail.

The "Japanization" of Reiki in 1970s North America

Takata's approach in the 1970s, which laid the foundation for the dominant forms of Reiki worldwide in the following decades, was based on an ambivalent form of universalism. At the same time that she described Reiki as "universal life energy" and its practice as available to all, regardless of religious or ethnoracial background, she also believed elements of Japanese culture were essential to its efficacious functioning. This belief exceeded the Orientalization at work in her claims that Reiki "is spoken of in the ancient history of Japan" and Reiki's "formula" came from a Buddhist sutra that Usui discovered while studying at a Zen temple.[74] Rather, Takata desired that her students internalize aspects of Japanese culture. She expressed this desire explicitly, assigning her 1970s students books on Japanese Buddhism to improve their Reiki practice, as she had in 1938 Chicago, and implicitly, changing Reiki instruction and practice to inculcate certain "Japanese values" into her students, including reverence of secret knowledge, authority, and reciprocity.[75] Yet at the same time that Takata used Oriental markers to exoticize Reiki's history and made changes to "Japanize" Reiki practice for her largely White students, she also incorporated hegemonic elements of Christian and professional culture to make Reiki more accessible and attractive to her audiences. In the terms of translation theory, Takata simultaneously "foreignized" Reiki as a practice derived from Japanese Buddhism and "domesticated" it with the discourses of Christianity and professionalism.[76]

Oral Tradition

One innovation Takata instilled in her students in the 1970s was the idea that Reiki is an oral tradition, to be passed directly from teacher to student without taking notes. This was particularly stressed regarding the symbols she taught in the Second Degree and Master training: any scrap of paper on which they were written during training was to be collected and burned. In the decades following Takata's death, the written word has held a contested position in Reiki communities, with many practitioners taking exception to books and websites that publish the symbols.

On the one hand, this resonates with Usui Reiki Therapy's derivation from other "oral transmission" (*kuden*) Japanese practices and the code of secrecy practiced in Usui's and Hayashi's organizations. However, as Takata took notes in her training, received copies of Hayashi's printed handbook (which she distributed in her early classes in Hawai'i), and received a personalized book from Hayashi in which he wrote the Second Degree symbols using a calligraphic brush, she also invented certain new conventions around how she wanted her students to honor the oral tradition.[77]

Takata's invention of Reiki's oral tradition had multiple motivations and effects, but one way to understand it is as a way of translating the practice of "secret transmission" (*hiden*) common to Japanese arts for American audiences. As described in chapter 2, this practice had roots in esoteric Buddhism but was professionalized in early modern Japan, where "secret teachings were commodified and made ready for retail."[78] Usui Reiki Therapy incorporated different aspects of secret transmission, including the idea that mastery could only be transmitted through physical practice, not writing, and that "abuse of words" could have catastrophic consequences.[79] The pedagogy and epistemology of secret transmission were local practices in prewar Japan, where Takata trained, and Usui's and Hayashi's handbooks made no mention of the practice of *reiju* or the advanced symbols. Still, by prohibiting note taking and the retention of the written symbols, Takata exceeded the proscriptions of her forebears to (over)compensate for her North American students' relative unfamiliarity with protocols around the treatment of secret knowledge.[80]

Respect for Authority

Takata's emphasis on oral tradition was but one of several changes she made in this period that strengthened her authority as "the only teacher of the Usui system of Reiki in the world today."[81] Around 1976, Takata added "Honor your parents, teachers, and elders" to Usui's five precepts (or the "Reiki Ideals," as she now called them), the most significant of several changes she made to the precepts over her teaching career.[82] Like Takata's emphasis on the direct transmission of oral culture, this ideal (still employed by many Takata-lineage Reiki practitioners today) told students to listen closely to her words and to accept her teachings without question. Its language combines the Mosaic "Honor your father and mother" with Confucian reverence for nonkin hierarchical relations.[83] Takata's predominantly first- and second-generation Nikkei students in Hawai'i, socialized in families with Confucian heritage, may not have needed this lesson, which she only developed after teaching on the mainland. With this new Reiki Ideal, Takata creatively combined foreignizing and domesticating elements to inculcate her predominantly White North American students with another "Japanese" value.

Exchange of Energies

A third example of Takata's creative bridging of cultural difference is her explanation of Reiki's operation via an "exchange of energies." She enshrined this value of reciprocity in a parable she developed of the founder's charitable work in a "beggars' camp." After developing Reiki, she said, Usui spent seven years healing the indigent, without payment, so they could be productive members of society. Eventually those he had healed returned to begging, and Usui was devastated. He realized "the spiritual is number one"—that is, that the beggars were unable to truly heal because, receiving treatments without giving anything in exchange, they were ungrateful. She reinforced this story with an account of her experience teaching Reiki for free to her in-laws after returning to Hawai'i from Japan but, because they learned it for free, they never valued their initiations and took their children to her for treatments rather than treating them themselves. After that, she said, she charged everyone, even her own sisters, because that helped them to cultivate the gratitude necessary to make their initiations and treatments effective.[84]

Takata developed this parable at some point in the postwar period, as when I recounted it to Takata's early Nikkei students in Hilo, they were dumbfounded. As described in chapter 3, Nikkei practitioners were critical of charging for Reiki, but their patients were socialized to give gifts of gratitude called *orei* after receiving treatments, sometimes for years after one's recovery. Hence, among other motivations (such as the justification of her commoditization of Reiki practice), the rhetoric of an "exchange of energies" helped Takata codify an ethic of reciprocity for her later, non-Nikkei students that went unsaid among her earlier, Nikkei ones.

It is tempting to read Takata's general refusal to allow students to document her words, her presentation of respect for one's teacher as a moral imperative, and her rhetoric of an "exchange of energies" to cultivate gratitude as moves to strengthen her authority and justify the high fees for Reiki training. However, in addition to the instrumentality of establishing absolute deference to her authority and sacralizing monetary payments, Takata's inculcation of her students with respect for secrecy, hierarchy, and reciprocity seems to have been at least partly rooted in anxiety about transmitting a "Japanese" healing art to non-Nikkei students socialized with quite different values, especially given the 1970s' countercultural values of questioning authority and sharing freely. In a sense, her experience teaching non-Nikkei students in the transwar decades may have led her to appreciate why Hayashi had initially hesitated to teach her, an American, in the 1930s: in some sense, the system of Usui Reiki Therapy relied on students' embodiment of "Japanese" values. Thus, Takata's adaptations of Reiki for North Americans added elements she understood to engender her predominantly White students with cultural values she associated with Japaneseness and, as such, resist neat interpretations of instrumentality and Westernization.

Japanizing Reiki under Christian Hegemony

This said, Takata's adaptations and her students' uptake of Reiki practice accommodated cultural aspects of their time and place. As seen in chapter 4, Takata took on perennialist language in the immediate postwar period, and by the 1970s, she began reinterpreting Reiki with Christian terminology, translating Reiki as "God-power" and referencing Christian scripture, developments that introduced tensions with her accounts of Reiki's Buddhist origin and its accessibility to people of all religions. As with her explanation of the "exchange of energies," Takata's chief tool to navigate this tension was the parable.

By the mid-1970s, Takata had fully developed the "master narrative" of Usui's biography.[85] In this story, Usui was a minister and educator at a Christian school in Kyoto in the late 1800s.[86] He was sent into crisis by a student's questions about how Jesus was able to perform healing and why the church no longer practiced this gift. He traveled "to study Christianity in a Christian country," enrolling at the University of Chicago but to no avail, as there too the secrets of this healing power seem to have been forgotten. Learning that the Buddha had also been a great healer, he returned to Kyoto to see if any temple retained his healing methods. He traveled to all of Kyoto's temples to no avail, so he entered a Zen monastery to study scripture. The Japanese versions yielded nothing, so he learned and studied the original Chinese; stymied again, he learned and studied the original Sanskrit, where he discovered Reiki's "formula" and decided he had to test it. He retreated to the mountains outside the city, fasting and meditating for twenty-one days. On the dawn of the final morning, a great light descended from the sky and struck him in the head, knocking him unconscious. When he came to and descended from the mountain, he discovered he had healing powers when he laid his hands on the injured and ill. He devoted his life to healing others and teaching his method to his disciples. Usui's successor, Hayashi, named Takata as his successor, and she was the world's sole remaining teacher of Usui's Reiki system.

This narrative combines the icon of the Oriental Monk with the logic of particular universalism. As described in chapter 4, the Oriental Monk is an aged Asian figure who transmits the spiritual wisdom of the ancient East to a "bridge figure"—a Western disciple in tension with the dominant culture—a transmission that represents the "future salvation of the dominant culture."[87] While Orientalism has long influenced American perceptions and appropriations of traditions ascribed to Asia, baby boomers' "seeker spirituality" particularly sought "personal experience and transformation" in "Asian religions . . . [and] their enigmatic teachers, who seemed to provide the discipline and attention without the stifling structures of church or synagogue."[88] Takata's narrative does not precisely follow Jane Iwamura's template, as she acted as an intermediate bridge to the absent Oriental

Monk of Usui, but many of her students found that Reiki practice fulfilled a need for spiritual transformation, even one of which they were previously unaware. Takata asserted that Reiki was a universal practice that underlay the healing powers of both Jesus and Buddha, uncovered by Usui from an ancient Sanskrit sutra, presenting a theosophical-style vision of Asia as a treasure house preserving a once-universal wisdom tradition. At the same time, her "Japanization" of Reiki is not purely perennialist but rather a form of particular universalism, in which one culture has privileged access to the reality toward which all cultures are oriented.

This model can be productively applied to the type of Japanese exceptionalism promoted in the postwar United States by Zen apologist D. T. Suzuki (among others). Suzuki explained Zen as an ostensibly uniquely Japanese "'spiritual technology' capable of inculcating the mystical experience that lay at the source of all authentic religious insight," and his American disciples took it as a therapeutic for the ills of Western modernity.[89] When Takata said that Usui discovered "a formula" in a Buddhist sutra in a Zen monastery, actualized that formula with austerities atop a sacred mountain, and passed down the boon he achieved through an initiation lineage, she framed Reiki as a path to gain the privileged access to the ground of Being—whether one calls it universal life energy or God-power—that the Japanese have uniquely retained from time immemorial.

Takata cast Usui as a Christian minister seeking the secret of Jesus' healing powers, which he could not find in his own church or in his scholarly pursuit of Christianity, making him a relatable hero figure for her North American audiences onto whom they could project their frustrations with their own religious communities. The fact that Buddhist monastics had also long forgotten the art of healing but preserved it within their sutras allowed Reiki to draw on Buddhism's cultural cachet without making students nervous that their initiation was a conversion to a foreign religion.

Particularly in the late 1970s, Takata's ministerial status and Christianized language of Reiki as "God-power" worked in tandem with her racialized features and heavy accent to reinforce "the logic of affiliation as well as difference" at the core of Cold War Orientalism.[90] For example, Paul Mitchell told me he never felt any conflict about Reiki's foreignness when he took his First Degree in 1978: "It was just like one of God's gifts, one of His blessings coming through this [practice]. . . . There's certain gifts of the Holy Spirit and one of them is healing." He sensed the Reiki initiation was a sacrament, in addition to the seven of Catholicism, a sense reinforced the following year, during his Master training, when he asked Takata the meaning of the kanji of the Master symbol. She replied, "For the Protestants it's like the Great Light, and for Catholics it would be the Holy Ghost, and for me it was like, oh yeah! So for me, it really is this universal practice."[91] Thus, Takata's addition of original practices to Reiki—practices she considered to help North American students internalize Japanese cultural values that she believed were essential to Reiki's efficacy—took place in a matrix of Christian hegemony.

Professionalization

Takata's development of the rhetoric of an "exchange of energies," symbolized in her parables and concretized in her significant fees for treatment and training, took another element of hegemonic culture to translate the value of reciprocity she considered lacking in her students. In this case, rather than Christianity, she borrowed from the fee structure of professionalized services. Her translation of Usui's precept *gyō o hageme* (fulfill your duty) into the Reiki Ideal, "Earn your living honestly," was tied up with a new vision of Reiki therapist as a professional vocation.[92] She advised students in this period to set fees for Reiki treatments by finding out what local massage therapists charged and charging slightly more, "because Reiki is more than massage," which operates strictly on the physical level. Reiki was of the utmost value, she taught, because "health is number one": without good health, nothing else is possible. The metaphysics of exchange suggest that the act of giving up something of value cultivates the gratitude needed to render a healing or initiation effective. Takata's class lists and financial records indicate that she often shared portions of her proceeds with her local organizers and made sizable donations to churches that hosted her classes. Reiki was never exactly a multilevel marketing organization, but these types of professional exchanges between the itinerant master and her local disciples, concretized in cash and symbolized as gratitude, add another dimension to Reiki's evolution.

That said, while perusal of the list of practitioners at any holistic health clinic in contemporary North America will probably reveal at least one professional Reiki therapist, Reiki is probably most often practiced without a cash fee. Self-treatment, of course, involves no exchange. Practitioners often treat friends and family without expectation of a particular exchange, justified by the fact that people in intimate relationships are always doing acts of service for one another. "Reiki circles" are sites where treatments are mutually exchanged, sometimes with a small fee or donation for the host's troubles (and to defray the cost of snacks). And countercultural communities that consciously chose to reject modern consumerism, like Takata's back-to-the-land students in the British Columbia interior, seem to have most often given Reiki treatments, even initiations, on the barter system. Even Takata had exceptions to her fee structure.[93]

But in the 1970s Takata was often insistent regarding the spiritual power of gratitude, concretized in a cash payment. In language reminiscent of prosperity theology, she insisted this fee would be returned many times over, not only by saving on doctors' bills but also in other forms of material success. During the conclusion of the free lecture she gave to recruit students for upcoming classes, she recounted how her sister, whom she charged for the Reiki class, "is a very, very successful woman. She has not failed in her business. She has her own business." In contrast, those whom she taught for free, "not one of them is a success. Not even in business nor in their health. And therefore my teachers were right, they were absolutely right."[94] Thus, she encouraged students to make whatever financial sacrifices were necessary in order to pay the fees for training, as they would be rewarded in time. Takata combined this metaphysical rhetoric with aspects of professionalization—such as the reinstatement of certificates, absent from her teaching from the late 1930s to the mid-1970s—as characteristic of her insistence, in her later years, that her students consider Reiki as a possible professional vocation as well as a path for holistic healing and spiritual development. And again, as Takata's teaching in the late 1970s was the foundation of what Reiki would become in subsequent decades, the entanglement that emerged at this time between practitioners seeing it as their "calling" both as spiritual practice and as profession continues today.

Takata as an Elder

In addition to the other factors that facilitated Takata's tremendous productivity in the last years of her career, in which she taught thousands of students and grossed hundreds of thousands of dollars, one must consider her embodied charisma as a wise and powerful elder. Every one of my interlocutors who studied with her in this late period spoke reverentially of her possessing "a presence" or an "energy" that was qualitatively different from the descriptions by those who studied with her in Hawai'i decades prior. The emergence of Takata's powerful charisma in her final years resulted from an intersection of exogenous and endogenous factors, including meanings her students projected onto her aging body and the bearing that comes from decades of experience as a spiritual therapist.

Takata already inspired adoration by the time of her 1951 trip to the US mainland; proclamations that one is "surely a messenger to humanity" do not come easily.[95] But her students increasingly commented on her charisma as she increased in age and experience. Describing her visits to British Columbia in her late seventies, Rick Bockner said, "She carried Reiki with her like a neon sign, without saying anything. Really, people would see her coming down the street when we were going somewhere and they would just stop. . . . They picked up on her energy."[96] Takata's diminutive stature, elegant bearing, and striking clothing choices were often commented on by my other interlocutors and in her print appearances, but Bockner insisted her conspicuousness had to do with her "energy," not that she was a petite, elderly Asian American with a predilection for brightly colored outfits in a predominantly working-class White region dominated by timber and agriculture.

In addition to Bockner's experience of Takata reenacting a prophetic dream, several other students from this period reported paranormal occurrences in conjunction with their first meeting of Takata. Bockner's friend Wanja Twan (1934–2019) took the Reiki course in 1978 after being led to Takata through a series of paranormal experiences. Twan's experiences (like Samdahl's) involved *Healers,* and (like Bockner's) they encouraged her to fight through initial resistance to taking the course. As Twan finally entered the home where the course was offered, she said, Takata descended the stairs in a fine gown, looked her in the eye, and said, "I knew you would come," causing her hair to stand on end and filling her with deep trust. Wanja later had Takata come teach classes in her home, including to her two daughters. Anneli Twan (b. 1968) told me, "When I met Takata, there was something with her presence. Like you know when you meet an Indian, like a guru, and there's something that strikes you that there's something with them. . . . I could just see this huge white light around Takata and just the strength that she carried."[97] Anneli's memory is interpreted through encounters with Indian gurus in the 1980s, but her immediate impression of Takata's bright aura told her, even at ten years old, that this elderly lady was special and possessed profound strength despite her frail stature.

A more mundane, oft-cited example of Takata's vitality was her regular golfing. She may have begun to pick up the game in her twenties, when

Saichi used it to fraternize with the planter families and other White elites of Kauaʻi, but she seems to have come into her own in her fifties and sixties, when she won a number of tournaments at the Ala Wai Golf Course near her Honolulu home.[98] In every newspaper article about her in the mid-1970s, she bragged about playing nine holes daily as an index of her energy. "'I've been playing golf every morning for nearly 30 years,' she declared. 'And I don't ride the cart either—I walk.'"[99] She told similar stories to her students, which perhaps influenced their perception of her as a preternaturally "energetic" septuagenarian.[100]

Takata's age inspired reverence as an index of her life experience and her impending mortality. Sally Hammond asked Takata in 1972 about the initiation process and "if there was any danger of the secret dying with her"; Takata replied, "Before I die I want to teach as many people as I can, spread it to as many people as possible and create many teachers."[101] The following year, Takata seems to have trained one of her first Masters, Eulalia Atkinson (1920–1997), but Atkinson may not have trained any students of her own due to personal struggles.[102] After Atkinson, Takata trained a total of twenty-two Masters between her first heart attack in 1975 and a second, ultimately fatal one in December 1980.[103] With two notable exceptions, these Masters resided in four locales: Hawaiʻi, Northern California, Chicago, and the British Columbia Interior.[104]

The sense that Takata was nearing the end of life lent urgency to the process of training Masters, both for her and for her students. John Harvey Gray recalls that her decision to train a number of Masters was spurred by her heart attack. She immediately taught the initiation method to her younger sister, Setsuko "Kay" Kawamura Hamamoto Yamashita (1912–1987), and told North American Master students in subsequent years that they could travel to Hawaiʻi to complete their training with Kay in case she died prematurely.[105] In late 1976, Takata sent her students a "Seasons Greetings" notice announcing her retirement and the continuation of her work by John Gray, Virginia Samdahl, and Ethel Lombardi.[106] However, she continued traveling and teaching up until her death. In these final years, concerned about her legacy, she privately asked several individuals to be her successor, contributing to contestation in the 1980s about who would follow Takata as Reiki's fourth "Grand Master."[107] Takata could have averted this "succession crisis" with a public announcement about her chosen successor before her death, and it is likely that she planned to do so but faded unexpectedly quickly.[108]

The Reiki currents that flowed through Takata into her grateful students branched out into many new streams in the years that followed her "transition" and continued to evolve through the bidirectional influences exhibited between practitioners and patients, Masters and disciples, as Reiki circulated around the globe. Helen Haberly employs this metaphor in the conclusion of her biography of her Master: "During [Takata's] time Reiki was brought from East to West, and through her, it flowed like a river, a single channel deep and broad . . . [but after her death] the river of Reiki which was a single channel in Mrs. Takata now flowed in two major streams," referring to the followers of Phyllis Lei Furumoto, Takata's granddaughter, and Barbara Weber Ray (1941–2020), Furumoto's chief challenger in succession. Haberly also mentions Masters who "work independently, without connection to any group," who came to far outnumber practitioners in the "two major streams."[109] Befitting a story about currents, Reiki's circulation has continued to diversify and transform in subsequent decades, so that today there are literally dozens of streams of Reiki, most of which trace their transmissions to Hawayo Takata.

The deep reverence Takata's students showed her in her final years demonstrates how her advanced age and deepened experience helped her fulfill their expectations of a spiritual teacher. The nature of these expectations appears differently from different perspectives. Emic narratives might attribute her growth in charisma to her strengthened connection to the cosmic source of Reiki's energy as she entered her fifth decade of practice and "transitioned" out of the physical realm altogether, but etic ones could explain them as a growth in symbolic power, as she further refined the techniques she used to establish authority and her time became an increasingly limited commodity.

Conclusion

Sally Hammond, whose story opens this chapter, does not seem to have ever learned Reiki and may never have seen Takata after their one fateful meeting in fall 1972. They corresponded for a couple of years, with Takata sending distance treatments to Hammond's sister, Marcelle (who enjoyed remarkable recovery through a combination of chemotherapy and holistic interventions), and Sally showing great interest in organizing classes for Takata in New York. However, these classes may never have come to fruition, especially as Hammond returned a check Takata sent her in advance as a thank-you. About a year later Marcelle's cancer returned, and she ultimately succumbed to it in 1976. Based on Takata's surviving correspondence, the letters from the Hammond sisters seem to have dwindled as Marcelle's condition worsened, and it is possible that their faith in Reiki declined with her health.

One bias built into studying the history of a current like Reiki is that the majority of the data—promotional media accounts, testimonials from grateful clients and students, interviews with longtime practitioners—highlights its successes. Its failings are mostly legible through negative spaces: gaps in the historical record, a sudden end to a robust exchange of letters. This is compounded by another bias for recentness. In terms of both archived materials and finding subjects for oral history interviews, I found more numerous and robust accounts of Takata's later years, with the exception of the brief, intense media coverage of Reiki in Honolulu's Japanese-language press during Hayashi's 1937–1938 visit.

Yet even considering these biases, Takata's successes teaching Reiki in the 1970s substantially exceeded those in prior decades both in their quantitative reach and in their qualitative depth of connection. Many of those whom I interviewed who studied Reiki in this period considered it a life-changing spiritual practice and, like Takata before them, dedicated their lives to its practice and teaching. Few in earlier generations had this long-term zeal. Even the most accomplished Reiki healers from transwar Hawai'i pursued it as a service they were happy to provide to others (and one that gained them local renown and social status), but their Reiki practice supplemented other spiritual and professional pursuits rather than forming the core of their identity. Thus, Reiki's professionalization between the 1930s and the 1970s went hand in hand with its transformation into a practice to which one might dedicate one's life. Takata's translation of Usui's fourth precept as, "Earn your living honestly," helped her postwar audiences to spiritualize their labor, and her 1970s discourse of an "exchange of energies," symbolized in the parable of Usui in the beggars' camp, tied payment for services to another of Reiki's core spiritual practices: the cultivation of gratitude. The potential to make one's living as a Reiki professional, whether one invested the substantial money to train as a Master and teach or simply as a practitioner, deepened the sense in which Reiki functioned as a complete system for Takata's students, particularly in a capitalist society that often equates one's profession with one's personal identity.

This connection between Reiki's potential as a professional and a spiritual vocation both supports and complicates claims that the cultural forms identified as "spirituality" in the late twentieth and early twenty-first centuries function as the "opiate of the bourgeoisie," helping the middle class adjust psychologically to late capitalism through sacralizing quietism and spiritualizing labor.[110] Reiki, as taught in this period, worked well with aspects of capitalist logics and systems, but its practitioners also critiqued commodification. When I asked Phyllis Furumoto and Paul Mitchell to explain why coverage of Reiki in commercial print media is compatible with Reiki as an "oral tradition" whereas advertising is not, Furumoto told me newspaper articles are an extension of word of mouth, while advertising reduces Reiki to "a product." Mitchell agreed, adding that advertising promises that a product will fulfill a consumer's need, whereas Takata and journalists told stories that allowed "prospective students to have a connection with the energy."[111] Thus, Takata not only withdrew from her prewar practice of advertising her treatments and classes in print media but trained her students in the 1970s to feel antipathy toward advertisement as overly commodifying, while at the same time considering the exchange of money to be capable of concretizing the spiritual value of gratitude.

As such, emic perspectives might describe the exchange of a treatment or initiation for cash as more closely resembling gift exchange than commodity exchange, as it comes from an "obligation to reciprocate" that establishes social relationships that can endure after the payment.[112] The asymmetrical relationship between therapist and patient or master and disciple can be mapped onto the capitalist relations of producer and consumer, but that does not exhaust their significance. Is Reiki the co-option of cultural critique by capitalist relations, or is it a translation of sacramental relationships for a society dominated by fee-for-service relationships? Examining Reiki's practice in localized communities that tended toward a barter economy and other cashless forms of exchange opens a third possibility for its economies to be counterhegemonic. Wanja Twan and others who practiced Reiki in the rural British Columbia interior describe the treatments and healing circles in their homes in ways that more closely resemble the unspoken assumption of reciprocity seen in earlier generations of Reiki practitioners than the explicit exchange of fee for service by more professionalized practitioners.

Finally, Takata's simultaneous foreignization and domestication of Reiki further complicates a simple understanding in terms of hegemony and counterhegemony. For example, her addition to Usui's precepts ("Honor your parents, teachers, and elders") may have been couched in the language of the Ten Commandments, but it was an attempt to instill her non-Nikkei students with the reverence of authority socialized in Japanese families. This reinforces a kind of quietism that serves the interest of the status quo and critiques the antiauthoritarianism of North American counterculture. But it also assigns a privileged position to "Japanese" values for those who desire to channel "universal energy," a mode that I call particular universalism. Takata's narrative of Usui finding the "formula" of Jesus' healing powers in an ancient Buddhist sutra, manifesting those powers through mountain-top austerities, and initiating students to similarly cultivate these powers inherits Orientalist and Occidentalist critiques of Western modernity as suffering from spiritual malaise due to its overemphasis of materialism. This follows a broader ambivalence to dominant cultural authorities in Takata's rhetoric that continues in Reiki and other spiritual therapies today. Takata called on multiple religious and medical authorities to help authorize her unorthodox practice for new audiences while also engaging in the rhetoric of cultural critique. This ambivalence is related to the ambivalence toward capitalist relations described earlier. Ultimately, Reiki in the 1970s gained symbolic capital in relation to but also in distinction from dominant systems.

The unprecedented success as a teacher that Hawayo Takata enjoyed in the final years of her life was related to a number of developments both within and outside her control. Broader social, cultural, and political developments led to shifts in the meanings of Japaneseness in postwar North America, and the 1970s saw growing interest in spiritual therapies ascribed to Asia. These factors, combined with broader interest in spiritual therapies as part of the growing movement that would come to be known as the New Age, helped facilitate Takata's use of print media, religious organizations, and universities to extend networks and build authority. Her innovations drew on the allure of Japanese culture, the familiarity of Christian rhetoric, and the professionalization of health services, situating Reiki in ambivalent relationships with cultural authorities that attracted middle-class audiences both enmeshed in and critical of mainstream culture. Finally, as a woman in her seventies entering her fifth decade of teaching a spiritual therapy, her authority grew with her mastery of her medium of storytelling and, as she became an elder nearing her mortal end, her spiritual capital became palpable to many whom she encountered.

Conclusion

Among the ironies of the so-called globalization era has been the resurgence of the importance of nations. Not long ago, scholars predicted that nations were in decline, giving way to regional or global systems, but today nativists and protectionists lash out against the transnational mobility of people and goods, dissolve trade agreements, and strengthen borders.[1] At the same time, nations are subject to the rise of other types of transnational mobility. At the macro scale, organizations like the International Monetary Fund and the World Bank exert tremendous influence on national economies; at the micro scale, internet connectivity and the ease of uploading user-generated content allow for the circulation of ideas and practices at unprecedented rates. Yet stark differences remain between haves and have-nots, many of which relate to national issues of infrastructure and regulation. Even the digital world, which seems like an apt metaphor for the immateriality of spirit in that it transmits knowledge and produces visions out of the flow of intangible electrons, is tied to material conditions at different scales ranging from the individual (socioeconomic level) to the community (broadband infrastructure) to the national (firewalls, public subsidies, etc.).

Nations also contribute their symbolic power to the potency of what I call transnational spiritual therapies, which include Reiki, meditation, and yoga, as well as (arguably) practices such as *curanderismo* (the folk healing traditions of Latin America) and healing practices derived from Afro-Caribbean and Indigenous religions. These are not simply spiritual therapies in transnational circulation (which they are), but rather their "nationality" is essential to their practices, enacted materially in practitioners' bodies, artifacts,

and spaces. Even when practiced in their ostensible land of origin, these practices' ancestral originators and imagined homelands (displaced in time, if not
in space) are "positive Others" crucial to practitioners' claims to spiritual and
therapeutic potency.[2] Furthermore, practicing a transnational spiritual
therapy affords practitioners a kind of imagined "citizenship" in a nonter-
ritorial nation that collectively desires a home that both is and is not the
geographical place attributed as the practice's origin.[3] This ambivalence of
the "spiritual homeland" is tangible in pilgrims' accounts of disappointment in discrepancies between expectation and reality, with which they must
grapple to make meaning of their journey.[4] These spiritual therapies are also
transnational in the sense that their modern forms (including, in many cases,
practitioners' attribution of potency to their ostensible sites of origin) have
developed out of transnational exchanges.[5]

This is not to flatten salient differences in the meanings practitioners
of these therapies assign to their "source" nations. As a transnational spiritual therapy primarily practiced outside its ostensible land of origin, by
people with few (if any) other ties to Japan or people of Japanese ancestry,
Reiki may be a particularly exoticized case, as opposed to *curanderismo* and
Afro-Caribbean practices, which have not spread as extensively from the
communities in which they developed. Furthermore, as noted in chapter 4,
the differences in the experiences of Japanese Americans with White settler
colonialism and those of Native Americans lead to different patterns of opinion in these communities regarding authorizing outsiders to experience or
practice their respective therapies.[6]

That said, Reiki can help make sense of this broader category of transnational spiritual therapy. Practitioners tactically position Reiki as neither
religion nor medicine, yet they selectively draw on religious and medical
idioms to gain authority. Being "spiritual but not religious" allows practitioners to employ the universalizing logic of secularity (as anyone can practice, regardless of their religion), and being "healing but not medicine"
allows them to work largely outside state regulation.[7] This contrasts with
similar healing practices that are part of transnational religious organizations, such as the *jōrei* and *okiyome* mentioned in the book's introduction. These practices share many of the attributes I have associated with
"alternate currents" and transnational spiritual therapies, but they are typically practiced within the settings of institutions that are registered with the
state (and receive benefits, such as tax exemption, denied to spiritual therapists). Thus, spiritual therapies' ambiguous status provides a certain freedom

and flexibility, although they lack certain benefits of "corporate forms" and they are open to attacks of being forms of "stealth religion."[8]

Practitioners of transnational spiritual therapies valorize the traditional cultures they consider the sources of their practices, effacing the fact that these practices' origins lie in modern "intersystems," in which cultures do not start and stop at national boundaries.[9] The promotion of Reiki as a "Japanese healing art" occludes its North Pacific character, just as projections of yoga as a product of ancient India and meditation movements as Asian traditions erase the impact of Americans and Europeans on their development. This occurs as much within Asia as outside it, as Asian promoters of these practices engage in Occidentalism and self-Orientalization when they reify "tradition" to critique modernity and "Western" influences.[10] At the same time, they cite foreign interest to increase prestige for domestic audiences.[11]

"Asian wisdom" becomes arguably even more exoticized when performed by people with little knowledge of the ostensible source culture. For example, Usui Mikao's recitation practices and use of symbols draw on older East Asian practices of fetishizing (both spoken and written) language, such as mantra recitation and talisman writing, but these practices clearly take on new meaning when taught to practitioners for whom Sino-Japanese characters (kanji) were completely foreign prior to their initiations. Similarly, chanting a Sanskrit mantra associated with the name of a Hindu deity likely affects White Americans differently than would chanting an English word.[12] The increased interactions between Japanese Reiki practitioners and the international Reiki community have caused some reevaluation of certain practices that spread widely in the 1980s and 1990s. For example, many Takata-lineage Reiki communities that transmitted a "Master symbol" that Takata taught near the end of her life and told her disciples to keep secret are currently coming to terms with the fact that this symbol is actually a combination of three common Japanese characters that form a fairly common phrase from Japanese religion meaning "enlightenment."

Some Reiki practitioners develop interest in other Japanese practices, like aikido or calligraphy, which they feel deepen their connection to their Reiki practice, or make pilgrimages to Japan, particularly Mount Kurama, where Usui had his mystical experience, and Usui's memorial in Tokyo. Similarly, practitioners of yoga, meditation, and Indigenous ceremony tend to value aspects of these spiritual therapies' "source cultures," adopting elements of their clothing, diets, and vocabularies. Reiki centers, yoga studios, and meditation halls often incorporate design elements to evoke their practices' "homelands" in order to transport those who enter into a foreignized space.[13]

This is not to say that all practitioners are purists or that all members of "source cultures" welcome outsiders' interest in their spiritual therapies. Part of Reiki's success in the 1980s and 1990s came from practitioners combining it with other practices, including those involving crystals and chakras (of Indian origin, but reinterpreted by Europeans and Americans), and practices ascribed to ancient Egypt (pyramid power and "elemental energies") or Tibetan Buddhism (deity yoga). Native American practices, particularly smudging, have been incorporated into the practices of spiritual therapists around the globe. Syncretism and cultural borrowing lead to (sometimes rightful) charges of appropriation and create backlashes, from Hindu nationalists' campaign to "take back yoga" to Native American shamans' denunciation of "plastic shamans" and "spiritual hucksters."[14]

Such contested questions about who is authorized to practice must be determined within practitioner communities, but scholarship can provide perspective on the terms of the debate. As such, I hope that practitioners and scholars alike find the model of transnational spiritual therapies arising out of modern intersystems provides insight into the nature of these practices. For example, I think this model complements Jeff Wilson's conclusion that the mindfulness movement is "an American Buddhist metaphysical religion." Wilson's study chiefly focuses on the American side of the intersystem that produced the mindfulness movement, examining how trends in American religion "influence what elements of Buddhism are chosen to be appropriated" and how Americans adapted these elements to their culture. While Wilson's use of this approach generates many insights, it also somewhat obscures how Asians internalized aspects of "American religion" in creating modern meditation movements in their own countries.[15] Promoters of Zen and Vipassanā, including Japan's D. T. Suzuki, Vietnam's Thich Nhat Hanh, Sri Lanka's Walpola Rahula, and Burma's Ledi Sayadaw, "drastically altered" their presentations of Buddhist practice "to reflect Western constructions and sensibilities."[16] Wilson reminds readers that the mindfulness movement emerged out of exchanges between "modern-minded Asian meditators and Western seekers," including Rahula, but this interactive model is largely undermined by the book's dominant model of the American reception of Buddhist meditation practices from Asia.[17] I do not mean to pick on an insightful scholar whose book has much to offer, but instead to point out how a model of practices circulating within a transnational intersystem can reveal complexities sometimes absent from accounts of unidirectional transmissions of "Asian" practices to the United States.

This book demonstrates that, contrary to the assumptions of earlier scholarship, Reiki is neither an American practice in Eastern trappings nor a Japanese practice that successfully adapted to meet the needs of Western practitioners. Instead, it arose out of North Pacific confluences that involved both Japanese and Americans, and it was repeatedly reimagined at different junctures of social forces and embodied agencies. After a chapter that presented the early life of Hawayo Takata, the woman whose lifework provided a frame for tracing this genealogy, this book traced Reiki's circulatory history from (1) a circle of social elites in 1920s–1930s Japan, where Japanese ethnoracial nationalism was bound up with its imperial projects; to (2) the Japanese labor diaspora in 1930s–1950s Hawaiʻi, where settler colonists from both sides of the Pacific operated within a White supremacist racial hierarchy; to (3) the US mainland of the 1950s–1970s, where the Cold War Orientalism of White society rearticulated the place of the Asian (and Asian American) Other in the racial hierarchy, creating opportunities for religious virtuosi like Takata to build networks and followings among middle-class and elite White Americans.

As Reiki circulated in these settings, teachers and practitioners adapted it to local needs and values while concomitantly introducing their students and patients to new forms of socio-spiritual connection. This became particularly pronounced after Reiki crossed the ethnoracial divide between Nikkei and White Americans. Takata did her best to inculcate her White students with "Japanese" values of respect for secrecy, hierarchy, and reciprocity, which she considered essential to Reiki practice, while also borrowing from Christian language to frame this "Japanization" in terms of North America's hegemonic religion. But Reiki practice also introduced students across the North Pacific, going back to the 1920s, to the elective kinship relations of lineage via a ceremony adapted from Buddhist monastic initiations. Thus, although Reiki practitioners vehemently resist the description of their practice as a "religion," its development resembles that of other "democratized" ritual practices that characterize new religious movements in modern Japan, including the popularization of laity practicing Zen meditation.[18]

Reiki shares other attributes with other transnational forms of body-oriented spiritual practice that grew out of so-called East-West interactions. Like forms of yoga and meditation practice, Reiki has been "universalized" in a number of ways. First, from the time of its founder Usui, Reiki's promoters have claimed that this therapy is based on a cosmic (and thus universal) power. This claim is related to its second universalism, which it acquired as it moved into the diverse society of Hawai'i: a rhetoric of being accessible to all, regardless of nationality, racioethnicity, or religion. Takata concisely combines these two universalisms in her statement that, "being a universal force from the Great Divine Spirit, it belongs to all who seek and a [sic] desire to learn the art of healing. It knows no color, nor creed, old or young."[19] A third way it was universalized was through a process that transnational studies calls deterritorialization: that is, the excision of elements that were culturally specific to Japanese audiences (such as the recitation of the poetry of the Meiji Emperor), which made it more accessible for people outside Japan (even if that was not the motivation behind that excision). These three interconnected forms of universalization have helped facilitate the transnational growth of Reiki, as they have for yoga and meditation.

Yet at the same time that advocates of Reiki, yoga, and meditation emphasize their global accessibility, they also posit (again, to varying degrees) a lineage that extends to an Asian source that possesses a kind of privileged access to the universal reality toward which all cultures are oriented.[20] To describe this tension between the particularist celebration of the culture where the practice originated and the universalism to which the practice aspires, I use the concept of "particular universalism," which Bruno Latour coined to describe the Western chauvinism inscribed in epistemologies that hold scientific knowledge to be a uniquely objective form of understanding the world.[21] Takata's form of particular universalism, which distinguished Reiki from other spiritual therapies by stressing its initiation lineage stretching back to Usui, identifies Japan as its potent site of origin. Her veneration of Japan and codification of values she identified as Japanese in Reiki practice helped solidify her own authority for North American students as a mediator to the authentic original, lost to time and the ravages of war.

Another important dimension of Reiki's development in this period is its changing relationship with capitalism. Reiki underwent a gradual process of commoditization over the course of the twentieth century. Within a couple of years of Usui's death in 1926, his disciple Hayashi introduced five-day training seminars in his own association so students paid for an initiation course that granted them certificates rather than learning the practice over a longer time and being awarded the certificates for passing practical examinations. It is not known whether Hayashi's organization charged for treatments, but

Takata appears to have done so shortly after completing her training, when she opened her first clinic in Kapaʻa in 1936. The professionalization of Reiki, which took some decades for Takata's students to accept, happened simultaneously with the growing recognition that Reiki could be a self-sufficient spiritual practice. Practitioners who studied with Takata in 1930s and 1940s Hawaiʻi complained about Reiki's commodification, but they also treated it more as a *technique* that supplemented their Buddhist practice or manifested values cultivated through their Buddhism. In contrast, Takata's students in North America who were drawn to becoming full-time Reiki therapists or teachers found Reiki to be more of a self-sufficient *practice,* capable of producing spiritual transformation.[22] Thus, not only did Reiki's professionalization not jeopardize its spiritual potential for North American audiences, but rather (at least by the 1970s) the two were deeply entangled.

Since Takata's death in 1980, Reiki has spread around the world, disproportionately among middle-class women, and has become even more entangled with global market forces as Masters form professional organizations, take out liability insurance, network, and self-promote online, even offering distance initiations that are paid for and performed online. Yet even prior to 1980, diverse forms of Reiki were being practiced across the North Pacific. The Usui and Hayashi Associations examined in chapter 2 survived the war, albeit in reduced capacity: the Usui Association continues to this day, and the teachings of an elderly Hayashi Association member became the basis for new Reiki lineages that were founded in the 1990s and 2000s.[23] Takata's students in Hawaiʻi practiced forms of Reiki based on what they learned in the 1930s for many decades, treating with a single hand in a single position for hours on end and rejecting the idea that Reiki treatment could be a commercial enterprise. Even after Takata reached a more or less finalized version of her teachings in the mid-1970s, Reiki practice took on different meanings from venue to venue, whether on massage tables in rented spaces or in clients' homes for set fees; in the massive Sunday-evening sessions in the ten-bed treatment area of the Trinity Metaphysical Center in the San Francisco suburbs, where donations were placed in envelopes for the church; in the rural British Columbia Interior, where friends and neighbors exchanged treatments or did them for barter; or in the hospital programs in which practitioners disregarded Takata's "exchange of energies" dictum by volunteering to give free treatments. Such diversity demonstrates the multidirectional influences on the evolution of practices in circulation.

This book's focus on circulation within networks is an attempt to resist some of the assumptions of uniformity and make sense of the structures that shape diverse communities of practice. As Latour poetically put it, networks of practice are "an Ariadne's thread that . . . allow us to pass with continuity from the local to the global" as they constitute "lines of force" that connect the microinteractions of interpersonal contact to the macrosystems of the state, economy, society, and culture, memorably concluding, "The Leviathan is a skein of networks."[24] As Latour indicated, network models allow scholars to examine interplays of agency and structure at different scales as individuals and organizations respond to and help constitute broader societal trends. In this way, networks function something like Pierre Bourdieu's habitus in that, like systems of embodied dispositions, they are created out of practice while also setting the possibilities for future practice.[25]

On the one hand, the structural frameworks of a socio-spiritual network's sociocultural environment influence that network's dynamics. For example, the fact that the quotas of US immigration policy largely led to the refusal of Japanese immigrants between 1924 and 1965 reinforced Takata's status as the only public teacher of Reiki outside Japan until she began initiating Masters in the 1970s. This example illustrates what Anna Tsing calls "friction": an encounter where tension between unequal parties produces motion, like the rubbing between a spinning tire and the road.[26] Friction can both reinforce and contest hegemony; it is employed by oppressor and oppressed alike. To wit, while Takata's racialized difference as a Japanese American limited her social mobility in the prewar and wartime Territory of Hawai'i, as well as her physical mobility during the war, it also identified her as an authoritative spiritual teacher in the postwar decades, particularly as she grew older and as American interest in "Oriental" medicine and spirituality grew.

On the other hand, agentive choices made within those structural frameworks and applied within networks of influence help form new network ties and have lasting impacts on other agents within that network. This is particularly true when ties in the network describe asymmetrical power relationships, as those between teachers and their students. Takata's influence on Reiki practice long outlasted her physical presence, as her teaching decisions continue to shape the values and possibilities inherited by subsequent generations. One student of Takata's, who completed her Master training with Wanja Twan (described in chapter 5), recalls a lesson Twan gave about making changes to the system they received: "When you have the idea that something would be added to the class . . . picture Takata in the class and say, would she be joyfully happy that you're doing this? . . . When people say, 'What would Jesus say about this?' . . . Well, we would say, 'What would Takata say about this?'"[27] Thus, the choices made by this influential hub in the network of Reiki's circulation—say, her development of the rhetoric of an "exchange of energies" to teach her students the value of reciprocity—continue to ripple through the Reiki world's "alternate currents" more than four decades after her death.

Glossary of Japanese Names and Terms

Note: In the main text, the names of Japanese Americans appear in the Western style, with the given name first. Here they appear in the Japanese style, with the family name first. In general, the simplified postwar *kanji* are used below.

abishahō	阿尾奢法
ajikan	阿字観
Akishima Rayla	昭島レイラ
Akiyama Saneyuki	秋山真之
ansei	安静
Aoyama Bunki	青山文記
Asano Wasaburō	浅野和三郎
bonji	梵字
butsudan	仏壇
byōgen	病源
byōkon	病根
byōsen	病腺
chinkon kishin	鎮魂帰神
chiryō shunin	治療主任
Chōsei Ryōjutsu	長生療術
Chūō Rengō	中央連合
Dainichi Nyorai	大日如来
Dai Nippon Seishin-dan	大日本精神団
dai-shihan	大師範
danna	檀那
Deguchi Onisaburō	出口王仁三郎
Dōtoku Kagaku	道徳科学
Eguchi Kaname	江口金馬
Eguchi Toshihiro	江口俊博
enkaku chiryō	遠隔治療
ēteru	エーテル
fujinkai	婦人会
Fukuoka Kōshirō	福岡甲旨郎
Furuya Keisei	古屋景晴
gachirinkan	月輪観

genki	元気
giri	義理
gō	業
gokai	五戒
goseiha	後世派
Gotō Konzan	後藤艮山
Gotō Shinpei	後藤新平
gyaku-yunyū	逆輸入
gyosei	御製
Hakuin	白隠
hanko	判子
hara	腹
Harada Shōsaku	原田正作
hatsurei-hō	発霊法
Hawai Bukkyōkai	布哇仏教会
Hayami Akira	速水融
Hayashi Chie	林知恵
Hayashi Chūjirō	林忠次郎
Hayashi Reiki Kenkyūkai	林霊気研究会
hibiki	響
hiden	秘伝
Hirano Naoko	平野直子
hō	法
Honpa Hong(w)anji	本派本願寺
hyōgiin	評議員
iemoto	家元
igakusha	医学者
Iino Kichisaburō	飯野吉三郎
Ikkisha	一記者
ikki tairyū-setsu	一気滞留説
Imaizumi Tetsutarō	今泉哲太郎
Imamura Yemyō	今村恵猛
imin no ko	移民の子
Imura Kōji	井村宏次
Ishii Tsunezō	石井常造
Issei	一世
Itō Gingetsu	伊藤銀月
Jintai Aura Reiki-jutsu	人体アウラ霊気術
Jintai Hōshanō Ryōhō	人体放射能療法
Jōdo Shinshū	浄土真宗

Jōdo-shū	浄土宗
jōrei	浄霊
jōshin kokyū-hō	浄心呼吸法
jumon	呪文
jūshoku	住職
Kaetsu Satoshi	嘉悦敏
kaji	加持
kaji kitō	加持祈祷
kami-sama	神様
kanji (characters)	漢字
kanji (secretary)	幹事
kanjō	灌頂
kanpō	漢方
kanzen sōden	完全相伝
katsu	活
Kawakami Mataji	川上又次
Kawamura Otogorō	河村音五郎
kechien kanjō	結縁灌頂
kenjinkai	県人会
kenkyūkai	研究会
ketsueki jōka-hō	血液浄化方
ketsueki kōkan-hō	血液交換法
Kenzen Tetsugaku	健全哲学
ki	気
kibei	帰米
kishōmon	起請文
Kōga Michiko	甲賀美智子
koiha	古医派
Kojima Miyoko	小嶋美代子
komon	顧問
komon riji	顧問理事
Kōmyōji	光明寺
Kondō Masaki	近藤正毅
kōryūkai	交流会
kōshūkai	講習会
Koyama Kimiko	小山君子
Kubokawa Kyokujō	窪川旭丈
kuchiyose kitō	口寄せ祈祷
kuden	口伝
kue issho	倶会一緒

kumiai	組合
Kurita Hidehiko	栗田英彦
kyōgi	教義
Maeda Geka Byōin	前田外科病院
Maeda Tomosuke	前田友助
Matsubara Kōgetsu	松原皎月
Matsuda Reiyō	松田靈洋
Matsui Shōō	松井松翁
Matsumoto Chiwaki	松本道別
Matsumoto Myōsei	松本妙清
Mikami Yoshitada	三上良忠
mikkyō	密教
miko	巫女
miteshiro otoritsugi	み手代お取次
Mitsui Kōshi	三井甲之
Mizuta Kin'ichi	水田謹一
Mochizuki Toshitaka	望月利隆
Moralogy	モラロジー
Morita Masatake	森田正馬
Moriya Tomoe	守屋友江
Murakami Aki	村上晶
Nagao Tatsuji	長尾辰二
Nagasawa Genkō	長沢玄光
Naha Shijinkai	那覇市人会
Nakamaki Hirochika	中牧弘允
Nakamura Tempū	中村天風
Nakano Genzō	中野玄三
Nakao Maika	中尾麻伊香
natori	名取
nenbutsu	念仏
nihonjinron	日本人論
Nikkei	日系
Nisei	二世
Nishi Honganji	西本願寺
Nishi Katsuzō	西勝造
Nishi-shiki Kenkō-hō	西式健康法
Noda Gikaku	野田義角
Noda Sae	野田サエ
Nukariya Kaiten	忽滑谷快天
nyūga ga'nyū	入我我入
Ogawa Fumio	小川二三夫

Okada Masayuki	岡田正之
Okada Mokichi	岡田茂吉
okiyome	お浄め
okuden	奥伝
Ōmoto	大本
onsen	温泉
orei	御礼
Ōtani Honbyō	大谷本廟
Purana Ryōhō	プラナ療法
reichi	霊知
reihō	霊法
reiji-hō	霊示法
reiju	霊授
reijukai	霊授会
reiju kitei	霊授規定
reijusha	霊授者
reijutsu	霊術
reijutsuka	霊術家
Reikai Kakusei Dōshikai	霊界廓清同志会
reiki	霊気
Reiki Ryōhō	霊気療法
reinō	霊能
Reiryō-jutsu Kenkyū-dan	霊療術研究団
reishi	霊子
Reishijutsu	霊子術
Rennyo	蓮如
riji	理事
Risshō Kōsei-kai	立正佼成会
roku-tō	六等
ryū	流
ryūha	流派
Sadanaga Kangorō	貞永勘五郎
saiminjutsu-shi	催眠術士
sanmitsu	三密
san-tō	三等
Seichō no Ie	成長の家
seiheki chiryō	性癖治療
seijō kokyū-hō	清浄呼吸法
seika tanden	臍下丹田
seikei geka	整形外科
Seiki Jikyō Ryōhō	生気自強療法

seishin	精神
seishin ryōhō	精神療法
seishin ryōhōka	精神療法家
seishin sekai	精神世界
seishin shūyō	精神修養
seiza gasshō	正座合掌
senbetsu	餞別
Senshin-ryū Shinrei Chiryō-jutsu	洗心流心霊治療術
seryō	施療
Shaku Sōen	釈宗演
shashin reiki	写真霊気
Shibata Junkō	柴田純宏
Shibusawa Eiichi	渋沢栄一
shihan	師範
shihan-kaku	師範格
shina jihen	支那事変
shin'netsu	芯熱
shinpiden	神秘伝
Shinshin Kaizen Usui Reiki Ryōhō Gakkai	心身改善臼井霊気療法学会
Shinshin Tōitsu-dō	心身統一道
Shinshū Chōsei-ha	真宗長生派
shoden	初伝
shōnen	正念
Shōninki	正忍記
Shufu-no-kai	主婦の会
shugorei	守護霊
Shunchōrō	春潮楼
shūshin	修身
shūyō	修養
sōke	宗家
supirichuaru serapii	スピリチュアルセラピー
Suzuki Bizan	鈴木美山
Suzuki Daisetsu Teitarō	鈴木大拙貞太郎
Taguchi Mugyū	田口無牛
taiki	大気
Taireidō	太霊道
Takagi Hidesuke	高木秀輔
Takahashi Ichita	高橋一太
Takai Shiomi	高井志生海
Takata Hawayo (Hiromi)	高田 布哇与 (浩美)

Takata Reiki Chiryōin	高田霊気治療院
Takata Saichi	高田佐一
Taketomi Kan'ichi	竹富咸一
Tamari Kizō	玉利喜造
Tamayose Hōun	玉代勢法雲
Tanaka Eihachirō	田中栄八郎
Tanaka Morihei	田中守平
Taniguchi Masaharu	谷口雅春
teate ryōhō	手当療法
Tenohira Ryōji	手のひら療治
Tōkyō Maiyū Shinbunsha	東京毎夕新聞社
Tomabechi Gizō	苫米地義三
Tomita Kaiji	富田魁二
Tomita-ryū Teate Ryōhō	冨田流手当て療法
tsubo	壺
Tsukada Hotaka	塚田穂高
Tsunematsu Kenzō	常松憲三
uchideshi	内弟子
uchū	宇宙
Ueshiba Morihei	植芝盛平
Ushida Jūzaburō	牛田従三郎
Usui Mikao	臼井甕男
Usui Reiki Ryōhō	臼井霊気療法
Usui Reiki Ryōhō Gakkai	臼井霊気療法学会
waka	和歌
Wanami Hōichi	和波豊一
wasei eigo	和製英語
yaito	灸
yakuin	役員
yamabushi	山伏
Yamada Shin'ichi	山田信一
Yamaguchi Chiyoko	山口千代子
Yamaguchi Tadao	山口忠夫
Yamazaki Kesaya	山崎今朝弥
yōjō	養生
yorigito	憑祈祷
yose kaji	寄加持
Yoshinaga Shin'ichi	吉永進一
zasshu	雑修
Zendōji	善導寺

Notes

Abbreviations

FHL   Family History Library, Salt Lake City

HSPAPA   Hawaiian Sugar Planters' Association Plantation Archives, University of Hawai'i at Mānoa Library

HTP   Hawayo Takata Papers, University of California, Santa Barbara, Special Research Collections, American Religions Collection Mss 86

NARA   United States National Archives and Records Administration, College Park, MD

RASRLR   Romanzo Adams Social Research Laboratory Records, University of Hawai'i at Mānoa Library

Introduction

1 The following story is based on Rick Bockner, interview by the author, Whaletown, BC, July 22, 2013; Rick Bockner to Hawayo Takata, August 20, 1980, Box 8, HTP; Bockner 2008; and Droog 2008.

2 Following Beeler (2016, 2017), I distinguish between the practice and the energy as "Reiki" and *reiki,* respectively.

3 The first Master Takata trained in British Columbia was Ursula Baylow (in August 1978), followed by Barbara Brown, Bethal Phaigh, and Wanja Twan, whom she trained together in October 1979. Fueston 2017: 222–229.

4 Rick Bockner to Hawayo Takata, February 7, 1980, Box 8, HTP.

5 This is the technical name for the language more commonly called pidgin in Hawai'i.

6 With a few exceptions (particularly Atlanta, New Jersey, and Puerto Rico in the late 1970s), Chicago marked the front line of Reiki's eastward advance until the 1980s.

7 This study is thus in the spirit of Anne Blackburn's microhistory of the networks of the Ceylonese monk Hikkaḍuvē Sumangala (1827–1911), which she "intended as an example of how to develop human-scale studies of modes of thought and practice in colonial times," recognizing the "deeply creative logic" of colonial subjects as well as "the force, and limits, of

colonial power in remaking local lives and social patterns" (Blackburn 2010: xiv). For racial rearticulation, see Omi and Winant 2014.

8   Hardacre 1998; Mohr 2014; Moriya 2000, 2001; Sharf 1993, 1995; Snodgrass 2003; Thomas 2019; Tweed 2005; J. Wilson 2009; Yoshinaga 2015.

9   Ama 2011; Esaki 2016; Masatsugu 2013; Moriya 2000, 2001, 2008a; Pereira and Matsuoka 2007; Shimizu 2019; Thomas 2019: 75–103; Williams 2019; Williams and Moriya 2010; J. Wilson 2009: 19–54; J. Wilson 2012: 62–81; Yoo 2000: 38–67.

10   Matory 2005; Takezawa and Okihiro 2016.

11   Buswell 2006; Tweed 2006: 59–60; Tweed 2012.

12   J. Stein 2017b: 44–45.

13   Blum 2002: 145n1; Teeuwen 2006: 9.

14   Matsui 1930; Tomita (1933) 1999: 78.

15   Csordas 2009: 5.

16   Albanese 1992; Fuller 2001: 101–121; Fuller and Stein 2014; Kalvig 2012; Pike 2004: 91–113; Skrivanic 2018.

17   Beeler 2016; Gaitanidis 2012, 2022; Lears 1981; Tweed 1992.

18   Taussig 1987: 44–45, 100.

19   Usui 1928: 4–9.

20   Asaki 1928: 16. This passage is examined in more detail in chapter 2.

21   Clara Mackler to Elsa Kane, postmarked September 18, 1951, Box 6, Folder 3, HTP; Thomas P. Mackler, "Testimony," unpublished document, 1965, personal collection of Shannon E. D. Mackler. The Macklers' story is further analyzed in chapter 4.

22   For Reiki as a "Buddhist secret," see Hammond 1973: 264. For its "spiritual" draw, see Schiller 2003: 21.

23   Committee on Doctrine 2009: 5–6; J. Stein 2022: 238.

24   Euteneuer 2010.

25   Quoted in Hirano 2016a: 71.

26   Takata 1948. This essay is examined in chapter 4.

27   Other examples of *wasei eigo* include "baby car" (*bebii kā*), meaning "stroller," and "magic tape" (*majikku tēpu*), meaning "Velcro."

28   For examples of primary sources, see Akishima 2012; Bodine 1997. For scholarship, see Gaitanidis 2010, 2012, 2022; Murakami 2017.

29   For examples from Reiki, see Klassen 2011: 186–188; Ray 1983: 35–38, 45–46; D. Stein 1995: 8–12, 141–142. See also the story of Takata's encounter with the AMA president in chapter 4.

30   For "third terms," see Hanegraaff 2016 and the special issue of *Method and Theory in the Study of Religion* 30, no. 1 (2018). For strategy versus tactics, see de Certeau 1984.

31 Neumann 2019; Singleton 2010; Soucy 2014: 27.

32 Borup 2015; Frøystad 2009; Joo 2011.

33 Beliso-De Jesús 2015; K. Clarke 2004; Matory 2005.

34 Palmié 2008; Willis and Murphy-Shigematsu 2008.

35 For "purification," see Latour 1993; for "intersystem," see Drummond 1980. Ama (2011: 5) recognized something similar when he asserted that Jōdo Shinshū Buddhism's modern "Japanization" continued after its movement to North America.

36 Azuma 2019: 10.

37 The thirty-five nations with the highest proportions of Google searches for "reiki" in the 2010s were (in descending order) Portugal, Uruguay, Argentina, Mauritius, Chile, Spain, Ireland, Estonia, Romania, Brazil, Mexico, Latvia, Switzerland, France, Serbia, Canada, Slovenia, the United Kingdom, Finland, Belgium, the Netherlands, Lithuania, Hungary, Australia, Czechia, New Zealand, Austria, Italy, Colombia, Costa Rica, the United States, Germany, Venezuela, Croatia, and South Africa. Google, n.d. These rankings do not take into account the sizable digital discourse about Reiki in languages such as Russian and Japanese that do not use Roman script. See note 45.

38 Jennings (2019: 54–55) points out that *reiki*'s indeterminacy is tied to broader trends in related forms of "subtle energy," such as mana or prana. See also Gaitanidis' (2019) discussion of Reiki's "grounding" in contemporary Japan. For the polysemy of "zen," see Levine 2017: 6–11.

39 Usui 1928: 8–9.

40 Hirano 2016b, 2019; Yoshinaga 2019: 4.

41 Sullivan and Sered 2005: 3813.

42 National Center for Complementary and Integrative Health 2018. There are likely several reasons for the development of this "hands-off" style, including concerns around liability, people being uncomfortable with the vulnerability of physical touch, or the practice's "spiritualization" (and dephysicalization). Whatever the reason, the growing association of Reiki with ethereality is linked to a reputation for being insufficiently physical, recently typified in the character on *The White Lotus* who, looking for a bodywork appointment at a busy luxury spa, says, "I'm not picky. . . . I don't have to have deep tissue or anything. I'd take anything at this point. Anything. Anything but Reiki, of course." White 2021.

43 J. Stein 2009.

44 J. Stein 2016a. See also chapter 2.

45 Precise counts of how many worldwide have received Reiki initiations are impossible. By the late 1990s, Reiki Masters estimated there were

approximately five million practitioners in 121 countries worldwide, with at least one million in the United States and another million in India. Mochizuki 1997: 14; Rand 1998: 58; Rand, n.d. Hirano Naoko also estimated the number of Reiki practitioners worldwide to be in the millions. Hirano 2016b: 81. These estimates cannot be confirmed, but worldwide interest in Reiki is supported by its substantial, multilingual internet presence: a June 2021 Google search for "reiki" yielded about eighty-two million hits, the Cyrillic "Рэйки" yielded over twenty-five million hits, and the Japanese katakana "レイキ" yielded almost two million as well.

Empirical data on Reiki practice has focused on recipients rather than practitioners. Two surveys by the US National Center for Complementary and Alternative Medicine found over one million Americans received Reiki or other forms of "energy healing therapy" annually. These surveys included non-Reiki modalities, but notably both studies described Reiki as the best-known example of this kind of therapy. P. Barnes, Bloom, and Nahin 2008: 12; T. Clarke et al. 2015: 10. Chile's Ministry of Health found that roughly 10 percent of Chilean urbanites had received Reiki, a number that, extrapolated to the country's urban population, would exceed five hundred thousand. Subsecretaría de Salud Pública 2012.

46   J. Stein 2015: 7–11; J. Stein 2016b; J. Stein 2019: 95–98; Takai 1986.

47   That said, Takata taught some of these "traditional Japanese Reiki" techniques to her Master students in the 1970s, although they are not widely practiced in Takata-lineage Reiki today. For example, Takata taught several of her Masters a "Reiki blessing" that resembles the initiation ritual but, like *reiju,* can be performed for students or others to support healing and/ or growth as practitioners. Jonker 2016: 403–405; Klatt 2006: 90–91. The chanting, meditation, and *reiju* practices are described in chapter 2.

48   See Nishina 2017b: 162–201.

49   Nishina 2017b: 107.

50   Williams 2008.

51   K. Brown 2001; Jain 2015; S. Palmer 1994.

52   In 2006, a Belgian court sentenced Dang to four years in prison for charges including fraud and criminal conspiracy. De Cordes 2014.

53   For details of these practices and the altars, see Baffelli and Reader 2019: 84–90.

54   Their roots are in Ōmoto (described in chapter 2), itself one of the first Japanese new religions to go overseas and make universalist claims. See J. Stein 2012; R. Young 1988. *Jōrei* is popular in Brazil, and *okiyome* has been growing in Africa. Lambertz 2017; Matsuoka 2018.

55   J. Stein 2012.

56   Campbell 2008.

57 Ray 1983: 45–46; D. Stein 1995: 8.

58 Yeshe 2001.

59 Lübeck, Petter, and Rand 2001; Petter 1997, 1998, 2012; Petter, Yamaguchi, and Hayashi 2003; Usui and Petter 2003.

60 For example, King 2007.

61 J. Stein 2009. I plan to update parts of that thesis as a kind of sequel to this book, addressing Reiki's development since 1980.

62 As of this writing, some materials, largely photographs, have yet to arrive in Santa Barbara.

63 Chandler 2008; Drescher 2016; Fuller 2001.

64 Harter, Japp, and Beck 2005; Kleinman 1988; Milne and Howard 2000; Sered and Agigian 2008.

65 For a book-length study of gender in contemporary Reiki, see Macpherson 2008. Like Sointu and Woodhead (2008), Macpherson argues that women are drawn to Reiki and other spiritual therapies because these therapies validate relational, caring work that has traditionally been considered "women's work," while providing an "alternative" social sphere in which women feel empowered. See also Kleeman and Jayne 2021.

66 Lepore 2013.

67 Urban 1998.

68 The decline of initiations in religious and artistic systems in early modern Japan was related to advancements in printing technology. Bodiford 2006: 309–310; Teeuwen 2006: 9.

69 Bodiford 2001: 488–490; Usui 1928: 17.

70 That said, several books and websites include the symbols, and they have been inscribed on commercial goods such as stones and pendants. Clay 1992; D. Stein 1995.

71 Personal email to the author, August 13, 2009. For the politics of human remains in Hawaiʻi, see Ayau 2000; Johnson 2007.

72 L. Wilson 2014.

73 Baffelli, Castiglioni, and Rambelli 2021: 3.

Chapter 1: Seeds of a Transpacific Network

1 The local expression for goosebumps in Hawaiʻi comes from the Japanese *torihada*. Shirai 2019: 8.

2 Takata 1981: tape 1, pp. 1–2. Throughout this book, when citing Takata's December 1979 recordings, I cite the corresponding pages in the unpublished transcript completed in 1981 by Helen Haberly (held in HTP, Box 5, Folder 1), although I sometimes change the wording to make it better accord with the actual recordings. As of January 2023, Takata's students

Paul and Susan Mitchell are planning to publish a revised version of the transcript under the title *Reiki Is God-Power.*

3 Matsuura 1974.

4 See Haberly 1990: 11.

5 The fact that Hatsu immigrated to Hawaiʻi in 1894 but did not marry Otogorō until 1897 suggests they met on the plantation. Shay 2019: 26–27.

6 Takata 1981: tape 1, p. 2. Takata appears to have taken Hawaiʻi statehood as a point of pride, mentioning it frequently in her stories, and her personal papers include memorabilia and documents issued on August 21, 1959 (the date of its admission), including commemorative stamps and an updated license from the new state board of massage.

7 For more on Asian settler colonialism in Hawaiʻi, see Fujikane and Okamura 2008; Saranillio 2013.

8 Kauai Plantation Railway 2007.

9 Feher 1969: 263. These investors were Charles Reed Bishop (1822–1915), who married into the royal family, became a Hawaiian citizen, and later founded the Kingdom's first chartered bank and served as the Kingdom's foreign minister; William Little Lee (1821–1857), a lawyer who became the first chief justice of the Kingdom's Supreme Court; and Henry A. Peirce (1808–1885), a merchant who became the US minister to the Kingdom.

10 Archer 2018: 2.

11 Soboleski 2007.

12 E. Wu 2014: 211–212.

13 University of Hawaiʻi at Mānoa Library, n.d.

14 Wichman 1998: 61–62.

15 Lo 2005; University of Hawaiʻi at Mānoa Library, n.d.

16 Conroy 1949: 14–15; Glenn 2002: 192; Kauai Plantation Railway 2007.

17 Daniels 1999: 5.

18 Irwin and Conroy 1972: 47–48; Spickard 2009: 11.

19 Irwin and Conroy 1972: 49–51; Lu 2019; Spickard 2009: 12–13.

20 1910 United States Federal Census, Hanamaulu, Kauai, Hawaii Territory, enumeration district 0005, page 9B, Ancestry.com, accessed June 20, 2014, http://www.ancestry.com (citing NARA microfilm publication T624; FHL microfilm 1375765); passenger lists of vessels arriving at Honolulu, Hawaii, compiled February 13, 1900–December 30, 1953, Ancestry.com, accessed June 20, 2014, http://www.ancestry.com (citing NARA microfilm publication A3422, roll 167; Records of the Immigration and Naturalization Service, 1787–2004, RG 85, NARA). See also Shay 2019: 23, 26.

21 Daniels 1999: 5–6; Kimura 1988: 5–6; Spickard 2009: 14.

22 Kimura 1988: 22.

23 Ayala 1999: 54–55; Kuykendall 1967: chaps. 20–21.

24 Asato 2006: 2.

25 Lihue Plantation Company, "Hanamaulu Labor Statements, 1902," HSPAPA 42/3. As one continues to read through the archived payroll records, Filipino names gradually supplant the Japanese ones.

26 Schmitt 1977: 25.

27 Fujikane and Okamura 2008; Lu 2019.

28 Glenn 2002: 194–195; emphasis in original.

29 Azuma 2005; Shimizu 2019.

30 Asato 2006.

31 Kawamura 1912.

32 Imai 2010: 77–80; Yano 2006: 42.

33 Carr 1972: 64; Reinecke 1969: 183–184.

34 Takata 1981: tape 1, pp. 2–5.

35 Van Bragt 2002.

36 In contrast to colonial Fiji, where the British imported indentured labor from India, Muslims were fairly rare in Territorial Hawai'i. The only significant Muslim population that immigrated to Hawai'i was Filipino Moros, whom Takata's classmates are unlikely to have directly encountered because (1) Filipino immigration to Hawai'i had barely begun by 1913, when this story took place; (2) early Filipino immigrants were almost entirely single men, so it is unlikely that any of Takata's classmates would have been Filipino; and (3) Filipino immigration to Hawai'i was disproportionately from the northern, predominantly Christian, Ilocos region. In 1915 (the first year for which there is data), only 84 of the 2,150 immigrants from the US Territory of the Philippines came from its predominantly Muslim region (Minandao, Palawan, and the Sulu archipelago). Sharma 1987. It is possible, however, that a small group of Filipino men had recently arrived on Kaua'i and that these "foreign" newcomers were a source of fascination for Nikkei, who circulated stories of Muslim practice.

37 Spickard 2009: 60–61; Tamura 1994: 207–208.

38 Soboleski 2007; "'Kauai's Emporium' Modernized Lihu'e Shopping," *The Garden Island* (Lihue, HI), November 12, 2010. Ads for the soda fountain where Hawayo washed ice cream dishes touted it as "the coolest place in town." *The Garden Island* (Lihue, HI), August 25, 1914.

39 The distance between Kealia Hongwanji Church and the Lihue Store seems to have been closer to ten miles (neither building still stands). If she actually walked both ways, it would likely have taken about four hours roundtrip.

40 Takata 1981: tape 1, pp. 5–6, 8–9, 12.

41   Julia Spalding and her four siblings were born in Hawai'i but lived in Europe as young adults and the three Spalding girls all married Italian men. Julia married Count Senni in 1900, from whom she reportedly separated soon after because of his cocaine use; she returned to Kaua'i a few years later. Stoddard 1991; "An Italian Nobleman," *The Pacific Commercial Advertiser,* September 17, 1903, 8.

42   Lihue Plantation Company, "Makee Sugar, Payroll Book Bonus—1916" and "Makee Sugar, Payroll Book Bonus, 1917–1932," HSPAPA v. 114–115; University of Hawai'i at Mānoa Library, n.d.; "Hawi Plantation to Make Fuel Alcohol," *The Garden Island* (Lihue, HI), October 12, 1920, 7.

43   The Valley House was built in the early 1880s by Julia's father, Zephaniah Swift Spalding (1837–1927), a Civil War colonel for the Union army sent to Hawai'i by the US government in the late 1860s. He married the daughter of James Makee (1813–1879), one of the early American sugar planters in Hawai'i, developed the Keālia plantation with financing from Makee and King David Kalākaua (1836–1891), and bought out their interests after Makee's death. Marley 2012; P. Young 2015.

44   Takata 1981: tape 1, pp. 9–13.

45   F. Brown 1992: 18.

46   Marley 2012.

47   Glenn 2002: 214.

48   Glenn 2002: 209.

49   Takata 1981: tape 1, p. 14.

50   Haberly 1990: 15; Takata 1981: tape 1, p. 14; "Well Known Citizen Dies of Heart Attack at Home in Kealia," *The Garden Island* (Lihue, HI), October 14, 1930. *Polk-Husted's Directory of Honolulu and the Territory of Hawaii* (Honolulu: Polk-Husted Directory) lists Saichi as an employee of the Makee Plantation Store (a.k.a. the Kealia Store) in every volume I found between 1914 and 1931. He is listed as a clerk (1914, 1916, 1918, 1920), assistant bookkeeper (1915), bookkeeper (1921, 1924), cashier and bookkeeper (1923), cashier (1927), and "warehouseman" (1930–1931).

51   Glenn 2002: 195–196.

52   Chris Faye, Kauai Museum, personal communication with the author, June 20, 2013.

53   Imamura 1918: 521–522.

54   "Expatriation in Wholesale, Plan," *Nippu Jiji,* March 23, 1925, names Saichi as SACJAK president, and Soboleski 2018 and "Well Known Citizen Dies" both name him SACJAK's founder.

55   The Takatas seem to have invested in stocks through this connection: Hawayo's diary from the period lists the purchase and sales of shares in

eleven local companies, including mills, between 1920 and 1926. The thousands of dollars involved, at a time when Nikkei laborers' day wages were one to two dollars, suggest that they were agents for wealthy White investors or community funds. Box 7, HTP.

56   "Well Known Citizen Dies."

57   In 1929, Wilfred Tsukiyama (who appears in chapter 3) became Hawai'i's first Nikkei to be appointed to government office. Tamura 1994: 241.

58   Takata 1981: tape 1, p. 15.

59   Okihiro 1992: 67–80, 130–131.

60   Spickard 2009: 98

61   Ichioka 2006: 46.

62   Quoted in Committee on Immigration 1924: 139–140; Duus 1999: 294; Okihiro 1992: 93.

63   Quoted in Okihiro 1992: 95; emphasis in original.

64   "Wailua Golf Club Holds First Tournament," *The Garden Island* (Lihue, HI), November 8, 1921, 3.

65   Soboleski 2013.

66   Lihue Plantation Company, "Makee Sugar, P, Payroll Book Bonus, 1917–1932" and "Makee Sugar Register of Employees, 1922–1925," HSPAPA v. 115, 120.

67   "Bureau of Conveyances," *Honolulu Star-Bulletin,* November 28, 1927, 3. As detailed in chapters 3–5, Hawayo would use her earnings from teaching Reiki to buy several properties.

68   This required the approval of county engineer R. L. Garlinghouse. "Three Kauai Officials In," *Honolulu Star-Bulletin,* January 7, 1931, 7.

69   Passenger lists of vessels arriving at Honolulu, Hawaii, compiled February 13, 1900–December 30, 1953, Ancestry.com, accessed June 20, 2014, http://www.ancestry.com (citing NARA microfilm publication A3422, roll 125; Records of the Immigration and Naturalization Service, 1787–2004, RG 85, NARA).

70   Takata 1981: tape 1, pp. 9–14.

71   Cooper and Daws 1990: 1–6, 42–43.

72   Azuma 2005: 112–113.

73   Bonacich and Modell 1980: 85–86.

74   The trip is documented in a photo album with notes written by their daughter Alice Takata Furumoto, currently held by Joyce Winough but to be donated to HTP. For Maeda's biography, see "Maeda Tomosuke" 2009.

75   Maeda opened his eponymous surgical clinic (Maeda Geka Byōin) in 1927. "Maeda Tomosuke" 2009.

76 Saichi's obituary attributes his death to a heart attack and Hawayo said the same to a reporter ("Well Known Citizen Dies"; Straub 1974), but her students from the late 1970s remember being told he died of a lung condition. Phyllis Furumoto said she thought it was pleurisy (personal communication, July 2014), which matches a note by her mother in a family photo album (see figure 1.2). Fran Brown cited lung cancer, and Rick Bockner remembered Takata saying it was tuberculosis. F. Brown 1992: 18; Fueston 2017: 76. It may have ultimately been some combination of factors, or this could be an example of Takata's fluid storytelling style.

77 Takata 1981: tape 1, pp. 16–17.

78 The idea that death is a transition is present in the discourse of Reiki Masters from the two major Reiki organizations established in the wake of Takata's death, as well as by one of the chief promoters of "Traditional Japanese Reiki." These examples often introduce this idea in stories of the Grand Masters (Usui Mikao, Hayashi Chūjirō, and Takata) but then extend it in discussions of end-of-life care to affirm that patients' deaths are not to be considered failures of Reiki treatment; rather, treatment can help ease the dying into a gentler transition. Fueston 2017: 19, 105, 145; Haberly 1990: 16, 41, 44; Morris 1999: 11–13, 15, 29, 31, 67, 69, 93; Petter 1997: 46, 94–95.

79 Godart 2017; McMahan 2008.

80 Haberly 1990: 56; Hammond 1973: 263; Takata 1948.

81 Although this idea would have resonated with the Law of Karma for the Buddhist Takata, that is not to say that it is of Buddhist origin; the same idea of "remove the cause and the effects will disappear" is expressed in the books of Yogi Ramacharaka (né William Walker Atkinson), which, translated into Japanese, (directly or indirectly) influenced the creation of Usui Reiki Therapy. See chapter 2 and Ramacharaka 1906: 13, 105, 145–146. Thank you to Paul Guillory for calling my attention to this connection.

82 Takata 1981: tape 22, p. 3.

83 McMahan 2008: 64.

84 Rowe 2011: 117–119.

85 Takata 1981: tape 22, p. 3. These instructions seem to reflect a canonical Buddhist concern for the doctrine of nonharm. In saying that they could "serve a little meat" but not "butcher anything for that purpose," Saichi echoes the monastic rules in the *Vinaya-piṭaka* that permit monks to eat meat if it is donated by a layperson and they do not know or suspect it was specifically killed for them. Stewart 2010: 110.

86 Takata 1981: tape 1, pp. 16–17.

87 Thank you to Mark Rowe for pointing out this connection. Also, like Shinran's, Saichi's request was ignored, and at least some of his ashes

were interred with Shinran's at the Ōtani Honbyō mausoleum in Kyoto, a practice called "meeting together in one place" (*kue issho*) that is supposed to help ensure a rebirth in the Pure Land. See chapter 2 and Blum 2000.

88 Wanja Twan, interview by the author, Sidney, BC, August 21, 2016.

89 Takata 1981: tape 1, p. 17; tape 2, p. 1.

90 Takata 1981: tape 22, pp. 3–4.

91 Matsuura 1974.

92 As mentioned in note 55, Hawayo Takata's diary indicates they bought and sold thousands of dollars' worth of shares; this would be worth over fifteen times that amount in 2022 dollars. Saichi's will indicates that she inherited the house in Kawaihau and Saichi's stockholdings. "Petition for Probate of Will," Probate No. 1039, Fifth Circuit Court, Territory of Hawaii, November 17, 1930.

Chapter 2: Drawn into the Current

1 They left Honolulu for Yokohama on October 8, 1935. Passenger lists of vessels arriving or departing at Honolulu, Hawaii, compiled February 13, 1900–December 30, 1953, Ancestry.com, accessed June 20, 2014, http://www.ancestry.com (citing NARA microfilm publication A3510, roll 110; Records of the Immigration and Naturalization Service, 1787–2004, RG 85, NARA).

2 Takata 1981: tape 1, p. 13.

3 Graham 1975.

4 Other Honpa Hongwanji churches in Hawai'i and the mainland formed Young Women's Buddhist Association groups by the 1930s (and eventually stopped dividing them by gender altogether, creating the Young Buddhist Association), but both men and women participated in Keālia's YMBA branch. For Saichi's participation, see Imamura 1918: 522. For Takata's election as secretary, see "Cohostesses Give Tea Honoring Mrs. Takata," *Honolulu Star-Bulletin,* March 23, 1934, 9.

5 J. Stein 2021, forthcoming.

6 "Proceedings of the First Canada-Hawaii-America Conference of the Young Buddhist's Associations," *Bhratri* 2, no. 2 (July 1934): 45.

7 On the way to San Francisco, Takata rode cabin class (between third class and first class) on the maiden voyage of the luxury liner SS *Monterey*, leaving Honolulu on July 14, 1932. Passenger lists of vessels arriving or departing at Honolulu, Hawaii, compiled February 13, 1900–December 30, 1953, Ancestry.com, accessed June 20, 2014, http://www.ancestry.com (citing NARA microfilm publication A3510, roll 094; Records of the Immigration

and Naturalization Service, 1787–2004, RG 85, NARA). Takata's autograph book from this trip is in Box 7, HTP. Photos are in the private collection of Joyce Winough and will be donated to the HTP.

8 Azuma 2005: 137–138.

9 Takata 1981: tape 2, p. 3.

10 Takata 1981: tape 2, p. 4.

11 Passenger lists of vessels departing from Honolulu, Hawaii, compiled June 1900–November 1954, Ancestry.com, accessed June 20, 2014, http://www.ancestry.com (citing NARA microfilm publication A3510, roll 110; Records of the Immigration and Naturalization Service, 1787–2004, RG 85, NARA).

12 This temple is the Ōtani Honbyō, where the remains of Shinran, founder of Jōdo Shinshū, are interred. See chapter 1, note 87.

13 Takata 1981: tape 2, pp. 4–11.

14 Bed rest (*ansei*) remains a common treatment in Japan, "recommended for almost all illnesses, including mild colds" (Ohnuki-Tierney 1984: 83).

15 Takata 1981: tape 2, pp. 11–12.

16 Takata 1981: tape 2, pp. 11–15; tape 3, pp. 6–7.

17 A 1928 book cataloged hundreds of such therapies and estimated some thirty thousand therapists at the time. Reikai Kakusei Dōshikai 2004 [1928]: 2–4, reproduced in Hirano 2019: 223–224.

18 Y.-C. Wu 2012: 131. Wu (2012) translates *seishin ryōhō* as "mental therapies," whereas Yoshinaga (2015) chooses "mind cures," emphasizing congruities between these therapies and those of the nineteenth-century United States. While the *rei* in *reijutsu* can literally mean "spirit," Yoshinaga argues that, in the first decades of the twentieth century, *rei* could also simply mean "excellent" without "spiritual" connotations, and thus translates *reijutsu* as "excellent art." Such translations elide the fact that (as both Wu and Yoshinaga point out) the practices they discuss—like Okada-style Quiet Sitting Method (Okada-shiki Seizahō) and Belly-Centered Medicine (Haradō Igaku)—have explicitly spiritual or religious aspects. This is more explicitly addressed in Yoshinaga's (2021) more recent translation of *seishin ryōhō* as "spiritual-psychic healing," *reijutsuka* as "spiritual/psychical healers," and *reijutsu* as "spiritual power." On the other hand, using "spiritual" to translate *seishin ryōhō* / *reijutsu* (as I do) risks anachronistically projecting late-modern understandings of spirituality onto the prewar period. For more on the early twentieth-century meanings of *rei, reijutsu, seishin,* and *seishin ryōhō,* see Gaitanidis and Stein 2019; J. Stein 2019; Yoshinaga, Hotaka, and Kurita 2019.

19 Albanese 2007: 6. See also Yoshinaga 2019: 17–18.

20 Hirano 2016a: 73–74. Spiritual therapies were called *seishin ryōhō* in the prewar period despite efforts by figures like Morita Masatake (1874–1938) to medicalize and scientize the field (while Morita also promoted his own Buddhist-inflected practice). McVeigh 2017: 101; Y.-C. Wu 2012: chap. 4; Yoshinaga 2019: 5–6. To help differentiate these popular healing practices from nascent forms of what we now consider psychotherapy, Yoshinaga (2019) suggests referring to the former as "folk psychotherapies" (*minkan seishin ryōhō*). While psychiatry and clinical psychology increasingly influenced psychotherapy in postwar Japan, psychotherapies with religious aspects, such as Morita therapy and Naikan, enjoy continued popularity. Harding 2015.

21 Kurita and Yoshinaga 2019: 352.

22 J. Sawada 2004: 3.

23 J. Sawada 2004: chaps. 2–3.

24 Ahn 2019; J. Sawada 2004: 67–68, 278n40; Y.-C. Wu 2012: 46–48.

25 This ritual was also sometimes called *kaji kitō, yose kaji,* or *kuchiyose kitō;* its Buddhist precedent was called *abishahō.* See Hardacre 1994: 142–149; Staemmler 2009: 60–72.

26 Josephson 2013: 122–123. See also Winfield 2005.

27 Hardacre 1994; Josephson 2013: 125–126.

28 Josephson 2012: 236–245; Josephson 2013: 129–131; Odaira 2018; Staemmler 2009: 44.

29 Garon 1997: 60–87; Josephson 2012: 238–240; Staemmler 2009.

30 Matsuoka 2018: 131–132. There has been much speculation about a connection between Usui Reiki Therapy and Okada's healing practice, *jōrei;* the clearest evidence for a direct connection is a report that Koyama Kimiko, the sixth Usui Association president, said that Okada's wife, Yoshi, studied under Usui. Petter 2012: 173.

31 Staemmler 2009: 104–108.

32 Yoshinaga 2021: 231–232.

33 Y.-C. Wu 2012: 138; Yoshinaga 2021: 233.

34 Hirano 2019: 226.

35 McVeigh 2017; Pincus 1996: 60–66; Treat 2018: chap. 4; Yoshinaga 2015.

36 Hirano 2016a: 73; Imura 1996: 300–301; Y.-C. Wu 2012: 30.

37 Josephson 2013: 131.

38 Chemouilli 2004; Hayami and Kojima 2004: 105; Saito 1996: 313.

39 Artemko 2015: 142–143; Johnston 1995: 4.

40 Ogasawara 2015.

41 Hayami and Kojima 2004: 117–119, 145; Nishimura and Ohkusa 2016.

42 Hirano 2019: 224–225.

43 Japanese Buddhists in this period also often did this to distinguish their religion from Christianity. See Godart 2017: chap. 3; Snodgrass 2003: 125.

44 Hardacre 1998; Hirano 2019: 226–229; Imura 1996; Okumura 2019; Person 2019: 94–99; Y.-C. Wu 2012: chap. 3; Yoshinaga 2015, 2021.

45 R. Young 1988: 274.

46 Y.-C. Wu 2012: 38, chap. 3.

47 Ambaras 2006: 30–31; Harootunian 2000; Silverberg 2009.

48 Hirano 2016a: 75, 79.

49 J. Sawada 2004.

50 Between 97 and 98 percent of Japan's adult male population was literate by 1920. Nishimura and Ohkusa 2016: 16.

51 Over one hundred books were published on hypnotism between 1903 and 1912. Hirano 2016a: 68.

52 Perhaps the largest was Taireidō, which a 1917 newspaper article estimated as having over one hundred thousand followers. Yoshinaga 2008: 40.

53 Hirano 2016a: 74–75.

54 Carrier 1995: 3.

55 M. Sawada 1996: 175. See also Esaki 2016: 41–43, 68–70; Ketelaar 1991; Snodgrass 2003.

56 Y.-C. Wu 2012: 181.

57 Ketelaar 1991; McMahan 2008; Snodgrass 2003.

58 Mendelson 2020: 290–340.

59 J. Stein 2015.

60 Petter 2012: 31–33.

61 Duke 2009: chap. 9.

62 Okada 1927.

63 Fukuoka 1974: 8. Fukuoka's text claims to be published by the Usui Association and has an introduction signed by the fifth Usui Association president, Wanami Hōichi. However, the current Usui Association president told me the organization does not consider it an authorized text and suspects Fukuoka used Wanami's name without permission. Takahashi Ichita, email to the author, September 24, 2016. Due to a dearth of biographical materials on Usui, I have chosen to selectively cite this disputed text.

64 Petter 2012: 42–44. Petter cites the memoir of Koyama Kimiko (1906–1999), the sixth Usui Association president, which I have been unable to obtain myself. The alleged Gotō connection is also described in Takai 1986.

65 Gotō was civilian governor of Taiwan, president of the South Manchurian Railway Company, director of Japan's Colonization Bureau, mayor of Tokyo, foreign minister, and home minister. At the time of the Great Kantō Earthquake, he was home minister and dedicated himself to Tokyo's

recovery efforts. Schencking 2013: 159–165, 178–180. He and Usui would have shared a passion for medicine; Gotō's initial background was as chancellor of Nagoya Medical School, and he initiated public health initiatives at home and in Japan's colonies. Lynteris 2011.

66   This is based on inquiries made by Hirano Naoko to the Gotō Shinpei Organization.

67   Okada 1927.

68   Fukuoka 1974: 8; Petter 2012: 44–51.

69   See photos of Usui with his students in Mochizuki 2001: 136; Petter 2012: 73.

70   Okada 1927.

71   Okada 1927.

72   Usui 1928: 8. I have argued elsewhere (J. Stein 2019: 86–87n15) that this passage could refer to being touched by "a great *ki*" (*daiki*) rather than the standard reading "atmosphere" (*taiki*). However, Takahashi Ichita and Kondō Masaki (the current and former Usui Association presidents) have advised me that it is read *taiki* and refers to a "cosmic air." Personal communication, August 2016. Thus, here, I translated *taiki* as "the ether," meant to correlate to the concept of *uchū* (cosmos), a key concept in Usui's cosmology. Japanese spiritual therapists, including Usui Reiki Therapy practitioners, used the term *ēteru* (ether) to explain their therapies' operation. See Matsui 1930; Yoshinaga 2019: 20.

73   Baffelli and Reader 2019: 35–69; J. Stein 2009. Kurita and Yoshinaga (2019) provide many examples of founder narratives in other spiritual therapies of the time.

74   Okada 1927; Tomita (1933) 1999: 7; Usui 1928.

75   Okada 1927.

76   A 1928 directory lists fifty-five regional branches in addition to the Tokyo headquarters (although two branches have no address or branch director listed); a circa 1930 directory lists sixty branches in addition to two Tokyo headquarters locations (again, two with no address or director); and a 1939 directory lists seventy-five regional branches (thirteen with no address or head, and seven branches in Okayama Prefecture all run by the same individual), including three branches in Japan's overseas empire: Busan (Korea), Dalian (Kwantung), and Taitung County (Taiwan). Usui 1939; Usui Reiki Ryōhō Gakkai 1928, ca. 1930.

77   Petter 2012: 73.

78   A 1928 directory and another circa 1930 directory both list five *dai-shihan* (great instructors), four of whom were naval officers: Ushida, Taketomi, Rear Admiral Eguchi Kaname (1877–1942), and Captain Tsunematsu

Kenzō (d. 1945). Under President Ushida served three directors (*riji*), all of whom were naval officers: Eguchi, Hayashi, and Rear Admiral Imaizumi Tetsutarō (1877–1945). Rear Admiral Harada Shōsaku (1874–1961), Rear Admiral Mikami Yoshitada (1880–1947), and Captain-Engineer Sadanaga Kangorō (d. 1944) were also *shihan* who served as councilors (*hyōgiin*). Usui Reiki Ryōhō Gakkai 1928: 1; Usui Reiki Ryōhō Gakkai ca. 1930: 1.

79 Takahashi Ichita, personal email to the author, October 2, 2016.

80 Yamaguchi 2007: 66.

81 Ōmoto's followers included high-ranking naval officers, such as Vice Admiral Akiyama Saneyuki (1868–1918), a renowned strategist of the Russo-Japanese War (1904–1905), and Ōmoto groups formed on naval vessels. After the so-called Ōmoto incident of 1921, in which leaders were imprisoned for lèse majesté and other charges, elite members such as former naval academy instructor Asano Wasaburō (1874–1937) distanced themselves from the group. Hardacre 1998: 146–147. Shortly before the 1921 incident, Ōmoto replaced the *chinkon kishin* possession ritual with a new healing practice called *miteshiro otoritsugi* (convey through a hand substitute) that, in turn, inspired other healing practices that use a hand to direct a spiritual force for healing, such as the *jōrei* practice of Okada Mokichi and the similar *okiyome* technique of Mahikari. Staemmler 2009: 261–274. Some suggest Usui adapted *reiju* from *chinkon kishin* or *miteshiro otoritsugi*. See Beeler and Jonker 2021: 178–181; Jonker 2016: 331. I find little evidence for such a direct connection, but I have argued elsewhere that the close timing of Ōmoto's rapid decline and Usui Reiki Therapy's rise in the early 1920s, coupled with their mutual naval connections, suggests that some of Usui's disciples from the Imperial Navy were primed for Usui Reiki Therapy through either membership in or knowledge of Ōmoto and its healing practices. J. Stein 2011, 2016b.

82 Tōkyō Maiyū Shinbunsha 1932, pt. 2: 274; Hirano 2019: 228.

83 Tōkyō Maiyū Shinbunsha 1932, pt. 2: 274.

84 Petter 2012: 72–78.

85 Tomabechi and Nagasawa 1951: 335–350. Tomabechi was the one *dai-shihan* in the 1928 directory who was not a naval officer. See note 78.

86 Otadon 2010.

87 Kadushin 2012: 19.

88 Association guidelines in a 1928 manual explain that a payment of thirty yen is due at the time of joining and ten yen more is due when one receives *okuden*. Furthermore, at meetings where the people administering *reiju* (*reijusha*) had to travel, attendees paid extra for travel expenses (five yen for *okuden* members and three yen for people at the lower ranks). Usui Reiki

Ryōhō Gakkai 1928: 17–18. At that time, high-level civil servants' monthly
salary was seventy-five yen, elementary schoolteachers' was forty to fifty yen,
and manual laborers made two yen a day. Hirano 2016a: 75n10; Kawana
2018: 212n35.

89   Nisbett and Wilson 1977.

90   Asaki 1928: 16. This article is reproduced and translated in Fueston 2017:
276–287. The other two of the "three fraudulent wizards" are "Kichisaburō
Iino and Taireidō." Iino (1867–1944), known as "Japan's Rasputin," was a
famous spiritual adviser who was said to have helped the Meiji state win
crucial battles in the Russo-Japanese War with his psychic powers and
gained notoriety in the mid-1920s for a series of scandals, some involving his
new religion, the Great Japan Psycho-Spiritual Association (Dai Nippon
Seishin-dan). Taireidō, founded by Tanaka Morihei, was the largest spiritual
therapy of its time. Some have speculated Usui was a Taireidō member, but
Hirano Naoko concluded that, while Usui and his students likely knew of
Tanaka and Taireidō, and there are similarities between their lives and
teachings, there is no evidence of a direct connection and Usui's therapy is
ultimately closer to other "prana therapies" (described later). Hirano 2014;
Jonker 2016: 311–313. That said, apparently an Usui Association member
claimed Tanaka had been among Usui's teachers. Petter 2012: 175.

91   Yoshinaga 2008; Yoshinaga 2021: 236.

92   Nomura 2019; J. Stein 2019: 85–86.

93   The Japanese *reiki* is derived from the Chinese *língqì,* traditionally
understood as the "pneuma" or "soul of life," and used in Chinese folk
religion to denote the "magical energy" associated with a deity's active
presence. Gu 2009: 29; Zavidovskaya 2012: 184. See J. Stein 2019 for
further discussion of *reiki*'s meanings and applications. Medical *qigong,* a
field of practice developed in China but distributed throughout the Sinitic
sphere, treats illness through the application of "humane *qi*" (*rénqì*) through
the hands, eyes, or breath. See J. Stein 2012: 130. Despite the outlawing of *kaji
kitō* in the Meiji era, Shingon Buddhist priests have recently revived it, and
some employ the word *reiki* to explain their efficacy. See Winfield 2005: 123.

94   For Kawakami, see Hirano 2019; Kurita and Yoshinaga 2019: 322;
Mochizuki 1995: 23; Otadon 2019. For Takagi, see Hirano 2016a, 2019;
Kurita and Yoshinaga 2019: 356–357; Takagi 1925. For Matsubara, see
Kurita and Yoshinaga 2019: 363–364; Reiryō-jutsu Kenkyūdan 1934:
236–253.

95   Horowitz 2015. At that time, Kurama's main temple was of the Tendai sect,
which performs this ritual, as do practitioners of Shugendō, also associated
with Kurama.

96 Horowitz 2015.

97 Okada 1927; Usui 1928: 8. See also note 72.

98 Usui 1928: 15.

99 Böhm (forthcoming) reproduces certificates from 1928–1930, when separate certificates were issued for each level. Takai (1986: 141) reproduces a certificate from 1942–1943 that has separate columns for each level from *roku-tō* to *okuden kōki* (explained later).

100 The text implies there was an exam. Usui 1928: 16. The certificates mentioned in note 99 suggest that *okuden* was split into a "first half" (*okuden zenki*) and "second half" (*okuden kōki*) sometime between 1930 and 1942.

101 Yamaguchi 2007: 188n9. This level may have been instituted after Usui's death.

102 Morinaga 2005. For Shinto *kanjō*, see Rambelli 2002.

103 Stone 1999: 109.

104 Morinaga 2005: 1–6.

105 Hurst 1998: chap. 8; Teeuwen 2006.

106 Bodiford 2001: 488–490; Usui 1928: 17.

107 Bodiford 2002.

108 Morinaga 2005: 71.

109 Hurst 1998: 177–179.

110 The first "regulation" reads, "The successors to the late founder Usui Mikao are called the *sōke* of the Usui Reiki Therapy Learning Association to Improve Mind and Body" (Ko-chōso Usui Mikao no kōkeisha o Shinshin Kaizen Usui Reiki Ryōhō Gakkai no sōke to shō su). Usui 1928: 15. Examples of Usui Association certificates with the term *sōke*, and the signature and seal of the association president, include the 1928 certificate published in Mochizuki (2001: 143), 1928–1930 certificates published in Böhm (forthcoming), and the 1993–2003 certificate published in Doi (2014: 152). However, the 1942–1943 certificate published in Takai (1986: 141) does not say *sōke* and was signed by a branch head (possibly due to wartime exigencies). A 1939 publication lists separate addresses for the *sōke*, the *honbu* (headquarters), and the *kaichō* (president). Usui 1939: 19.

111 A 1928 directory lists sixteen officers (*yakuin*): the president, three directors (*riji*), and twelve councilors (*hyōgiin*). Another directory, circa 1930, lists twenty-one officers: the president, four directors, fifteen councilors, and a secretary (*kanji*). A 1939 publication also contains a list of officers including the president, three consulting directors (*komon riji*), one director, four advisers (*komon*), and a secretary. Usui Reiki Ryōhō Gakkai 1928: 1–2; Usui Reiki Ryōhō Gakkai ca. 1930: 1–2; Usui 1939: 19–24. See also note 78.

112 Baffelli and Reader 2019: 80–87, 166–167; Hardacre 1994.

113 Petter 2012: 234–236.

114   Josephson 2013: 122. See also Winfield 2005.

115   Josephson 2013: 122–123.

116   Rambelli 2002.

117   Winfield 2005.

118   That said, it could be based on a cursive form of the character for *kami.* Stiene 2016.

119   Nakano 1972: 22–25.

120   Stiene and Stiene (2010) point out this talisman's appearance in the late seventeenth-century ninjutsu text *Shōninki.* Paul Guillory alerted me to its reproduction in an early twentieth-century ninjutsu manual, possibly where Usui found it. Itō 1917: 196.

121   Petter 2012: 262.

122   Okada 1927; Usui 1928: 7.

123   Petter (2012: 52) says these poems were recited during *reiju* in the Usui Association, and Yamaguchi (2007: 83) says they were recited before *reiju* in the Hayashi Association (discussed later). As *reiju* was received in *seiza gasshō,* it stands to reason that the poems would also be recited in this position. Moreover, Tomita Kaiji ([1933] 1999: 63; also discussed later) emphasizes the importance of reciting *gyosei* in *seiza gasshō* to purify one's heart-mind. This recitation was part of a meditation practice called *hatsurei-hō* (method for activating *reiki*).

124   Koyama 1991; Ushida, Imaizumi, and Harada 1926. See Böhm forthcoming.

125   Ushida, Imaizumi, and Harada 1926. My translations were informed by those of Rika Saruhashi, which appear in Böhm (forthcoming). The postwar association replaced these nationalistic *gyosei* with more anodyne ones.

126   Gluck 1985: 53–54, chap. 5; Khan 1997. The Rescript on Education was enshrined with the Emperor's and Empress's photos, and in at least one school where they were damaged in a fire, the principal committed ritual suicide; in other schools, people risked their lives to save them from fire. Khan 1997: 73.

127   Tomita (1933) 1999: 63.

128   Mitsui (1930) 2003: iv. Mitsui may have inspired the Usui Association to start *gyosei* recitation through a 1925 article on the practice in the magazine *Japan and the Japanese* (*Nihon oyobi Nihonjin*). See Mitsui (1930) 2003: 25. For more on Mitsui and his hand-healing, see Person 2019; Tsukada 2019.

129   J. Stein 2011, 2016b.

130   Garon 1997: 81.

131   King 2007; Petter 2012: 213–248; Petter, Yamaguchi, and Hayashi 2003; Stiene and Stiene 2003: 189–217; Stiene and Stiene 2005; Yamaguchi 2003, 2007.

132   Hirano 2016a: 70–71.

133   McMahan 2008: 69–72; Mohr 2014; Volk 2010.

134   Josephson 2012: 24–28. See also Masuzawa 2008; Pincus 1996; R. Young 1988.

135   Deslippe 2019: 84; Zoehrer 2020: 164–170.

136   Deslippe 2019.

137   Nukariya 1913; Ozaki 2017.

138   Hirano 2014; Hirano 2016a: 80–81; Hirano 2019: 232–233. Ramacharaka's practices were similarly localized in Europe without attribution. Zoehrer 2021.

139   Ramacharaka 1906, 1916.

140   Hirano (2016a: 80–81; 2019: 233) points out that Usui uses quite similar language to Yamada's to talk about emitting prana/*reiki* through touch, exhalation, and gaze, so Yamada is one likely source for Usui to have learned about prana therapy. Usui 1928: 7; Yamada (1920) 1985: 289. However, Ramacharaka also repeatedly named these three methods (see 1906: 52, 67–69; 1916: 69–70, 93–94).

141   Hirano 2016a: 81; Hirano 2019: 234. For *seijō kokyū-hō*, see Yamada (1920) 1985: 279–280. For one account of *jōshin kokyū-hō,* see Petter 2012: 221–227.

142   As esoteric Buddhism tends to consider the practitioner and the deity "only nominally existent" but ultimately as empty as any other phenomena, this process can also be more of a realization of their nonduality rather than a fusion of the two. Dalai Lama 1987: 22. See also Winfield 2005: 110. The rhetoric of "I am the universe" is found in the teachings of Ueshiba Morihei (1883–1969), founder of aikido, which he began teaching at Ōmoto's headquarters in 1920. Staemmler 2009: 225. However, at that time it was used more broadly by spiritual therapists as well. See Taguchi 1918.

143   Thanks, Paul Guillory, for drawing my attention to the depth of these connections.

144   Ramacharaka 1906: 81–83; Ramacharaka 1916: 112–116.

145   See Petter 2012: 244–245, 246–248.

146   Ramacharaka 1906: 81–83, 87–88; 1916: 112–116, 122. For *reiji-hō* and *byōsen,* see Petter 2012: 190–207, 227–229.

147   Okada 1927; Ramacharaka 1916: 23.

148   Usui 1928: 1.

149   Okada 1927.

150   The *gokai* and Usui's portrait likely hung alongside an altar (*kamidana* or *butsudan*), a practice that was common in martial arts and other lineage-based Japanese arts. Hurst 1998: 179–180. Hawayo Takata had a large

portrait of Usui framed with the caption, "Usui-sensei, founder of Usui Reiki Therapy" (Usui Reiki Ryōhō chōso Usui-sensei), that seems to have been printed and distributed for this purpose. Box 19, HTP.

151   Suzuki 1914: 27. Hirano (2016a: 81) demonstrates the closeness of Suzuki's, Takagi's, and Usui's texts by reproducing them side by side. For Suzuki's Christian Science connections, see Hirano 2019: 230, 234–235.

152   A 1919 guide to spiritual therapies lists Suzuki as the progenitor of "philosophic principles therapies" (*tetsuri ryōhō*) in Japan (Furuya 1919: 209–210), and a famous lawyer, after reading Suzuki's *Principles of Health* (*Kenzen no genri*), described Suzuki as "the Japanization of Mrs. Eddy" (Yamazaki 1921: 67), referring to the founder of Christian Science.

153   See Kleeman and Jayne 2021: 19; Petter 2012: 83. Evidence for Hayashi's medical training remains wanting. Despite accounts of his training as a naval surgeon, his name is not listed among the records of Imperial Naval Medical School graduates in Japan's National Archives. Hirano Naoko, personal communication with the author, December 7, 2012. Moreover, Hayashi's clinic does not appear in the contemporary Japanese medical directory (Tanaka, n.d.). That said, Hayashi's tax records reportedly listed his occupation as doctor. Nishina 2017b: 87. Takata consistently referred to him as "Dr. Hayashi" and claimed he was a retired naval surgeon. See "Reiki Ryōhō no Hayashi Chūjirō-shi raiha, zaikyō kaigun gun'i taisa, jūnigatsu made taizai" (Reiki Therapy's Mr. Hayashi Chūjirō arrived in Hawaii: Ex–naval surgeon and captain, will stay until December), *Hawaii Hochi*, October 2, 1937. Some of the hand positions in the Hayashi Association handbook suggest he may have been trained in Sino-Japanese medicine (*kanpō*). See Fueston 2017: 70–71; Gray and Gray 2002: 184–185.

154   Tōkyō Maiyū Shinbusha 1932, pt. 2: 274.

155   Usui Reiki Ryōhō Gakkai 1928: 1.

156   The names of Hayashi and his wife Chie appear in the 1928 Usui Association directory but are gone by the 1930 edition. Usui Reiki Ryōhō Gakkai 1928, 1930. The profile of Hayashi in Tōkyō Maiyū Shinbusha (1932, pt. 2: 274) says Hayashi founded his association in 1927.

157   Yamaguchi (2007) describes all of these methods in detail except the breathing method. Hawayo Takata's diary and handwritten course notes indicate she learned this meditation from Hayashi. Boxes 5, 7, HTP.

158   Petter 2012: 63–64. See also Mochizuki (2001: 138–139), who writes that, at branches outside Tokyo, the Usui Association offered five-day workshops (*kōshūkai*) that gave students *shoden*.

159   Yamaguchi 2007: 27–33. See also Petter 2012: 85–86.

160   Yamaguchi 2007: 30.

161 Petter 2012: 272. Midwifery in prewar Japan could be lucrative, with popular midwives making forty to fifty times the salary of a teacher or bank clerk; the fierce competition led many to distinguish themselves by becoming early adopters of new medical products or practices. A housewife in one of modern Japan's new middle-class nuclear families was "expected, as a 'good wife, wise mother' (*ryōsai kenbo*), to assume the role of a guardian of health for her husband and children" (Homei 2012: 280, 286–287).

162 Matsui 1928.

163 A 1937 edition of this handbook is reprinted in A. Furumoto 1982. The Usui Association, influenced by Hayashi, eventually developed its own *Therapy Guidelines,* which were incorporated into the postwar association *Handbook* (*Hikkei*). Olaf Böhm, personal correspondence with the author, June 30, 2021.

164 For example, to treat "peritoneum diseases," the reader is told to treat the liver, pancreas, stomach, intestines, peritoneum, bladder, heart, and kidneys, before finishing with the Blood Exchange Method. Petter, Yamaguchi, and Hayashi 2003: 77. For the 1928 edition of the Usui Association's *Treatment Methods Outline* (*Chiryō-hō Taii*), see Böhm forthcoming. The Usui Association manual focuses less on organs and more on the spine, including references to specific vertebrae, suggesting possible influence by chiropractic theory. Yamaguchi 2007: 127–128.

165 Takata's chart is in Box 19, HTP. The other Hayashi Association student, Tatsuji Nagao, is described in chapter 3, and the information about his anatomical charts came from an interview with his daughter, Yoshie Kimura, and family, Hilo, HI, June 12, 2012. The 1937 edition is reprinted in A. Furumoto 1982.

166 Asaki 1928: 15.

167 See Lang 1984; Petter, Yamaguchi, and Hayashi 2003: 99. Two photos of Takata teaching in 1930s Hawai'i show her demonstrating this *katsu* technique; in them, she stands behind a seated student who has their arms crossed over their chest, pulling backward on their elbows with a knee in their back. Private collection of Joyce Winough, to be donated to HTP.

168 An article on the Hayashi Association opening a branch in Honolulu says the association had about four thousand members and its biggest branch was in Osaka, followed by Kyoto, Nagoya, Daishōji (Ishikawa), Chichibu (Saitama), Sendai, Morioka (Iwate), and Aomori. About half of these branches are in small towns and cities in northeast Honshu (Japan's main island). This list of branches omits the Tokyo headquarters. It mentions that Hayashi approved of thirteen *shihan,* including Takata, the only one outside Japan. "Reiki Ryōhō no shibu, sakuya soshiki, yakuin mo sentei"

(Branch of *reiki* therapy organized last night, officers selected), *Hawaii Hochi,* January 11, 1938. In Hayashi's farewell address the following month, he cited five thousand members. "Mina-sama no go-kōjō ni chūshin yori kansha su: Hayashi-shi no kokubetsu hōsō" (Grateful from the bottom of my heart for everyone's kindness: Mr. Hayashi's farewell broadcast), *Hawaii Hochi,* February 22, 1938, 8 (reproduced and translated in Fueston 2017: 293–296).

169 See Ikkisha [pseud.] 1938; Takata 1981: tape 3, p. 6.

170 Shimura became a member of the Hayashi Association after Hayashi's treatments helped her recover from a coma while at Keio University Hospital. Takata 1981: tape 3, pp. 6–7.

171 The subject he taught, *seikei geka,* covers both orthopedic surgery and plastic surgery. "Maeda Tomosuke" 2009.

172 Kleeman and Jayne 2021: 123.

173 Takata 1981: tape 2, pp. 16–17; tape 3, pp. 1–3.

174 Takata 1981: tape 3, pp. 2–3.

175 Usui 1928: 3; Okada 1927.

176 Albanese 2007; Hirano 2016a.

177 See J. Stein 2019 for more on this translation choice and *reiki*'s cosmic nature.

178 Usui 1928: 8.

179 *Kanpō* theorists generally divided *ki* into innumerable varieties correspond-ing with *yin-yang* theory, Five Phases theory, and physiological conceptions of the body and its functions, but Usui's monist portrayal of a universal *reiki* underlying all phenomena somewhat resembles the "one *ki* stagnation theory" (*ikki tairyū-setsu*) pioneered by the influential medical scholar Gotō Konzan (1653–1733) of the "ancient medicine school" (*koiha*), which attributed all disease to the stagnation of vital *ki* (*genki*). Although Usui's understanding of *ki* seems influenced by this etiology, his emphasis on connections between morality and health also resembles that of the "latter-day school" (*goseiha*), which considered disease to result from an immoral lifestyle as well as "vital force imbalances." Deal 2006: 234–235. This apparent contradiction can be understood by considering that Usui and his contemporary therapists built their theory at the juncture of a rich tradition of "nurturing life" (*yōjō*) traditions to cultivate, preserve, and circulate *ki* and modern concerns about the nervous system, neurasthenia, and electromagnetism. Nakao 2019; Y.-C. Wu 2012.

180 Diary entry dated December 10, 1935, Box 7, HTP. The Japanese "r" sound is sometimes transliterated as "l," hence "Leiki." See also A. Furumoto 1982; Kono 1954. Hayashi and Takata's reference here to an internal repository of

reiki, corresponding to the *hara* or *seika tanden* center in the lower abdomen, exists in some tension with Takata's later teaching that Reiki is a universal energy channeled by the practitioner. However, in an audio recording of a 1980 First Degree class, Takata taught the universal source recharges a "battery" in the abdomen, which is the proximate source of the energy for Reiki treatments. Fueston 2017: 116–119.

181   Diary entry dated ~~April 1936~~ May 1936 [strikethrough in original], Box 7, HTP. Even earlier, another student of Hayashi's, Matsui Shōō, offered his opinion that Usui Reiki Therapy's efficacy was an entirely physical phenomenon (and not spiritual, despite what the word *reiki* might suggest), explicable with recourse to the vibrations of the therapist's blood affecting the vibrations of the patient's blood. See Matsui 1928, 1930.

182   Albanese 2007; Klassen 2011, 2018; Yoshinaga 2015.

183   She also said she continued to receive treatments from Hayashi and his students "every day for one year." Takata 1981: tape 3, p. 13. This period was probably closer to eight months (October 1935–June 1936).

184   Takata 1981: tape 3, p. 7.

185   Mitsui (1930) 2003: iv.

186   Takata 1981: tape 3, pp. 4–5.

187   Takata 1981: tape 3, p. 5.

188   Ichioka 2006: 61.

189   Azuma 2005: 152.

190   On "double consciousness" in the Black Atlantic, see Gilroy 1993. For "triple consciousness," see Jiménez Román and Flores 2010: 14–15; Welang 2018.

191   In addition to the death of her eldest sister, Kawayo, as an infant and her younger sister Fusae the previous year, Takata's older brother Kazuo had died in February 1920. The timing of Kazuo's death suggests it could have been from the Spanish influenza epidemic that ravaged the Territory that year, particularly Kauaʻi. Kazuo had briefly served in the Hawaiian Department of the US Army in 1918–1919. Most of the soldiers who served in Hawaiʻi prior to World War II were White, but Kazuo enlisted during a period of intense recruitment. For statistics on Spanish influenza in Hawaiʻi, see Schmitt and Nordyke 1999. For the army in prewar Hawaiʻi, see Byers 2019: chap. 5. For Kazuo's service and dates, see Applications for Headstones for U.S. Military Veterans, 1925–1941, Ancestry.com, accessed June 20, 2014, http://www.ancestry.com (citing NARA microfilm publication M1916; Records of the Office of the Quartermaster General, RG 92, NARA).

192   Takata 1981: tape 3, pp. 9–12.

193   The notes in the back of Takata's copy of the Hayashi Association handbook
       are dated December 10–13, 1935. Her *shoden* and *okuden* certificates are
       both dated December 13, 1935. Box 5 and Frames 2–3, HTP.

194   Takata 1981: tape 3, p. 12; Yamaguchi 2007: 27–30.

195   Takata 1981: tape 3, pp. 12–13; diary entry dated March 28, [1936], Box 7,
       HTP.

196   Deacon (2010) 2015.

197   Diary entry dated April 2, 1936, Box 7, HTP.

198   Diary entry dated May [1936], Box 7, HTP.

199   Takata 1981: tape 3, p. 14.

200   Diary entry dated ~~April 1936~~ May 1936 [strikethrough in original] and
       May 21, 1936 (on subsequent pages), Box 7, HTP. Her *shinpiden* certificate,
       dated October 1, 1936, states that Takata practiced treatment at the Hayashi
       Association from December 10, 1935, to May 8, 1936. Frame 5, HTP. It is
       unclear why the dates of Takata's certificate and diary do not correspond or
       why the certificate itself is dated four months after she had already returned
       to Hawai'i. It is possible that Hayashi only wrote out the certificate once he
       received payment for the *shinpiden* training, something Takata did later in
       her teaching career. Fueston 2017: 84–85. Takata's writing "Mr. Hayashi"
       (instead of "Dr. Hayashi") here seems to be a unique occurrence.

201   Passenger lists of vessels arriving at Honolulu, Hawaii, compiled
       February 13, 1900–December 30, 1953, Ancestry.com, accessed June 20,
       2014, http://www.ancestry.com (citing NARA microfilm publication
       A3422, roll 169; Records of the Immigration and Naturalization Service,
       1787–2004, RG 85, NARA).

202   I use here the English term "Reiki Master" to translate the Japanese *shihan*,
       although it is not clear whether Takata was a full *shihan* at this point,
       authorized to teach all levels of the practice, or a kind of "teacher-in-training"
       (referred to in some Japanese Reiki lineages as *shihan-kaku*), authorized to
       teach just the beginner classes. See Nishina 2017a. Another possibility is
       that she was authorized to teach the beginner and intermediate classes,
       but only a "great instructor" (*dai-shihan*) was authorized to make other
       Masters, and she did not receive this status until February 1938. See
       Fueston 2017: 86–87. At least three people are reported to have practiced
       Usui Reiki Therapy in Hawai'i before Takata: Kan Higuchi, minister
       of the Hilo Japanese Christian Church; his wife, Tsuya Higuchi; and a
       Mr. Tahara, who seems to have been Hiroshi Tahara, principal of the
       Papaikou Japanese School on the Papaikou plantation near Hilo. "Reiki
       Ryōhō no Hayashi Chūjirō-shi raiha: reijō Kiyoe-san dōhan, doyōbi
       Chichibu Maru de" (Reiki Therapy's Mr. Hayashi Chūjirō comes to

Hawaii: Accompanied by his daughter Kiyoe, arrives Saturday on the Chichibu Maru), *Hawaii Hochi,* September 30, 1937, 7.

203   "Mina-sama no go-kōjō."

204   Stoddard 1991.

205   "Mina-sama no go-kōjō." She left Honolulu on June 29 and returned on September 24, 1937. Passenger lists of vessels arriving or departing at Honolulu, Hawaii, 1900–1954, Ancestry.com, accessed June 20, 2014, http://www.ancestry.com (citing NARA microfilm publication A3422, roll unknown and roll 186; Records of the Immigration and Naturalization Service, 1787–2004, RG 85, NARA).

206   Jung 1954: 116.

207   Takata 1981: tape 22, p. 4.

208   Selberg 1995.

209   For charismatic entrepreneurship, see Stalker 2008.

210   Blacker 2004: 105–113; Dorman 2012: 67.

211   Matsui 1928.

212   Y.-C. Wu 2012: 11.

213   Usui 1928: 9–11.

214   Ketelaar 1991: 38.

215   Venuti 2008.

Chapter 3: Healing at the Hub of the Transwar Pacific

1   "Mina-sama no go-kōjō ni chūshin yori kansha su: Hayashi-shi no kokubetsu hōsō" (Grateful from the bottom of my heart for everyone's kindness: Mr. Hayashi's farewell broadcast), *Hawaii Hochi,* February 22, 1938, 8 (reproduced and translated in Fueston 2017: 293–296). "Hayashi's Farewell Broadcast," op. cit. They also taught two courses on Kaua'i, for a total of sixteen. From November to February, they held a class every week, with a two-week break for the holidays, a schedule Takata maintained for a month after Hayashi's departure. See Nishina 2017a for analysis of this schedule. This teahouse still operates today under the name Natsunoya. See Ohira 1999.

2   Going-away gifts, called *senbetsu,* were common among Nikkei in Hawai'i. They often gave money for a person's travels, generally to Japan, which would be reciprocated either with souvenirs or with a *senbetsu* of the same amount in the future. Ogawa 1973: 76. Takata's diary from the 1930s has a section called "Senbetsu" that lists fifty-three people who each donated between one and ten dollars for a total of $110 (over $2000 in 2022 dollars). It is unclear if this was money she received before one of her trips to Japan or money she collected for Hayashi's *senbetsu.* Box 7, HTP. Nikkei plantation

laborers in 1939 Hawai'i made an average of 26 cents an hour. Shoemaker 1940: 45. The details of the gifts are from Takata 1981: tape 5, p. 11.

3 However, rumors spread that Hayashi took home between $6,000 and $7,000 (roughly $125,000–$150,000 in 2022 dollars). See Ikkisha [pseud.] 1938.

4 Natsunoya Tea House, n.d.; Savela 2011.

5 Williams 2019: 19–37.

6 Ogawa and Fox 2008: 32. My inquiries to the US National Archives and Records Administration did not locate files for either Hawayo or Julia Takata, but correspondence from the US Department of Justice two decades after the war indicates that Julia (under her Japanese name, Sayoko) had money seized by the US Office of Alien Property Custodian, which suggests that the government classified her as a "resident enemy alien," despite her being an American citizen. This was probably related to her having studied in Japan in the 1930s. John W. Douglas, US Department of Justice, to Hawayo Takata, July 20, 1964, Box 6, HTP.

7 Hunter 1971: 186, 189; Ogawa and Fox 2008; Williams 2019, chap. 2. Only about 1,250 Nikkei (less than 1 percent of the roughly 150,000 who lived in Hawai'i) were incarcerated, much different from the US West Coast, where the federal government incarcerated nearly all Nikkei in concentration camps. US officials decided that incarcerating the entire Hawaiian Nikkei population would devastate the local economy. Okamura 2000. For the importance of using the terms "incarceration" and "concentration camp" rather than the more anodyne "internment" and "internment camp," see Daniels 2005.

8 Abel 2015; Fujitani 2011.

9 This is addressed in chapter 4.

10 "Reiki Ryōhō no Hayashi Chūjirō-shi raiha: Reijō Kiyoe-san dōhan, doyōbi Chichubu Maru de" (Reiki Therapy's Mr. Hayashi Chūjirō comes to Hawaii: Accompanied by his daughter Kiyoe, arrives Saturday on the *Chichibu Maru*), *Hawaii Hochi,* September 30, 1937, 7; "Reiki Ryōhō no Hayashi Chūjirō-shi raiha, zaikyō kaigun gun'i taisa, jūnigatsu made taizai" (Reiki Therapy's Mr. Hayashi Chūjirō arrived in Hawaii: Ex-naval surgeon and captain, will stay until December), *Hawaii Hochi,* October 2, 1937. Coverage of Kiyoe invariably described her as an adept of tea ceremony and ikebana and said she would instruct interested students. The *Hawaii Hochi* was published by Fred Kinzaburō Makino (1877–1953), an immigration and labor rights activist who was at the forefront of numerous political issues facing the Nikkei community; he and Takata grew friendly through the period of Hayashi's stay and he became an advocate for her and for Reiki.

See Nakamura 2017a; Takata 1981: tape 5, p. 4; tape 6, pp. 1–4. In the five months of Hayashi's stay, the *Hochi* published dozens of articles about Reiki and advertisements for Hayashi and Takata's lectures and training courses. I am indebted to Hirano Naoko for initially locating roughly three dozen of these articles and ads and transcribing the faded microfilm into postwar characters, and to Nishina Masaki for locating even more and hosting them on his website. Nishina 2017a.

11 "Reiki Ryōhō kōen: Tadai no kanmei atau, chōshū nihyakuyo-mei no seikyō" (Reiki Therapy lecture leaves big impression: Success with over 200 attending), *Hawaii Hochi,* November 27, 1937, 4. In transwar Hawai'i, Usui Reiki Therapy was commonly called "Usui-style Reiki Therapy" (Usui-shiki Reiki Ryōhō) or simply "Reiki Therapy" (Reiki Ryōhō) in Japanese and "Reiki" (or "Leiki") in English, so these terms will be used interchangeably throughout this chapter.

12 As described in chapter 1, Jōdo Shinshū is by far the most common Buddhist sect among Nikkei Americans and is the sect to which Takata and her family belonged; in Hawai'i, the Honpa Hongwanji (Nishi Honganji) denomination is much more common than the Ōtani-ha (Higashi Honganji) denomination.

13 Matsui 1928: 14.

14 For more on the Chūō Rengō, see Imai 2010: 6.

15 Gulick 1914; Millis 1915; A. Palmer 1924: chap. 5.

16 Committee on Immigration 1920: 34; Duus 1999; I. Lind 1984: 29–30; Millis 1915; Nakamura 2003; A. Palmer 1924: chap. 5; Wakukawa 1938: 361–364.

17 Takata 1981: tape 5, pp. 9–10. See also note 28.

18 In "Mina-sama no go-kōjō," Hayashi says there were 350 practitioners in the Hawaiian Islands and that Takata taught "over fifty" before his arrival. If he and Takata taught approximately 300 students in the sixteen classes they taught together (two on Kaua'i and fourteen on O'ahu), that averages 18.75 students per class.

19 "Mina-sama no go-kōjō." Yoshie Kimura also remembered that her father's class in prewar Hilo was in Japanese. Interview by the author, Hilo, HI, June 13, 2012.

20 Takata 1981: tape 5, p. 6.

21 Schmitt 1977: 25.

22 Private collection of Joyce Winough, to be donated to HTP. Two photos fell out of the album, so there are eighty-two names total.

23 In the late 1930s and early 1940s, the standard fee for Takata's First Degree Reiki class was fifty dollars; an unsalaried male plantation laborer in 1939

Hawaii averaged about forty-nine dollars a month, and women made less. Shoemaker 1940: 48, 56.

24 "Hoken chibyō no fukuin: Reiki Ryōhō kōenkai, kuru nijūyonnichi gogo shichiji, kōensha Hayashi Chūjirō" (The gospel of preserving health and healing disease: Reiki Therapy lecture, the coming 24th, 7 p.m., lecturer Hayashi Chūjirō), *Hawaii Hochi,* November 20, 1937, 5.

25 Ikkisha [pseud.] 1938.

26 Bonacich and Modell 1980.

27 This biography of Alice Sae Noda is based on Imai 2010; Peterson 1984; Lillian Emiko Noda Yajima, phone interview by the author, May 23, 2017; and Lenny Yajima Andrew, email to the author, September 10, 2017.

28 Takata later told her students stories about "Sadie," a character based on Noda who extorted Takata for money and reported Hayashi to immigration authorities. In those stories, Takata met Sadie in Tokyo in 1936 and treated her there. See F. Brown 1992: 31–38. However, as other aspects of these stories contradict evidence about Takata's relationship with Noda, they cannot be taken as depicting literal events and (like other stories Takata told in the 1970s) are likely parables used for teaching purposes.

29 The newspaper article ("Reiki Ryōhō no Hayashi Chūjirō-shi raiha") says Noda was on the same ship as the Hayashis, but ship registries indicate Noda sailed on the *Taiyo Maru* with Takata a week prior, leaving Yokohama on September 15 and arriving September 24, while the Hayashis traveled on the *Chichibu Maru,* leaving Yokohama on September 24 and arriving October 2. Passenger lists of vessels arriving or departing at Honolulu, Hawaii, 1900–1954, Ancestry.com, accessed June 20, 2014, http://www.ancestry.com (citing NARA microfilm publication A3422, rolls 186–187; Records of the Immigration and Naturalization Service, 1787–2004, RG 85, NARA).

30 "Reiki Ryōhō no taika: Hayashi Chūjirō-shi raitō, Waimea to Kapaa de no kōshūkai hidori kettei" (Reiki Therapy authority, Mr. Hayashi Chūjirō visits island: Waimea and Kapaa seminar dates decided), *Hawaii Hochi,* October 7, 1937, 6. The article suggests Noda accompanied Hayashi's daughter, Kiyoe, so it is possible she also wanted to learn tea ceremony or ikebana, in which Kiyoe was skilled.

31 Advertisements in *Hawaii Hochi,* October 29, 1937, 5, and February 5, 1938, 2, reproduced in Nishina 2017a.

32 Over 60 percent of the photos and names in the album cited in note 22 were female.

33 Advertisement in *Hawaii Hochi,* February 5, 1938, 2.

34 "Mrs. Steere Noda to Address Members of Shufu-no-Kai Sunday," *Nippu Jiji,* April 6, 1940, 2.

35 Lillian Emiko Noda Yajima, phone interview by the author, May 23, 2017.

36 Untitled, undated (ca. summer 1938) clipping of a Japanese-language magazine from Hawaii, p. 32, Box 2, Folder 7, HTP.

37 It is even possible that Noda introduced Takata and Reiki to one of their most important patrons: the wealthy heiress Doris Duke (described in chapter 4). Lillian Yajima recalled her mother holding events for the Girl Scouts at Doris Duke's Honolulu estate in the prewar period. Phone interview by the author, May 23, 2017.

38 "Reiki Ryōhō no shibu, sakuya soshiki, yakuin mo sentei" (Branch of Reiki Therapy: Organized last night, officers selected), *Hawaii Hochi,* January 11, 1938; "Mina-sama no go-kōjō"; "Reiki kenkyūkai, sakuya reikai seikyō, shussekisha hyakugojūyomei" (Reiki Research Association—last night's regular meeting a success—over 150 in attendance), *Hawaii Hochi,* March 15, 1938, 7.

39 He bought a property on Fort and Kukui, in downtown Honolulu, in 1913 and did construction there, but in 1914 this property was seized for failure to pay. "Real Estate Transactions," *Honolulu Star-Bulletin,* March 10, 1913, 11, and November 21, 1913, 3; "High Sheriff's Sales Notice," *Honolulu Star-Bulletin,* April 27, 1914, 5. The *Polk-Husted Directory* for the Territory of Hawaii (Honolulu: Polk-Husted Directory Co.) lists him as a launderer (1928–1931), as a restaurateur (1932–1933), and as renting furnished rooms at the Nuuanu address where Takata and Hayashi stayed (1937–1942).

40 "Teikoku kantai hōshisha: Aoyama Bunki-shi to sono katei" (Imperial fleet volunteer: Bunki Aoyama and his family), *Jitsugyo-no-Hawaii,* June 1, 1936, 12. My gratitude to Aoyama's granddaughter Karen Kikukawa for this source.

41 "Hayashi-shi kokubetsu ni raisha: Tsugi de kaigun bochi tenba" (Mr. Hayashi's farewell visits: Next, a visit to the naval cemetery), *Hawaii Hochi,* February 22, 1938, 6; no title, *Hawaii Hochi,* February 23, 1938, 6.

42 "Teikoku kantai hōshisha"; "Mina-sama no go-kōjō"; "Reiki Ryōhō no kenkyūkai soshiki saru: Sakuya Hayashi-shi sōbetsukai sekijō, kōshūsei ichidō ni yotte" (Reiki Therapy study group organized: At Hayashi's farewell party last night, by all students from training courses), *Hawaii Hochi,* December 14, 1937, 7.

43 "Mina-sama no go-kōjō"; "Reiki Ryōhō no shibu"; "Reiki kenkyūkai"; "Reiki kōshūkai no shūsaisha ni tsuite" (About sponsors of Reiki seminars), *Hawaii Hochi,* February 28, 1938, 8. Farewell photos are in Boxes 12, 19, HTP.

44 "Teikoku kantai hōshisha."

45 See Nishina 2017a; "Reiki Kenkyūkai: Sakuya reikai seikyō" (Reiki Research
Association: Last night's regular meeting well-attended), *Hawaii Hochi,*
March 15, 1938, 7.

46 Takata said that Kubokawa was in retirement in Japan for seven years
because he had lost his voice from laryngitis until Hayashi treated him; she
herself traveled to Kamakura to treat him while she was in Japan, so when
he recovered and was assigned to be the bishop of the Jōdō Mission of
Hawai'i, he remembered her and asked her to join their trip to California.
Takata 1981: tape 6, p. 2. In 1934, Kubokawa had been abbot of Kōmyōji,
an important Jōdō temple in Kamakura. Ives 1999: 87n18. Kubokawa was
incarcerated in Hawai'i on the day of the Pearl Harbor attacks and was held
at the Sand Island Detention Center until he was transferred to a mainland
concentration camp. Williams 2019: 86, 271n18.

47 "Reiki Ryōhō no Takata-joshi torai: Beijin fujin tō no shōsei nite" (The visit
of Reiki Therapy's Mrs. Takata: Invited by American women and others),
Hawaii Hochi, April 16, 1938, 12; "Reiki Ryōhō no Takata fujin: Beitairiku
no tabi kara kiha, shikago de ōini nihon o senden" (Reiki Therapy's
Mrs. Takata returns to Hawaii from U.S. mainland: Greatly publicized
Japan in Chicago), *Hawaii Hochi,* July 2, 1938; Nishina 2017a.

48 "Reiki Ryōhō no Takata-joshi torai"; untitled, undated (ca. summer 1938)
clipping of a Japanese-language magazine from Hawaii, p. 32, Box 2, Folder
7, HTP. The latter article says that Takata left Alice Saeko Noda in charge of
Maui and Kin'ichi Mizuta in charge of Hawai'i Island.

49 "Reiki Ryōhō no Takata fujin." These "schools" were "a religious organization" (likely the Saint Germain Foundation, described in the following
section) and "medical scientists," who seem to have been a group
experimenting with radionics (also described later).

50 Takata 1981: tape 6, p. 3. Further evidence that this was not a spur-of-the-
moment decision comes in the recollection of Julia Spalding's nephew that
Spalding had funded Takata's "medical training" on the mainland,
suggesting she had petitioned for these monies from her Keālia benefactor
months in advance. Stoddard 1991.

51 Fueston 2017: 70–71.

52 "Reiki Ryōhō no Takata fujin"; Takata 1981: tape 6, p. 4. She does not seem
to have acquired a certificate there, or if she did, she never mentioned it and
it has not survived.

53 Takata 1981: tape 6, p. 6.

54 Kitagawa 1948.

55 See "Mrs. Takata to Open Office," *Hawaii Tribune-Herald,* May 28, 1939;
"An Announcement," *Hawaii Tribune-Herald,* May 29, 1939.

56 "Mrs. Takata to Open Office."

57 Haberly 1990: 46; Streich 2007: 15; Takata 1981: tape 15, p. 2; tape 16, pp. 12–13; tape 21, p. 7. Takata's juice recipes were likely influenced by juicing pioneer Norman W. Walker, who wrote that watercress juice "should be used with other juices" such as carrot or celery. Walker 1955: 66. Takata traveled to Walker's retreat center in Wickenburg, Arizona, in June 1959, but as the first edition of his book was published in 1936 and she was recommending students to purchase juicing machines by around 1940, she may have encountered his ideas in 1938 Chicago.

58 For Takata attributing juicing to Hayashi's clinic, see Graham 1975. For a history of beets in Japan, see Aoba 2013. Walker (1955: 18) also called beet juice an excellent blood tonic.

59 The text of the certificate is reproduced in Gray and Gray 2002: 67–68.

60 That said, the question-and-answer section of the Usui Association handbook mentions that his method "requires no bitter medicines" (contrasting it with *kanpō*). See Usui 1928: 9. Takata also described Reiki as "absolutely drugless" in her 1936 ad.

61 Baer 2001: 86–87; Dodds 1915; Whorton 2002: 159, 204–205, 215–217.

62 Takata 1981: tape 5, pp. 10–11. Tsukiyama was a local Nisei, World War I veteran, and University of Chicago Law School graduate who was among the first Nikkei attorneys and first to serve in public office. He was appointed city and county deputy attorney in 1929 and city and county attorney in 1933. Nakamura 2017b; Tamura 1994: 241. On the tape, Takata just said "a license," but a handwritten note on the transcript clarifies that it was a massage license. See also F. Brown 1992: 65.

63 Her earliest extant massage license, issued by the Territory of Hawai'i Board of Massage, is dated September 22, 1947, but she saved a mailing tube for what appears to have been an earlier license, postmarked July 7, 1943. Boxes 3, 14, HTP. However, she had been professionally practicing since the late 1930s: from 1938 to 1942, Hawayo Takata was listed in the *Polk-Husted Directory* for the Territory of Hawaii (Honolulu: Polk-Husted Directory Co.) as providing "massage"; in 1942 her listing changed from Honolulu to Hilo. In a newspaper article on Hawai'i residents traveling to Japan, she is listed as "masseur." "5 Excursion Parties Sail for Nippon," *Honolulu Star-Bulletin*, March 21, 1940, 11. See also figure 3.3.

64 Kanemitsu said some women from the interrupted class on Maui later studied *jōrei*, the spiritual healing technique developed by Usui's contemporary Okada Mokichi (mentioned in chapter 2), which projects "God's light" from a raised hand without touch. She dates this story to before Takata's Chicago naturopathy course, which would place it in early 1938,

and speculates it may be related to a story Takata told of treating a policeman from Lahaina (Maui) for a carbuncle, who may have told a colleague who took offense to an unlicensed healer laying hands. However, as Takata claims that healing the policeman caused "Reiki to spread on the Island of Maui," it is also possible that she treated the policeman years later, once she was more established and had her massage license. Kanemitsu, personal conversation with the author, August 2016, and follow-up emails, January 2017; Takata 1981: tape 21, pp. 16–17.

65 F. Brown 1992: 65.

66 Tatsuyama 1948: 1–2.

67 Advertisements in *Hawaii Tribune-Herald,* May 29, 1939, 5, and November 11, 1939, 3. See also "Mrs. Takata to Open Office."

68 Takata 1948.

69 Kanemitsu, n.d.: 3.

70 Skrivanic 2017: 85–86.

71 Gregory 1982; Skrivanic 2017.

72 Advertisement in *Hawaii Hochi,* June 22, 1938, 2. The address where Takata's clinic was is now on the Hawaii State Capitol grounds.

73 Class photos are in the private collection of Joyce Winough, to be donated to the HTP. The class photos each list the time and place, and I have tried to determine what churches they were held at. To the best of my knowledge, the classes were held at Waimea Hongwanji Mission on Kauaʻi (October 7, 1938), Kahuku Hongwanji Mission on Oʻahu (October 23, 1938, and January 19, 1939), Kurtistown Jodo Mission on Hawaiʻi (December 26, 1938), Ōkala Jodo Mission (January 30, 1939), and Ninole Hongwanji Mission (May 19, 1939). She had several clinical spaces in Hilo between May 1939 and December 1940.

74 The *onsen* is mentioned in the Japanese text in figure 3.5; the "cabinet baths" in an English-language ad in the *Hilo Tribune-Herald,* December 7, 1940, 3.

75 The information about Tatsuji Nagao in this paragraph comes from interviews by the author with Yoshie, Art, and Rene Kimura in Hilo in June 2012 and June 2013; Robert Nagao in Hawaii Kai in January 2013; and Yoshie Kimura, "Memories of Jitchan," unpublished, undated essay in author's collection.

76 To "get" or "acquire" Reiki (*reiki o ukeru*) was a common phrase used by Takata's Hilo students and their families to describe having received the initiations.

77 Yoshie, Art, and Rene Kimura, interview by the author, Hilo, HI, June 13, 2012.

78 Yuda family, interview by the author, Hilo, HI, June 30, 2013.

79   Fujimoto 2012: 56.

80   Robert Nagao, interview by the author, Hawaiʻi Kai, HI, January 5, 2013.

81   Mauss 1990. Dennis Ogawa ties this concept of the gift to the Hawaiian Nikkei concept (imported from Japan) of *giri* (obligation). Ogawa 1973: chap. 4.

82   Takata 1981: tape 5, pp. 6–10.

83   *Hawaii Hochi,* February 5, 1938, 2, reproduced in Nishina 2017a.

84   J. Stein 2017a.

85   Haberly 1990: 35; Takata 1981: tape 6, p. 8.

86   Kitagawa 1948. Takata actually did not sell her share in the Waimea Hotel (a.k.a. the Waimea Ranch Hotel) until the late 1950s, although she leased it to a Hollywood-based holding firm from 1953 to 1956. See "Hotelmen Urge HVB Launch Ad Campaign for Tourists," *Honolulu Advertiser,* July 16, 1947, 9; "Hotel Men Meet: Travel Agents Cited to Boost Island Tours," *Honolulu Advertiser,* September 14, 1947, 11; "Hotel, Contractors' Groups Incorporate," *Honolulu Advertiser,* October 25, 1947, 13; Chun 1953; Greaney 1957.

87   Financial records for 623 Pumehana Street and 620 McCully Street, Honolulu, Box 1, Folders 5–6, HTP; advertisement for "Open House . . . Ala Wai Manor," *Honolulu Advertiser,* June 26, 1965. These buildings would be Takata's primary residences beginning in the 1950s, when she sold the Hilo house to her sister and moved back to Honolulu. Takata also bought four lots in Waikiki in September 1939 and constructed another three-story apartment building (423 Nāmāhana Street) there in 1958. See "Land Court Deeds," *Honolulu Star-Bulletin,* October 24, 1939, 10; "Legal Notices," *Honolulu Star-Bulletin,* December 30, 1958, 17.

88   This store, located in the Damon Building on the corner of Hotel and Alakea in downtown Honolulu, was first called B & T Health Foods Store and then Honolulu House of Health. They dissolved their partnership in December 1947 and Bergau continued it under the name Sophie Bergau Health Food Store. "Legal Notices," *Honolulu Star-Bulletin,* November 26, 1946, 18; "Legal Notices," *Honolulu Star-Bulletin,* December 20, 1947, 35; 1940 United States Federal Census, Honolulu, Hawaii, census tract 22, enumeration district 2-50, p. 28A, Ancestry.com, accessed September 15, 2018, https://www.ancestry.com.

89   Takata's efforts to open a health resort in California are described in chapter 4. In the 1970s, she told reporters that she planned to build a Reiki center on land she owned in ʻŌlaʻa (on the island of Hawaiʻi, south of Hilo), which she would then bequeath to the county government, "so it can belong to all the people." Matsuura 1974; Nickerson 1974.

90   For *byōsen,* see Fukuoka 1974: 66–67; Petter 2012: 190–211; Yamaguchi 2007: 73–75. An article published by one of Takata's early students in Hilo

circa 1939 also mentions *byōsen,* so she must have also taught that term in Hawai'i. See Mizuta ca. 1939. For *byōgen,* see Matsui 1928. Robert Nagao told me that his father Tatsuji used the term *shin'netsu* ("root of the fever"). Interview by the author, January 5, 2013. Another Reiki student, Sawami Koshiyama, used the expression "'root' of the illness" (*byōkon*). Kenneth Ogata, "Kogata Theories on Healing," unpublished, undated essay in author's collection. The Yuda family used the term "root of the pain." Interview by the author, June 30, 2013.

91   Gray and Gray 2002: 93; Streich 2007: 12–14; Takata 1948.
92   Haberly 1990: 57.
93   Takata 1948.
94   Fueston 2017: 175–176.
95   Another version of the foundation treatment has fifteen positions, creating a seventy-five-minute treatment.
96   "'Reiki'—A Healing System," May 1953, Journals J-3, Folder 14, RASRLR.
97   Kitagawa 1948.
98   Kono 1954.
99   Follow-up email from "Mrs. B.," August 3, 2015.
100   Yamaguchi 2007: 83.
101   Kimura, "Memories of Jitchan."
102   For details of Nagao's training in postwar Tokyo, see Kleeman and Jayne 2021: 32–34.
103   Ogata, "Kogata Theories."
104   This is a simplified version of the *hatsurei-hō* practice described in Tomita (1933) 1999: 59–70. See p. 233n123.
105   Williams 2019: 41.
106   Classified ad, *Hilo Tribune-Herald,* March 3, 1941.
107   "Reiki Ryōhō no Takata fujin."
108   See International Association for the Preservation of Spiritualist and Occultist Periodicals 2020.
109   Ironically, the original author of Reiki's five precepts was a Japanese promoter of Christian Science. See chapter 2.
110   "Reiki Ryōhō no Takata fujin." Her report of the I Am Movement's eager uptake of *zazen* in 1938 is all the more fascinating because of the fervent American patriotism expressed in their monthly journal, the *Voice of the I Am,* at that time.
111   Takata told students it was possible to lose their ability to perform Reiki if they abused the system. This idea also apparently existed in the Usui Association. See Fueston 2017: 119n224.

112 This is something I heard in many conversations with Takata's students. See also Fueston 2017: 116–119. That said, Takata did teach some students to perform a "Reiki blessing" that resembles *reiju* in its form and usage. See the introduction, note 47.

113 Whorton 2002: 234. Of course, receiving a naturopathy license required much more coursework than a First Degree Reiki certificate (four years as opposed to Takata's four days), but the logic of licensure is the same.

114 On Abrams and the Oscilloclast, see DeVries, n.d.; Raines 1996. Takata named the Oscilloclast in her ad announcing her clinic's opening. *Hawaii Tribune-Herald,* December 7, 1940, 3. This ad is reproduced in Shay 2019: 61.

115 "Reiki Ryōhō no Takata fujin." I have been unable to confirm the identity of A. R. Williamson, but there was an NBC radio executive by that name in Chicago at that time. The article says Williamson conducted his research in an area called Teffin with lots of "radiocraft and radionics manufacturing."

116 Exodus 7:8–12; K. Brown 2001: 226–228, 263; Hendrickson 2014: 61–62. Another of Takata's showdowns appears in chapter 4.

117 Ikkisha [pseud.] 1938.

118 Reader and Tanabe 1998: 94–95, 134–135; Yoshida 2006: 404–405.

119 Yoshida 2006: 405.

120 Moriya 2008b: 122.

121 Reader and Tanabe 1998: 51, 95.

122 Buddhist priests from the Jōdo and Jōdo Shin sects also appear to have organized Takata's first class on the island of Hawai'i. Ikkisha [pseud.] 1938.

123 Tamayose also founded the Hawaii Buddhist Association (Hawai Bukkyōkai) and served as president of the Naha Municipal Association (Naha Shijinkai). Center for Oral History and Hawai'i United Okinawa Association 2009: 182, 185–186, 315–316, 564; Oshiro 2007: 55; Territory of Hawai'i Legislature 2012.

124 "Reiki Ryōhō kōen"; "Reiki Ryōhō no shibu."

125 This said, a small Yokohama-based Shin sect founded by Shibata Junkō (1899–1954) called Shinshū Chōsei-ha (True Sect Longevity School) taught a Longevity Healing Method (Chōsei Ryōjutsu) that claimed to deliver "salvation of the united spirit and flesh" (*reiniku ittai no kyūsai*) through a form of spinal adjustment, explained with the language of the prana therapies described in chapter 2. Interestingly, Shibata, like Tamayose, was a Higashi Honganji minister, and the two were contemporaries, with Shibata introducing his health method in 1931. See Shibata 1988. Thanks to Yoshinaga Shin'ichi for informing me of Shibata.

126 "Lesson 2 Foundation Book," HTP, Box 5. This may have been the minister of the Jōdo Mission in Laupāhoehoe, a plantation town on the Hamakua coast of Hawai'i Island. In Takata's autobiographical recordings, she tells a related story of a Buddhist minister in Laupāhoehoe bringing her to treat a man who had not walked for years, although the details differ from this version. Takata 1981: tape 7, pp. 3–6.

127 Susan Ledesma, interview by the author, February 10, 2023.

128 Abel 2015; Williams 2019.

129 "'Reiki'—A Healing System."

130 Interview by the author, June 30, 2013.

131 Kleinman 1988.

132 Ohnuki-Tierney 1984: 98–99.

133 Interviews by the author with the Yuda family, June 30, 2013, and Susan Ledesma, February 10, 2023.

134 Nishi-shiki Kenkō-hō predated Reiki in Hawai'i, and practitioners wondered how their own laying on of hands therapy (called Nishi-shiki Shokushu Ryōhō) compared to Reiki. See "Nishi-shiki Shokushu Ryōhō to Reiki Ryōhō" (Nishi-style Hands-on Therapy and Reiki Therapy), *Hawaii Hochi,* January 19, 1938.

135 Takata 1981: tape 23, pp. 1–2. The date Takata recalled in this story (January 1, 1943) was before that battle (which began January 22, 1944) or even to the 100th's arrival in Europe (September 1943).

136 A. Lind 1946: 208. See also Hunter 1971: 195.

137 Irene Eshin Matsumoto, conversation with the author, January 2019; Nakamaki 1980: 330–331.

138 Census records list Kekela as "Asiatic Hawaiian," but the same census lists her father, James, a police officer, as a Pacific Islander from Tahiti, and her mother, Mary, as "Asiatic Hawaiian," so it seems that most of her ancestry was Pacific Islander. US Census Bureau, "1930 United States Federal Census, Hilo, Hawaii, Hawaii Territory" and "1930 United States Federal Census, Honolulu, Hawaii, Hawaii Territory," in *Fifteenth Census of the United States, 1930* (Washington, DC: National Archives and Records Administration, 1930), http://www.ancestry.com.

139 Esther Kekela to Hawayo Takata, postmarked June 16, 1943, Box 6, Folder 3, HTP.

140 Takata 1948.

141 Bowler 2013, chaps. 1–2.

142 Takata's diary from this period is in Box 7, HTP. The note above Taniguchi's name and address says, "March 29–1937 / The Law of Karma, so true according to the teachings, when we meet, it is the beginning of parting."

This translates the Japanese expression *au wa wakari no hajimari,* which emphasizes the Buddhist concept of impermanence.

143   This account of Taniguchi's career comes from Staemmler 2013.

144   Holmes 1925, 1926. Holmes, in turn, was inspired by William Walker Atkinson, whose writings as Yogi Ramacharaka seem to have strongly influenced Mikao Usui in the creation of Usui Reiki Therapy. Satter 1999: 249.

145   In volume 3 of the twenty-volume 1935 edition of *Truth of Life,* Taniguchi writes briefly about Mikao Usui and Usui Reiki Therapy while giving background to the Palm Healing Treatment (Tenohira Ryōji) of Eguchi Toshihiro, which he repeatedly uses as a foil for his own method of curing disease by correcting the deluded thinking at the root of illness. Following Eguchi, Taniguchi criticized the high fees Usui charged for training in his methods and noted that Eguchi popularized this technique by decreasing the fees, but ultimately denigrates both for relying on physical *ki* rather than a purely mental approach. Taniguchi 1935: 41–42.

146   Takata transformed Usui's "Be grateful" (Kansha shite) into "Be grateful to every living thing," which resembles Taniguchi's teaching, "Be grateful to all things in heaven and earth" (Tenchi no manbutsu ni kansha seyo), contained in his inaugural issue of *Seichō no Ie.* Also, her Reiki Ideal of "Honor your parents, teachers, and elders" echoes not only the language of the Ten Commandments but also Taniguchi's filial piety. He taught, "The person who is ungrateful to their parents does not realize the heart-mind of God" (Fubo ni kansha shienai-sha wa kami no kokoro ni kanawanu).

147   Box 7, HTP.

148   Mengzi 6A16.

149   Takata seems to have also traveled to a Moralogy event on her way to Saichi's memorial service in Kyoto in March 1936; in her diary she recounts taking an overnight train from Tokyo to Gifu, where she was greeted by her "Moralogy friends" before attending a religious service attended by about one hundred people, run by a Rev. Yamada. Box 7, HTP.

150   For progressivism in early twentieth-century New Thought in the United States, see Hickey 2019; Satter 1999: chap. 6. For affinities between prosperity theology and neoliberalism, see Gutterman and Murphy 2016: chap. 4.

151   Cadge 2005: 10.

152   Wong et al. 1948.

153   Kitagawa 1948.

154   "Mrs. T.," interview by the author, June 11, 2012.

155   A. Lind 1946: 208.

156　"1654J," May 1953, Journals J-3, Folder 12, RASRLR.

157　Baer 2001: 110–120, 167–170.

158　Bonacich and Modell 1980: 85–86.

159　In our interview (June 13, 2012), Yoshie Kimura called *reiki* an "invisible power" (*mienai chikara*).

160　"Lesson 2 Foundation Book," HTP, Box 5.

Chapter 4: Building Authority in the Cold War United States

1　The originals of these certificates and the traveling cases described here are in Box 3, Folders 1–3; Box 16; and Frames 2–3, HTP. Takata continued carrying these cases throughout her teaching career: they appear in a photograph from her 1979 teaching tour in Puerto Rico. "'Sanadora' Hawaiana Explica sus Métodos," *El Vocero* (San Juan), June 20, 1979, 20. It is also possible Takata was only made a so-called *shihan-kaku* at this point. See p. 239n202.

2　This story is analyzed later in the chapter.

3　Benjamin 1969.

4　Weber 1978: 223–224.

5　Chidester 2005.

6　For example, Gray and Gray 2002: 71. The sole example I have found of a report of Takata teaching on the mainland before 1970 is in Morris 1999: 13.

7　Granovetter 1973, 1983.

8　"Reiki Ryōhō no Takata fujin: Beitairiku no tabi kara kiha, shikago de ōini nihon o senden" (Reiki Therapy's Mrs. Takata returns to Hawaii from U.S. mainland: Greatly publicized Japan in Chicago), *Hawaii Hochi,* July 2, 1938; untitled, undated (ca. summer 1938) clipping of a Japanese-language magazine from Hawai'i, Box 2, Folder 7, HTP.

9　Untitled, undated (ca. summer 1938) clipping.

10　Matsui 1928.

11　Kitagawa 1948.

12　The name was inspired by the lavishly produced Frank Capra film *Lost Horizon,* released the same year (based on the 1933 novel of the same name). It depicts an idyllic lamasery in the Himalayas whose residents live to be hundreds of years old. Shangri-La's faux Tibetan name underscores Duke's goal to create an idealized Oriental setting by mixing architecture and décor from across the Muslim world. Karlins (2009) argues Duke was as inspired by opulent "Moorish homes" in New York as she was by sites she had visited in India.

13　Mansfield 1992: 161, 202–203.

14　They could have met between 1938 and 1940 through their mutual connection Alice Saeko Noda. See chapter 3, note 37.

15 Doris Duke to Hawayo Takata, April 28, 1952, Box 6, Folder 3, HTP.

16 Takata founded Springboard Farms with dietician and physiotherapist Charles Benson in 1955, but by the summer of 1956, Takata wanted out of the deal and Duke's lawyers demanded Benson repay this money in full. T. L. Perkins to Dr. Charles W. Benson, July 30, 1956, Box 95, Folder 1, Doris Duke Papers, David M. Rubenstein Rare Book and Manuscript Library, Duke University. Thanks to Robert Fueston and Elayne Crystal for photographs from this archive.

17 Yoshihara (2003: 18) notes that White women's collection of Asian art and goods "packaged the mixed interests Americans had about Asia—Asia as seductive, aesthetic, refined culture, and Asia as foreign, premodern, Other—and made them into unthreatening objects for collection and consumption."

18 Takata 1981: tape 21, pp. 11–14. Takata left Honolulu on February 25 and returned on June 14, 1957.

19 This tendency, which sociologists call homophily, is discussed further later.

20 Box 6, Folder 3, HTP, contains correspondence from Hutton and Todd; the Huxley connection is less substantiated but was reported by two students of Takata's in 1950s Los Angeles, where Huxley socialized with Duke. See Morris 1999: 13.

21 Sylvia Fine Kaye to Hawayo Takata, August 9, 1961, Box 6, Folder 3, HTP.

22 See Hammond 1973: 263; Klatt 2006: 71; Matsuura 1974; Morris 1999: 13; Stiene and Stiene 2003: 149.

23 Kray 2016.

24 This story relies on a phone interview by the author with Ted Vento, June 15, 2015; Takata 1981: tape 9, p. 8; and early typewritten drafts of Takata's autobiography, Box 5, Folders 7–8, HTP. See also Haberly 1990: 100–101. Ted was ten, which is about as young as Takata would initiate anyone. Larisa Stow (b. 1968) attended a class around 1979 where Takata declined to initiate her eleven-year-old friend because after "scanning" the two of them, she decided her friend's "energetic system wasn't fully developed" and it could harm her to take the class. Robert Fueston connects this story to Hayashi's statement in his farewell speech that anyone can learn Usui Reiki Therapy "from the age of twelve or thirteen," as the *ki* meridians of Sino-Japanese medicine (*kanpō*) are only fully developed in "the teen years." However, in 1979, Takata initiated Anneli Twan (b. 1968) at age ten and Kristina Twan (b. 1970) at age nine. Fueston 2017: 294n365; Stow, n.d.; Anneli Twan, interview by the author, Nanaimo, BC, July 25, 2013, and email to the author, July 9, 2017.

25 Ted Vento, phone interview by the author, June 15, 2015.

26 Esther Vento to Hawayo Takata, postmarked August 4, 1942, Box 6, Folder 3, HTP.

27 Vento to Takata.

28 Entries in guest log: Stephen Opsata, August 14, 1951, and Edwin and Neva Opsata, undated, Box 2, Folder 5, HTP.

29 Granovetter 1973.

30 Granovetter 1983: 202.

31 Early typewritten drafts of Takata's autobiography, Box 5, Folders 7–8, HTP.

32 Thomas P. Mackler, "Testimony," unpublished document, 1965, p. 2, personal collection of Shannon E. D. Mackler. This is also the source of the information about the $150 fee and the Macklers' meeting of Takata. Thanks, Shannon Mackler, for sharing this document with me.

33 L. Wilson 2014: 188.

34 Isabel Carden Griffin to Hawayo Takata, postmarked October 8, 1951, Box 6, Folder 3, HTP.

35 Obermer is chiefly remembered as the lover of and muse for the British painter Hannah Gluckstein, a.k.a. Gluck. Lockard 2004.

36 Gitelman and Cronin 2010.

37 Irene Kane Mable, phone conversation with the author, August 25, 2014.

38 Clara Mackler to Elsa Kane, postmarked September 18, 1951, Box 6, Folder 3, HTP.

39 Mae T. Pool to Hawayo Takata, September 22, 1951, Box 6, Folder 3, HTP; Carol Pool, personal emails with the author, August 2014 and May 2017.

40 McPherson, Smith-Lovin, and Cook 2001: 420.

41 Yano 2006: 42.

42 Bender 2010.

43 Red Fox was a prominent early twentieth-century figure in pan-Indian rights organizations and movements. He went by a number of names throughout his life, including Francis St. James, Frances Fox James, Chief Red Fox Skiuhushu, and Dr. Barnabas Sa-Hiuhushu, but I call him Red Fox in this chapter, as that name appears throughout his career. Red Fox claimed to be Blackfoot (some sources say Blackfeet), but a number of his contemporaries, including Sioux activist Zitkála-Šá, doubted his heritage. In 1914 he traveled the United States on horseback to gain signatures from political and cultural elites on a petition for full citizenship for Native Americans and a national holiday for American Indian Day; he delivered this to President Woodrow Wilson with significant press coverage, and he was known as "the father of American Indian Day." He began giving

"Indian names" to non-Natives at least by the summer of 1920 when, as "Rev. Red Fox Skiuhushu, chief of the Federated Tribes of Indians," he "adopted" the Republican presidential candidate Warren G. Harding and his wife, Florence. See Chief Red Fox Skiuhushu to Richard Henry Pratt, January 5, 1920, Richard Henry Pratt Papers, Beinecke Rare Book and Manuscript Library, Yale University; "Indians Adopt G.O.P. Nominee," *Bismarck (ND) Tribune,* July 9, 1920, 3; Carpenter 2005; Hertzberg 1971: chap. 9; Seward 1998.

44   The intertwining of these organizations is evidenced by their joint publication of a magazine called *American Indian Tipi* (also *Tepee* and *Teepee* and, briefly, *American Indian Advocate*) from 1920 to 1927. While the AIA performed charitable works benefiting Native Americans, particularly those in urban areas, its formation seems to have been tied up with Red Fox's desire to gain control of the legacy of the Society of American Indians (SAI), the first pan-Indian association. The founding of the AIA in 1922 came at a time when the SAI was floundering, and it disbanded entirely the following year. One of the SAI's founding executives, archaeologist and ethnologist Arthur C. Parker, blamed Red Fox and his associates for its decline and asserted that they sought to usurp SAI's reputation. Parker's assertion became a reality as, in time, the AIA cited its founding date as 1911, the year of SAI's founding, and listed the early SAI officers as those of the AIA. Moreover, the name "American Indian Association" was what had been used during the planning of the SAI in 1911, suggesting Red Fox willfully conflated the two organizations. Hertzberg 1971: 193–194, 220–221. It is unclear exactly when Red Fox formed the IAA to synthesize the TOA's esoteric fraternal order with the AIA's promotion of Native culture and political activism, but it was sometime between 1932, when Red Fox became the AIA's great sachem at Sherman Coolidge's death, and 1936, when he published a pamphlet under the new name. See M. Brown 1946; Skiuhushu 1936.

45   Adele and Webb 2015: 44–47; Cowger 1999: 18–19; Deloria 1998; Hertzberg 1971: chap. 9.

46   I say "more integrated" because both organizations barred Black people from joining, which the TOA upheld even if the prospective member was of mixed Black and Native heritage.

47   While the undercounting of racial minorities is a perennial issue, census data records the US population as 89.5 percent White in 1950. Gibson and Jung 2005: table A-1. Photo is in Box 16, HTP.

48   C. Wilson 2014.

49   C. Wilson 2014: 79.

50   "Red Fox, Lecturer, to Become Priest," *New York Times,* December 28, 1925, 4; Societas Rosicruciana in America, n.d. This church may be the "Ecumenical Eastern Orthodox Churches" referenced on Takata's ministerial certificate.

51   "Dr. Ralph M. Lewis, Ph.D., F.R.C. (Strong Beaver)" is also listed on the IAA letterhead among their national councilors and advisers. Dr. B. Sa-Hiuhushu—Red Fox to Hawayo Takata, October 16–December 14, 1948, Box 6, Folder 3, HTP (italicized text underlined in original).

52   At the turn of the century, an estimated 40 percent of US adult males were members of fraternal organizations and, by the 1920s, that number rose to nearly half of all US adults, fueled by the rise of women's organizations like the Order of the Eastern Star. Moore 2011: vii; Schmidt 1980: 3.

53   Takata's students from the late 1970s told me similar renditions of this story, but these quotes are from Haberly 1990: 94–95; and Takata 1981: tape 23, pp. 1–2.

54   See Dr. B. Sa-Huihushu to Hawayo Takata, October 16, 1948–December 14, 1948, Box 6, Folder 3, HTP.

55   Most of the names of the national officers on the IAA letterhead are followed by their respective tribal affiliations, but several of them, including Red Fox and "THE GREAT SACAJAWEA—Bird Woman" (a.k.a. Lady Chinquilla, Princess Chinquilla), had had their heritage questioned since at least the 1920s. See Carpenter 2005; Skiuhushu 1936. For "playing Indian," see Deloria 1998.

56   Matsumoto 2014: 31.

57   Morris 1999: 13.

58   Ted Vento, phone interview by the author, June 15, 2015.

59   Takata 1948; "Statement of Mrs. Hawayo Hiromi Takata, Senior Citizen," in *Problems of the Aging: Hearings before the Subcommittee on Federal and State Activities of the Special Committee on Aging, United States Senate Eighty-Seventh Congress, First Session, Part 12.—Hilo, Hawaii, December 1, 1961* (Washington, DC: US Government Printing Office, 1962), 1601–1603.

60   Cf. "Cathedral Contacts," *Rosicrucian Digest,* May 1948, 153. The language of the "cosmic wave" also resembles the "energy wave" of the I Am Movement, which she encountered in 1938 in Chicago. "Reiki Ryōhō no Takata fujin."

61   Hotten 1948. Takata wrote the essay sometime between November 20, 1948, when Red Fox asked for "an essay of 2,000 words in art of healing [*sic*]" as her "examination" for the doctor of naturopathy diploma, and December 11, when he wrote a second letter, enclosed with her diploma.

62   J. Stein 2019.

63 Takata 1948.

64 Palazzotto 1949.

65 Fueston 2017: 48.

66 C. Wilson 2014: 82.

67 C. Wilson 2014: 82.

68 Lears 1981.

69 Jacobson 1998.

70 Jenkins 2004: chap. 7.

71 Huxley (1954) 1970: 9, 18–19, 58.

72 Cheah 2011; Deloria 1998; Owen 2008; Tweed 1992.

73 McPherson, Smith-Lovin, and Cook 2001.

74 Samuels 1970: 112–113; Tamura 1994: 189–192.

75 Okamura 2000: 135.

76 T. Suzuki et. al. 1972: 13.

77 Tamura 1994: 175.

78 Dower 1986: 9.

79 Dower 2012: 35.

80 Janssens 2015: 135–136.

81 Feraru 1950: 101.

82 Feraru 1950: 103.

83 That said, Chinese Americans, especially those with leftist ties, faced
    surveillance and threats of deportation in the 1950s Red Scare. E. Wu 2014:
    119–122.

84 E. Wu 2014: 97–98, 145–146.

85 Klein 2003: 226.

86 Jacobson 1998: 96–99, 234–236.

87 Cheah 2011; Omi and Winant 2014; E. Wu 2014.

88 Yoo 1999: 6–7.

89 Iwamura 2011.

90 See Okamura 2014, chap. 4, for the transformation of Hawaiian Nikkei
    "from race to ethnicity," and Yu 2001, chap. 10, for the model minority
    myth as a legacy of earlier depictions of unassimilable "Orientals."

91 Omi 2016: 43.

92 War Relocation Authority 1945: 36.

93 Bellah 1957; Petersen 1966; E. Wu 2014: 168–174; Yu 2001: 188–189.

94 Klein 2003: 16, 226.

95 Fujitani 2011: 210–211, 230–231. See also Shibusawa 2006; E. Wu 2014.

96 Lani Vento, phone interview by the author, March 10, 2015; Ted Vento,
    phone interview by the author, June 15, 2015.

97 Okamura 2014.

 98 A notable exception is Patsy Takemoto Mink (1927–2002), a local Sansei (third-generation Nikkei) who, in 1964, became the first woman of color elected to the US Congress. See Okamura 2014: 98–100.

 99 Tamura 1994: 222, 232.

100 Wanja Twan, interview by the author, Sidney, BC, August 21, 2016.

101 For "iron maiden," see Kanter 1977: 236; for "dragon lady," see Hearn 2016: 18–19; for the "wise woman" and "crone," see Conway 1994.

102 Iwamura 2011: 20–21.

103 Iwamura 2011: chap. 2.

104 Mettler 2018.

105 Graham 1975.

106 Quoted in Iwamura 2011: 56.

107 Iwamura 2011: 6, 18, 31–32, 59–62.

108 Iwamura 2011: 28–32; Shibusawa 2006; Yoshihara 2003: chap. 7.

109 Uchida 1998: 169.

110 Iwamura 2011: 60.

111 Jaffe 2018.

112 Quoted in Harrell 1985: 479.

113 Peale 1952: 3, 30, 33.

114 Epstein 1993: 181–193; Sutton 2007: 16.

115 Bowler 2013: chaps. 1–2.

116 Albanese 2007: 370.

117 Yogananda 1985: 81, 88–89.

118 Yogananda 1985: 294–307.

119 By 1920, Yogananda preached to Americans about the unity of all religions, while rereading Christianity through Hindu theology, which "in his view provided uniquely satisfying answers to the anomie of a modern materialistic society" (Neumann 2019: 73). This closely resembles what I call "particular universalism" in chapter 5.

120 The 1951 address book is in Box 7, HTP. The books she noted include *Yoga and Self Culture* (1947) by Sri Deva Ram Sukul, who entered the public consciousness two decades prior when actress Mae West claimed he healed her of chronic abdominal pain by laying his hands on the afflicted area. Watts 2001: 115. Takata also noted two books by Yogi Ramacharaka: *The Science of Psychic Healing* (1906) and his translation of the Bhagavad Gita. Ramacharaka was the pen name of New Thought author William Walker Atkinson (which Takata evidently knew, as for *Science of Psychic Healing* she wrote, "by Yogi Ramacharaka by W.W. Atkinson"), and he (directly or indirectly) influenced Reiki's formation in 1920s Japan. See chapter 2.

121   Yogananda's guru Pranabananda ended his life consciously in front of a gathering of his students using breath and concentration. Yogananda 1972: 295. Similarly, Takata told her students that Hayashi summoned a gathering of his students to bid them farewell before using his concentration to burst his arteries and end his life consciously. F. Brown 1992: 58–59; Haberly 1990: 38–41. Moreover, she claimed that Hayashi's body lay in state for a week with no signs of deterioration; the SRF also published a notarized letter from a mortuary director stating that Yogananda's body did not deteriorate normally after embalmment while he lay in state. Haberly 1990: 42; Self-Realization Fellowship 1958: 121–124. Thanks, Robert Fueston, for alerting me to these connections.

122   Mansfield 1992: 233, 259.

123   Takata 1981: tape 21, pp. 12–13.

124   "Takata Hawayo fujin reiki ryōhō o kataru" (Mrs. Hawayo Takata discusses Reiki Therapy), *Hawaii Hochi,* October 17, 1957.

125   Takata 1948.

126   Takata 1948.

127   Gertrude Underwood Kilgore to Esther [Vento], September 8, 1949, Box 6, Folder 3, HTP.

128   Clara Mackler to Elsa Kane, postmarked September 18, 1951, Box 6, Folder 3, HTP.

129   Shannon Mackler, phone interview by the author, August 7, 2014.

130   Takata 1981: tape 18, pp. 8–9.

131   Takata 1981: tape 18, pp. 10–12.

132   See, for example, Hammond 1973: 262.

133   For example, the cover story of the March 1952 issue of Oral Roberts' *Healing Waters* magazine showed "three great medical doctors congratulating" the Pentecostal faith healer. Similar to Takata's story of the anonymous American Medical Association president, it claimed one of these men was an "outstanding medical doctor and president of a medical society of over 20,000 physicians," although a critic of Roberts was unable to substantiate that man's existence. Harrell 1985: 163. A disciple of Yogananda's also recalls how, when "Master conversed with medical doctors . . . the others there obviously accepted him as one of their own" (Swami Kriyananda 2004: 270–271).

134   Clara Mackler to Elsa Kane, postmarked September 18, 1951, Box 6, Folder 3, HTP.

135   Margaret A. Paul to Hawayo Takata, postmarked October 17, 1961, Box 6, Folder 3, HTP.

136   Wuthnow 1997: 19–20.

137   Williamson 2010: 40.
138   Hudnut-Beumler 1994.
139   Deslippe 2018: 20–21.

Chapter 5: Coupling Universalism and "Japanese" Values

1   Jain 2015: 70, 84–87; J. Wilson 2014: 31–36. I use this language of ascribed origins rather than identity (e.g., "Asian religion" or "Asian medicine") to highlight how practices like Reiki, yoga, and meditation movements were produced through Asians' engagement with practices developed in the North Atlantic and continued developing during their circulation outside Asia. Braun 2013; Sharf 1993; Singleton 2010; Strauss 2005.

2   Hammond 1973; Sally Hammond to Hawayo Takata, postmarked November 10, 1972, Box 6, HTP.

3   Hammond 1973: 238.

4   "Worrall, Olga Nathalie Ripich," 2001.

5   Worrall 1972: 24.

6   Hammond 1973: 261.

7   Hammond 1973: 261, 264.

8   Hammond 1973: 261–262.

9   Latour 1993: 104–106. Particular universalism might be considered another way to think about Josephson's "hierarchical inclusion," which deals with alterity by "subordinating marks of difference into a totalizing ideology" that assimilates the Other "while preserving external, and supposedly superficial, difference" and "privileging one interpretive frame over another" (Josephson 2012: 26–27). One related example from prewar East Asia is Ōmoto's promotion of the idea that all religions are one, and it is the foundation. R. Young 1988. Another from the 1940s United States is the movement to declare universal human rights, rooted in "Judeo-Christian" American values. Gaston 2019; Loeffler 2015. Spanning the Pacific, George Tanabe Jr. (2004) discusses a similar kind of "sectarian universalism" present in early twentieth-century Japanese and Japanese American Buddhism.

10   J. Stein 2009.

11   Takata's discourse actually switches between aspects of Occidentalism and Orientalism, which we might consider another form of "oscillation." Brett Esaki's (2016) study of Japanese American artists shows a similar kind of "non-binary" use of silence that appeals to Japanese and White American audiences for different reasons. I plan to explore this further in a future publication.

12   Previously, it had been assumed that Takata trained twenty-two Masters, but my research (presented later in the chapter) indicates that she trained at least one more.

13   Venuti 2008.

14   Stalker 2008: 3.

15   Morris 1999: 13. Morris paraphrases her personal communication with Phyllis and Sidney Kristal, who studied with Takata in 1950s Los Angeles.

16   The 1970 census reports Honolulu's population as 324,871. US Bureau of the Census 1972: pt. 13, p. 10. In Takata's final years, they began forwarding this correspondence to Keosaqua, Iowa, where she spent much of the year when she was not traveling, being cared for by her younger daughter Alice Takata Furumoto.

17   Boxes 6–7, HTP. Many more must have either been marked as undeliverable or been lost somewhere between Honolulu and Green Valley, Arizona, where we unpacked, organized, and archived these letters four decades later.

18   For more on the role of these "middlemen" in the publishing industry to shape spirituality culture, see Gaitanidis 2022: chap. 3.

19   Bone 1975. Despite Takata's exhortation, Gibbs ran an ad for the class beside the article.

20   Twan 2005: 17–22.

21   Wanja Twan, whose story is told later, has been particularly influential, as she and her students were the first to introduce Reiki to Scandinavia, the Netherlands, and India, places where it is fairly common today. Boräng 2013: 17–20; Jonker 2016: 429.

22   Hammond 1973: 263.

23   Nickerson 1974.

24   Hammond 1973: 263; Matsuura 1974.

25   Albanese 2007.

26   The first of these organizations was the Louis Foundation, a spiritual commune led by Louis Gitter on Orcas Island in Washington State. Gitter channeled wisdom from "The Source." Steiger 1975. The foundation's secretary, Helen Haberly, became close with Takata in her final years and was one of two individuals (the other being Marta Getty) whom Takata intended to train as a Master at the time of her death. Fueston 2017: 100. As described in the introduction, Haberly transcribed the December 1979 audio recordings that were to be the basis of Takata's autobiography and ended up writing Takata's first biography. Haberly 1990; Takata 1981. The second organization was a Bay Area–centered personal development group

called Creative Consciousness, headed by Nick Buchanan, who had also been an instructor with the human potential training group Lifespring. Takata taught classes at the Louis Foundation and at the homes of Creative Consciousness members in California and New Jersey, and both organizations published notices about her classes and testimonials about Reiki in their newsletters. Box 6, HTP.

27 Takata had made her sister Kay Yamashita a Master the previous year and may have trained other Masters earlier. See Fueston 2017: 209.

28 Rauscher 1970; "Spiritual Frontiers Fellowship," 1990.

29 Lugenbeel 1984: 1–2; "1974–1975 Mainland Class Lists #2," "Certificate of Merit," and Virginia Samdahl to Hawayo Takata, postmarked September 7, 1974, Box 9, HTP.

30 This number represented about one-third of the SFF's national membership, which peaked in the mid-1970s. Shortly after Takata's first visit, the headquarters moved to Kansas City. J. Gordon Melton, email message to the author, September 25, 2009.

31 Melton, email message to the author.

32 Despite Samdahl's claim to be "the first occidental to obtain the rank of Reiki Master in [Reiki's] 2500 years" (Bartges 1979: 33), Takata had likely trained at least two Masters already: her sister Kay Yamashita (see note 27) and Eulalia Atkinson (described later in this chapter).

33 This new generation of Masters and those they initiated also adapted Reiki in new ways and for new audiences. Lombardi was particularly innovative, teaching over a hundred students at once and employing multiple Masters to give the initiations. Fueston 2017: 213. In 1983, after the contested succession following Takata's death, Lombardi created one of the first Reiki-inspired therapies: a Christian form called Mari-El, combining the name of Jesus' mother with a Hebrew name for God.

34 Gray and Gray 2002: 27–28.

35 Beth Gray and some other Trinity members attended Takata's First Degree class at the home of Wally and Jenny Richardson, in Woodside, California, on June 2–7, 1974. At Beth's recommendation, John Harvey Gray and more Trinity members attended a second class at the Richardsons', held June 12–16. Jenny Richardson, phone interview by the author, June 12, 2017; "Book #1, Mainland, U.S.A., Reiki Class—June 2nd to Sept. 16th 1974," Box 7, HTP.

36 John Harvey Gray Center for Reiki Healing, n.d.

37 With two sessions and ten beds, up to thirty-five practitioners treated up to twenty patients every Sunday before the evening services. While Trinity only offered treatments weekly instead of daily, its capacity was larger than the

Hayashi Reiki Research Association's Tokyo headquarters, which hosted eight beds and sixteen practitioners. Gray and Gray 2002: 31; Takata 1981: tape 2, p. 15.

38 Gray and Gray 2002: 31. This practice of donation envelopes resembles that of *jōrei,* a form of hands-based healing with divine energy that also formed in prewar Japan and spread to the United States in the postwar period. J. Stein 2012: 120.

39 John Harvey Gray Center for Reiki Healing, n.d.

40 Howlett 2008.

41 F. Brown 1992.

42 Sally Okura Lee, interview by the author, Honolulu, HI, July 12, 2013.

43 The Mormon concept of priesthood Lee draws on here is not a clerical title but a mediational role between God and humanity open to any person in the proper relationship with God. Andersen 2013.

44 Sally Okura Lee, interview by the author, Honolulu, HI, July 12, 2013.

45 See her "retirement" letter, signed "Rev. Hawayo Takata," original in HTP, reproduced in Takata, n.d.

46 "Universal Church of the Master Test Questionnaire for Ordained Minister," undated (ca. 1975), Box 6, HTP.

47 These notes have circulated in a number of Reiki teaching manuals and are reproduced in Deacon (2010) 2015: 18. Their original source has yet to be confirmed, but students of Takata's have told me they seem consistent with Takata's language at the time, although they do not recall her citing Bible verses per se.

48 The notes are dated August 29, 1975, which does not correlate with any class in Takata's notebook of class lists, but it includes classes just before and just after that date in Woodside, California. "Mainland Reiki Class May 12th 1975 to [*sic*]," Box 7, HTP.

49 Paul Mitchell, interview by the author, Green Valley, AZ, July 28, 2014; Susan Mitchell, email to the author, September 10, 2017.

50 J. Gordon Melton, email to the author, September 25, 2009.

51 Graham 1975; Straub 1974.

52 "1976 University of Hawaii Paystubs and Class Register," Box 7, HTP.

53 Vivian Kimura, interview by the author, Honolulu, HI, December 20, 2014. For examples of Takata citing teaching at the University of Hawaiʻi at Mānoa, see Bone 1975; Matsuura 1974; Nickerson 1974; Straub 1974.

54 Harlan Mittag, phone interview by the author, June 12, 2017; George Araki to Hawayo Takata, May 9, 1978, Box 8, HTP.

55 Paul Mitchell, interview by the author, Green Valley, AZ, July 28, 2014; Nancy Araki, phone interview by the author, July 17, 2015.

56 For the secularization of American public universities in the mid-twentieth century, see Marsden 1994. Transcendental Meditation is currently engaged in a similar therapeutization process to get into public schools. See Wendt et al. 2015; Williamson 2010.

57 Graham 1975.

58 Altman 2016; Whorton 2002: 260–264.

59 Hing 2004: 93–96.

60 Burnham 1982; Roof 1993.

61 Baer 2001: 106.

62 Iwamura 2011.

63 Reston 1971.

64 Li 2014.

65 Albanese 2007: 489; Whorton 2002: 265.

66 L. Barnes 2013; D. Palmer and Siegler 2017.

67 Nickerson 1974.

68 Straub 1974.

69 Gray and Gray 2002: 66; Nickerson 1974.

70 Gray and Gray 2002: 27, 51.

71 Gray and Gray 2002: 70.

72 Patricia Elders to Takata, April 12, 1978, Box 6, HTP. Showing the tendency among American metaphysicals to combine Asian-descent practices with Christian referents, the same author, apparently having received word of Takata's intention to retire, also says she can no more believe that Takata would retire "from the use of one of God's greatest gifts . . . than I could imagine Jesus giving up on his healing work."

73 Rick Bockner, interview by the author, Whaletown, BC, July 22, 2013.

74 Graham 1975.

75 That Takata recommended books on Japanese Buddhism came from an interview of Phyllis Furumoto by the author, Green Valley, AZ, July 21, 2014, although I have not been able to identify what books they were.

76 Venuti 2008.

77 The book with the symbols is currently in the private collection of Joyce Winough but is to be donated to the HTP.

78 Morinaga 2005: 6.

79 Morinaga 2005: 6–7.

80 The culture of oral tradition Takata created has spawned anxieties within the Reiki community about the proper relationship between orality and writing that continue to the present day. Takata's granddaughter and successor, Phyllis Furumoto, told me that for years she resented any book on Reiki for undermining the direct relationship between master and disciple. Interview

by the author, Green Valley, AZ, July 21, 2014. This mistrust of the written word was related to Furumoto's decision to privately retain the over twelve hours of recordings that Takata made in December 1979 in preparation for her autobiography, which she planned to call *Reiki Is God-Power*. Takata 1981. Forty years later, Takata's students Paul and Susan Mitchell are working on publishing that autobiography, indicating another shift in the relationship between Reiki's leaders and the written word.

81   Bone 1975; Graham 1975.

82   This new "Ideal" sometimes replaced an older one and was sometimes combined with one of them, as Takata experimented with different versions over the last five years of her life. Thank you to Robert Fueston for helping date this addition. For examples of various forms of the Ideals over time, see Jonker 2016: 355–357.

83   The Reiki Ideals contained in the 1948 "Art of Healing" essay analyzed in chapter 4 are an intermediate step toward this innovation, containing self-consciously King Jamesian language (e.g., "Thou Shalt not Anger"), but not the line about honoring one's elders. Takata 1948. As mentioned in chapter 3, it is possible that the filial piety of Seichō no Ie, to which Takata may have been exposed in her time in Japan, had some influence here.

84   Both of these stories were staples of the free lecture and demonstration Takata gave to recruit students for her subsequent four-day classes. See Deacon (2010) 2015: 34–38; Fueston 2017: 45–51.

85   J. Stein 2009: chap. 3. Transcriptions of Takata telling this story are included in Deacon (2010) 2015: 27–38 and Fueston 2017: 35–51. Even articles that cite more historically accurate tellings of Usui's biography continue to cite discredited elements of this story. See Coakley and Barron 2012.

86   She sometimes said this school was Dōshisha University and other times that it was a "boys school." She also often said Usui lived in the "eighteenth century," by which she likely meant the 1800s. See Graham 1975.

87   Iwamura 2011: 20.

88   Iwamura 2011: 20.

89   Sharf 1993: 39.

90   Klein 2003: 16.

91   Paul Mitchell, interview by the author, Green Valley, AZ, July 28, 2014.

92   She had begun experimenting with similar translations by the immediate postwar period; in "The Art of Healing" she renders it, "Earn thy livelihood with honest labor." Takata 1948.

93   Her archived class lists record discounted or free instruction to the elderly or children, and one family is marked as having received free instruction

because someone had cancer. Furthermore, she sometimes allowed Master students to arrange classes for her and count those students' tuitions against their $10,000 fee. Wanja Twan paid the entirety of her Master's training by organizing classes for Takata in the rural British Columbia interior. Takata wanted payments in US cash, which the tree planters and farmers in these classes had difficulty locating, as local banks did not carry it; Wanja recalled piles of crumpled bills scrounged from friends, gas stations, and restaurants. Interview by the author, Sidney, BC, August 21, 2016. See also the case of Rick Bockner in the introduction.

94   Fueston 2017: 51.

95   Clara Mackler to Elsa Kane, postmarked September 18, 1951, Box 6, Folder 3, HTP.

96   Rick Bockner, interview by the author, Whaletown, BC, July 22, 2013.

97   Wanja Twan, interview by the author, Victoria, BC, July 24, 2013; Anneli Twan, interview by the author, Nanaimo, BC, July 25, 2013.

98   Takata won or tied for first in the "ace tournament" of the Ala Wai Women's Golf Club in 1958, 1965, and 1970, and she won their "President Jordan" trophy in 1966. "Hawayo Takata Wins Ace Play," *Honolulu Advertiser*, December 6, 1958, 9; "Hawayo Takata Ace Victor," *Honolulu Advertiser*, November 10, 1965, 24; "Hawayo Takata Wins Tourney," *Honolulu Star-Bulletin*, January 16, 1966, 49; "Ala Wai Ace," *Honolulu Advertiser*, September 21, 1970, 25.

99   Matsuura 1974. See also Bone 1975; Graham 1975; Nickerson 1974 (to whom she said almost exactly the same quote, word for word).

100   See Breedlove 1975.

101   Hammond 1973: 263–264.

102   Eulalia Atkinson to Hawayo Takata, July 14, 1973, Box 6, HTP; Teri Apodaca, Atkinson's daughter, phone interview by the author, June 2016. It is possible Takata trained Masters before the 1970s. Ted Vento (chapter 4) told me Takata offered to make him a Master in 1951, when he was nineteen years old and moving to Alaska, but he turned her down; this suggests she may have trained others who never gained renown. Phone interview by the author, June 15, 2015.

103   Fueston (2017: 100) attributes Takata's death to a heart attack. However, Gretchen Munsey, Takata's student and friend, told me that Takata did not die from a cardiac episode but an aneurysm. Interview by the author, Edmonds, WA, October 7, 2022.

104   The two outliers, Phyllis Furumoto of Winter Park, Colorado, and Barbara Weber of Atlanta, Georgia, would become the two main claimants to be Takata's successor after her death. At least two more Master students were

waiting to finish training at the time of her death, two weeks before her eightieth birthday. Fueston 2017: 100.

105   Gray and Gray 2002: 178.
106   Original in HTP, reproduced in Takata, n.d.
107   Fueston 2017: chap. 6.
108   See Melton 1991 for discussion of succession crises in new religious movements.
109   Haberly 1990: 111–112.
110   Carrette and King 2005; Martin 2014.
111   Phyllis Furumoto and Paul Mitchell, email to the author, June 9, 2017.
112   Gregory 1982; Mauss 1990.

Conclusion

1   Guéhenno (1993) 2000; Stiglitz 2017.
2   Hammer 2004.
3   Brah 1996: 188; Bremer 2006: 33; Matory 2005.
4   Petsalis-Diomidis 2002; Rogers 2011.
5   Beliso-De Jésus 2015; Clearwater 2014; Hendrickson 2014; Matory 2005; Owen 2008; Ramirez 2007; Singleton 2010; Strauss 2005; Williamson 2010; J. Wilson 2014.
6   For analysis of controversies of appropriating Native practices, see Owen 2008.
7   That said, some do obtain licensure for legal protections (as Takata did), from receiving a massage therapy license to becoming a minister of the Universal Life Church (which offers free online ordinations). Hoesly 2018: 175–184.
8   For "corporate forms," see McLaughlin et al. 2020; for "stealth religion," see C. Brown 2013.
9   Drummond 1980.
10   See chapter 2.
11   Joo 2011.
12   Williamson 2010: 89–90.
13   Hoyez 2007.
14   Chidester 2005: 173; Jain 2015: 142–148; Owen 2008: 88–110.
15   J. Wilson 2014: 191–192.
16   Soucy 2014: 27. See also Braun 2013; DeVido 2009; McMahan 2008; Sharf 1995.
17   J. Wilson 2014: 23–27.
18   Hardacre 1994; Sharf 1995.
19   Takata 1948.

20 Braun 2013: 160; Lucia 2018: 58–59; Schedneck 2019; Sharf 1993; Williamson 2010: 12–20.

21 Latour 1993: 104–106.

22 This distinction between technique and practice is found in the teachings of Phyllis Furumoto, although she placed the earlier practitioners of Reiki in a third category she called "folk art." P. Furumoto 1997.

23 J. Stein 2016b. The challenges posed by these non-Takata lineages and information about how Takata adapted Reiki have provoked some Takata-lineage practitioners to change their practice, such as by (re)incorporating recitation of the *gokai* (five precepts) in Japanese with hands in *gasshō* (prayer position) or reframing the "Master symbol" as a tool rather than a symbol (like the three symbols learned in Second Degree).

24 Latour 1993: 120–122.

25 Bourdieu 1990: 53.

26 Tsing 2005.

27 Droog 2008.

References

Abel, Jessamyn R. 2015. *The International Minimum: Creativity and Contradiction in Japan's Global Engagement, 1933–1964.* Honolulu: University of Hawai'i Press.

Adele, Lynne, and Bruce Lee Webb. 2015. *As Above, So Below: Art of the American Fraternal Society, 1850–1930.* Austin: University of Texas Press.

Ahn, Juhn Y. 2019. "Hakuin." In *The Dao Companion to Japanese Buddhist Philosophy,* edited by Gereon Kopf, 511–535. Dordrecht: Springer Netherlands.

Akishima Rayla. 2012. *"Kōun no tobira o hiraku": Supirichuaru serapī* ("Open the door of good fortune": Spiritual therapy). Tokyo: Gentōsha.

Albanese, Catherine L. 1992. "The Magical Staff: Quantum Healing in the New Age." In *Perspectives on the New Age,* edited by James Lewis and J. Gordon Melton, 68–84. Albany: State University of New York Press.

———. 2007. *A Republic of Mind and Spirit: A Cultural History of American Metaphysical Religion.* New Haven, CT: Yale University Press.

Altman, Michael J. 2016. "The Construction of Hinduism in America." *Religion Compass* 10, no. 8:207–216.

Ama, Michihiro. 2011. *Immigrants to the Pure Land: The Modernization, Acculturation, and Globalization of Shin Buddhism, 1898–1941.* Honolulu: University of Hawai'i Press.

Ambaras, David R. 2006. *Bad Youth: Juvenile Delinquency and the Politics of Everyday Life in Modern Japan.* Berkeley: University of California Press.

Andersen, Elder Neil L. 2013. "Power in the Priesthood." Church of Jesus Christ of Latter-day Saints. https://www.lds.org/general-conference/2013/10/power -in-the-priesthood?lang=eng.

Aoba Takashi. 2013. "Tēburu biito" (Beets). In *Nihon no yasai bunkashi jiten* (Cultural history encyclopedia of Japanese vegetables), edited by Aoba Takashi, 334–336. Tokyo: Yasaka Shobō.

Archer, Seth. 2018. *Sharks upon the Land: Colonialism, Indigenous Health, and Culture in Hawai'i, 1778–1855.* Cambridge: Cambridge University Press.

Artemko, Oleg. 2015. "ИСЦЕЛЕНИЕ СИЛОЙ 'ХАРА'— ЭТНОМЕДИЦИНСКИЕ ПРЕДСТАВЛЕНИЯ О 'ЗДОРОВЬЕ' В ЯПОНИИ" (Healing with the power of "hara": Ethnomedical representations of "health" concepts in Japan). In *МЕДИЦИНСКАЯ*

АНТРОПОЛОГИЯ: ПРОБЛЕМЫ, МЕТОДЫ, ИССЛЕДОВАТЕЛЬСКОЕ ПОЛЕ (Medical anthropology: Problems, methods, research field), edited by Valentina Kharitonova. Moscow: Russian Academy of Sciences.

Asaki [pseud.]. 1928. "Sekishu ryōhō jikken no tame: Mizukara kanja to naru no ki" (For the sake of testing single-hand therapy: A personal account of becoming a patient). *Sandē mainichi* (Sunday mainichi), March 4, Shōwa 3 [1928], 15–16. Reprinted and translated in Fueston 2017: 276–287.

Asato, Noriko. 2006. *Teaching Mikadoism: The Attack on Japanese Language Schools in Hawaii, California, and Washington, 1919–1927.* Honolulu: University of Hawaiʻi Press.

Ayala, César J. 1999. *American Sugar Kingdom: The Plantation Economy of the Spanish Caribbean, 1898–1934.* Chapel Hill: University of North Carolina Press.

Ayau, Edward Halealoha. 2000. "Native Burials: Human Rights and Sacred Bones." *Cultural Survival,* March 2000. https://www.culturalsurvival.org/publications/cultural-survival-quarterly/native-burials-human-rights-and-sacred-bones.

Azuma, Eiichi. 2005. *Between Two Empires: Race, History, and Transnationalism in Japanese America.* Oxford: Oxford University Press.

———. 2019. *In Search of Our Frontier: Japanese America and Settler Colonialism in the Construction of Japan's Borderless Empire.* Oakland: University of California Press.

Baer, Hans A. 2001. *Biomedicine and Alternative Healing Systems in America: Issues of Class, Race, Ethnicity, and Gender.* Madison: University of Wisconsin Press.

Baffelli, Erica, Andrea Castiglioni, and Fabio Rambelli, eds. 2021. *The Bloomsbury Handbook of Japanese Religions.* London: Bloomsbury Academic.

Baffelli, Erica, and Ian Reader. 2019. *Dynamism and the Ageing of a Japanese "New" Religion.* London: Bloomsbury Academic.

Barnes, Linda L. 2013. "A World of Chinese Medicine and Healing: Part One." In *Chinese Medicine and Healing: An Illustrated History,* edited by TJ Hinrichs and Linda L. Barnes, 284–333. Cambridge, MA: Harvard University Press.

Barnes, Patricia M., Barbara Bloom, and Richard L. Nahin. 2008. *Complementary and Alternative Medicine Use among Adults and Children: United States, 2007.* National Health Statistics Reports 12. Hyattsville, MD: National Center for Health Statistics.

Bartges, Jonna R. 1979. "Reiki: An Ancient Art." *Psychic Dimensions,* January 1979, 32–33, 36.

Beeler, Dori-Michelle. 2016. *An Ethnographic Account of Reiki Practice in Britain.* Newcastle upon Tyne: Cambridge Scholars.

———. 2017. "Reiki as Surrender: Evidence of an External Authority." *Journal of Contemporary Religion* 32, no. 3:465–478.

Beeler, Dori-Michelle, and Jojan Jonker. 2021. *Reiki Practice and Surrender: An Intersection of Body, Spirituality and Religion.* Zurich: Lit Verlag.

Beliso-De Jésus, Aisha M. 2015. *Electric Santeria: Racial and Social Assemblages of Transnational Religion.* New York: Columbia University Press.

Bellah, Robert N. 1957. *Tokugawa Religion: The Values of Pre-industrial Japan.* Glencoe, IL: Free Press.

Bender, Courtney. 2010. *The New Metaphysicals: Spirituality and the American Religious Imagination.* Chicago: University of Chicago Press.

Benjamin, Walter. 1969. "The Work of Art in the Age of Mechanical Reproduction." In *Illuminations,* edited by Hannah Arendt, translated by Harry Zohn, 217–251. New York: Schocken Books.

Blackburn, Anne M. 2010. *Locations of Buddhism: Colonialism and Modernity in Sri Lanka.* Chicago: University of Chicago Press.

Blacker, Carmen. 2004. *The Catalpa Bow: A Study in Shamanistic Practices in Japan.* 3rd ed. London: RoutledgeCurzon.

Blum, Mark L. 2000. "Stand by Your Founder: Honganji's Struggle with Funeral Orthodoxy." *Japanese Journal of Religious Studies* 27, no. 3–4:179–212.

———. 2002. *The Origins and Development of Pure Land Buddhism: A Study and Translation of Gyonen's "Jodo Homon Genrusho."* Oxford: Oxford University Press.

Bockner, Rick. 2008. Interview by Phyllis Furumoto. November 27, 2008. http://www.reikitalkshow.com/files/shows/20081127.mp3.

Bodiford, William M. 2001. "Religion and Spiritual Development: Japan." In *Martial Arts of the World: An Encyclopedia,* edited by Thomas A. Green, 472–505. Santa Barbara, CA: ABC-CLIO.

———. 2002. "Soke: Historical Incarnations of a Title and Its Entitlements." Koryu. https://www.koryu.com/library/wbodiford1.html.

———. 2006. "When Secrecy Ends: The Tokugawa Reformation of Tendai Buddhism and Its Implications." In *The Culture of Secrecy in Japanese Religion,* edited by Bernhard Scheid and Mark Teeuwen, 309–330. London: Routledge.

Bodine, Echo. 1997. *Supirichuaru serapī: Jinsei o ikinaosu iyashi no gaidansu* (Spiritual therapy: Guidance to heal and revive your life). Translated by Kōga Michiko. Tokyo: Nihon Kyōbunsha.

Böhm, Olaf. Forthcoming. *A Journey to Oneness with the Universe: Early Documents and Practices of Usui Mikao Sensei's Reiki Therapy.* Self-published.

Bonacich, Edna, and John Modell. 1980. *The Economic Basis of Ethnic Solidarity: Small Business in the Japanese American Community.* Berkeley: University of California Press.

Bone, Sonni. 1975. "Are We All Healers? Yes, Says Reiki Teacher." *Penticton Herald* (Penticton, BC), August 27, 1975, 5.

Boräng, Kajsa Krishni. 2013. *Principles of Reiki.* Rev. ed. London: Singing Dragon.

Borup, Jørn. 2015. "Easternization of the East? Zen and Spirituality as Distinct Cultural Narratives in Japan." *Journal of Global Buddhism* 16:70–93.

Bourdieu, Pierre. 1990. *The Logic of Practice.* Translated by Richard Nice. Stanford, CA: Stanford University Press.

Bowler, Kate. 2013. *Blessed: A History of the American Prosperity Gospel.* New York: Oxford University Press.

Brah, Avtar. 1996. *Cartographies of Diaspora: Contesting Identities.* London: Routledge.

Braun, Erik. 2013. *The Birth of Insight: Meditation, Modern Buddhism, and the Burmese Monk Ledi Sayadaw.* New York: Oxford University Press.

Breedlove, Lynn. 1975. "Reiki." *Imagination Plus* 1, no. 3:2–3.

Bremer, Thomas S. 2006. "Sacred Spaces and Tourist Places." In *Tourism, Religion, and Spiritual Journeys,* edited by Dallen J. Timothy and Daniel H. Olsen, 25–35. London: Routledge.

Brown, Candy Gunther. 2013. *The Healing Gods: Complementary and Alternative Medicine in Christian America.* New York: Oxford University Press.

Brown, Fran. 1992. *Living Reiki: Takata's Teachings.* Mendocino, CA: LifeRhythm.

Brown, Karen McCarthy. 2001. *Mama Lola: A Vodou Priestess in Brooklyn.* Rev. ed. Berkeley: University of California Press.

Brown, Mary. 1946. "Noted Indian to Give Talk Here." *Waukesha Daily Freeman* (Waukesha, WI), October 17, 1946, 2.

Burnham, John C. 1982. "American Medicine's Golden Age: What Happened to It?" *Science* 215, no. 4539:1474–1479.

Buswell, Robert E., Jr., ed. 2006. *Currents and Countercurrents: Korean Influences on the East Asian Buddhist Tradition.* Honolulu: University of Hawai'i Press.

Byers, Andrew. 2019. *The Sexual Economy of War: Discipline and Desire in the U.S. Army.* Ithaca, NY: Cornell University Press.

Cadge, Wendy. 2005. *Heartwood: The First Generation of Theravada Buddhism in America.* Chicago: University of Chicago Press.

Campbell, Joseph. 2008. *The Hero with a Thousand Faces.* 3rd ed. Novato, CA: New World Library.

Carpenter, Cari. 2005. "Detecting Indianness: Gertrude Bonnin's Investigation of Native American Identity." *Wicazo Sa Review* 20, no. 1:139–159.

Carr, Elizabeth Ball. 1972. *Da Kine Talk: From Pidgin to Standard English in Hawaii*. Honolulu: University of Hawai'i Press.

Carrette, Jeremy, and Richard King. 2005. *Selling Spirituality: The Silent Takeover of Religion*. London: Routledge.

Carrier, James G., ed. 1995. *Occidentalism: Images of the West*. Oxford: Clarendon Press.

Center for Oral History and Hawai'i United Okinawa Association. 2009. *Uchinanchu: A History of Okinawans in Hawaii*. 3rd ed. Honolulu: Center for Oral History.

Chandler, Siobhan. 2008. "The Social Ethic of Religiously Unaffiliated Spirituality." *Religion Compass* 2, no. 2:240–256.

Cheah, Joseph. 2011. *Race and Religion in American Buddhism: White Supremacy and Immigrant Adaptation*. New York: Oxford University Press.

Chemouilli, Philippe. 2004. "Le choléra et la naissance de la santé publique dans le Japon de Meiji: 1. Modernité, choléra, and pensée hygéinique." *M/S: Médecine Sciences* 20, no. 1:109–114.

Chidester, David. 2005. *Authentic Fakes: Religion and American Popular Culture*. Berkeley: University of California Press.

Chun, Ella. 1953. "Mainland Firm to Take Over Waimea Ranch Hotel." *Honolulu Advertiser,* September 1, 1953, 13.

Clarke, Kamari Maxine. 2004. *Mapping Yorùbá Networks: Power and Agency in the Making of Transnational Communities*. Durham, NC: Duke University Press.

Clarke, Tainya C., Lindsey I. Black, Barbara J. Stussman, Patricia M. Barnes, and Richard L. Nahin. 2015. *Trends in the Use of Complementary Health Approaches among Adults: United States, 2002–2012*. National Health Statistics Reports 79. Hyattsville, MD: National Center for Health Statistics.

Clay, A. J. MacKenzie. 1992. *The Challenge to Teach Reiki: Hands-on Healing That Promotes Physical Wellbeing and Mental, Emotional and Spiritual Extension*. Byron Bay, New South Wales: New Dimensions.

Clearwater, Brian. 2014. "'No Lock on the Tipi Door': Extending Religion in the American Indian Urban Diaspora: Healing, Renewal, and Decolonizing Spaces." PhD diss., University of California, Santa Barbara.

Coakley, Amanda Bulette, and Anne-Marie Barron. 2012. "Energy Therapies in Oncology Nursing." *Seminars in Oncology Nursing* 28, no. 1:55–63.

Committee on Doctrine. 2009. "Guidelines for Evaluating Reiki as an Alternative Therapy." United States Conference of Catholic Bishops, March 25, 2009. http://www.usccb.org/about/doctrine/publications/upload/evaluation-guidelines-finaltext-2009-03.pdf.

Committee on Immigration. 1924. *Japanese Immigration Legislation: Hearings before the Committee on Immigration.* S. 2576, First Session. United States Senate, Sixty-Eighth Congress, Washington, DC.

Conroy, Francis Hilary. 1949. "The Japanese Expansion into Hawaii: 1868–1898." PhD diss., University of California.

Conway, D. J. 1994. *Maiden, Mother, Crone: The Myth and Reality of the Triple Goddess.* Saint Paul, MN: Llewellyn.

Cooper, George, and Gavan Daws. 1990. *Land and Power in Hawaii: The Democratic Years.* Honolulu: University of Hawai'i Press.

Cowger, Thomas W. 1999. *The National Congress of American Indians: The Founding Years.* Lincoln: University of Nebraska Press.

Csordas, Thomas J. 2009. "Introduction: Modalities of Transnational Transcendence." In *Transnational Transcendence: Essays on Religion and Globalization,* edited by Thomas J. Csordas, 1–29. Berkeley: University of California Press.

Dalai Lama. 1987. "Heart of Mantra." In *Deity Yoga: In Action and Performance Tantra,* by Dalai Lama, Tsong-ka-pa, and Jeffrey Hopkins, 1–35. Ithaca, NY: Snow Lion.

Daniels, Roger. 1999. *The Politics of Prejudice: The Anti-Japanese Movement in California and the Struggle for Japanese Exclusion.* Berkeley: University of California Press.

———. 2005. "Words Do Matter: A Note on Inappropriate Terminology and the Incarceration of the Japanese Americans." In *Nikkei in the Pacific Northwest: Japanese Americans and Japanese Canadians in the Twentieth Century,* edited by Louis Fiset and Gail Nomura, 183–207. Seattle: University of Washington Press.

Deacon, James. (2010) 2015. "The Takata-Files . . . Vol. 2." James Deacon's Reiki Pages, Version 1.0.3. http://www.aetw.org/pdf/Reiki_Takata-files _vol_2.zip.

Deal, William E. 2006. *Handbook to Life in Medieval and Early Modern Japan.* Oxford: Oxford University Press.

de Certeau, Michel. 1984. *The Practice of Everyday Life.* Translated by Steven Rendall. Berkeley: University of California Press.

de Cordes, Henri. 2014. "The Dang Case: When *Chakras* Opening Leads to a Belgian Court Case." In *Legal Cases, New Religious Movements, and Minority Faiths,* edited by James T. Richardson and François Bellanger, 199–127. Surrey, UK: Ashgate.

Deloria, Philip J. 1998. *Playing Indian.* New Haven, CT: Yale University Press.

Deslippe, Philip. 2018. "The Swami Circuit: Mapping the Terrain of Early American Yoga." *Journal of Yoga Studies* 1:5–44.

———. 2019. "Uiriamu Uōkā Atokinson: Betsumei Yogi Ramacharaka" (William Walker Atkinson, a.k.a. Yogi Ramacharaka). In Yoshinaga, Tsukada, and Kurita 2019: 79–108.

DeVido, Elise A. 2009. "The Influence of Chinese Master Taixu on Buddhism in Vietnam." *Journal of Global Buddhism* 10:413–458.

DeVries, Bob. n.d. "Some Memories of a Hewlett Packard Product Designer: Part 6, Microwave Lab, 1973–79." HP Memory Project. Accessed April 18, 2022. https://web.archive.org/web/20150103003452/http://www.hpmemory.org/timeline/bob_devries/some_memories_06.htm.

Dodds, Susanna W. 1915. *Drugless Medicine: Hygeiotherapy.* Passaic, NJ: The Health-Culture Company.

Doi, Hiroshi. 2014. *Iyashino Gendai Reiki Ho: A Modern Reiki Method for Healing.* Rev. ed. Southfield, MI: Vision Publications.

Dorman, Benjamin. 2012. *Celebrity Gods: New Religions, Media, and Authority in Occupied Japan.* Honolulu: University of Hawaiʻi Press.

Dower, John W. 1986. *War without Mercy: Race and Power in the Pacific War.* New York: Pantheon Books.

———. 2012. *Ways of Forgetting, Ways of Remembering: Japan in the Modern World.* New York: New Press.

Drescher, Elizabeth. 2016. *Choosing Our Religion: The Spiritual Lives of America's Nones.* New York: Oxford University Press.

Droog, Inger. 2008. "Reiki: Balancing Form and Essence, with Phyllis Lei Furumoto." December 4, 2008. http://www.reikitalkshow.com/files/shows/20081204.mp3.

Drummond, Lee. 1980. "The Cultural Continuum: A Theory of Intersystems." *Man* 15, no. 2:352–374.

Duke, Benjamin C. 2009. *The History of Modern Japanese Education: Constructing the National School System, 1872–1890.* New Brunswick, NJ: Rutgers University Press.

Duus, Masayo Umezawa. 1999. *The Japanese Conspiracy: The Oahu Sugar Strike of 1920.* Berkeley: University of California Press.

Epstein, Daniel Mark. 1993. *Sister Aimee: The Life of Aimee Semple McPherson.* San Diego: Harcourt Brace.

Esaki, Brett J. 2016. *Enfolding Silence: The Transformation of Japanese American Art under Oppression.* New York: Oxford University Press.

Euteneuer, Thomas J. 2010. "To the Editor." *New Oxford Review,* March. https://www.newoxfordreview.org/documents/letter-to-the-editor-march-2010/.

Feher, Joseph. 1969. *Hawaii: A Pictorial History.* Honolulu: Bishop Museum Press.

Feraru, Arthur N. 1950. "Public Opinion Polls on Japan." *Far Eastern Survey* 19, no. 10 (May): 101–103.

Frøystad, Kathinka. 2009. "The Return Path: Anthropology of a Western Yogi." In *Transnational Transcendence: Essays on Religion and Globalization,* edited by Thomas J. Csordas, 279–297. Berkeley: University of California Press.

Fueston, Robert. 2017. *Reiki: Transmissions of Light.* Vol. 1, *The History and System of Usui Shiki Reiki Ryoho.* Twin Lakes, WI: Lotus Press.

Fujikane, Candace, and Jonathan K. Okamura, eds. 2008. *Asian Settler Colonialism: From Local Governance to the Habits of Everyday Life in Hawaiʻi.* Honolulu: University of Hawaiʻi Press.

Fujimoto, Ruth Kikuko. 2012. *Chapters of My Life.* 2nd ed. Hilo: Hawaii Japanese Center Press.

Fujitani, T. 2011. *Race for Empire: Koreans as Japanese and Japanese as Americans during World War II.* Berkeley: University of California Press.

Fukuoka Kōshirō, ed. 1974. *Reiki Ryōhō no shiori* (Reiki Therapy guidebook). Tokyo: Shinshin Kaizen Usui Reiki Ryōhō Gakkai.

Fuller, Robert C. 2001. *Spiritual but Not Religious: Understanding Unchurched America.* New York: Oxford University Press.

Fuller, Robert C., and Justin B. Stein. 2014. "Alternative Medicine: I. Social History." In *Bioethics,* 4th ed., edited by Bruce Jennings, 1:163–172. Farmington Hills, MI: Macmillan Reference.

Furumoto, Alice Takata, ed. 1982. *Leiki: A Memorial to Takata-sensei.* Self-published.

Furumoto, Phyllis Lei. 1997. "A Letter from Phyllis Furumoto." James Deacon's Reiki Pages, March 7, 1997. https://www.aetw.org/reiki_furumoto_letter.htm.

Furuya Keisei. 1919. *Seishin ryōhō kōgi-roku: Dai-san-shū* (Spiritual therapy lecture records, vol. 3). Tokyo: Seishin Kenkyūkan.

Gaitanidis, Ioannis. 2010. "Spiritual Business? A Critical Analysis of the Spiritual Therapy Phenomenon in Contemporary Japan." PhD diss., University of Leeds.

———. 2012. "Spiritual Therapies in Japan." *Japanese Journal of Religious Studies* 39, no. 2:353–385.

———. 2019. "'Haikeika' suru Reiki: Gendai no supirichuaru serapii ni okeru ichidzuke" (The "grounding" of Reiki among contemporary spiritual therapists). In Yoshinaga, Tsukada, and Kurita 2019: 269–290.

———. 2022. *Spirituality and Alternativity in Contemporary Japan: Beyond Religion?* London: Bloomsbury.

Gaitanidis, Ioannis, and Justin B. Stein. 2019. "Japanese Religions and the Global Occult: An Introduction and Literature Review." *Japanese Religions* 44, no. 1–2:1–32.

Garon, Sheldon M. 1997. *Molding Japanese Minds: The State in Everyday Life.* Princeton, NJ: Princeton University Press.

Gaston, K. Healan. 2019. *Imagining Judeo-Christian America: Religion, Secularism, and the Redefinition of Democracy.* Chicago: University of Chicago Press.

Gibson, Campbell, and Kay Jung. 2005. "Historical Census Statistics on Population Totals by Race, 1790 to 1990, and by Hispanic Origin, 1970 to 1990, for Large Cities and Other Urban Places in the United States." Population Division Working Paper No. 76, US Census Bureau, Washington, DC. https://www.census.gov/content/dam/Census/library/working-papers/2005/demo/POP-twps0076.pdf.

Gilroy, Paul. 1993. *The Black Atlantic: Modernity and Double Consciousness.* London: Verso.

Gitelman, Lisa, and Holly Cronin. 2010. "Hamilton Heights." In *The Encyclopedia of New York City,* 2nd ed., edited by Kenneth T. Jackson, 568. New Haven, CT: Yale University Press.

Glenn, Evelyn Nakano. 2002. *Unequal Freedom: How Race and Gender Shaped American Citizenship and Labor.* Cambridge, MA: Harvard University Press.

Gluck, Carol. 1985. *Japan's Modern Myths: Ideology in the Late Meiji Period.* Princeton, NJ: Princeton University Press.

Godart, G. Clinton. 2017. *Darwin, Dharma, and the Divine: Evolutionary Theory and Religion in Modern Japan.* Honolulu: University of Hawai'i Press.

Google. n.d. "Reiki." Google Trends. Accessed December 7, 2022. https://trends.google.com/trends/explore?date=2010-01-01%202019-12-31&q=reiki.

Graham, Vera. 1975. "Mrs. Takata Opens Minds to 'Reiki.'" *Times* (San Mateo, CA), May 17, 1975.

Granovetter, Mark S. 1973. "The Strength of Weak Ties." *American Journal of Sociology* 78, no. 6:1360–1380.

———. 1983. "The Strength of Weak Ties: A Network Theory Revisited." *Sociological Theory* 1:201–233.

Gray, John Harvey, and Lourdes Gray. 2002. *Hand to Hand: The Longest-Practicing Reiki Master Tells His Story.* Xlibris.

Greaney, Edward. 1957. "Big Island Mountain Hotel Up for Sale or Lease." *Honolulu Advertiser,* December 12, 1957.

Gregory, C. A. 1982. *Gifts and Commodities.* London: Academic Press.

Gu, Ming Dong. 2009. "From *Yuanqi* (Primal Energy) to *Wengqi* (Literary Pneuma): A Philosophical Study of a Chinese Aesthetic." *Philosophy East and West* 59, no. 1 (January): 22–46.

Guéhenno, Jean-Marie. (1993) 2000. *The End of the Nation-State.* Translated by Victoria Elliott. Minneapolis: University of Minnesota Press.

Gulick, Sidney L. 1914. *The American Japanese Problem.* New York: Charles Scribner's Sons.

Gutterman, David S., and Andrew R. Murphy. 2016. *Political Religion and Religious Politics: Navigating Identities in the United States.* New York: Routledge.

Haberly, Helen J. 1990. *Reiki: Hawayo Takata's Story.* Olney, MD: Archedigm Publications.

Hammer, Olav. 2004. *Claiming Knowledge: Strategies of Epistemology from Theosophy to the New Age.* Leiden: Brill.

Hammond, Sally. 1973. *We Are All Healers.* New York: Harper and Row.

Hanegraaff, Wouter. 2016. "Reconstructing 'Religion' from the Bottom Up." *Numen* 63:576–605.

Hardacre, Helen. 1994. "Conflict between Shugendō and the New Religions of Bakumatsu Japan." *Japanese Journal of Religious Studies* 21, no. 2–3:137–166.

———. 1998. "Asano Wasaburō and Japanese Spiritualism in Early Twentieth-Century Japan." In *Japan's Competing Modernities: Issues in Culture and Democracy, 1900–1930,* edited by Sharon A. Minichiello, 133–153. Honolulu: University of Hawai'i Press.

Harding, Christopher. 2015. "Religion and Psychotherapy in Modern Japan: A Four-Phase View." In *Religion and Psychotherapy in Modern Japan,* edited by Christopher Harding, Fumiaki Iwata, and Shin'ichi Yoshinaga, 25–50. New York: Routledge.

Harootunian, Harry. 2000. *Overcome by Modernity: History, Culture, and Community in Interwar Japan.* Princeton, NJ: Princeton University Press.

Harrell, David Edwin, Jr. 1985. *Oral Roberts: An American Life.* Bloomington: Indiana University Press.

Harter, Lynn M., Phyllis M. Japp, and Christina S. Beck. 2005. *Narratives, Health, and Healing: Communication Theory, Research, and Practice.* Mahwah, NJ: Lawrence Erlbaum.

Hayami Akira, and Kojima Miyoko. 2004. *Taishō demogurafi: Reikishi jinkōgaku de mita hazama no jidai* (Taishō demography: The "gap era" as seen by historical demography). Tokyo: Bungei Shunjū.

Hearn, Mark Chung. 2016. *Religious Experience among Second Generation Korean Americans.* New York: Palgrave Macmillan.

Hendrickson, Brett. 2014. *Border Medicine: A Transcultural History of Mexican American Curanderismo.* New York: New York University Press.

Hertzberg, Hazel W. 1971. *The Search for an American Indian Identity: Modern Pan-Indian Movements.* Syracuse, NY: Syracuse University Press.

Hickey, Wakoh Shannon. 2019. *Mind Cure: How Meditation Became Medicine.* New York: Oxford University Press.

Hing, Bill Ong. 2004. *Defining America through Immigration Policy.* Philadelphia: Temple University Press.

Hirano Naoko. 2014. "Taireidō to Usui Mikao no reiki ryōhō no kankei ni tsuite no kōsatsu: Seishin ryōhōka / reijutsuka no keifu no naka de" (An inquiry into the relationship between Taireidō and Usui Mikao's Reiki Ryōhō—in the context of psycho-spiritual therapists). Paper distributed at the joint meeting of the Theosophical Society Research Group and the Buddhism and Modernity Research Group, Ryūkoku University, Kyoto, February 1, 2014.

————. 2016a. "The Birth of Reiki and Psycho-spiritual Therapy in 1920's–1930's Japan: The Influence of 'American Metaphysical Religion.'" *Japanese Religions* 40, no. 1/2:65–83.

————. 2016b. "'Supirichuaru' no keifu o kakinaosu: Hīringu gihō 'reiki' no tanjō kara gendai jiko keihatsu gensetsu made" (Rewriting the genealogy of 'the spiritual': From the birth of the healing technique 'Reiki' to contemporary self-development discourse). *Ōyō Shakkaigaku Kenkyū* 58:81–92.

————. 2019. "Taishō-ki no Usui Reiki Ryōhō: Sono kigen to hoka no seishin ryōhō to no kankei" (Taisho-era Usui Reiki Therapy: Its origins and relation to other spiritual therapies). In Yoshinaga, Tsukada, and Kurita 2019: 217–240.

Hoesly, Dusty. 2018. "A Religion of Convenience: The Universal Life Church, Religious Freedom, and Contemporary Weddings." PhD diss., University of California, Santa Barbara.

Holmes, Fenwick L. 1925. *Ikaniseba unmei o shihai shi eru ka* (How to control your destiny). Translated by Taniguchi Masaharu. Tokyo: Jitsugyō no Nihon-sha.

————. 1926. *Kami to minna ni ikuru michi: Kurisuchan Saiensu no shinkō oyobi tetsugaku* (The way to live with God: The faith and philosophy of Christian Science). Translated by Taniguchi Masaharu. Tokyo: Keiseisha Shoten.

Homei, Aya. 2012. "Midwives and the Medical Marketplace in Modern Japan." *Japanese Studies* 32, no. 2:275–293.

Horowitz, Liad. 2015. "גנאקהיו סקט של שי ינרדומ לוגלגכ יקיירה תכינח :תודוסו םילמס םיסקט יירטוזאה" (Rituals, symbols, and secrets: The Reiki initiation ceremony as a modern incarnation of esoteric *kanjō*). MA thesis, Tel Aviv University.

Hotten, M. L. 1948. "Electronics in Medicine." *Rosicrucian Digest,* May 1948, 127–130.

Howlett, Scott. 2008. "Tribute to Rev. Beth Gray." *Reiki Australia,* July 2008.

Hoyez, Anne-Cécile. 2007. "The 'World of Yoga': The Production and Reproduction of Therapeutic Landscapes." *Social Science and Medicine* 65:112–124.

Hudnut-Beumler, James David. 1994. *Looking for God in the Suburbs: The Religion of the American Dream and Its Critics.* New Brunswick, NJ: Rutgers University Press.

Hunter, Louise. 1971. *Buddhism in Hawaii: Its Impact on a Yankee Community.* Honolulu: University of Hawai'i Press.

Hurst, G. Cameron, III. 1998. *Armed Martial Arts of Japan: Swordsmanship and Archery.* New Haven, CT: Yale University Press.

Huxley, Aldous. (1954) 1970. *The Doors of Perception.* New York: Perennial Library.

Ichioka, Yuji. 2006. *Before Internment: Essays in Prewar Japanese American History.* Edited by Gordon H. Chang and Eiichiro Azuma. Stanford, CA: Stanford University Press.

Ikkisha [pseud.]. 1938. "Shinshin kaizen reiki ryōhō ni tsuite: Kōshi Takata fujin o otonau" (About Reiki Therapy to improve mind and body: Visiting instructor Mrs. Takata). *Hawai Shōgyō,* November 15, 1938, 6.

Imai, Shiho. 2010. *Creating the Nisei Market: Race and Citizenship in Hawai'i's Japanese American Consumer Culture.* Honolulu: University of Hawai'i Press.

Imamura Yemyō. 1918. *Hawai kaikyō-shi* (A history of missionization in Hawaii). Honolulu: Hawai Honpa Honganji Kyōdan.

Imura Kōji. 1996. *Shin reijutsuka no kyōen* (New feast of spiritual healers). Tokyo: Shinkōsha.

International Association for the Preservation of Spiritualist and Occultist Periodicals. 2020. "Voice of the I AM." Last updated July 16, 2020. http://www.iapsop.com/archive/materials/voice_of_the_i_am/.

Irwin, Yukiko, and Hilary Conroy. 1972. "R. W. Irwin & Systematic Immigration to Hawaii." In *East across the Pacific: Historical and Sociological Studies of Japanese Immigration and Assimilation,* edited by Hilary Conroy and T. Scott Miyakawa, 40–55. Santa Barbara, CA: Clio.

Itō Gingetsu. 1917. *Ninjutsu no gokui* (The secrets of ninjutsu). Tokyo: Bugyō Sekai-sha.

Ives, Christopher. 1999. "The Mobilization of Doctrine: Buddhist Contributions to Imperial Ideology in Modern Japan." *Japanese Journal of Religious Studies* 26, no. 1–2:83–106.

Iwamura, Jane Naomi. 2011. *Virtual Orientalism: Asian Religions and American Popular Culture.* New York: Oxford University Press.

Jacobson, Matthew Frye. 1998. *Whiteness of a Different Color: European Immigrants and the Alchemy of Race.* Cambridge, MA: Harvard University Press.

Jaffe, Richard M. 2018. "D.T. Suzuki and the Two Cranes: American Philanthropy and Suzuki's Global Agenda." *Kōeki Zaidan Hōjin Matsugaoka Bunko Kenkyū Nenhō* (Annual report of research in the Matsugaoka Library Public Interest Foundation) 32:29–58.

Jain, Andrea B. 2015. *Selling Yoga: From Counterculture to Pop Culture.* Oxford: Oxford University Press.

Janssens, Ruud. 2015. "'Because of Our Commercial Intercourse and . . . Bringing about a Better Understanding between the Two Peoples': A History of Japanese Studies in the United States." In *Reassessing Orientalism: Interlocking Orientologies during the Cold War,* edited by Michael Kemper and Artemy M. Kalinovsky, 120–152. London: Routledge.

Jenkins, Philip. 2004. *Dream Catchers: How Mainstream America Discovered Native Spirituality.* Oxford: Oxford University Press.

Jennings, Jessica Laura. 2019. "Reiki in London: The Vibrant Individual." PhD diss., University College London.

Jiménez Román, Miriam, and Juan Flores. 2010. Introduction to *The Afro-Latin@ Reader: History and Culture in the United States,* edited by Miriam Jiménez Román and Juan Flores, 1–15. Durham, NC: Duke University Press.

John Harvey Gray Center for Reiki Healing. n.d. "John Harvey Gray." Accessed April 18, 2022. https://web.archive.org/web/20160206190340/http://learnreiki.org/john-harvey-gray.htm.

Johnson, Greg. 2007. *Sacred Claims: Repatriation and Living Tradition.* Charlottesville: University of Virginia Press.

Johnston, William. 1995. *The Modern Epidemic: A History of Tuberculosis in Japan.* Cambridge, MA: Harvard University Press.

Jonker, Jojan. 2016. *Reiki: The Transmigration of a Japanese Spiritual Healing Practice.* Zurich: Lit Verlag.

Joo, Ryan Bongseok. 2011. "Countercurrents from the West: 'Blue-Eyed' Zen Masters, Vipassana Meditation, and Buddhist Psychotherapy in Contemporary Korea." *Journal of the American Academy of Religion* 79, no. 3:614–638.

Josephson, Jason. 2012. *The Invention of Religion in Japan.* Chicago: University of Chicago Press.

———. 2013. "An Empowered World: Buddhist Medicine and the Potency of Prayer in Japan." In *Deus In Machina: Religion, Technology, and the Things in Between,* edited by Jeremy Stolow, 117–141. New York: Fordham University Press.

Jung, Carl. 1954. "Fundamental Questions of Psychotherapy." In *The Practice of Psychotherapy,* vol. 16 of *Collected Works of C. G. Jung,* 111–125. London: Routledge.

Kadushin, Charles. 2012. *Understanding Social Networks: Theories Concepts, and Findings.* New York: Oxford University Press.

Kalvig, Anne. 2012. "Facing Suffering and Death: Alternative Therapy as Postsecular Religious Practice." *Scripta Instituti Donneriani Aboensis* 24:145–164.

Kanemitsu, Harue. n.d. "Reiki Teachings: Part I." Unpublished class materials. Text is partially reproduced in "The Art of Healing," Reiki Threshold, last updated May 27, 2005. http://www.threshold.ca/reiki/Art-of-Healing.html.

Kanter, Rosabeth Moss. 1977. *Men and Women of the Corporation.* New York: Basic Books.

Karlins, N. F. 2009. "A Visit to Shangri La." *Artnet Magazine,* June 8, 2009. http://www.artnet.com/magazineus/features/karlins/doris-duke6-8-09.asp.

Kauai Plantation Railway. 2007. "Kauai Sugar Plantations." https://web.archive .org/web/20140708135906/http://www.kauaiplantationrailway.com/agplan tations.htm.

Kawamura, Hawa. 1912. "English Composition." *The Garden Island* (Lihue, HI), November 26, 1912, 6.

Kawana, Sari. 2018. *The Uses of Literature in Modern Japan: Histories and Cultures of the Book.* London: Bloomsbury.

Ketelaar, James Edward. 1991. "Strategic Occidentalism: Meiji Buddhists at the World's Parliament of Religions." *Buddhist-Christian Studies* 11:37–56.

Khan, Yoshimitsu. 1997. *Japanese Moral Education Past and Present.* Madison, NJ: Fairleigh Dickenson University Press.

Kimura, Yukiko. 1988. *Issei: Japanese Immigrants in Hawaii.* Honolulu: University of Hawai'i Press.

King, Dave. 2007. *O-Sensei: A View of Mikao Usui.* 2nd ed. Lulu.com.

Kitagawa, Michiko. 1948. "Reiki." In Wong et al. 1948.

Klassen, Pamela E. 2011. *Spirits of Protestantism: Medicine, Healing, and Liberal Christianity.* Berkeley: University of California Press.

———. 2018. *The Story of Radio Mind: A Missionary's Journey on Indian Land.* Chicago: University of Chicago Press.

Klatt, Oliver. 2006. *Reiki Systems of the World: One Heart, Many Beats.* Twin Lakes, WI: Lotus Press.

Kleeman, Silke, and Amanda Jayne. 2021. *Women in Reiki: Lifetimes Dedicated to Healing in 1930s Japan and Today.* Norderstedt, Germany: BoD—Books on Demand.

Klein, Christina. 2003. *Cold War Orientalism: Asia in the Middlebrow Imagination, 1945–1961.* Berkeley: University of California Press.

Kleinman, Arthur. 1988. *The Illness Narratives: Suffering, Healing, and the Human Condition.* New York: Basic Books.

Kono, Emiko. 1954. "Practice of Leiki among the Japanese." Journals J-4, Folder 26, Romanzo Adams Social Research Laboratory Records, University of Hawai'i at Mānoa Library.

Koyama Kimiko, ed. 1991. *Reiki ryōhō hikkei* (Reiki Therapy handbook). Tokyo: Shinshin Kaizen Usui Reiki Ryōhō Gakkai.

Kray, Thorn R. 2016. "On Name-Dropping: The Mechanisms behind a Notorious Practice in Social Science and the Humanities." *Argumentation* 30:423–441.

Kurita Hidehiko and Yoshinaga Shin'ichi. 2019. "Minkan seishin ryōhō shuyō jinbutsu oyobi chosaku gaido" (Guide of leading figures and authors in folk psycho-spiritual therapies). In Yoshinaga, Tsukada, and Kurita 2019: 297–384.

Kuykendall, Ralph S. 1967. *The Hawaiian Kingdom,* vol. 3, *The Kalakaua Dynasty, 1874–1893.* Honolulu: University of Hawai'i Press.

Lambertz, Peter. 2017. *Seekers and Things: Spiritual Movements and Aesthetic Difference in Kinshasa.* New York: Berghahn.

Lang, Thomas. 1984. "*Katsu:* Traditional Japanese Resuscitation Methods." *Annals of Emergency Methods* 13, no. 1:40–44.

Latour, Bruno. 1993. *We Have Never Been Modern.* Translated by Catherine Porter. New York: Harvester Wheatsheaf.

Lears, T. Jackson. 1981. *No Place of Grace: Antimodernism and the Transformation of American Culture, 1880–1920.* New York: Pantheon Books.

Lepore, Jill. 2013. "The Prodigal Daughter." *New Yorker,* July 8, 2013.

Levine, Gregory P. A. 2017. *Long Strange Journey: On Modern Zen, Zen Art, and Other Predicaments.* Honolulu: University of Hawai'i Press.

Li, Yongming. 2014. "Acupuncture Journey to America: Turning Point in 1971." *Journal of Traditional Chinese Medical Sciences* 1, no. 2:81–83.

Lind, Andrew W. 1946. *Hawaii's Japanese: An Experiment in Democracy.* Princeton, NJ: Princeton University Press.

Lind, Ian Y. 1984. "Ring of Steel: Notes on the Militarization of Hawaii." *Social Process in Hawaii* 31:25–48.

Lo, Catherine Pascual. 2005. "Lihu'e Plantation and Hanama'ulu." Hanama'ulu Town Celebration, February/June 2005. http://poipuwebdesigns.tripod.com /id3.html.

Lockard, Ray Ann. 2004. "Gluck." In *The Queer Encyclopedia of the Visual Arts,* edited by Claude J. Summers, 156–158. San Francisco: Cleis.

Loeffler, James. 2015. "The Particularist Pursuit of American Universalism: The American Jewish Committee's 1944 'Declaration on Human Rights.'" *Journal of Contemporary History* 50, no. 2:274–295.

Lu, Sidney Xu. 2019. *The Making of Japanese Settler Colonialism: Malthusianism and Trans-Pacific Migration, 1868–1961.* Cambridge: Cambridge University Press.

Lübeck, Walter, Frank Arjava Petter, and William Lee Rand. 2001. *The Spirit of Reiki.* Twin Lakes, WI: Lotus Light Press.

Lucia, Amanda. 2018. "Saving Yogis: Spiritual Nationalism and the Proselytizing Missions of Global Yoga." In *Asian Migrants and Religious Experience: From Missionary Journeys to Labor Mobility,* edited by Bernardo E. Brown and Brenda S. A. Yeoh, 35–70. Amsterdam: Amsterdam University Press.

Lugenbeel, Barbara Derrick. 1984. *Virginia Samdahl: Reiki Master Healer.* Norfolk, VA: Grunwald and Radcliffe.

Lynteris, Christos. 2011. "From Prussia to China: Japanese Colonial Medicine and Gotō Shinpei's Combination of Medical Police and Local Self-Administration." *Medical History* 55, no. 3:343–347.

Macpherson, Judith. 2008. *Women and Reiki: Energetic / Holistic Healing in Practice.* London: Equinox.

"Maeda Tomosuke." 2009. In *Dijitaru-han Nihonjinmei daijiten* (Digital-version Japanese name dictionary). Tokyo: Kodansha.

Mansfield, Stephanie. 1992. *The Richest Girl in the World: The Extravagant Life and Fast Times of Doris Duke.* New York: G. P. Putnam's Sons.

Marley, Roni. 2012. "A Focal Point in the Social Aspects of the Kauai Sugar Cane Business—A Narrative of the Valley House Estate (Part 2)." *Hawaiʻi Life* (blog), August 18, 2012. https://www.hawaiilife.com/blog/valley-house-estate-part2/.

Marsden, George M. 1994. *The Soul of the American University: From Protestant Establishment to Established Nonbelief.* New York: Oxford University Press.

Martin, Craig. 2014. *Capitalizing Religion: Ideology and the Opiate of the Bourgeoisie.* London: Bloomsbury.

Masatsugu, Michael K. 2013. "'Bonded by Reverence toward the Buddha': Asian Decolonization, Japanese Americans, and the Making of the Buddhist World, 1947–1965." *Journal of Global History* 8:142–164.

Masuzawa, Tomoko. 2008. *The Invention of World Religions: Or, How European Universalism Was Preserved in the Language of Pluralism.* Chicago: University of Chicago Press.

Matory, J. Lorand. 2005. *Black Atlantic Religion: Tradition, Transnationalism, and Matriarchy in the Afro-Brazilian Candomblé.* Princeton, NJ: Princeton University Press.

Matsui Shōō. 1928. "Sekishu manbyō o ji suru ryōhō" (A therapy that heals all disease with one hand). *Sandē mainichi* (Sunday mainichi), March 4, Showa 3 [1928], 14–15. Reprinted and translated in Fueston 2017, 246–275.

———. 1930. "Reiki ryōhō no kagaku-teki genri" (The scientific principles of Reiki Therapy). *Shufu no tomo* (The housewife's companion) 24, no. 8:66–67.

Matsumoto, Valerie J. 2014. *City Girls: The Nisei Social World in Los Angeles, 1920–1950.* Oxford: Oxford University Press.

Matsuoka, Hideaki. 2018. "Sekai Kyūseikyō." In *Handbook of East Asian New Religious Movements,* edited by Lukas Pokorny and Franz Winter, 128–143. Leiden: Brill.

Matsuura, Patsy. 1974. "Mrs. Takata and Reiki Power." *Honolulu Advertiser,* February 25, 1974, B-2.

Mauss, Marcel. 1990. *The Gift: The Form and Reason for Exchange in Archaic Societies.* Translated by W. D. Halls. London: W. W. Norton.

McLaughlin, Levi, Aike P. Rots, Jolyon Baraka Thomas, and Chika Watanabe. 2020. "Why Scholars of Religion Must Investigate the Corporate Form." *Journal of the American Academy of Religion* 88, no. 3:693–725.

McMahan, David L. 2008. *The Making of Buddhist Modernism.* New York: Oxford University Press.

McPherson, Miller, Lynn Smith-Lovin, and James M. Cook. 2001. "Birds of a Feather: Homophily in Social Networks." *Annual Review of Sociology* 27:415–444.

McVeigh, Brian. 2017. *The History of Japanese Psychology: Global Perspectives, 1875–1950.* London: Bloomsbury.

Melton, J. Gordon. 1991. "When Prophets Die: The Succession Crisis in New Religions." In *When Prophets Die: The Postcharismatic Fate of New Religious Movements,* edited by Timothy Miller, 1–12. Albany: State University of New York Press.

Mendelson, Rebecca. 2020. "Fierce Practice, Courageous Spirit, and Spiritual Cultivation: The Rise of Lay Rinzai Zen in Modern Japan." PhD diss., Duke University.

Mettler, Meghan Warner. 2018. *How to Reach Japan by Subway: America's Fascination with Japanese Culture, 1945–1965.* Lincoln: University of Nebraska Press.

Millis, H. A. 1915. *The Japanese Problem in the United States.* New York: Macmillan.

Milne, Derek, and Wilson Howard. 2000. "Rethinking the Role of Diagnosis in Navajo Religious Healing." *Medical Anthropology Quarterly* 14, no. 4 (December): 543–570.

Mitsui Kōshi. (1930) 2003. *Te-no-hira ryōji* (Palm healing). Tokyo: Vorutekkusu.

Mizuta Kin'ichi. ca. 1939. "Shōfuku no hihō, manbyō no reiyaku: Reiki-jutsu chiryō gaiyō" (The secret method of inviting happiness, the miracle drug for all disease: An outline of the Art of Reiki Treatment"). Possibly self-published or newspaper clipping. Box 2, Folder 7, Hawayo Takata Papers, Special Research Collections, University of California, Santa Barbara.

Mochizuki Toshitaka. 1995. *Iyashi no te: Uchū enerugī "reiki" katsuyō-hō* (Healing hands: How to use "reiki" universal energy). Tokyo: Tama.

———. 1997. *Uchū enerugī: "Reiki" no kiseki* (The miracle of "reiki" universal energy). Tokyo: Goma Shobō.

———. 2001. *Chō-kantan iyashi no te: Nikka de "ki" ga deru "reiki" katsuyō-hō* (Super easy healing hands: How to use "reiki" and emit "ki" in two days). Tokyo: Tama.

Mohr, Michel. 2014. *Buddhism, Unitarianism, and the Meiji Competition for Universality.* Cambridge, MA: Harvard University Press.

Moore, William D. 2011. Introduction to *Secret Societies in America: Foundational Studies in Fraternalism,* edited by William D. Moore and Mark A. Tabbert, vii–xiii. New Orleans: Cornerstone.

Morinaga, Maki Isaka. 2005. *Secrecy in Japanese Arts: "Secret Transmission" as a Mode of Knowledge.* New York: Palgrave Macmillan.

Moriya, Tomoe. 2000. *Yemyo Imamura: Pioneer American Buddhist.* Translated by Tsuneichi Takeshita. Edited by Alfred Bloom and Ruth Tabrah. Honolulu: Buddhist Study Center Press.

———. 2001. *Amerika Bukkyō no tanjō: Nijū seiki shotō no bunka hen'yō* (The birth of American Buddhism: Cultural transformation in the early twentieth century). Tokyo: Gendai Shiryō Shuppan.

———. 2008a. "Buddhism at the Crossroads of the Pacific: Imamura Yemyō and Buddhist Social Ethics." In *Hawaii at the Crossroads of the U.S. and Japan before the Pacific War,* edited by Jon Thares Davidann, 192–216. Honolulu: University of Hawaiʻi Press.

———. 2008b. "Senzen no Hawai ni okeru Nikkei Bukkyō kyōdan shosō" (Various aspects of Buddhist organizations in prewar Hawaii). *Ritsumeikan gengo bunka kenkyū* 20, no. 1:115–128.

Morris, Joyce J. 1999. *Reiki: Hands That Heal.* Boston: WeiserBooks.

Murakami Aki. 2017. *Fusha no iru nichijō: Tsugaru no kamisama kara toshin no supirichuaru serapisuto made* (The everyday being of spirit mediums: From the *kami* of Tsugaru to the downtown spiritual therapist). Yokohama: Shunpūsha.

Nakamaki Hirochika. 1980. "Hawai ni okeru Nikkei reinōsha to minkan shinkō: Oafu-tō no josei reinōsha no jirei" (Japanese religious mediums and folk belief among Japanese Americans in Hawaii: Female mediums on Oahu island). *Kokuritsu minzokugaku hakubutsukan kenkyū hōkoku* 5, no. 2:317–375.

Nakamura, Kelli Y. 2003. "Murder, Rape, and Martial Law: A Dual-System of Justice for Hawaiʻi's Japanese, 1928–1944." MA thesis, University of Hawaiʻi at Mānoa.

———. 2017a. "Hawaii Hochi (Newspaper)." *Densho Encyclopedia.* http://encyclopedia.densho.org/Hawaii%20Hochi%20%28newspaper%29/.

———. 2017b. "Wilfred Tsukiyama." *Densho Encyclopedia.* http://encyclopedia.densho.org/Wilfred%20Tsukiyama/.

Nakano Genzō. 1972. *Kurama-dera* (Kurama Temple). Tokyo: Chūō Kōron Bijutsu Shuppan.

Nakao Maika. 2019. "Butsuri ryōhō no tanjō: Fukashi enerugii o meguru kindai Nihon no i, ryō, jutsu" (The birth of physics therapy: The medicine, therapy, and techniques of invisible energy in modern Japan). In Yoshinaga, Tsukada, and Kurita 2019: 27–49.

National Center for Complementary and Integrative Health. 2018. "Reiki." US Department of Health and Human Services. Last updated December 2018. https://nccih.nih.gov/health/reiki-info.

Natsunoya Tea House. n.d. "History." Accessed April 9, 2022. https://www .natsunoyahawaii.com/about-us/history/.

Neumann, David J. 2019. *Finding God through Yoga: Paramahansa Yogananda and Modern American Religion in a Global Age.* Chapel Hill: University of North Carolina Press.

Nickerson, Roy. ca. 1974. "She Is Gentle Healer." *Maui News.* [Day and month unknown.]

Nisbett, Richard, and Timothy D. Wilson. 1977. "The Halo Effect: Evidence for Unconscious Alteration of Judgments." *Journal of Personality and Social Psychology* 35, no. 4:250–256.

Nishimura, Hidekazu, and Yasushi Ohkusa. 2016. "Verification of the Overestimation of the 'Deaths Associated with Influenza Pandemic of 1918–1919, Japan' Claimed in a Demographic Study." *Japanese Journal of Infectious Disease* 69:12–17.

Nishina Masaki. 2017a. "Hayashi's Activities in Hawaii." Jikiden Reiki, January 2017. http://jikiden-reiki-nishina.com/hawaii/.

———. 2017b. *Reiki and Japan: A Cultural View of Western and Japanese Reiki.* CreateSpace.

Nomura Hideto. 2019. "Tamari Kizō no reiki-setsu no keisei katei to sono engen" (The formation of and influences on Tamari Kizō's *reiki* theories"). In Yoshinaga, Tsukada, and Kurita 2019: 145–165.

Nukariya Kaiten. 1913. *Yōki renshin no jikken* (Experiments for cultivating *ki* and training the mind). Tokyo: Tōado Shobo.

Odaira, Mika. 2018. "Female Shrine Priests and Doctrinal Instructors in the Early Meiji Moral Edification Campaign." *Monumenta Nipponica* 73, no. 2:213–244.

Ogasawara, Kota. 2015. "Decline in Infant Mortality: Japan's Historical Experience." In *Tojōkoku Nihon no kaihatsu kadai to taiō: Keizai-shi to kaihatsu kenkyū no yūgō, chūkan-hōkoku-sho* (Developing nations and Japan, development issues and responses: Fusing economic history and development research, an interim report), edited by Arimoto Yutaka, 170–191. Chiba: IDE-JETHRO.

Ogawa, Dennis. 1973. *Jan-Ken-Po: The World of Hawaii's Japanese Americans.* Honolulu: University of Hawai'i Press.

Ogawa, Dennis, and Evarts C. Fox Jr. 2008. "Japanese Internment and Relocation: The Hawaii Experience." Presented at the International

Conference of Relocation and Redress: The Japanese American Experience, Salt Lake City, March 10–13, 1983. Reproduced in Japanese Cultural Center of Hawaii, *Japanese American Internment Unit for Modern History of Hawai'i, 2013*, 31–34. http://hawaiiinternment.org/sites/default/files /Modern%20History%20of%20Hawaii_0.pdf.

Ohira, Rod. 1999. "Alewa Teahouse One of the Last of Its Kind." *Honolulu Star-Bulletin*, April 12, 1999. http://archives.starbulletin.com/1999/04/12/news /story7.html.

Ohnuki-Tierney, Emiko. 1984. *Illness and Culture in Contemporary Japan: An Anthropological View*. Cambridge: Cambridge University Press.

Okada Masayuki. 1927. "Reihō chōso Usui-sensei kudoku no hi" (Memorial of the merit of Usui-sensei, founder of the spiritual method"). Wayback Machine. https://web.archive.org/web/20181119055152/http://okojo.b.la9 .jp:80/voda/kudokuhi_1.htm.

Okamura, Jonathan Y. 2000. "Race Relations in Hawai'i during World War II: The Non-internment of Japanese Americans." *Amerasia Journal* 26, no. 2: 117–141.

———. 2014. *From Race to Ethnicity: Interpreting Japanese American Experiences in Hawaii*. Honolulu: University of Hawai'i Press.

Okihiro, Gary Y. 1992. *Cane Fires: The Anti-Japanese Movement in Hawaii, 1965–1945*. Philadelphia: Temple University Press.

Okumura, Daisuke. 2019. "Matsumoto Chiwaki's Theory of Human Radioactivity: A Case of Reception of Western European Science in Japan." *Japanese Religions* 44, no. 1–2:65–88.

Omi, Michael. 2016. "The Unbearable Whiteness of Being: The Contemporary Racialization of Japanese/Asian Americans." In *Trans-Pacific Japanese American Studies: Conversations on Race and Racializations*, edited by Yasuko Takezawa and Gary Y. Okihiro, 39–59. Honolulu: University of Hawai'i Press.

Omi, Michael, and Howard Winant. 2014. *Racial Formation in the United States*. 3rd ed. New York: Routledge.

Oshiro, George M. 2007. "Hawai'i in the Life and Thought of Ifa Fuyū, Father of Okinawan Studies." *Social Process in Hawai'i* 42:35–60.

Otadon [pseud.]. 2010. "Shibusawa Eiichi to reijutsuka" (Shibusawa Eiichi and spiritual therapists). *Jinbōchō-kei otaota nikki* (blog), January 19, 2010. https://jyunku.hatenablog.com/entry/20100119/p1.

———. 2019. "Kyūkyoku no seishin ryōhō: Kawakami Mataji 'Nihon Shinzō Gakkai' ni yoru enkaku shijutsu" (The ultimate *seishin ryōhō*: Distance treatment in Kawakami Mataji's "Japan Mental Phenomena Study Association"). *Jinbōchō-kei otaota nikki* (blog), March 27, 2019. https:// jyunku.hatenablog.com/entry/2019/03/27/211812.

Owen, Suzanne. 2008. *The Appropriation of Native American Spirituality.* New York: Continuum.

Ozaki, Shunsuke. 2017. "American and Japanese Self-Help Literature." *Oxford Research Encyclopedia of Literature.* https://doi.org/10.1093/acrefore/9780190201098.013.164.

Palazzotto, John. 1949. "Relationship in World's Religions." *Rosicrucian Digest,* October 1949.

Palmer, Albert W. 1924. *The Human Side of Hawaii.* Boston: Pilgrim Press.

Palmer, David A., and Elijah Siegler. 2017. *Dream Trippers: Global Daoism and the Predicament of Modern Spirituality.* Chicago: University of Chicago Press.

Palmer, Susan Jean. 1994. *Moon Sisters, Krishna Mothers, Rajneesh Lovers: Women's Roles in New Religions.* Syracuse, NY: Syracuse University Press.

Palmié, Stephan, ed. 2008. *Africas of the Americas: Beyond the Search for Origins in the Study of Afro-Atlantic Religions.* Leiden: Brill.

Peale, Norman Vincent. 1952. *The Power of Positive Thinking.* New York: Prentice-Hall.

Pereira, Ronan Alves, and Hideaki Matsuoka, eds. 2007. *Japanese Religions in and beyond the Japanese Diaspora.* Berkeley: University of California Press.

Person, John. 2019. "Palm Healing and the Japanese Right: *Tanasue no Michi* and the Body of the Imperial Japanese Subject." *Japanese Religions* 44, no. 1–2:89–110.

Petersen, William. 1966. "Success Story, Japanese-American Style." *New York Times Magazine,* January 9, 1966, 20–21, 33, 36–43.

Peterson, Barbara Bennett. 1984. *Notable Women of Hawaii.* Honolulu: University of Hawai'i Press.

Petsalis-Diomidis, Alexia. 2002. "Narratives of Transformation: Pilgrimage Patterns and Authorial Self-Presentation in Three Pilgrimage Texts." *Journeys* 3, no. 1:84–109.

Petter, Frank Arjava. 1997. *Reiki Fire: New Information about the Origins of the Reiki Power: A Complete Manual.* Twin Lakes, WI: Lotus Light Press.

———. 1998. *Reiki: The Legacy of Dr. Usui.* Twin Lakes, WI: Lotus Light Press.

———. 2012. *This Is Reiki: Transformation of Body, Mind and Soul—From the Origins to the Practice.* Twin Lakes, WI: Lotus Press.

Petter, Frank Arjava, Yamaguchi Tadao, and Hayashi Chujiro. 2003. *The Hayashi Reiki Manual: Traditional Japanese Healing Techniques from the Founder of the Western Reiki System.* Twin Lakes, WI: Lotus Press.

Pike, Sarah M. 2004. *New Age and Neopagan Religions in America.* New York: Columbia University Press.

Pincus, Leslie. 1996. *Authenticating Culture in Imperial Japan: Kuki Shūzō and the Rise of National Aesthetics.* Berkeley: University of California Press.

Raines, Ken. 1996. "Dr. Albert Abrams and the ERA." *JW Research Journal* 3, no. 2:4–11.

Ramacharaka, Yogi. 1906. *The Science of Psychic Healing.* Chicago: Yogi Publication Society.

———. 1916. *Saishin seishin ryōhō* (The latest spiritual therapy). Translated by Matsuda Reiyō. Tokyo: Kōhōsha.

Rambelli, Fabio. 2002. "The Ritual World of Buddhist 'Shinto': The *Reikiki* and Initiations on Kami-Related Matters (Jingi Kanjō) in Late Medieval and Early-Modern Japan." *Japanese Journal of Religious Studies* 29, no. 3–4:265–297.

Ramirez, Renya K. 2007. *Native Hubs: Culture, Community, and Belonging in Silicon Valley and Beyond.* Durham, NC: Duke University Press.

Rand, William Lee. 1998. *Reiki for a New Millennium.* Southfield, MI: Vision Publications.

———. n.d. "Reiki in India." International Center for Reiki Training. Accessed April 18, 2022. http://www.reiki.org/reikinews/india.html.

Rauscher, William V. 1970. "Spiritual Frontiers Fellowship." *Psychic Magazine,* September/October 1970. Reprinted as an undated brochure, Box 2, Folder 3, Hawayo Takata Papers, Special Research Collections, University of California, Santa Barbara.

Ray, Barbara Weber. 1983. *The Reiki Factor: A Guide to Natural Healing, Helping, and Wholeness.* Smithtown, NY: Exposition Press.

Reader, Ian, and George J. Tanabe Jr. 1998. *Practically Religious: Worldly Benefits and the Common Religion of Japan.* Honolulu: University of Hawai'i Press.

Reikai Kakusei Dōshikai. 2004 [1928]. *Reijutsu to reijutsuka* (*Reijutsu* and *reijutsu* therapists). Tokyo: Nishōdō Shoten. In *Nihonjin no mi-shin-rei: Kindai minkan seishin ryōhō sōsho 8* (The Japanese body, mind, and spirit: Modern popular spiritual therapies, volume 8), edited by Yoshinaga Shin'ichi. Tokyo: Kuresu Shuppan.

Reinecke, John E. 1969. *Language and Dialect in Hawaii: A Sociolinguistic History to 1935.* Honolulu: University of Hawai'i Press.

Reiryō-jutsu Kenkyū-dan. 1934. *Reiryō-jutsu seiten* (The bible of spiritual healing techniques). Tokyo: Tengendō Hon'in.

Reston, James. 1971. "Now, about My Operation in Beijing." *New York Times,* July 26, 1971, A1.

Rogers, Stephanie Stidham. 2011. *Inventing the Holy Land: American Protestant Pilgrimage to Palestine, 1865–1941.* Lanham, MD: Lexington.

Roof, Wade Clark. 1993. *A Generation of Seekers: The Spiritual Journeys of the Baby Boom Generation.* San Francisco: HarperCollins.

Rowe, Mark. 2011. *Bonds of the Dead: Temples, Burial, and the Transformation of Contemporary Japanese Buddhism.* Chicago: University of Chicago Press.

Saito, Osamu. 1996. "Famines and Epidemics: A Comparison between India and Japan." In *Local Agrarian Societies in Colonial India: Japanese Perspectives*, edited by Peter Robb, Kaoru Sugihara, and Haruka Yanagisawa, 311–320. Surrey, UK: Curzon.

Samuels, Frederick. 1970. *The Japanese and the Haoles of Honolulu: Durable Group Interaction*. New Haven, CT: College and University Press.

Saranillio, Dean Itsuji. 2013. "Why Asian Settler Colonialism Matters: A Thought Piece on Critiques, Debates, and Indigenous Difference." *Settler Colonial Studies* 3, nos. 3–4:280–294.

Satter, Beryl. 1999. *Each Mind a Kingdom: American Women, Sexual Purity, and the New Thought Movement, 1875–1920*. Berkeley: University of California Press.

Savela, Edward. 2011. "The Spy Who Doomed Pearl Harbor." HistoryNet, November 8, 2011. https://www.historynet.com/the-spy-who-doomed-pearl -harbor/.

Sawada, Janine Tasca. 2004. *Practical Pursuits: Religion, Politics, and Personal Cultivation in Nineteenth-Century Japan*. Honolulu: University of Hawai'i Press.

Sawada, Mitziko. 1996. *Tokyo Life, New York Dreams: Urban Japanese Visions of America, 1890–1924*. Berkeley: University of California Press.

Schedneck, Brooke. 2019. "The Promise of the Universal: Non-Buddhists' Accounts of Their Vipassanā Meditation Retreat Experiences." *Religion* 49, no. 4:636–660.

Schencking, J. Charles. 2013. *The Great Kanto Earthquake and the Chimera of National Reconstruction in Japan*. New York: Columbia University Press.

Schiller, Robert. 2003. "Reiki: A Starting Point for Integrative Medicine." *Alternative Therapies in Health and Medicine* 9, no. 2:20–21.

Schmidt, Alvin J. 1980. *Fraternal Organizations*. Westport, CT: Greenwood Press.

Schmitt, Robert C. 1977. *Historical Statistics of Hawaii*. Honolulu: University Press of Hawaii.

Schmitt, Robert C., and Eleanor C. Nordyke. 1999. "Influenza Deaths in Hawai'i, 1918–1920." *Hawaiian Journal of History* 33:101–117.

Selberg, Torunn. 1995. "Faith Healing and Miracles: Narratives about Folk Medicine." *Journal of Folklore Research* 32, no. 1:35–47.

Self-Realization Fellowship. 1958. *Paramahansa Yogananda: In Memoriam*. Los Angeles: Self-Realization Fellowship.

Sered, Susan, and Amy Agigian. 2008. "Holistic Sickening: Breast Cancer and the Discursive Worlds of Complementary and Alternative Practitioners." *Sociology of Health and Illness* 30, no. 4:616–631.

Seward, Adam. 1998. "Biographical Background for Red Fox Skiuhushu." Indian Country. http://electricindian.50megs.com/redfox2.htm.

Sharf, Robert H. 1993. "The Zen of Japanese Nationalism." *History of Religions* 33, no. 1:1–43.

———. 1995. "Sanbōkyōdan: Zen and the Way of the New Religions." *Japanese Journal of Religious Studies* 22, no. 3–4:417–458.

Sharma, Miriam. 1987. "Towards a Political Economy of Emigration from the Philippines: The 1906 to 1946 Ilocano Movement to Hawaii in Historical Perspective." *Philippine Sociological Review* 35, no. 3–4:15–33.

Shay, Shoshana. 2019. *Reiki History: Real Reiki® from Japan to the Western World.* St. Petersburg, FL: Radiance Associates.

Shibata Junkō. 1988. *Shin-chōsei igaku* (New longevity medicine). Yokohama: Chōseiji.

Shibusawa, Naoko. 2006. *America's Geisha Ally: Reimagining the Japanese Enemy.* Cambridge, MA: Harvard University Press.

Shimizu, Karli. 2019. "Religion and Secularism in Overseas Shinto Shrines: A Case Study on Hilo Daijingū, 1898–1941." *Japanese Journal of Religious Studies* 46, no. 1:1–29.

Shirai, Yukiko. 2019. "Japanese Immigrant Workers and the Formation of Hawaiian Pidgin English." *Osaka Gakuin University Foreign Linguistic and Literary Studies* 77:1–15.

Shoemaker, James H. 1940. *Labor in the Territory of Hawaii, 1939.* Seventy-Sixth Congress, Third Session, H.D. 838. Washington, DC: Government Printing Office.

Silverberg, Miriam. 2009. *Erotic Grotesque Nonsense: The Mass Culture of Japanese Modern Times.* Berkeley: University of California Press.

Singleton, Mark. 2010. *Yoga Body: The Origins of Modern Posture Practice.* New York: Oxford University Press.

Skiuhushu, Barnabas [Red Fox]. 1936. *General Indian Information: The Indian Association of America, Inc.* Lisle, IL: St. Procopius College Press.

Skrivanic, Peter. 2017. "The Therapeutic Hour: Locating Shiatsu Subjectivities between Gift and Commodity." *Inochi no mirai* (The future of life) 2:84–105.

———. 2018. "Medicine and Religion are Not-Two: Sensory Economies of Knowledge in 'Zen Shiatsu.'" *Studies in Religion / Sciences Religieuses* 47, no. 2:201–222.

Snodgrass, Judith. 2003. *Presenting Japanese Buddhism to the West: Orientalism, Occidentalism, and the Columbian Exposition.* Chapel Hill: University of North Carolina Press.

Soboleski, Hank. 2007. "Island History: Gov. Kaikioʻewa." *The Garden Island* (Lihue, HI), February 18, 2007.

———. 2013. "Wailua Golf Course History." *The Garden Island* (Lihue, HI), July 14, 2013.

————. 2018. "Kauai's Spalding Monument." *The Garden Island* (Lihue, HI), April 29, 2018.

Societas Rosicruciana in America. n.d. "George Winslow Plummer." Accessed December 13, 2022. http://www.sria.org/george-winslow-plummer/.

Sointu, Eeeva, and Linda Woodhead. 2008. "Spirituality, Gender, and Expressive Selfhood." *Journal for the Scientific Study of Religion* 47, no. 2:259–276.

Soucy, Alexander. 2014. "Buddhist Globalism and the Search for Canadian Buddhism." In *Flowers on the Rock: Global and Local Buddhisms in Canada,* edited by John S. Harding, Victor Sōgen Hori, and Alexander Soucy, 25–52. Montreal: McGill–Queen's University Press.

Spickard, Paul. 2009. *Japanese Americans: The Formation and Transformations of an Ethnic Group.* Rev. ed. New Brunswick, NJ: Rutgers University Press.

"Spiritual Frontiers Fellowship (SFF)." 1990. In *New Age Encyclopedia,* edited by J. Gordon Melton, Jerome Clark, and Aidan A. Kelly, 287. Detroit: Gale Research.

Staemmler, Birgit. 2009. *Chinkon Kishin: Mediated Spirit Possession in Japanese New Religions.* Berlin: Lit Verlag.

————. 2013. "Seichō no Ie." World Religions and Spiritualities Project. https://wrldrels.org/2016/10/08/seicho-no-ie/.

Stalker, Nancy. 2008. *Prophet Motive: Deguchi Onisaburō, Oomoto, and the Rise of New Religions in Imperial Japan.* Honolulu: University of Hawai'i Press.

Steiger, Brad, ed. 1975. *Words from the Source: A Metaphysical Anthology of Readings from the Louis Foundation.* Englewood Cliffs, NJ: Prentice Hall.

Stein, Diane. 1995. *Essential Reiki: A Complete Guide to an Ancient Healing Art.* Freedom, CA: Crossing Press.

Stein, Justin. 2009. "The Many Lives of Usui Mikao: Authority and Authenticity in Stories of Reiki's Founder." MA thesis, University of Hawai'i at Manoa.

————. 2011. "The Story of the Stone: Memorializing the Benevolence of Usui-sensei, Founder of Reiki Ryoho." Paper given at the International Conference of the European Association for Japanese Studies. Tallinn, Estonia, August 26, 2011.

————. 2012. "The Japanese New Religious Practices of *Jōrei* and *Okiyome* in the Context of Asian Spiritual Healing Traditions." *Japanese Religions* 37, no. 1–2:115–141.

————. 2015. "Usui Reiki Ryōhō to Reiki: Nijū seiki Nihon ni okeru supirichuaru hīringu ni tsuite no gensetsu kūkan" (Usui Reiki Ryōhō and Reiki: The discursive space of spiritual healing in twentieth-century Japan). Paper presented at the Nanzan Seminar, Nanzan Institute for Religion and Culture, Nagoya, Japan, May 31, 2015.

————. 2016a. "Die Historische Bedeutung von Mikao Usui in Japan, Teil 1" (The historical significance of Mikao Usui in Japan, Part 1). Translated by Jürgen Nietzke and Elke Porzucek. *Reiki Magazin* 2016, no. 4:26–29.

————. 2016b. "Usui Reiki Ryōhō (Reiki, Japan)." World Religions and Spiritualities Project. http://www.wrldrels.org/profiles/Reiki(Japan).htm.

————. 2017a. "Die Historische Bedeutung von Mikao Usui in Japan, Teil 2" (The historical significance of Mikao Usui in Japan, Part 2). Translated by Jürgen Nietzke and Elke Porzucek. *Reiki Magazin* 2017, no. 1:22–25.

————. 2017b. "Global Flows of Universal Energy? Aquatic Metaphors, Network Theory, and Modeling Reiki's Development and Circulation in North America." In *Eastspirit: Transnational Spirituality and Religious Circulation in East and West,* edited by Jørn Borup and Marianne Q. Fibiger, 36–60. Leiden: Brill.

————. 2019. "'Universe Energy': Translation and Reiki Healing in the Twentieth-Century North Pacific." *Asian Medicine* 14, no. 1:81–103.

————. 2021. "Nationalism and Buddhist Youth Groups in the Japanese, British, and American Empires, 1880s–1930s." *Journal of Global Buddhism* 22, no. 2:341–359.

————. 2022. "Energy Healing: Reiki, Therapeutic Touch, and Healing Touch in the United States and Beyond." In *Routledge Handbook of Religion, Medicine, and Health,* edited by Dorothea Lüddeckens, Philipp Hetmanczyk, Pamela Klassen, and Justin B. Stein, 229–243. London: Routledge.

————. Forthcoming. "Japanese Imperialism and the Chinese Delegation to the Second General Conference of Pan-Pacific Young Buddhists' Associations (1934)." *Modern Asian Studies.*

Stewart, James J. 2010. "The Question of Vegetarianism and Diet in Pāli Buddhism." *Journal of Buddhist Ethics* 17:100–140.

Stiene, Bronwen, and Frans Stiene. 2003. *The Reiki Sourcebook.* New York: O Books.

————. 2005. *The Japanese Art of Reiki.* New York: O Books.

————. 2010. "Distance Healing Symbol?" International House of Reiki, January 24, 2010. https://ihreiki.com/blog/distance_healing_symbol/?v=3e8d115eb4b3.

Stiene, Frans. 2016. "The Hidden Meaning of the First Symbol." International House of Reiki, June 3, 2016. https://ihreiki.com/blog/the_hidden_meaning_of_the_first_symbol/?v=3e8d115eb4b3.

Stiglitz, Joseph. 2017. *Globalization and Its Discontents Revisited: Antiglobalization in the Era of Trump.* New York: W. W. Norton.

Stoddard, Sandol. 1991. "Biography of Col. Spaulding." Unpublished manuscript, Kauai Historical Society, Lihue, Hawaii.

Stone, Jacqueline I. 1999. *Original Enlightenment and the Transformation of Medieval Japanese Buddhism.* Honolulu: University of Hawaiʻi Press.

Stow, Larisa. n.d. "Larisa Stow about Her Reiki Experience." Reiki—the Healing Touch. Accessed April 18, 2022. http://www.reiki-healing-touch.com/&art_takata.

Straub, Mary. 1974. "Reiki: Japanese Method of Healing Could Spark Public Interest Similar to Chinese Acupuncture." *Tinley Park (IL) Times Herald,* November 13, 1974, 13.

Strauss, Sarah. 2005. *Positioning Yoga: Balancing Acts across Cultures.* Oxford: Berg.

Streich, Marianne. 2007. "How Hawayo Takata Practiced and Taught Reiki." *Reiki News,* Spring 2007, 10–18. https://www.reiki.org/sites/default/files/resource-files/TakataArticle.pdf.

Subsecretaría de Salud Pública. 2012. *Estudio sobre conocimiento, utilización y grado de satisfacción de la población chilena en relación a las medicinas complementarias alternativas.* Ministerio de Salud de Chile. http://web.minsal.cl/portal/url/item/cdc107bdcfc3bff6e040010164015ba5.docx.

Sukul, Sri Deva Ram. 1947. *Yoga and Self-Culture.* New York: Yoga Institute of America.

Sullivan, Lawrence E., and Susan Sered. 2005. "Healing and Medicine: An Overview." *Encyclopedia of Religion,* 2nd ed., edited by Lindsay Jones, 6:3808–3816. Detroit: Macmillan Reference.

Sutton, Matthew Avery. 2007. *Aimee Semple McPherson and the Resurrection of Christian America.* Cambridge, MA: Harvard University Press.

Suzuki Bizan. 1914. *Kenzen no genri* (Principles of health). Tokyo: Teikoku Kenzen Tetsugaku-kan.

Suzuki, Tatsuzo, Chikio Hayashi, Sigeki Nishira, Hirojiro Aoyama, Kikuo Nomoto, Yasumasa Kuroda, and Alice K. Kuroda. 1972. "A Study of Japanese-Americans in Honolulu, Hawaii." *Annals of the Institute of Statistical Mathematics* supplement 7:1–60.

Swami Kriyananda. 2004. *Conversations with Yogananda.* Nevada City, CA: Crystal Clarity.

Taguchi Mugyū. 1918. *Uchū soku ware no jitsugen* (The realization that the universe is oneself). Tokyo: Chūgai Shuppansha.

Takagi Hidesuke. 1925. *Danshoku-hō oyobi reiki-jutsu kōgi* (Lectures on fasting methods and *reiki* techniques). Yamaguchi City: Reidō Kyūsei-kai.

Takai Shiomi. 1986. "Reiki chiryō no rūtsu o saguru: Usui-shiki Ryōhō to wa? Reiki wa Nihon kara Amerika ni watatta" (Searching for the roots of Reiki: What is Usui-Style Reiki Therapy? Reiki went from Japan to America). *Towairaito Zōn* (Twilight zone), April 1986, 140–143.

Takata, Hawayo. 1948. "The Art of Healing." Unpublished essay, reprinted in A. Furumoto 1982. Original manuscript in Box 5, Folder 6, Hawayo Takata Papers, Special Research Collections, University of California, Santa Barbara. Also available at http://www.threshold.ca/reiki/Handouts/Threshold -Reiki-Takata-Diary.pdf.

―――. 1981. "Reiki Is God-Power: The Story of Hawayo K. Takata." Edited by Helen J. Haberly. Transcript of a series of audio recordings from December 12–19, 1979, Hawayo Takata Papers, Special Research Collections, University of California, Santa Barbara.

―――. n.d. "A Letter from Hawayo Takata." James Deacon's Reiki Pages. Accessed April 18, 2022. https://www.aetw.org/reiki_takata_retirement _letter.html.

Takezawa, Yasuko, and Gary Y. Okihiro, eds. 2016. *Trans-Pacific Japanese American Studies: Conversations on Race and Racializations.* Honolulu: University of Hawai'i Press.

Tamura, Eileen H. 1994. *Americanization, Acculturation, and Ethnic Identity: The Nisei Generation in Hawaii.* Urbana: University of Illinois Press.

Tanabe, George J., Jr. 2004. "Grafting Identity: The Hawaiian Branches of the Bodhi Tree." In *Buddhist Missionaries in the Era of Globalization,* edited by Linda Learman, 77–100. Honolulu: University of Hawai'i Press.

Tanaka Satoshi. n.d. "Hayashi Chūjirō-sensei no kanji hyōki." (The character notation of Hayashi Chūjirō-sensei). Reiki Network Yokohama. Accessed April 18, 2022. http://okojo.b.la9.jp/hayashi.html.

Taniguchi Masaharu. 1935. *Seimei no jissō, dai-san-kan: Seirei-hen, jisshō-hen* (The truth of life, vol. 3: The Holy Spirit and concrete evidence). Tokyo: Nippon Kyōbunsha.

Tatsuyama, Tamiko. 1948. "Faith Healing Practices." In Wong et al. 1948.

Taussig, Michael. 1987. *Shamanism, Colonialism, and the Wild Man: A Study in Terror and Healing.* Chicago: University of Chicago Press.

Teeuwen, Mark. 2006. Introduction to *The Culture of Secrecy in Japanese Religion,* edited by Bernhard Scheid and Mark Teeuwen, 1–34. London: Routledge.

Territory of Hawai'i Legislature. 2012. "House Resolution No. 61, 1955." In *Voices of the Asian American and Pacific Islander Experience,* edited by Sang Chi and Emily Moberg Robinson, 1:403–404. Santa Barbara, CA: Greenwood Press.

Thomas, Jolyon Baraka. 2019. *Faking Liberties: Religious Freedom in American-Occupied Japan.* Chicago: University of Chicago Press.

Tōkyō Maiyū Shinbunsha. 1932. "Hayashi Chūjirō." In *Dai Tōkyō no gensei* (The present state of great Tokyo), vol. 2, 274. Tokyo: Tōkyō Maiyū Shinbunsha.

Tomabechi Gizō and Nagasawa Genkō. 1951. *Tomabechi Gizō kaikoroku* (Tomabechi Gizō's memoirs). Tokyo: Asada Shoten.

Tomita Kaiji. (1933) 1999. *Reiki to jinjutsu: Tomita-ryū teate ryōhō* (Reiki and benevolent healing: Tomita-Style Healing Method). Tokyo: BAB Japan.

Treat, John Whittier. 2018. *The Rise and Fall of Modern Japanese Literature.* Chicago: University of Chicago Press.

Tsing, Anna Lowenhaupt. 2005. *Friction: An Ethnography of Global Connection.* Princeton, NJ: Princeton University Press.

Tsukada Hotaka. 2019. "Reijutsu, shintai kara shūkyō he: Mitsui Kōshi no 'te-no-hira ryōji'" (Reijutsu, from body to religion: Mitsui Kōshi's "Palm Healing"). In Yoshinaga, Tsukada, and Kurita 2019: 167–189.

Twan, Anneli, ed. 2005. *Early Days of Reiki: Memories of Hawayo Takata.* Hope, BC: Morning Star Productions.

Tweed, Thomas A. 1992. *The American Encounter with Buddhism, 1844–1912: Victorian Culture and the Limits of Dissent.* Bloomington: University of Indiana Press.

———. 2005. "American Occultism and Japanese Buddhism: Albert J. Edmunds, D. T. Suzuki, and Translocative History." *Japanese Journal of Religious Studies* 32, no. 2:249–281.

———. 2006. *Crossing and Dwelling: A Theory of Religion.* Cambridge, MA: Harvard University Press.

———. 2012. "Tracing Modernity's Flows: Buddhist Currents in the Pacific World." *The Eastern Buddhist* 43, no. 1/2:35–56.

Uchida, Aki. 1998. "The Orientalization of Asian Women in America." *Women's Studies International Forum* 21, no. 2:161–174.

University of Hawai'i at Mānoa Library. n.d. "Lihue Plantation Company History." Hawaiian Sugar Planters' Association Plantation Archives. Accessed April 18, 2022. http://www2.hawaii.edu/~speccoll/p_lihue.html.

Urban, Hugh B. 1998. "The Torment of Secrecy: Ethical and Epistemological Problems in the Study of Esoteric Traditions." *History of Religions* 37, no. 3: 209–248.

US Bureau of the Census. 1972. *Census of Population: 1970.* Vol. 1, pt. A, sect. 1. Washington, DC: US Government Printing Office.

Ushida Juzaburō, Imaizumi Tetsutarō, and Harada Shōsaku, eds. 1926. *Meiji Tennō gyosei hyakushu* (100 poems by the Meiji Emperor). Self-published.

Usui Mikao. 1928. *(Shinshin kaizen) Usui Reiki Ryōhō oyobi kōkai denju setsumeisho* (Usui Reiki Therapy [to Improve Mind and Body] public explanation of instruction). Tokyo: Katsubunsha.

———. 1939. *(Shinshin kaizen) Usui Reiki Ryōhō kōkai denju setsumeisho* (Usui Reiki Therapy [to Improve Mind and Body] public explanation of instruction). 15th ed. Tokyo: (Shinshin Kaizen) Usui Reiki Ryōhō Gakkai Honbu.

Usui Mikao, and Frank Arjava Petter. 2003. *The Original Reiki Handbook of Dr. Mikao Usui*. 4th English ed. Translated by Christine M. Grimm. Twin Lakes, WI: Lotus Press.

Usui Reiki Ryōhō Gakkai. 1928. *(Shinshin Kaizen) Usui Reiki Ryōhō Gakkai nyūmonsha meibo* (Usui Reiki Therapy Learning Society [to Improve Mind and Body] member directory). No publisher.

———. ca. 1930. *(Shinshin Kaizen) Usui Reiki Ryōhō Gakkai nyūmonsha meibo, dai-ichigō* (Usui Reiki Therapy Learning Society [to Improve Mind and Body] member directory, first issue). Self-published.

van Bragt, Jan. 2002. "Multiple Religious Belonging of the Japanese People." In *Many Mansions? Multiple Religious Belonging and Christian Identity*, edited by Catherine Cornille, 7–19. Eugene, OR: Wipf and Stock.

Venuti, Lawrence. 2008. *The Translator's Invisibility: A History of Translation*. 2nd ed. New York: Routledge.

Volk, Alicia. 2010. *In Pursuit of Universalism: Yorozu Tetsugoro and Japanese Modern Art*. Berkeley: University of California Press.

Wakukawa, Ernest Katsumi. 1938. *A History of the Japanese People in Hawaii*. Honolulu: Toyo Shoin.

Walker, Norman W. 1955. *Raw Vegetable Juices: What's Missing in Your Body?* Wickenburg, AZ: Norwalk Press.

War Relocation Authority. 1945. *Myths and Facts about the Japanese Americans: Answering Common Misconceptions Regarding Americans of Japanese Ancestry*. Washington, DC: Department of the Interior.

Watts, Jill. 2001. *Mae West: An Icon in Black and White*. New York: Oxford University Press.

Weber, Max. 1978. *Economy and Society: An Outline of Interpretive Sociology*. Edited by Gunther Roth and Claus Wittich. Berkeley: University of California Press.

Welang, Nahum. 2018. "Triple Consciousness: The Reimagination of Black Female Identities in Contemporary American Culture." *Open Cultural Studies* 2, no. 1:296–306.

Wendt, Staci, Jerry Hipps, Allan Abrams, Jamie Grant, Laurent Valosek, and Sanford Nidich. 2015. "Practicing Transcendental Meditation in High Schools." *Contemporary School Psychology* 19, no. 4:312–319.

White, Mike, director and writer. 2021. *The White Lotus*. Season 1, episode 1, "Arrivals." Aired July 11, 2021, on HBO.

Whorton, James C. 2002. *Nature Cures: The History of Alternative Medicine in America*. Oxford: Oxford University Press.

Wichman, Frederick B. 1998. *Kauai: Ancient Place Names and Their Stories*. Honolulu: University of Hawai'i Press.

Williams, Duncan Ryūken. 2008. "At Ease in Between: The Middle Position of a Scholar-Practitioner." *Journal of Global Buddhism* 9:155–163.

———. 2019. *American Sutra: A Story of Faith and Freedom in the Second World War.* Cambridge, MA: Harvard University Press.

Williams, Duncan Ryūken, and Tomoe Moriya, eds. 2010. *Issei Buddhism in the Americas.* Urbana: University of Illinois Press.

Williamson, Lola. 2010. *Transcendent in America: Hindu-Inspired Meditation Movements as New Religion.* New York: New York University Press.

Willis, David Blake, and Stephen Murphy-Shigematsu, eds. 2008. *Transcultural Japan: At the Borderlands of Race, Culture, and Identity.* London: Routledge.

Wilson, Cecile. 2014. "Is AMORC Rosicrucian?" *Aries* 14, no. 1:73–94.

Wilson, Jeff. 2009. *Mourning the Unborn Dead: A Buddhist Ritual Comes to America.* Oxford: Oxford University Press.

———. 2012. *Dixie Dharma: Inside a Buddhist Temple in the American South.* Chapel Hill: University of North Carolina Press.

———. 2014. *Mindful America: The Mutual Transformation of Buddhist Meditation and American Culture.* Oxford: Oxford University Press.

Wilson, Liz. 2014. "Buddhism and Family." *Religion Compass* 8, no. 6:188–198.

Winfield, Pamela D. 2005. "Curing with *Kaji:* Healing and Esoteric Empowerment in Japan." *Japanese Journal of Religious Studies* 32, no. 1:107–130.

Wong, Dorothy, Tamiko Tatsuyama, Michiko Kitagawa, Tomiye Komatsubara, Bobbe Greaves, June Morigaki, Sadao Miyashiro, and George Uesato. 1948. *Faith Healing in Hawaii.* Romanzo Adams Social Research Laboratory Records, Box A-6, Folder 25, University of Hawai'i at Mānoa Library.

Worrall, Olga. 1972. "Healing by Unconventional Methods." In *The Dimensions of Healing: A Symposium,* 22–28. Los Altos, CA: Academy of Parapsychology and Medicine.

"Worrall, Olga Nathalie Ripich (1906–1985)." 2001. In *Encyclopedia of Occultism and Parapsychology,* vol. 2, *M–Z,* 5th ed., edited by J. Gordon Melton, 1688. Detroit: Gale Group.

Wu, Ellen D. 2014. *The Color of Success: Asian Americans and the Origins of the Model Minority.* Princeton, NJ: Princeton University Press.

Wu, Yu-Chuan. 2012. "A Disorder of Ki: Alternative Treatments for Neurasthenia in Japan, 1890–1945." PhD diss., University College London.

Wuthnow, Robert S. 1997. *The Fifties Spiritual Marketplace: American Religion in a Decade of Conflict.* New Brunswick, NJ: Rutgers University Press.

Yamada Shin'ichi. (1920) 1985. *Yamada-shiki Seitaijutsu kōgi-roku, dai-ikkan: Purana ryōhō* (Lecture records on Yamada-Style Osteopathy, vol. 1: Prana Therapy). Tokyo: Entapuraizu.

Yamaguchi Tadao. 2003. *Jikiden Reiki: Reiki no shinjitsu to ayumi* (Jikiden Reiki: Reiki's truth and history). Tokyo: BAB Japan.

———. 2007. *Light on the Origins of Reiki: A Handbook for Practicing the Original Reiki of Usui and Hayashi.* Twin Lakes, WI: Lotus Press.

Yamazaki Kesaya. 1921. *Bengoshi ōyasuuri* (Bargain lawyer). Tokyo: Shūeikaku.

Yano, Christine. 2006. *Crowning the Nice Girl: Gender, Ethnicity, and Culture in Hawai'i's Cherry Blossom Festival.* Honolulu: University of Hawai'i Press.

Yeshe, Lama. 2001. *Medicine Dharma Reiki: An Introduction to the Secret Inner Practices with Extensive Excerpts from Dr. Usui's Journals.* Delhi: Full Moon.

Yogananda, Paramahansa. 1972. *Autobiography of a Yogi.* Los Angeles: Self-Realization Fellowship.

———. 1985. *Man's Eternal Quest and Other Talks.* Los Angeles: Self-Realization Fellowship.

Yoo, David K. 1999. Introduction to *New Spiritual Homes: Religion and Asian Americans,* edited by David K. Yoo, 1–15. Honolulu: University of Hawai'i Press.

———. 2000. *Growing Up Nisei: Race, Generation, and Culture among Japanese Americans of California, 1924–1949.* Urbana, IL: University of Illinois Press.

Yoshida, Tomoko. 2006. "Kuroda Toshio (1926–1993) on Jōdo Shinshū: Problems in Modern Historiography." *Japanese Journal of Religious Studies* 33, no. 2:379–412.

Yoshihara, Mari. 2003. *Embracing the East: White Women and American Orientalism.* Oxford: Oxford University Press.

Yoshinaga, Shin'ichi. 2008. "Tairei to kokka: Taireidō ni okeru kokka-kan no imi" (Great Spirit and the state: The meaning of the view of the state in Taireidō). *Jintai kagaku* (Science of the human body) 17, no. 1:35–51.

———. 2015. "The Birth of Japanese Mind Cure Methods." In *Religion and Psychotherapy in Modern Japan,* edited by Christopher Harding, Fumiaki Iwata, and Shin'ichi Yoshinaga, 76–102. New York: Routledge.

———. 2019. "Joron" (Introduction). In Yoshinaga, Tsukada, and Kurita 2019: 3–23.

———. 2021. "Spiritualism and Occultism." In *The Bloomsbury Handbook of Japanese Religions,* edited by Erica Baffelli, Fabio Rambelli, and Andrea Castiglioni, 229–239. London: Bloomsbury Academic.

Yoshinaga Shin'ichi, Tsukada Hotaka, and Kurita Hidehiko, eds. 2019. *Kingendai Nihon no minkan seishin ryōhō: Okaruto-na enerugī no shosō* (Folk spiritual therapies in modern and contemporary Japan: Various forms of occult energy). Tokyo: Kokusho Kankōkai.

Young, Peter T. 2015. "Colonel Zephaniah Swift Spalding." Images of Old Hawai'i, February 3, 2015. http://imagesofoldhawaii.com/colonel-zephaniah-swift-spalding/.

Young, Richard Fox. 1988. "From *Gokyō-dōgen* to *Bankyō-dōkon:* A Study in the Self-Universalization of Ōmoto." *Japanese Journal of Religious Studies* 15, no. 4: 263–286.

Yu, Henry. 2001. *Thinking Orientals: Migration, Contact, and Exoticism in Modern America.* New York: Oxford University Press.

Zavidovskaya, Ekaterina A. 2012. "Deserving Divine Protection: Religious Life in Contemporary Rural Shanxi and Shaanxi Provinces." *St. Petersburg Annual of Asian and African Studies* 1:179–197.

Zoehrer, Dominic S. 2020. "Pranic Healing: A Mesmerist Echo in the New 'Holistic' Age." *Religion in Austria* 5:139–199.

———. 2021. "From Fluidum to Prāna: Reading Mesmerism through Orientalist Lenses." In *The Occult Nineteenth Century: Roots, Developments, and Impact on the Modern World,* edited by Lukas Pokorny and Franz Winter, 85–110. Cham, Switzerland: Palgrave Macmillan.

Index

acupuncture, 54, 118, 180–182
Afro-Caribbean religion, 12, 198–199
aikido, 118, 200, 234n142
"alternative" and "unorthodox" medicine, 8, 139, 218n45. *See also* acupuncture; chiropractic; *kanpō* (Sino-Japanese medicine); moxibustion; naturopathy; osteopathy; radionics; spiritual therapies
ancestor veneration, 45, 116–117
Ancient Mystical Order Rosae Crucis (AMORC), 141–147, 158–160, 164
anti-Black racism. *See* racial hierarchy
anti-Japanese racism. *See* Japanese Americans; racial hierachy
Aoyama, Bunki, 97–98
Araki, George, 179
Atkinson, Eulalia, 193, 263n32, 267n102
Atkinson, William Walker. *See* Yogi Ramacharaka
Atlantis, 16, 20

biomedicine: as foil for spiritual therapies, 54, 59, 85, 161–163, 246n60; Hayashi Chūjirō and, 75, 235n153, 236n164; hegemony of, 55–57; perceived limitations of, 48, 57, 84, 162, 167, 180; public health initiatives, 228n65; spiritual therapies' ambiguous / ambivalent relationship with, 9, 11–12, 60, 84, 199

Black Atlantic religion, 12, 238n190. *See also* Afro-Caribbean religion
Bockner, Richard "Rick," 3–4, 183–184, 192, 224n76, 267n93
breathing techniques, 13, 55, 57–58, 71–72, 74, 147–148, 231n93, 260n121
bridge figure. *See* Oriental Monk, icon of the
Brown, Barbara, 172, 215n3
Brown, Fran, 175, 224n76
Buddhism: Buddhist modernism, 45, 59, 85, 201; *butsudan* (home altar) practice, 37, 45, 110–111, 116–117, 177, 234n150; in Hawai'i (postwar), 122; in Hawai'i (prewar), 36, 40, 44, 98–99, 115–116, 261n9; in Hawai'i (wartime), 27, 90, 92, 110–111, 117; and Hawayo Takata, 30–31, 36–37, 42, 44–46, 53, 120, 150, 163, 177, 251n142; lineage in, 14–15, 25, 67, 137, 202; and Native American religion, 149; and Nikkei Reiki practitioners, 110–111, 115–117, 124, 137, 166, 178, 204; Orientalism / Occidentalism, 25, 59, 130, 149–150, 157, 169, 184; Reiki as "Buddhist," 9, 112, 125, 168–171, 182, 184–185, 187–189; Reiki taught in Hawaiian Buddhist "churches," 25, 103, 116, 131, 140, 247n73, 250n122, 251n126; and Saichi Takata, 40, 47–48, 224n85; and spiritual therapies, 115,

About the Author

Justin B. Stein received his PhD from the University of Toronto in the study of religion and is on the faculty of the Asian Studies Program at Kwantlen Polytechnic University in British Columbia.